A Different Way Forward

Social Market Capitalism and Social Partnership in Europe, Austria and the USA

Edward France

Copyright © 2025 by Edward France

All rights reserved. No part of this publication may be reproduced, distributed, or transmitted in any form or by any means, including photocopying, recording, or other electronic or mechanical methods, without the prior written permission of the publisher, except in the case of brief quotations embodied in critical reviews and certain other noncommercial uses permitted by copyright law.

Dedication

To my wife and two daughters,
Family and friends near and far, and to
Everybody, especially those folks in town,
living on the other side of the tracks

Acknowledgments

Many gave support, were interviewed and/or consulted in the research and writing of this book. First, I want to thank readers who previewed the text – Duluth, MN collaborative counsel, Pat Francisco; former St. Louis County commissioner, Frank Jewell; brother, Montana state legislator, Tom France; professor of Mathematics, American College of Greece, philosopher, and fisherman, Miltos Gikas, and North Carolina, Jr. High School Social Studies teacher, Chris Mason. I also want to thank my daughter, Melissa, who helped with interview translations.

Many in Vorarlberg, Austria also granted interviews and gave perspective on different facets of Austria's Social Partnership: Representatives of Vorarlberg's Chambers of Labor and Commerce; social worker and works council representative, Karl Pakorny; state personnel administrator, Eva Pammer; IT programmer and Works Council representative, Martin Pammer; graphic editor and works council representative, Christian Stuppner; Milke Chocolate Worker-Management liaison, Hubert Duelli; national labor union (ÖGB) provincial director, Reinhard Stemmer; Dutch Business Manager and CEO, Felix Rippe; IT business owner and Commerce Chamber member, Christian Bickel; grocery store /manager/owner, Arno Riedmann; business executive, Roland Zangerle; Vorarlberg Green Party representative, spokesman, Bernie Weber. Last but not least, I want to thank the editors at Ace Book Writers.

Table of Contents

Dedication i

Acknowledgments ii

About the Author xii

A Foreword to A Different Way Forward: Social Market Capitalism and Social Partnership in Europe, Austria and the USA xiii

Introduction: Social Partnership & Historical Materialism xxi

Part I 27

    Chapter One: Take the European Bull by Its Horns 28

        Growing Pains Indeed 34

Part II American Survey I 40

    Chapter One: Economic and Political Divides 41

        Private and Public Goods — Wealth and Poverty 48

        The GINI Index & Inequality Rankings 55

        Piketty's Inequality Treaties 61

        Economic Class, and the Escape from Freedom 68

        Taxation Matters 73

Part III Historial Materialism 76

    Chapter One: Historical Materialism 77

        Marx's Precursor(s), Ideology & Progress 79

        The Hegelian State and Liberalism 98

        Marxist Class Analysis 100

Surplus Value 102

Material Incentive Matters 105

Class Allegiances 108

Chapter Two: Ebenezer's Exploitation 110

Trade Unions and Purchasing Power 112

Producers and Consumers 113

Chapter Three: A Glance Backward: Democratic Capitalism 119

Chapter Four: The Marxist Account Revisited: A Post-Marxist Perspective 124

Post-Marxism 125

The Humanist View 126

Ideology and Marx 128

Contemporary Marxism 130

The Way Forward 131

The Dialectic Zombie 132

Dialectic Issues Today 134

Part IV Golden Jocks 140

Chapter One: Historical Materialism and the NFL 141

The Roster Depreciation Allowance — RDA 144

Philanthropy 148

Ticket Costs 149

Chapter Two: Historical Materialist Analysis Revisited 155

iv

Part V Austrian Legacies 160

    Chapter One: A Dive into History 162

        Austrian Class Conflict 166

        World War II Aftermath 172

        Austrian Neo-Corporatism/Social Partnership 173

        Wages and Prices in Austria 180

Part VI American Survey II 186

    Chapter One: Polarization Roots and Realities 187

        Modern American Economic History 190

        Social Values & Public Goods 195

        Taxation Doesn't Pay 196

        Tax Policy 200

        Political Process Impact 206

Part VII Modern Austria 208

        Austrian Trade-Union Milestones 213

        Austrian Business Status — Pre-distribution 217

        The Tax Accountant and the Social Worker 223

Part VIII American Survey III 227

    Chapter One: The Welfare State & Slavery 228

        Racism 236

        The Tenets of Critical Race Theory 240

        The Sum of Us 245

Chapter Two: Legacies of Racism Continued — Health Care Insurance 254

    Education 257

    Status and the American Ethos 259

    Chapter Three: *Political* Polarization- Roots and Realities 263

    Recent Political History 270

    Citizens United 275

    Schedule F 276

    Class War and Politics 279

    Reagan Revisited 281

    Economics Reconsidered-Collective Bargaining 284

Part IX European Social Market Capitalism 288

    Chapter One: Austrian Echoes 289

    Chapter Two: Social Partnership Origins and Development 293

    Social Polarization and Immigration 294

    The Austrian School of Economics and Social Market Capitalism 295

    The Social Market Economy and its Origins 296

    Social Market Capitalism 298

    Chapter Three: Competitive Economy — Ludwig von Mises Revisited 302

    Monopoly Control 304

    Europe's Social Market Revisited 305

    Europe's Competition Law 309

    American Anti-Trust Enforcement 312

    Social Market/Austrian Anti-Trust Review 314

Part X American Survey IV 319

  Chapter One: *Socio-Psychological* Polarization 320

  Chapter Two: Straits of Poverty 323

    The Poor and Indigent Poor 326

    World Economic Forum Measures 329

    Stakeholder Capitalism 331

  Chapter Three: The Bicycle Reaction 333

Part XI European Overview 338

  Chapter One: European Social Partnership Appraisal 339

  Chapter Two: European Collective Bargaining 343

    European Social Dialogue 345

  Chapter Three: Social Partnership Status Survey 348

  Chapter Four: Social Market Economy Law 353

    Court of Justice of the European Union (CJEU) 354

Part XII American Survey V 361

  Chapter One: Polarization Profiles Continued… 362

  Chapter Two: Authoritarian Personality/Cult 365

    Status and Inequality 372

    Austrian Parallels 374

Chapter Three: The New Executive Class 378

    Democrats 386

    Dystopian Interlude 388

    Practical Idealism Reborn 389

Part XIII Post-War European Treaties 394

    The Treaty of Paris (1951) 394

    The Treaty of Rome (1957) 395

    The Merger Treaties/The Treaty of Belgium (1965) 395

    The Maastricht Treaty (1992) 396

    GATT Negotiations (1994) 397

    Chapter One: The Eurozone 399

    The Lisbon Treaty (TFEU) 2007-2009 400

    EU Courts Revisited 404

    Conclusion 406

Part XIV Social Partnership Over Polarization 408

    Chapter One: European and the American Contrast 409

    Chapter Two: Compare European/American Market Conditions .. 413

    American Trade-Unions 416

    Health Insurance 418

    American Higher Education Conditions 423

    American Student Debt Relief 426

Part XV Finance Interludes 428

Chapter One: Education, Deficits, Debts, GDP Interlude 429

    Education Finance Loses Out 430

    Out of the Debt/Deficit Funding Impasse 431

    The Cost of Universal Tuition-Free Higher Education 433

Chapter Two: Compare Higher Ed/VoTech Education 434

Chapter Three: Debt, Deficit & Taxation 444

    The American Contrast 448

    Alternative Deficit Platforms 450

    Social Market/ Partnership Platforms 452

Part XVI Contemporary American Realities 456

Chapter One: The Social Contract 457

    Financialization and Private Equity Frenzy 460

    A New Social Contract 465

    Welfare Revisited 468

Part XVII The Old New Deal Social Contract 473

Chapter One: American Labor History 474

    Collective Bargaining in America 478

    Post-World War II Labor Conditions 481

    Golden Age Capitalism 484

Chapter Two: Labor Movement Plight 487

    Racketeering 488

    The State and Legal System 491

    Card-Checks 492

  Chapter Three: Employer Offensives I 495

    Today's (PRO) Act: Protecting the Right to Organize 497

    Right-to-Work Laws 500

Part XVIII Austrian and European Parallels 505

  Chapter One: Social Partnership Institutions and Agencies 506

  Chapter Two: Social Partnership on the Ground in Austria 510

    A Works Council Graphic Design Editor 511

    European Works Councils 513

    Chambers of Labor 515

    Social Partnership Parliamentary Involvement 517

    Austrian National Trade-Union 524

    Provincial Representation 526

    Political Influence 527

    A Social Partnership Business Owner 529

Part XIX More American Labor History 533

  Chapter One: Right-to-Work Revisited 534

  Chapter Two: Trade-Union Role Retrospective 537

    Anti-communism 539

    Trade-Union Historical Hang-Ups/Divisions 540

    AFL-CIO 542

    Walter Reuther & the Alliance for Labor Action 545

Chapter Three: Employer Offensive II... 551

    GE & Jack Welch.. 553

    Old Social Contract Torn 558

Part XX The Modern World in America and Europe................. 561

    Chapter One: Comparisons 562

    Chapter Two: M&A in Europe 567

    Chapter Three: Competition Law Revisited................... 573

        Conclusion 575

Part XXI 578

    Chapter One: The Tragedy of Russian Autocracy 579

        Putin's Reign... 581

        Russian Nationalist Fabrications.............................. 583

Appendices 589

    Appendix 1: Environmental Consciousness p. XIV 590

    Appendix 2: Collective Bargaining and Wage Inequality pp. 29, 86 591

    Appendix 3: Net National Wealth Chart p. 40 592

    Appendix 4: World-Wide Income Shares p. 186 593

Bibliography... 594

    Citations 595

Index 596

About the Author

I grew up in a political household during the 1960's and 70's in Duluth, Minnesota. My father was long active in Republican politics as a State Representative and federal government official, and my mother, during and after the Vietnam War, became a die-hard liberal Democrat. The political observations and arguments around the dinner table were ongoing and often heated; some of the lightening wore off on me.

I married an Austrian woman, and spent many of the last 30 years or so residing in Austria, working as an educator, raising a family and finally retiring. I was well and fully acquainted with Austrian society, but didn't really understand the design and function of its unique economic system. This compelled me to find out more about my second home, about its particular history, governmental and economic institutions and why Austrian society hangs together in some ways like a harmonious, if at times halting Viennese waltz.

I combine a background in liberal arts (Kenyon College, Political Science, 1980) and a master's degree in Education, (Open University, 2007) with life-long, amateur interest in Politics, History, Economics, Philosophy, and Sociopsychology. Each and all help me arrive at some clarity and convictions about why Austria and Europe generally stand as promising beacons to guide further modern historical development.

A Foreword to A Different Way Forward:
Social Market Capitalism and Social Partnership in Europe, Austria and the USA

The book's title refers to historical progress broadly demonstrated by Europe's social democracies, and by Austria, in particular. This progress is somewhat tenuous, especially as turmoil over issues such as immigration, political alignments, or the Ukrainian War dominate European headlines. Is Europe bedeviled as of yore by the same old divisions and conflicts? Yes and No. The continent has always been hard to harmonize, with its 33 distinct 'and dominant nationalities, or ethnic groups, not counting the other 54 minority ethnic groups sharing ancestry, language and culture. "(Ron Perarca, European Ethnic Groups/Region, Language and Minorities, study.com, November 21, 2023) No, Europe has remarkably transcended many historic shadows. It maintains broad social unity and greater shared material prosperity.

The title does two things. First, it proposes that as American political and economic developments have veered off in faulty directions, a 'different' route can and should be sought and adopted. Second, it proposes a different way forward. What does this different way look like? What makes it different? There are standards by which such propositions and historical progress itself can be measured and judged. Most of us are just trying to find our way home for dinner at night, but now and then it's important to believe that all our individual and collective efforts may also be contributing to a viable and sustainable future. The book is dedicated to giving an appraisal of such things and their respective developments in America, Europe, and Austria.

The idea of having a standard or gauge to judge historical progress was perhaps most currently and famously raised by Francis Fukuyama, whose views came to the fore in the 1990's. He proposed that history had reached some kind of outstanding and final culmination. "The state that emerges at the end of history;" he contended, "is liberal insofar as it recognizes and protects through a system of law the universal human right to freedom, (sic) and democratic insofar as it exists only with the consent of the governed. "(Francis Fukuyama, The End of History? JSTOR, the National Interest- #16, Summer 1989, p. 5)

This conclusion seemed warranted at the time by the western world's apparent triumph over Soviet Communism in what had been the post-war world, epic civilizational contest, the Cold War. Additionally, many other countries at the time increasingly embraced forms of democratic government. Liberal-democratic economic and political organization ultimately and finally seemed best suited to serve the collective and individual interests of humanity.

Technological progress and economic development in all spheres of production appeared manifest. Prosperity seemed to prevail. The individual's competence to be more rather than less self-governing was vouchsafed. Governmental legitimacy rested squarely on popular consent. As interpreted by the Political Scientist, Yascha Mounk, the successful implementation of liberal-democratic precepts, cited by Fukuyama, represented a kind of „end of ideological evolution." (Yascha Mounk, The End of History Revisited, Journal of Democracy, journalofdemocracy.org, January 2020)

Mounk further elaborated Fukuyama's view that 'purposive evolution 'is abetted by the progressive "human ability to accumulate knowledge. "(ibid) That accumulation is grounded in the 'scientific method' which safeguards rational development from random impulse, or overweening instinct, and assures social and economic change that is 'directional'; moving gradually, progressively forward. Such change would prevent, or at least impair historical regression visited upon humanity by past cyclical rises and falls of all prior governmental systems.

Subsequent economic researchers even posed the argument that when countries adopt stable democratic processes, continuous fair elections and achieve a certain (sic) level of annual per capita income, "democracy is certain to survive, come hell or high water." (ibid, Przeworski, Alvarez, Cheibub, Limongi, What Makes Democracies Endure? Journal of Democracy #7, January 1996, p. 48) Liberal-democracies appeared to resolve internal divisions or contradictions implicit in any governmental and/or economic system, with regard especially to wealth distribution and political succession.

Systemic stability and legitimacy are great attributes. The 'liberal-democratic' model is hoisted higher by Fukuyama, however, because it is rooted in human social consciousness. "The human desire for recognition, and respect (sic), pushes societies in the direction of greater equality." (Jascha Mounk, ibid) The promotion and gratification of this need provides the capstone to liberal-democratic durability. Fukuyama did admit, however, that such gains remain contingent. He admitted that the „victory of liberalism had (sic) occurred primarily in the realm of ideas or consciousness and is as yet incomplete in the real or material world." (ibid) Here, of course, is the rub.

This essay seconds Fukuyama's reservations. Real progress must also take place in the material world. To measure material matters and matters of consciousness, the present essay partially adopts the respective, not necessarily complimentary ideational and materialist perspectives of Friedrich Hegel (1770-1831) and Karl Marx (1818-1883). You might question invoking such old views, but they still retain relevance. First, they have a lot to do with elaborating modern historical development, and second, materialist and ideational frameworks still offer valid and compelling prisms for interpreting and guiding human affairs. The social and economic material challenges of the world will always throw up unforeseen obstacles and goads for human consciousness and human society to contend with and resolve.

To note just two realms of challenge since Fukuyama's time, the leaps and bounds accomplished by information technology and the internet, and now of AI promote all kinds of associations and purvey massive amounts of information and knowledge, but not always of the socially constructive sort. Further, the sheer quantity of information may downgrade the veracity and utility of knowledge. This upsets the social and moral realm of ideals, values and beliefs. Second, the deployment of the ‚scientific method 'in all fields of production allows efficient exploitation of earth resources and phenomenal economic development, but all this productivity generates the release of gases that threaten the earth's ecosystem. The scientific method calls out for greater ethical and spiritual grounding. **(See Appendix 1: Environmental Consciousness)**

Mounk identifies "3 further (sic) challenges to Fukuyama's ,triumphalist view: 1) the spread of democratic government appears to recede; 2) there is greater openness toward authoritarian, or illiberal movements and regimes; and 3) populist forces upend the basic rules and norms of liberal democracy." (ibid) A fourth challenge involves the widening gaps of social and economic inequality, especially in America. Each of these challenges reveal internal contradictions which call into question the liberal-democratic and market capitalist order. These contradictions can be addressed and resolved. It is essential to reform and so save both systems.

The challenge posed by massive income and wealth inequality produced over the past 40 years or so, especially in the USA, is a central focus of this essay. The liberal market economy still produces great incentives, but its rewards are unevenly and jaggedly shared, foreshadowing civic conflict. This contradiction stokes self-centered entitlement and downgrades the principles and precepts of democratic equality and aspiration. The avowed human desire for recognition, respect and social equality becomes distorted. Fukuyama's 'end of ideology', in this case, would not be benign, but signal a tragic loss of guidance and inability to address the human condition and its affairs. A revival of pragmatic ideology is called for.

As counterpoint, this essay proposes that the social democracies of Europe and Austria, in particular, have significantly addressed, if not overcome the contradictions that drive massive economic inequality. They have done so pragmatically without thwarting productive economic enterprise. These adaptations point a different way forward, out of impasses, among others, in the realms of healthcare, education and wage compensation that thwart and threaten modern civilization.

Austrian Impasse But neither Europe, nor Austria are immune from polarizing, illiberal, populist forces. In Austria's recent 2024 national election, as a matter of fact, the insurgent, populist Freedom Party gained ,28.8% of the vote and a 2%+ majority over the Conservative Party's vote of 26.3%. The Socialist Party won 21.1%, the Neos (a neo-capitalist party) 9.1% and the Green Party, 8.2% (Wikipedia, Austrian Legislative Election, September 30, 2024) The Freedom Party share of the vote jumped 13+% from 2019. The vote reflects many issues.

Economic inflation in Austria, resulting from the Covid epidemic's economic bailouts, and the Ukrainian War-shutdown of Russian oil exports, rose from 1.5% in 2019 to 8.5% in 2022. (Macrotrends, Austrian Inflation Rates, 1960-2024, World Bank data source) Borrowing interest rates grew correspondingly. Mandatory Covid vaccination policies caused widespread resentment of governmental intrusion. Moreover, since 2015, Austria welcomed more than 150,000 Syrian and Afghani immigrants as well as 80,000 Ukrainians, making it „one of the countries which receives the most refugees per capita in the EU. "(Jean-Baptiste Chastand, In Austria, Migration Dominates the

General Election Campaign, LeMonde, Sept. 29, 2024) The right-wing Freedom Party, however, exploits such immigration numbers to incite insecurity and prejudice. Yes, in Austria too, the racist ‚great replacement 'theory is deployed to demonize recent waves of Islamic and foreign immigration as a threat to „white, Christian populations."(ibid) In this, alignment between the Freedom Party and illiberal, authoritarian movements in Hungary and Russia, becomes evident. History, to contradict Fukuyama, ain't over. It appears inescapable, but also always capable of remedy.

In Austria, as in the U.S., illiberal rhetoric serves to distract the populace and mainstream media outlets from all the ‚brigandage 'being perpetrated by hyper-capitalist economic interests. The insinuated social unrest makes people anxious about their bank accounts and perhaps more inclined to support illiberal policies. As Donald Trump appears preoccupied with advancing the oligarchic interests of high finance, so is Austria's Freedom Party similarly a front for oligarchic designs. (Konrad Lachmayer, Austria's Populist Turn, Constitutional Blog, verfassungblog.de, January 16, 2025)

Liberal democratic guardrails remain in America to restrain, if not defeat the oligarchic flim-flam, but only just. Eventual exit from, or remedy of contemporary economic and political conditions appears nonetheless elusive. In Austria, likewise, social market economy and parliamentary system guardrails have held the Freedom Party at bay. But here, in addition, society remains largely unified. Whatever the momentary and in part local advantage of Austria's Freedom Party, 72% of Austrian voters still support

Austria's 'social state'. This fact contributed to the ultimate 2025 formation of the governing coalition between Conservative, Socialist and Neo-Capitalist parties. The Freedom Party is boxed out. Austria's Social Market Capitalist economy and Social Partnership system of government abide.

Despite gathering glooms, the lanterns of social and historical progress are notably upheld by the social democracies of Europe and Austria.

Introduction: Social Partnership & Historical Materialism

Modern-day Europe exemplifies an affirmative social dynamism from which to draw critical new economic and political perspectives. Taking hold in various forms between state, business, and trade-union labor interests across the European continent, the phenomenon of Social Partnership is too little recognized for the institutional and practical contributions it makes to political economy and the modern capitalist welfare state. "Social partnership (sic) involves coordinating the collaboration of key interests, freeing the state from deep involvement in organizing work and wages while overcoming economic distortions and solving collective action problems such as training" (Scott Green, Michelle Falkenbach, *Social Partnership, Civil Society and Healthcare,* National Library of Medicine, 2016). It stands in its various permutations as a model by which the current impasse and polarization between democratic-social and conservative capital interests in America can be positively resolved; it offers a different way forward.

The development of Social Partnership in Europe has its roots in national and multi-faceted pre- and post-World War II confrontations between organized labor and capital interests. The Social Partnership pursued in most of its member states was endorsed by the E.U.'s original treaties and institutions. Support was redoubled after the inauguration of the E.U. monetary union in 2000. Social Partnership is now confirmed as a central component of E.U. social and economic policy. It has a particular and unique construction in Austria, whose special design warrants

xxi

detailed investigation. Among other factors, the phenomenon of Social Partnership embodies what British historian Tony Judt describes as "Europe's emergence at the dawn of the 21st century as a paragon of international virtues: a community of values and a system of interstate relations held up by Europeans and non-Europeans alike as an exemplar for all to emulate" (Post-War, A History of Europe Since 1945, Tony Judt, p. 799, Penguin Books, 2005). Social Partnership is a means by which Europe's social market economy is enacted.

The phenomenal, historical transformation in Europe since the end of World War II was certainly not predicted, nor is it currently a panacea. Europe is just as subject to the low and high tides of historical events as it ever was. Post-war economic and political conditions required continuous adjustment and adaptation — through periods jolted by inflation and recession - clear through to the Great Recession of 2008-2011, and Russia's military invasion of Ukraine in 2022; and now, after the Covid Pandemic, amidst tides of immigration from Africa, the Middle East and Ukraine, the resurgence of populist movements across the continent.

Non-Militarized States Nonetheless, Europe abides as a community of diverse but still united interests and values. Its' novel Social Partnership adaptations represent the conjunction and broad resolution of big historical, economic, and political issues: between, for example, nationalism and non-militarized nation-state co-existence, between liberal and conservative philosophies and most tellingly, between economic and political interests associated with capitalism and democracy. Not that any such over-arching issues can ever be fully addressed or finally resolved (history doesn't work that way), but Europe brings each issue to a new and different level. To take but one example, perhaps now consigned to a foregone era, the emergence of provisionally *non-militarized states* in Europe demonstrates a remarkable coincidence of national interest and historical trajectory. Admittedly, and at the crux of the matter, after World War II, Europe was able to develop relatively, non-militarily only under the aegis of America's protective defense umbrella. That history may now be catching up to Europe (and America). "Total defense expenditure of the European Defense Agency (EDA) Member States was €214 billion in 2021, which was 1.5% of the 26 EDA Member States' GDP, the same percentage as in 2020" (Wikipedia, *List of countries in Europe by military expenditures,* wikipedia.org, March 13, 2024). U.S. military spending as a percent of GDP, by contrast, is 3.5%, or roughly $957 billion (Marcus Lu, *Which Countries Meet NATO's Spending Target,* visual capitalist.com, February 25, 2024). To a great extent, this arrangement restrained European foreign policy initiative, just as American global interests, presumably, wanted it.

Nonetheless, the relatively non-militarized European states demonstrate what can be accomplished when substantial financial resources are used for social, non-military expenditure. Even at this fevered moment, Europe's record over the past 75 years indicates at least a path forward to that long-held aspiration of peaceful nation-state co-existence, and to a broadly hopeful and extended future. A new era dawns, however, as the second Trump administration brandishes unilateral, nationalist interest that may eclipse old alliances. It may turn out that Europe's record of more-or-less peaceful co-existence is nothing but a short-lived historical chimera; all the more reason to recall and extol its accomplishments and insist on its continued, if imperiled, relevance.

Historical Materialism To get a better handle on this and other historical conjunctions and resolutions, this essay surveys Historical Materialism. You might say that citing philosophical theory risks tedium, irrelevance, or both. But it was the philosophy of Historical Materialism, along with such things as the invention of the steam engine, which kindled the flames of modern industrial development. Historical Materialism proposes in profound ways how material relations between owners, employers, and workers are not only self-evidently central to industrial and business enterprises but also largely configure the historical eras in which they take place, for good and for bad.

The mode of production — what sort of industrial relations between employers and employees dominate and with what sort of technology things get produced — from the stone flint to the microchip — significantly configures such things as social class, social consciousness, and the very viability of society. The Social Partnerships of social market capitalism in Europe between labor, capital, and governmental interests constitute a managed resolution of tensions inherent in the capitalist mode of production. It may sound utterly foreign at the moment to American ears, but the issues of Social Partnership and the pragmatic-ideological adaptation it represents can be taken up in any land.

In today's world, the tenets of Historical Materialism may seem outmoded and/or inapplicable. Globalization and expansion of markets transform and occlude traditional class relations and interests – massive volumes of foreign trade influence, if not contort local economic conditions and labor relations. Whatever the case, relations between workers and owners/employers, the focus of Historical Materialism, always need to adapt and come abreast of market developments. Issues between workers and employer/owners, after all, account for much of the upheaval, resolution, and/or irresolution that has occurred in Europe and/or America over the past 150 years. Over this period, class interests gripped Europe and America in different ways. Business and capital interests have had the upper hand in America, but as long as work needs to get done, the labor interest is always vital. In Europe, class interests of labor and capital were thrust into a struggle that finally reached a certain climax in the war-torn conditions that throttled Europe at the close of World War II. At that moment, it was as if the materialist history of industrial class relations clutched the whole continent figuratively by the scruff of the neck and demanded submission. And for just one historical moment, Europe relented, and the *materialist* grip of history was released. It found a new resolution, or balance by which democratic processes guide capitalist development and bound into a purged future.

A confederation of states was born, and what would become the European Union. The system stands four-square behind capitalist enterprise but within certain pre-defined social parameters and, among other things, commitments to welfare, medical care, education, and collective bargaining. 'Social Market Capitalism', as it is here described (in contrast to American market capitalism), offers a variety of what are termed *coordinated market economies*, free markets that are coordinated to support broad social interests; Each of these coordinated markets bears the influence of long *historical materialist* struggle and development whose end is not what its philosopher, Marx, prophesied — the overthrow of capitalism by the working class — but reconciled capital and labor interests and sustainable productivity and prosperity for the future — upholding democratic processes that effectively manage economic relations, staving off economic inequality and the destructive forces of modern polarization.

Part I

Chapter One:
Take the European Bull by Its Horns

This foregoing being said, the proverbial bull needs to be taken by the horns. Contemporary European economic and political affairs must stand down historic trends and face what appear to be more than transitory challenges.

Productivity The European Union (E.U.) counts 27-member states, 20 of which are a part of the Euro monetary zone, who share the Euro as a common currency. These states include Nordic Denmark, Sweden, and Finland, better-known Western countries such as France, Germany, and Italy, and newly arrived eastern European countries, such as Hungary, Bulgaria, Romania, Poland, and the Czech Republic, as well as states of the Mediterranean south, Greece, Spain, and Portugal. As such, the zone comprises a burgeoning confederation of four distinct and separate regions, each with histories of different, unequal economic development. This makes judging Europe as a single entity difficult. Broadly speaking, Eurozone, Euro-sharing countries have undergone considerable growing pains in the past 25, or so years.

Eurozone status at the moment provokes raised eyebrows on both sides of the Atlantic and dire concerns in other quarters. However obscure, these matters are serious. As the seminal French newspaper Le Monde reported, "In 2008, the eurozone and the U.S. had equivalent gross domestic products (GDP) at current prices of $14.2 trillion and $14.8 trillion respectively (€13.1 trillion and €13.6 trillion). Fifteen years on, in 2023, the eurozone's GDP is just over $15 trillion, while US GDP has soared to $26.9 trillion. As a result, the GDP gap is now 80%!" (Arnaud Leparmentier, *The GDP gap between Europe and the United States is now 80%,* Le Monde, September 24, 2023). As widely known, GDP numbers provide a composite scoresheet to measure and compare economies, not to mention guide governmental and financial policy-makers. The GDP is comprised of taking the "quantities of all final goods and services produced and sold in markets, multiplying them by their current prices, and adding up the total" (Khan Academy, *Measuring the size of the economy: gross domestic product,* Khan Academy.org).

The definition may be straightforward, but the interpretation is complex, depending on whether the sum of what is purchased in the economy is measured, known as the *expenditures approach,* or if the *income approach* is adopted, which measures "income earned on what is produced" (ibid). Whatever, it's a huge number and don't forget to throw in foreign trade deficits and/or surpluses into the balance. Avoiding the miasma that too much economic detail often produces (leave that to high finance bankers and professional economists), GDP numbers reflect all sorts of other indicators. The *productivity gap* between the Eurozone and the U.S. economy over the last 15 years involves European shortfalls in *corporate-level spending on R&D, corporate and banking (sic) profitability, stock market valuation, technological innovation,* and *per capita income growth* (Eric Albert, *Europe trails behind the United-states in economic growth,* Le Monde, Nov. 1, 2023).

Such dour appraisals, however, are not universally shared. Other commentators, such as Zsolt Darvos, insist that global comparisons be measured in terms of *Purchasing Power Parity* (PPP), that is, "the rate at which the currency of one country would have to be converted into that of another country to buy the same amount of goods and services in each country" (Zsolt Darvos, The European Union's remarkable growth performance relative to the United States, Bruegel, Oct. 26, 2023). By this measure, Darvos argues, "E.U. output is just slightly falling behind U.S. output" (ibid), and gaps in *per-capita income* and *output per hour* in many parts of the E.U. and the Eurozone have narrowed considerably. Thus, he finds "the narrative wrong that asserts (sic) the E.U. has significantly fallen behind the U.S. in terms of output. The crucial question is why the E.U. economy performs so well despite its many well-known weaknesses" (ibid).

Differences of opinion and perspective about European economic performance reveal complexities of measurement and assessment. Circumstances such as the shutdown of cheap Russian oil exports to Germany and supply chain interruptions because of Covid and the Ukraine War also play a definitive role. Then there is Brexit and all the economic and political challenges it unleashes. Eurozone GDP may not have grown as much as the GDP in the United States, but since 2007, it has grown in 13 of the past 16 years. *(World Bank Open Data, GDP growth (annual %) — Euro area, 2023)* This timeframe includes 2008, when European financial institutions and banks were blindsided by the sub-prime mortgage meltdown in the United States, the attendant banking industry crisis, and the pandemic-stricken years of 2020/2021. An economic downturn in Europe is as much circumstantial and episodic as systemic.

Supposed European economic weaknesses still require further explication. The vulnerability associated with the issues of productivity and unemployment exposes the European project to taunts that it is *insufficiently competitive*; code, as the Financial Times would have it, for dismantling European progressive labor, taxation, and welfare policies. Measures to mitigate both shortfalls are underway — without sacrificing the broader commitments of Europe's social market economies. But doubts still come to the fore. Critical voices and perspectives are cogently and concisely if somewhat abstractly, represented by Chartbook's Adam Tooze in his essays 1 & 2 on *the Euro at 25*.

The driving force behind European unification over the past 75 years has been to achieve a continent-wide monetary union. But the E.U. is loose in the joints. There is no United States of Europe. Instead, there are, more or less, 27 sovereign state E.U. economies that are united only by treaty, circumspectly monitored and directed by federal E.U. authority, and circumspectly presided over by the European Central Bank (ECB). As yet, there is no European Union Constitution. Lines of authority are still being drawn. The outcome is uncertain. As Tooze notes, "Negotiations over banking and capital market unions have been ongoing for years. The need for a substantial (E.U., sic) fiscal capacity, backed by (ECB, sic) common debt, is both so obvious and seemingly so impossible in political terms that it induces eye-rolling and handwaving talk of the difficulty of *"treaty change"* (Adam Tooze, Chartbook 260 Beyond failing forward? The Euro at 25 [Part 1], Substack Chartbook, January 11, 2024).

There's a lack of EU/ECB centralized economic authority to finance common or aggregate European debt. It is quite complex, but it would essentially mean getting each individual national economy into the same harness to guarantee debt finance, putting some states more on the hook to cover debt than others. The lack thereof resulted in ineffective ECB monetary and national government fiscal policy coordination in the aftermath of the 2007 banking crisis. In what Tooze describes as a *perverse policy mix*, "the ECB and European governments willfully hiked interest, imposed austerity, and allowed confidence in bond markets to evaporate" (ibid). National economies were blind-sided by sudden credit shortages and debt *call-ins*. Starting with Greece, followed by Ireland, Portugal, Cyprus, and Spain, a *sovereign debt crisis* erupted in which state finances had to be rescued by deficit spending. Borrowing interest rate costs were so high that national economies verged on bankruptcy and had to be *bailed out* by the ECB, which could only supply limited funds. The E.U. financial system almost crashed. Austerity measures were imposed on the affected countries. This triggered cutbacks in public spending, economic recession, and, as noted above, higher unemployment. As Tooze concludes, "Europe's banks suffered a disastrous shock after 2007 from which they, unlike their U.S. counterparts, have not fully recovered" (ibid).

Such *disastrous* policies led to a credit crisis in Europe between 2015 and 2019 in which the ECB introduced *negative interest rates-* of all things! — in order to counter deflationary economic trends and reinvigorate investment. When things got tough, more coordinated and *common* approaches to finance debt foundered on issues of trust and, ultimately, who would have to underwrite national shortfalls associated with suspected profligacy. As Tooze notes, "proposals for common E.U. spending programs pushed by France and other member states did not meet with a warm reception in Berlin" (ibid). Germany's economic power and strength give it preponderant influence in determining the extent of European integration and the nature of economic policy. Germans and Europeans generally favor the Euro and monetary union. It fosters market expansion, greater trade, and all-around economic growth. At the same time, Germany (and other European countries) is loath to surrender too much political and economic independence and autonomy. Hence, no constitution, no common debt, just treaties and negotiations. National pride and politics, independence and autonomy prevent the concentration of outright federal EU/ECB power. And yet issues emerge that demand a common response.

The Pandemic of 2020/2021 provoked more coordinated federal E.U. *Recovery and Resilience Plans*, but Tooze cautions, "Europe's governments interpret the new policy institutions and processes created in 2020 very differently." (ibid) Other assessments, noted as well by Tooze, see these plans as a "qualitative step forward in E.U. governance — demand-driven and performance-based (sic) that act as an amplifier of economic transitions in member states" (Chartbook 260, ibid). Other authors conclude that the design of plans fostered "a national ownership (in countries, for example, like Spain and Italy) which was previously lacking" (C. Korinek and L. Bertram, *Building Back Better: a Promise Fulfilled?* socialeurope.eu, February

19, 2024). This indicates closer integration between the E.U., the ECB, and member states. Tooze remains doubtful.

Growing Pains Indeed

He concedes that "the E.U. is a highly original political project and European Monetary Union — the Euro — is a work in progress, so getting the balance between fiscal, monetary and regulatory structures right, is tricky" (ibid, Chartbook 261, January 20, 2024). But he also casts broad aspersion and argues that the European project is a regime "organized essentially around the interests of a politico-business elite and their political constituencies…" and goes so far as to denigrate the E.U. as just "a loosely and liberally articulated, state capitalism" (ibid, Chartbook 261). Compared to what?

State capitalism is a global phenomenon where governments "play a strong role, (either *predatory* or *developmental*, sic) in supervising and administering capital accumulation, allocation and ownership (sic)" (A. Dixon, R. Gonzales-Vicente, et al., *Geopolitics and the New State Capitalism,* Taylor & Francis Online — Geopolitics, Vol 27, 2022). Due to the crisis induced by American capitalist, bank overreach in 2007/2008 and the more recent Covid public health crisis of 2020/2021, national states have had to exercise economic prerogatives in excess of those "that are merely expected from capitalism's intrinsic properties" (M. Wright, G. Wood, A. Musacchio, et al., *State capitalism in an international context: varieties and variations,* Journal of World Business, Volume 56, issue 2, February 2024). State intervention into market affairs in the last 15 years is relatively unprecedented, but it's no great secret: states intervene to support capital and corporate interests — oligopolies in Russia, for example; or, if it's not the same thing, the pharmaceutical and health insurance (and banking) industries in America. For Tooze, then, the E.U. system is just one among many regimes "in which state and business interests, elite politics, and the functioning of capitalism are inextricably interwoven" (Tooze, ibid). State capitalism has many variants from *China to America, to Japan, South Korea, Saudi Arabia, and Russia*, "none of them self-contained, all combined and interlinked in a process of uneven and combined development" (ibid). Still, state capitalism does strain, if not undermine, capitalist free market competitive precepts, principles, and operations. The state is not supposed to pick winners.

Tooze's intent is to burst the balloon of European pretension about its *history and purpose*. E.U. advocates should "pass the smelling salts" (ibid) and wake up to the perils and straits that their policies and organizational structures bring about. Compared to the robust American recovery from economic crises over close to two decades, the European response, in Tooze's view, has been muddled and wrong-headed. The (sic) "featherbedding of European finance should not be confused with saying that the euro area's policy-makers managed the crisis in such a way as to provide a strong platform for the recovery or long-run growth of European financial capital. Everything suggests the opposite. In this sense, the euro area crisis truly was an instance of (state intervention) Keynesian policy failure. Everyone could have been better off with better policies and better institutions. The mismatch of institutions, policies, politics, and economic realities is a problem at every level, for *ordinary citizens*, for the balance of European democratic capitalism, but also for the success of the E.U. as an elite state capitalist project" (Tooze, Chartbook 261, ibid).

All this, for Tooze, confirms his observation that Europeans have a self-perception that their affairs are only the "sum of the solutions to each of its crises" (ibid). Central coordination is lackluster. But Europe and the E.U. *are* different. Besides being capitalist-minded and to some extent all these things Tooze alleges, it also confirms his analysis, as a "polity with an economy to govern according to certain norms and principles:" It is an ideology in transition, whose postulates seek to avoid rigidity, on the one hand, and Capitalist capture on the other. The EU is wary of joining the hyper-capitalist global moment in which all or most economic matters are federally managed, commodified, and market-driven. The hyper-capitalist trend, as currently construed in different ways by the likes of the USA and China, lacks social and political security. The E.U.'s structural and institutional design places built-in constraints that allow a certain degree of European member-state autonomy and independence. The E.U. just needs time and more fortuitous circumstances to work out its own systemic growing pains. (as many recent developments indicate, however, especially those related to NATO expenditures and alignments, this time may be running out)

Tooze admits his views may be *jaundiced* in their skepticism of the European project. His purpose is to "disrupt the standard liberal distinctions between state-politics-policy and economy, etc." (ibid). But he is simply on the wrong foot when he says, as noted, "The E.U. (sic) is one regime of *state capitalism* in a world shaped by other political economies in all of which state and business interests, elite politics and the functioning of capitalism are inextricably interwoven" (ibid); this admission is jaundiced indeed. The E.U. is explicitly not one regime, perhaps most pointedly because the European states don't want to be coerced or managed by one excessive federal power. They have other social *norms and principles* to uphold. Tooze's 2-part analysis ignores or underestimates the quantum leap executed by the E.U. and, to a greater and lesser degree, its 27 states in establishing viable social democracies. The *social partnerships* that abide in most of these countries between state, business, and labor interests are anchored in the democratic process and participation, in defiance and contradiction of *state capitalist* intrusions and the *state capitalist* epitaph. Democratic interest, after all, is the one great counterpoint to state-capitalist interest. It provides assurance that capitalist markets for the free movement of goods, services, labor, and capital serve an approximate public interest. Despite its ungainly arrangements between the federal E.U., state interests, and the ECB, Europe has managed to concoct a new political economy — as noted, social market capitalism. It has different ideological dimensions that are, however, still grounded in the brute realities of national and international marketplaces.

The social market capitalist system is, for better and for worse, also staunchly oriented to and mediated by the economic and political policy input of the EU's member states. Austria, in particular, shouldered the economic headwinds in the slack Pandemic year of 2020 to grow its GDP in 2021 and 2022 by over 4% (Statistics Austria, *Gross Domestic Product grew by 4.8% in 2022,* statistik.at,

September 2023). Austria, along with the Eurozone in general, grew its GDP in 14 of 16 years since 2007 (Macrotrend, *Austria GDP 2007-2023,* macrotrends.net, 2024). Tooze's sharpest rebuke is that „European capitalism does not self-regulate, it does not deliver the right kind of investment in the right places, or the right level of activity and employment, (A. Tooze, Chatbook 261, ibid). In other words, it fails as a state capitalist enterprise, the very thing; in other passages, he accuses it of being. Europe, apparently, is more de-centralized than he prefers. This is more a matter of systemic design than a random outcome of historic drift. European member states navigate their national and regional political and economic affairs in semi-autonomy. Perhaps this provides a certain resiliency and adaptability when global economic downturns occur. Tooze himself cites one account that acknowledges this propensity. "The dispersal and generally limited policy resources of the E.U. combined with the E.U. Commission's (executive branch, sic) status as a non-elected bureaucracy allows for a constructive political dynamic: member states come to rescue the center because it is not a party-political rival. Its very fragility provided incentives to prop it up so that it can serve its essential purpose of concertation (coordination, sic) and moderation in crisis management" (A. Tooze, Chartbook 260, *Maintaining the E.U.'s Compound polity during the long crisis decade*, M. Ferrera, H. Kriesi, W. Shelkle, ibid).

This points, in Tooze's words, to a one European outcome scenario "between outright failure and deeper integration: resilience without ostentatious change" that can mean "gradual transformation or mere survival in anticipation of the next crisis" (A. Tooze, ibid). The relatively young E.U. arrangements and pragmatic ideology may yet find its way. The foregoing discussion of European economic conditions and institutional adaptation conveys some of the tension, challenge and opportunity with which European affairs are involved. Since the onset of Trump II, such systemic topics should hold particular interest for American eyes, as America itself is now faced with singular systemic challenges and adaptations of its own. The conditions for such challenges and adaptation need to be identified.

Part II
American Survey I

Chapter One:
Economic and Political Divides

Political stalemate and social polarization in America have long been noticed. The extent to which they result from unresolved systemic contradictions of labor relations in the economic sphere is inexcusably neglected. The dialectic depicting their development has been building for decades. It is coming to a head at the moment in growing cataclysmic and unprecedented political terms. Militant capitalists and Republicans pursue what appears to be a plutocratic interest, or rule by the richest classes of society. This interest finds uncanny alignment with large sectors of middle and lower-middle-class echelons of American society who bizarrely identify with the success of their economic overlords, even though that success is bought at the expense of their own exploitation. American market capitalism exerts a powerful hold. The MAGA movement ramps up polarization in which leaders and followers dance a rabbit-hole tango. Sometimes, you can't tell who is leading who. In any case, such polarization appears to prevent broad, bi-partisan evolution and resolution of economic relations at the heart of America's turmoil, much less of a prospective social partnership.

On the other side of the polarized, dialectic divide, the Democratic Party and its many liberal adherents from all walks of life backpedal in defense of what remains of our democratic republic and the social welfare state. This divide sharpens the perennial debate over rightful private and public goods into what could become civil conflict. Adding to the puzzle of stalemate and polarization, over a longer period, the labor movement and labor interests have foundered. This contributes mightily to ongoing and disruptive economic inequality in which the haves have ever more and the have-nots ever less. Positive resolution of this economic contradiction and a society at odds with itself depends on the revival of a robust labor movement and the invocation of a different kind of social welfare state.

The dialectic of historical materialist analysis is a useful tool in this effort because it identifies opposed economic class interests, not in frozen, disused and discredited Marxist terms, but in terms of basic sociology and functional understanding of economic class dynamics. Marxist ideologists errantly postulated the ultimate and historic, zero-sum resolution of class conflict. This misuse of dialectic analysis forecloses its basic utility. The dialectic proposes continuous evolution and adaptation of economic interests. 'Class' divisions in society are subject to reconciliation and more-or-less peaceful resolution. Further, dialectic analysis provides perspective and prospect that patterns of historical development are comprehensible and manageable. It offers relief from the self-inflicted blur and tangle of contemporary affairs, and provides invaluable reference points for evolution. Dialectic analysis applies to the polarization bedeviling America's current political and economic impasse – to its outdated form of democratic capitalism – as well to social market capitalism in Europe. Martin Wolf, Chief Economics Commentator for The Financial Times, utilizes similar analysis. The societies that have been most successful in combining both "universal democratic suffrage and a market economy" and in "serving the interests of the people at large," Wolf finds, are exemplified by the "welfare capitalist" or "social market economies" (sic) of Europe, or of what remains of "liberalism" in America (Martin Wolf, *The Crisis of Democratic Capitalism*, Penguin Book, p. 218, 2023). Such findings are based at least in part on dialectic scrutiny, which parses the historic tango between democracy and capitalism.

At this mounting-tide moment, America's social welfare state has been outmoded and is in the process of being dismantled by Donald Trump's second presidential administration. Whether deserved or not, this dismantling indicates a certain inadequacy, brought on not by a lack of funding, but by a deficiency of systemic adaptation. As a Kaiser Family Foundation report shows, federal government outlays "amounted to $4.63 trillion" to cover programs and services such as Medicare and Medicaid, income security, education and infrastructure in 2024. (sic, J. Cubanski, A. Burns, C. Cox, *What Does the Federal Government Spend on Health Care?* Medicaid, February 24, 2025) These monies roughly constituted 67% of all federal outlays in 2024 (ibid) and represented massive, if only partial 'state' investment in the economy. Whatever purported and undocumented 'waste', 'fraud', and 'abuse' may be at play, the actual issue involves economic efficiency.

Europe and America present two different, if not opposed social welfare models. As will be considered later in more detail, America's public spending/welfare outlays relative to GDP are comparably less than those in other developed western economies. In 2022, for instance, so-called 'public spending' in America measured "36,7% of GDP, compared with 57.2% in France and 48.9% in Germany" (Arnaud Leparmentier, *The US's Ambivalent*

Relationship to a Welfare State, Le Monde International, lemonde.fr, October 23, 2024). European welfare outlays, though, are much more extensive. They include social investments in healthcare, education and employment compensation support. Their tax rates are correspondingly higher. In France, for example, the "public pension burden is 14.5% compared to a 7.5% rate in the USA" (ibid, sic) In such terms are public goods and interests measured.

The inadequacy, or inefficiency of America's social state lies more in the make-up of policy choices and values and the design of the overall economic system. $4.76 trillion should buy a lot of social program delivery and efficacy, yet the USA doesn't even deliver comprehensive, or effective health insurance for everybody, nor adequate support to ensure universal access to higher education and/or technical training. One reason for this, on the face of it, is the co-existence of private and public economies, which are, however, insufficiently integrated.

The U.S. Congress, for example, and more particularly, the private health insurance industry didn't allow for the inclusion of a 'public option' in Affordable Care Act legislation. Health insurance reform, as a result, is still riddled by half-measures. The competition and cost efficiencies that might have resulted by integrating public and private services are lost. The private health insurance industry still recoups $billions in profits, but at the expense of larger social cost, benefit and utility. Part of the current impasse in American affairs and impending downgrade of its social state is attributable to its citizens being unsatisfied customers. The Trump administration currently exploits that dissatisfaction for all its worth, as if there are no alternatives to the total privatization of the American economy. Make no mistake, private business enterprise is central to social prosperity. By more or less sequestering its affairs and function from public obligation and service, however, and especially from the obligations it has to the interests of labor, America will remain prone to social polarization and growing economic inequality. To right this balance, economic analysis must utilize the dialectic to identify class interests and reconcile and resolve their opposition. The economy must be re-politicized, not in the anti-government manner that the Reagan revolution putatively accomplished, nor now in what Trump pursues, but in the name of better sharing and allocating the country's immense wealth. Taxation levels are indeed at the heart of the matter.

Private control of business enterprise enables dynamism geared to market exigencies that produce market efficiency. When allowed overweening purview and control of social, consumer and public interests, however, this efficiency comes at considerable, historically proven expense: the devolution of civic standing, increasing pauperization, and the gradual and now paramount capitalist overthrow of democratic processes. The writing for such developments has long been on the wall.

Just try figuring out what conditions are covered by your health insurance policy, or having to make inquiries about it, or applying for higher education financial aid, or making ends meet on a paltry salary – each symptomatic of larger market mismanagement. The American business economy gets hoisted by its own petard. The all-consuming profit quest and apparent market hegemony overruns the delivery of affordable, decent services. Wide affluence and visible material abundance, if not prosperity, collides with social and economic, dysfunction, impoverishment and division.

The point of this essay is not to bash capitalism too much, but to help create an atmosphere and terms for its reformation. It may be, as Adam Tooze argues, that the US has ‚recovered' from the economic and public health shocks of the past 16 years. The U.S. government was certainly able to infuse the economy with $trillions of Federal Reserve monetary and Congressional fiscal stimulus, not to mention a sizable and costly tax cut. The book is still out on whether such measures were constructive, or simply bail-outs for a foundering economic system, unmoored from its social-welfare, free-enterprise heritage. That system is increasingly hamstrung in meeting the everyday needs for safety, sustenance, and future prospects of its citizenry. To that point - now that the gargantuan 2017 tax cut has been extended in 2025, its record and legacy should be critically examined. Has it delivered the promised goods?

The latest analysis of the 2017 Corporate Tax Cuts produces ambiguous conclusions. Researchers from Princeton University, the University of Chicago, Harvard, and the Treasury Department concluded that tax-cut benefits fall way short of those hailed and promised at the time. The tax cuts boosted corporate investment in the U.S. economy and contributed to wage gains of "about $750 per worker per year on average." But this was well below the "$4,000-$9,000" predicted and promised by Trump administration officials who lobbied in Congress for the bill. The analysis further finds that "the corporate tax cuts came nowhere close to paying for themselves, as conservatives insisted, they would. More to the point, the very premise that tax cuts contribute to economic growth is highly suspect. In a well-researched Economic Policy Institute article, Josh Bivens concludes that "there is essentially no robust relationship between post-tax profit rates and productivity-enhancing business investment in the U.S. economy. (Josh Bivens, *Cutting Corporate Taxes Will Not Boost American Wages*, Economic Policy Institute, epi.org, October 25, 2017).

Instead, tax cuts are adding more than $100 billion a year to America's $34 trillion-and-growing national debt." (Jim Tankersley, *Trump's Tax Cut Fueled Investment but Did Not Pay for Itself, Study Finds,* NYT, March 4, 2024) Chalk up the whole venture, to prolonging the life span of an invalid patient. Republicans talk out of both sides of their mouth. When it serves their purposes in other venues, they decry the debt and deficit funding for government programs, not to mention how it raises credit borrowing rates. But with the tax cuts, private corporate interests take the upper hand. As a result, public debt and financial solvency are put further at risk, not to mention prospects for greater public investment in things like affordable healthcare and higher educational and vocational opportunities. Current media coverage fails to delineate the clear stakes involved in such transactions, which would be highlighted by greater dialectic analysis of public and private interests. As it is, deficit increases, even when they result from Republican policy, help those very same Republicans decry deficits. Such things are at the crux of American polarization and economic dysfunction.

Besides lowering the corporate tax rate from 35 to 21%, the 2017 Trump tax cut also lowered the "top individual income tax rate from 39.6 to 37% and extended other tax advantages for the very wealthy. (C. Marr, S. Jacoby, G. Fenton, *The 2017 Trump Tax Law Skewed to the Rich, Expensive and Failed to Deliver on its Promises,* Center on Budget and Policy Priorities, cbpp.ort, June 13, 2024. Now, the tax cuts of 2025 follow suit.

Corporate tax cuts, somewhat self-evidently, contribute to growth in governmental deficit spending The Reuters news agency reported, "the U.S. government on Friday posted a $1.695 trillion budget deficit in fiscal 2023, a 23% jump from the prior year as revenues fell and outlays for Social Security, Medicare and record-high interest costs on the federal debt rose" (David Lawder, *US Budget Gap Soars to $1.7 trillion, the Largest Outside of Covid Era*, reuters.com, October 20, 2023). Even as such deficit numbers appear ominous, they do fluctuate. They were comparably huge during the COVID year of 2021, at $2.78 trillion, and then declined "during President (sic) Biden's first two years in office" (ibid). Whatever their number, all this deficit spending upsets balanced-budget orthodoxy, which seeks to balance tax revenues and spending obligations — the allocation and distribution of public and private goods.

Private and Public Goods — Wealth and Poverty

As noted, understanding the issues of private and public interests, or goods is critical not only in itself, but for restraining and resisting the oncoming 'privatization' onslaught. There should be essential agreement between public and private goods, to maintain balance between the complimentary, but competing interests of democratic equality and economic freedom. Goods and services, such as for clean air and water, roads and bridges, public education, the judicial system and public welfare, for example, should be provided as matters of public interest, to assure equality of access and use. Especially since the 2007 financial crisis, however, increased deficit spending (and erratic twists of Federal Reserve Bank interest rates) beleaguers the efficiency of government spending. Privatization of such services and the profit incentive on which it depends, however, threatens to limit broad public access, still further bifurcating and dividing society.

By now, after months in office, the actual Trump agenda heaves into clear view. The naked object portends to eviscerate public services, the federal departments that deliver them, and Congressional-provisions that allocate their finance. Cuts in spending are meant to underwrite pronounced and massive cuts in taxes. The abject interest is to restore control of the economy to private economic interests. In dialectical terms, this indicates that the old public goods, and public-welfare consensus has been outflanked, as a casualty mostly of political fiat, but also of outmoded public spending policies. This diagnosis must call those who care for democratic equality and social unity to reconceive and reassert ideals and policies that uphold a new public goods, and public interest agenda – that will renew democratic government. This agenda must enact a public-goods vision of economic freedom, to reign in hyper-capitalist distortions brought on by globalization and the militancy of MAGA economic designs. The alleged object of Trump's tariffs and privatization agenda is to increase American productivity, but at prospectively dear cost. To say nothing of the domestic economy, the system of international trade, which has engendered mostly long-standing peace and prosperity, is likely to founder.

Globalization of the American economy left the barn decades ago. The promise of larger markets induced widespread business and multi-national corporations to support the re-location of production facilities beyond American borders. The attendant integration of national economies proceeded apace into what now has become a world economy. The Trump administration aims to turn back the hands of time and reverse the terms of this evolution, at whatever the cost to global markets and the world trading system. Perhaps the motivation for Trump's tariff policies, in particular, is honorable. But it is a high-stakes gamble whose dimensions and designs are obscure. The repatriation of thousands, if not millions of domestic, manufacturing jobs lost to global market expansion might restore a semblance of economic equality and vitality. But the maneuver flaunts market equilibrium. It takes more than honorable intentions to return economic enterprise into the barn of domestic employment, economic control and direction. Successful execution of such a plan requires strategic calculation, not the blunderbuss, haphazard approach thus far exhibited.

Poverty In the meantime, outright poverty persists and grows, itself an outright indictment of the skewed 'private goods' market economy. Renowned sociologist, Matthew Desmond points out, "according to the latest national data, one in eighteen people in the United States lives in deep poverty, a subterranean level of scarcity. In 2022, the poverty line was drawn at $13,590 a year for a single person and $27,750 a year for a family of four. Take the poverty line and cut it in half: Anything below that is considered deep poverty. In 2020 (sic), almost 18 million people in America survived under these conditions." (Desmond, Matthew, *Poverty Isn't a Line,* Plough, July 8, 2024)

The operative word in his analysis is *subterranean*. These people are dispersed and practically invisible, but their struggle, along with those living in simple poverty, altogether totaling "37.9 million people or 11.5%" (sic) of the American population, capitalist admonitions aside, is flagrantly indefensible. (United States Census Bureau, *National Poverty in America Awareness Month,* January 2024, census.gov, January 2024).

In the United States, according to Sanda Ojiambo, "almost 23% of the workforce labors in low-paying jobs, more than twice the level found in Chile, France or Japan. , (*Why companies who pay a living wage create wider societal benefits,* World Economic Forum, May 14, 2024)

The country arrives at an endpoint, or crossroads. It is exceedingly obvious that "short-changing workers is in nobody's interest. Low wages erode trust in our political, economic and social systems. They tear at the fabric of society and constrain economic growth. In the business context, low wages are not a cost advantage – they are a cause of systemic risk." (ibid) Strict business interests would, of course, dispute this conclusion by asserting that moderating wages (and taxes) do provide a cost advantage, thereby allowing capital investment and expansion. In actuality, however, lower wages and taxes has not reduced prices; to the contrary. Market capitalism currently produces an abundance of income inequality and relatively high prices.

On the other side of the 'private goods' ledger, conditions are apparently reversed. Here, growing abundance and affluence for large sectors of the American populace appear to validate the hyper-capitalist moment — defined here provisionally as corporate and global economic interests colluding to overtake domestic market systems and democratic provision of public-interest expenditures. These were designed and implemented to restrain inequality and promote social unity. But they have grown wobbly - unable to restrain income and wealth inequality and sustain the time-honored social welfare consensus. This induces moral lassitude, enflamed and perpetuated by fevered capitalist overreach and entitlement — tough luck to the vague, less fortunate masses. President Joe Biden's 2024 State of the Union speech addressed at least the need for updating and re-balancing the American economy. Among other things, he outlined several tax increase proposals — a "25% minimum income tax for "anyone worth at least $100 million," for "raising corporate minimum taxes from 15-21%," and "for quadrupling taxes on stock buybacks for companies" (Noah Kirsch, *Billionaires Are Raging About Biden's SOTU (sic) Tax Proposals,* Daily Beast, March 8, 2024). These proposals clearly asserted a public goods agenda. Not surprisingly, such an agenda raised the indignation of several billionaires.

The article cites grocery billionaire-magnate, John Catsimatidis, in particular, as one who makes it plain for whom the U.S. government should work, "I think it sounds like President Biden doesn't want a capitalist government. He wants a government for socialism. And socialism doesn't work. Ask the people in Russia, ask the people in Cuba, ask the people in Venezuela" (ibid). In this, Catsimatidis voices the current plutocratic capture of the U.S. government and, more broadly, the capitalist capture of American society — one in which MAGA polarization actually serves the perpetuation of economic inequality and the impoundments of poverty. As Biden's proposals indicated, however, U.S. government commitment to the broader social interests of American society could still be made paramount — such are the stakes and dynamic dialectic between public and private goods, between democracy and capitalism. Now that they are definitively out of power, the Democratic Party and any sober-minded conservative must reconceive a regime in which the public interest in health, education, and fair wages, among other things, can be renewed.

The backdrop for that dialectic and the economic contradiction to which it applies, while billionaires make their billions, features economic inequality, powerlessness, and disenfranchisement taking greater hold. Biden simply meant to re-balance the economy's dialectic, not at all in the direction of Cuba, Russia, Venezuela, et al., but perhaps toward the social market national economies of the European Union. Biden's response recognized the terrible systemic contradictions driving the country into deeper polarization and political impasse. His speech would perhaps have carried more punch had he directly addressed the post-pandemic inflation surge. Inflation upsets large swaths of the American public, who carry enough economic burden as it is. That burden would be more tolerable if, in the first place, the people had higher wages to buffer against inflationary tides. The pathetic $7.25 federal minimum wage hasn't risen since 2009. In the meantime, it has been overtaken by more than half the states in which minimum wages range from $8.75 in West Virginia to $16.00 in California (US Department of Labor, *State Minimum Wage Laws,* dol.gov., 2023). Biden and the Democratic Party weren't apparently ready to mount a concerted and 4-square campaign to couple minimum wage increases to the inflation rate, dour economic prognostications to the contrary be damned. In the meantime, greater and wider-spread wage parity languishes, awaiting a shift in political winds that never quite comes to pass. Instead, protests over inflationary conditions are enflamed by misdirected populist retribution.

Something is out-of-whack. The people feel it in their bones, but most are at a loss as to explaining and understanding that the current state of affairs is a result of misjudgment, or blatant capitalist overreach, or both, against the provision of living wages for the American people. In his Letter to the editor Duluth News Tribune, Martin Rhoads put his finger on it, before the calamity of Trump's second presidency occurred. The writing was on the wall. "Support for former President Donald Trump is not rocket science. The working and labor class was ignored by our party system for years. Trump came along at the right time to ride and use the wave of hate (and neglect, sic) to his advantage" (Martin Rhoads, *Trump a Wolf in Sheep's Clothing,* Duluth News Tribune, January 26, 2024). Skewed American economic development over at least the past 40 years is a result, among other things, of confusion over the allocation of public and private goods. This confusion and the social unrest to which it relates is rooted in outmoded and retarded ideological developments. The foregoing diagnosis outlines the urgent need for America to follow a different way forward.

The lapse in 'public goods' consciousness is perhaps nowhere better seen than in the downfall of collective bargaining associated with the decline of the American trade union movement. Appendix 2 cites chapter and verse the corresponding erosion of labor income over the last 40 years, lost as support for and involvement in trade union membership dwindled. **(See Appendix 2, Collective Bargaining & Wage Inequality)** As the appendix indicates, wage loss over this period has especially fallen out on middle- and lower-income earners, driving the growth of economic inequality, so decidedly contributing to the polarization of American society. Such developments are amply demonstrated by verifiable, empirical data and analysis, which convey the extent of inequality in America on a world-wide comparative basis.

The GINI Index & Inequality Rankings

In comprehensive, 2023 worldwide inequality rankings calculated by WiseVoter, the USA is 47th among all nations of the world. Its GINI index rating is 41.5. This indicates substantially high-income disparity, where a rate of 50 is considered ominous and intolerable. South Africa, still smarting from its heritage of apartheid, has an index rating of 63, the highest income inequality of all countries. It is joined at the top by Hong Kong, Botswana, and many other African nations. Countries with the lowest GINI index include Slovakia, the Czech Republic, Ukraine, Iceland, and Belgium, ranging from 23.2 to 27.2. Other European countries pertinent to the current treatise find Austria's GINI score at 30.2, Germany at 31.7, France at 32.4, Italy at 35.2, and Sweden at 29.3 (Wisevoter *High-Income Countries*, wisevoter.com).

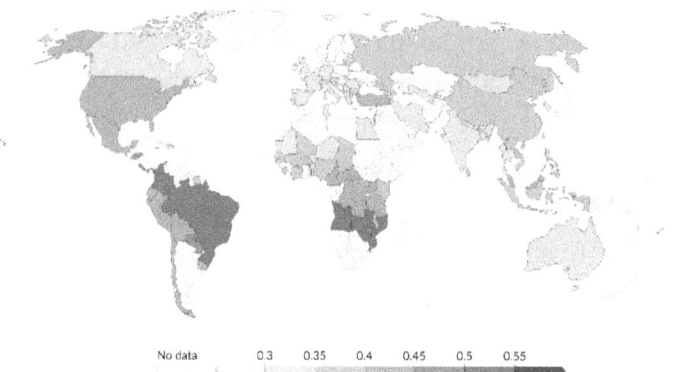

These GINI statistics might appear antiseptic, but they do provide a useful lens for interpreting economic conditions in America and the status of, and relation between public and private goods. Income inequality measures cross-population, income distribution differences in a particular year. Income refers to household disposable income. Now all this wouldn't be such a big deal except that income inequality supercharges social polarization, now so disturbing and evident in America. Besides less discernible racial and ethnic attitudes, economic inequality provides an ongoing pretext for distrust and division. You might say if economic inequality were such a big part of polarization, you would see and hear more outcry from those most deprived. More than anything, this indicates market capitalism's capture and lack of awareness of viable alternatives. Economic discontent in America finds other, misdirected expression.

A direct correlation is scant, in fact, between the bottom 20-30% of wage earners, those who daily endure the fallout of economic inequality, and involvement in the MAGA movement. There are definitely overlaps. After the 2020 election, studies by the University of Washington revealed (sic) "that almost half of purported MAGA supporters earn less than $50,000, (half earn more), and 70% do not have a college education" (Kim Eckart, *New Nationwide Survey Shows MAGA Supporters' beliefs about the Pandemic, the Election, and the Insurrection,* washington.edu, February 5, 2021) The American economic system exerts an enormous captive influence. People are to a large extent constrained by their economic system from seeing, let alone advocating, alternative economic designs. As prominent linguist and social philosopher, Noam Chomsky put it, the economic order of things is driven and promoted by all media arms "manufacturing consent." Manufactured consent is further reinforced by all sorts of 'conservative' and militant Republican mouth organs. Their take on 'public-goods in the economy' can be strident. They hold that welfare redistribution, or so-called 'wealth transfer,' among other things, enervates initiative and enterprise. There is no excuse, even for those who've worked hard but still can't seem to find employment or afford health care, higher education, housing, food, etc. Apparently, these people, much less the indigent, should have little or no claim to government-paid benefits. This trope of capitalist ideology still claims wide appeal, despite the economic conditions and social polarization it produces.

The GINI inequality numbers tell only part of the story. Interestingly, American redistributive expenditures, by reliable counts, covering formal, social welfare outlays, are even higher than states in Europe, who are identifiably social-democratic- that is, these states reinforce the viability of democratic governance by recognizing and incorporating definitive socio-economic interests. And yet, the mayhem of American society, seen in the rates of crime, drug abuse, poverty, and other indicators of social dysfunction, continues to be maddeningly unsolved. The vehemence in the country against the Democratic Party and the liberals who support it, is an outgrowth of this frustration. Democrats are increasingly caught with their pants down in defense of a bloated, 'public-goods' welfare system that doesn't quite live up to its promise of reducing the sharp edges and inequalities of the competitive marketplace. Claims that more extensive welfare is necessary to finally ameliorate harsh conditions sound increasingly tinny. The fact is that the Democratic Party's positioning and policies over at least the past 40 years have been wrong-footed. Democratic Party leaders, too, it seems, have been inducted into the system's 'manufactured consent'. However, grudgingly or unwittingly, the party came around to accept the economic analysis imposed by the go-go capitalist marketeers of the Reagan era. It got drafted into the wrong argument back in the 80s, which centered on the level and extent of taxation.

The spectacle of the Democratic Party losing its working-class roots is sad and ominous. It reveals ideological timidity, inefficacy, confusion, or all three, over how best to address economic conditions, and so strengthen the viability of American democracy. Perhaps it means adopting social and economic policies that are ardently pragmatic and non-, or even anti-ideological. The argument that the party should have gotten into, and might have, but for the fatal capitulation to apparent market and political realities during the Clinton years, is that the market alone is inadequate to the task of maintaining decent wages and conditions of employment. It manages lower unemployment on the cheap, to the long-term detriment of social cohesion and ultimate economic viability.

Here, for example, instead of listening to their respective Treasury Secretaries, Robert Rubin and Larry Summers under Clinton, and Timothy Geithner under Obama, it might have worked out much better if either one, or both of them said, "Gee, gentlemen, I know how important the central banks and Wall Street are, but they're taking us for a ride. Tell me how I can challenge their power, without losing too much economic traction, and share the wealth better, to serve the broader interests of the American people in a fair and resilient economic system."

On account of this epochal failure, economic inequality has grown to consume the country. The GINI index is more than a number. It is a lever that should drive economic debate and policy. It shouldn't support any ideological agenda, but identify and proclaim the social interest in conclusive and objective terms. Despair is in the wings, if not on center stage. Capitalism isn't all bad. The Democratic Party simply got seduced by its sinewy limbs and forgot to keep in mind the sharpness of its fangs. Muscles have gone slack. The tendons of modern Democracy are tested as never quite before, but can still be revived.

Part and parcel of the competitive marketplace is to broker winners and losers. One hallmark of its success is to reward productivity and efficiency and thereby sustain market dynamism and growth. Inequality is a necessary, if unfortunate, byproduct of the competition. It is taken for granted. But a failure to notice the extent to which income and wealth inequality has grown, or to minimize it, augers ill fate. Indices of economic inequality float in and out of awareness like trial balloons, prompting attention but then fading off onto another horizon, to be replaced by other figures rambling by. As noted, other frameworks are needed by which all the data can be reinvigorated, providing new contexts to address the issues of economic distribution and inequality.

Such a framework and findings are gleaned in a well-documented report. *"Why is Europe More Equal than the United States?"* spells out the differences between the United States and European economies in terms of wage distribution. At the upper end, "The average national income per adult stood at e52,700 in the US at purchasing power parity, compared to e44,900 in Northern Europe, e35,300 in Western Europe, and e21,700 in Eastern Europe. Things look very different at the bottom of the pretax income distribution. The bottom 50% earned only about e12,300 in the US in 2017, compared to e21,600 in Northern Europe and e14,600 in Western Europe. Of the twenty-seven countries considered in this paper, the US ranks third in terms of average national income per adult but nineteenth when it comes to the average income of the poorest 50%" (Ibid, T. Blanchet, L. Chancel, A. Gethin, World Inequality Lab – Working Paper No. 2020/19, P. 19). Such figures measure systemic differences with regard to the distribution, deployment and utilization of income. (Measures of wealth portray similar differences) In the normal course of things, such measurements may be unremarkable. At this momentous moment, however, they reveal the economic roots of social polarization, particularly in America. The rightfully renowned French economist Tom Piketty (and what must be his huge research team) provides telling historical perspective of what happens when economic inequality gets out of hand.

Piketty's Inequality Treaties

Piketty surveys historical tax data and national economic development in great and cautionary detail. First, in his book *Capital in the 21st Century,* Piketty explores the historical lineage of economic analysis, as it focuses on the phenomenon of wealth concentration. Each of Piketty's precursors, from Malthus, to Ricardo, to Karl Marx, detected the threat that capitalism poses: "Arbitrary and unsustainable inequalities that radically undermine the meritocratic values of democratic society" (p.1). First, in the early 1800s, it was Thomas Malthus and the economist, David Ricardo who identified the challenges posed by overpopulation. Ricardo defined the 'scarcity principle' of economics. He identified overpopulation as leading to land scarcity and the consequent increase and concentration of landlord wealth at the expense of everybody else. This would disturb social equilibrium.

Then it was Karl Marx, who from 1848 and the publication of his 'Communist Manifesto' seemed to prove, as will be noted, the categorical untenability of capitalism as an economic system. The 'principle of infinite accumulation' defined in his influential treatise, *Capital* (1867), predicted, as a matter of systemic necessity, the overaccumulation of wealth for industry and business owners, the capitalists, and the pauperization of everybody else. This had particularly ominous repercussions as more and more people were involved in the operations and machinations of industrialization.

Though their principles are still insightful, neither Marx' nor Ricardo's predictions were entirely born out. For Ricardo, the value of land did climb as predicted, but it didn't skyrocket. As a society of manufacturing emerged, instead, "the value of farmland inexorably declined relative to other forms of wealth" (ibid, p.6). The apocalyptic all-out war between capitalists over ever-diminishing returns on capital investment that Marx foretold didn't quite pan out either. Nor did inequality ever quite reach such proportions that worldwide revolutions ensued (except in Russia, but that's another story). In Piketty's words, "Marx totally neglected the possibility of durable technological progress and increasing productivity which counterbalance excessive wealth concentration" (ibid, p.10). Marx foresaw these developments, but discounted their ability to fundamentally shift the systemic realities of capitalism.

He was convinced instead that the over-accumulation and concentration of wealth would persist as an ongoing threat to social life, social equilibrium, and overall social development. It can't be wished or rationalized away. For all its benefits, the capitalist system still generates massive contradictions between wealth and penury, for instance which are not self-regulating. Adam Smith, the great, early theorist of capitalism, believed that the system's 'invisible hand,' "was always capable of achieving equilibrium (of supply and demand, sic) on its own, without major deviations" (ibid, p.9). Though the workings of supply and demand in the economy are ever useful in determining wages and prices, they don't preclude large and lasting disparities and inequities of destabilizing wealth distribution. Disequilibrium is structural. Even in the long-term, it doesn't right itself. While praising him in some respects, Piketty dismisses the "fairy-tale or at any rate happy ending" prognostications of Simon Kuznets, the 20th-century American economist. Kuznets postulated in 1955 that "income inequality decreases automatically in advanced capitalist societies," which engendered the oft-cited trope of the 1980s and 90s that "(economic, sic) growth is a rising tide that lifts all boats" (ibid p.11).

Piketty recognizes Kuznets as a pioneer, but one hoisted by his own petard. To make his point, Piketty employs two sources of data that had previously been unavailable for economic analysis: "US federal income tax returns (which did not exist before the creation of the income tax in 1913) and Kuznets' own estimates of US national income" (ibid, p 12). This data took economic analysis out of the realm of incomplete economic citation and theory and provided a comprehensive and accurate measurement of actual, unequal income distribution. Such data can now gauge the evolution of income distribution over time. This marks a major contribution not only to scientific measurability and knowledge but to 'democratic transparency.' On the basis of Piketty's analysis, it turns out that Kuznets's optimism about advanced capitalist societies was unfounded. Piketty's data constructs new frameworks whose details and prescriptions are not, however, uncontroversial. They challenge traditional paradigms, and at least offer the prospect of conclusive economic explanation and enduring resolution. Piketty revamps and upgrades the cited customary GINI coefficient for measuring economic inequality. By doing so, he reinforces the credibility of empirical analysis. Now, for a little Piketty economics.

Among many formulae, one $r > g$ measures the way in which the rate of return on capital wealth — r — (stocks/bonds/rents, etc.) and existing wealth owned (disproportionately) by the rich exceeds > (exceeds) the rate of growth in the economy as a whole g. This analysis explains economic vicissitudes, especially characteristic of market capitalist systems, undergone by countries over time and up to the present day. It also accounts for the periodic and historical cataclysms that are the result of widespread and deeply rooted economic and social inequality. As Piketty writes in his seminal work, *Capital and Ideology*, post-1848 European ownership societies promised "individual emancipation and social harmony…associated with universal access to property and to the protection of the state." (ibid, Belknap Press of Harvard University. 2020 p. 479) Such developments gradually overcame the prior historical order, which was characterized by castes of clergy, warrior-nobility, and peasanty, "inequalities of status" (ibid). As Piketty further notes, "these new ownership societies largely conquered the world thanks to the military, technological, and financial power they derived from intra-European competition." (ibid) But these societies (sic) "failed for two reasons: first, in the period 1880-1914, they attained a level of inequality and concentration of wealth even more extreme (than in the prior landed gentry-late mercantile period, sic), which they purported to replace; and second, the nation-states of Europe ultimately self-destructed and were replaced by other states (such as Nazi Germany and the Soviet Union, sic) organized around new political and ideological projects" (ibid 76).

Piketty's research extends to the post-World War II era as well. At first, as disparities between wealth and income declined after the vast war outlays, greater income equality ensued in the period between 1950 and 1980. In a New Yorker article, Idrees Kahloon cites Piketty's analysis in describing that period as demonstrating conscious social and political policy decisions to "reduce the social influence of private property" (The New Yorker, *The Leveller* 3/9/2020, p.76) "Steeply progressive income and estate taxes shaped income distributions" (ibid) during those 'Trente Glorieuses" — the 30 glorious years. These were years of American Greatness, aside from the catastrophe of the Vietnam War, among other ill developments, such as seething racial discrimination. Piketty's analysis reveals the extent to which greater income parity, or equality, has been reversed in the current period up to 2020.

Amplified by findings given above, rendered by the World Inequality Lab and those of the American Economic Association that the "richest 10% of Americans today take home (a historically high) 48% of all domestic income" (sic) (ibid), Piketty has another formula to measure key economic performance outcomes. This is denoted $a = r \times ß$. It is a quantification formula that reveals "the importance of capital (as opposed to income) for an entire country"

(Piketty, *Capital,* p. 54). (ibid). Hang on to your hats. It is complex. As noted, r is the rate of return on capital (stocks, bonds, rents) and existing wealth. a = the share of income from capital in national income, GDP (the value of all goods and services produced by a country) minus capital depreciation required for production, or 10% of GDP. ‚ß' = the capital wealth/income ratio. Without going into the computation, Piketty shows that ß = 500-600% in the major industrial countries of France, the USA, and Japan, to name but a few. This number, for Piketty, represents untenable, if not disastrous, economic conditions, especially in America where economic clefts between top 10% and bottom 50% income levels have grown so formidably wide **(See Appendix 3, Net National Wealth Chart).**

The combination of income and wealth inequality drives social discontent, now coming to dominate American affairs. In other words, most people are working hard, but not getting ahead. This is the combustible element that should be kept front and center in formulating alternative economic and taxation policy.

In all its complexity, Piketty maintains that this formula comprises the "first fundamental law of capitalism" (ibid, p.52). It combines the 3 most important concepts for capitalist system analysis: 1) the capital/income ratio, 2) the share of capital in national income, and 3) the rate of return on capital. Through it, he shows that income from capital (profits, interests, dividends, rents, etc.) "generally hovered around 30% of national income" (ibid p.53).

Overall, his analysis provides ample and conclusive (though not uncontroversial) grounds for programs he claims would usher the modern world into post-capitalist democratic prosperity — the 'broad, sunlit uplands,' as Winston Churchill put it, of a future in which wealth is more equitably distributed and thereby social unity more assured. Piketty lambasts current EU social democratic regimes as 'glaringly inadequate' (sic) and weak in advancing truly sustainable progressive agendas. The current essay disputes Piketty's more categorical prognostications. Despite the persuasive clarity of his analysis on inequality, Piketty's policy recommendations challenge some of the basic conditions and incentives that foster wealth generation and productivity in the first place. Piketty doesn't give European social market economies enough credit. They recast purely market capitalist economies, and advance greater wage parity economies, to the benefit both of the people and long-term economic development. In general, they have engineered agreement between public-and-private goods interests, and thereby strengthen the fusion between democracy and capitalism.

Other studies further elaborate American wage parity dereliction. A Brookings Institution report, for example finds that "53 million Americans ages 18 to 64—44% of all workers—earn low hourly wages. Their median hourly earnings are $10.22, and for those working full time year-round, median annual earnings are about $24,000." (M. Ross, N. Bateman, A. Friedhoff, *A Closer Look at Low-Wage Workers across the Country*, brookings.ed, March, 2020) The power of the economic system ordains such outcomes and leaves little recourse for those affected. People are led to accept such conditions, reinforced by an inadequacy of information and/or awareness of alternative options.

When it comes to over-compensation, conversely, "seventy-four percent of Americans believe that CEOs are paid too much relative to the average worker—even as they underestimate the annual compensation of large-company CEOs. According to the report *"Americans and CEO Pay: 2016 Public Perception Survey on CEO Compensation"* (Stephen Miller, *CEO's Vastly Overpaid, Most Americans Say Society for Human Resource Management (SHRM)*, shrm.org, March 13, 2016). Both reports get at the meat and bones of wage and compensation issues. These issues are obviously complex and depend on skill levels, market factors of supply and demand and the productivity, or revenues rates generated by given businesses, or industries. Essentially, however, they reveal the striking cleft left over from market capitalist finagling. Perception of pay scales is scandalously distorted. "The typical American would limit CEO pay to no more than 6x that of the average worker. This figure is significantly below current pay multiples, which are approximately 210x the average worker's pay, based on Equilar's compensation figures" (ibid). Such discrepancies amplify Piketty's warning about the civilizational consequences of untoward income and wealth inequality! Somebody is taking the money and running.

Economic Class, and the Escape from Freedom

Even as now amply described, the issue of economic inequality demands still greater definition. The philosophy of Historical Materialism and its dialectical class analysis magnifies the focus on basic modes of production. It reveals the structural sources of unsustainable income and wealth inequality. It may yet have a thing or two to say about events and economic relations, even in America, where class analysis never really caught on. Class struggle in America, as such, has often been deferred or dispersed by incessant market gyrations. Except perhaps in the Depression years of the 1930s, the struggle never quite reached climactic resolution. America's open frontiers, individualist belief system, and mostly sustained productivity growth provided a great outlet valve by which society partially sidestepped the conflicts of class. Of course, American economic and social classes always existed and still do, whether defined by income and wealth, or educational attainment, but class interest and conflict have only intermittently shown sharp teeth. Now is one of those times when income and wealth inequality and ever-growing marketplace commodification come glaring to the fore. These put class interest on the line.

Social division and polarization in America are mostly driven by manifest economic contradiction and inequality and the ascendance of capital class interests over hollowed-out labor class standing. Yet, somehow, the nature and scope of economic inequality don't quite register. Just what is going on in your town, on the other side of the economic tracks? The authoritative Pew Research Center reports that in "1989 the richest 5% of families had 114 times as much wealth, (sic) based in ownership of stocks and property assets, as families in the second quintile" (the next 20% of the population on the wealth scale); to say nothing of these other quintiles below. (Katherine Schaeffer, *6 facts about economic inequality in the U.S.*, Pew Research Center, February 2020) Such numbers leave the social cohesion and unity supposed to be provided by an economic system, especially in a democratic society, in tatters. They bear out Piketty's income/wealth analysis, in scathing terms. But numbers can also be numbing. They don't quite convey the massive social/psychological and economic fallout they perpetrate, nor the market capitalist calculations they reflect.

In more recent times, the Pew report continues, "the richest families are (sic) the only ones whose wealth increased in the years after the start of the Great Recession (2007-2009). Discrepancies between the top and bottom become more pronounced, with those in the upper tiers gaining more in income and those in the lower tiers losing more." Fortunes ebb and flow. For those above the 50% of the population threshold, there is perhaps still enough dynamism in the market to produce a sense of opportunity and economic class mobility. But for the rest, as the data indicates, the party petered out a long time ago. It's not fun anymore, and it's time to go home. The American Dream of renewed generational prosperity becomes for too many a nightmare. Median middle-class incomes have risen, but barely enough to keep up with inflation and far behind median income gains for upper-tier households. Economic inequality and social polarization festers.

On the one side, it appears that entitlement and privilege are justified and deserved, while on the other, social resentment grows. Immigrants and minorities offer an obvious pretext as a threat to job and social status but come nowhere close to the discrete and indiscrete threats to place and position posed by economic anxiety and despondency. The capture and power of modern-day American market capitalism forestall cries for systemic change, but the fear of falling behind or simply not keeping up roils under the surface. It results from unevolved and unresolved market capitalist contradictions that undermine the broad social interest. Raw class interest, through which people perceive shared economic experience, appears dispersed and largely unarticulated. It awaits galvanizing events and voices. In the meantime, this lull, or void before the storm, is being filled by the taunts and revanchist policies of a demagogue, and a militant capitalist agenda.

The analysis provided by Piketty and others, the present essay no exception, are by themselves not about to move the American electorate. But as conditions on the ground begin to radically shift, people are bound to consider their options. This is the case, even though America's economic markets are massive and appear intractable, and the stock market 'appears to be doing great – at least for those who can afford it; even though it's a patent, obvious fact that large and significant segments of the American population enjoy ballooning wealth – and the personal security and satisfaction it allows – representing itself a commanding, if not monolithic, dialectic interest; even though the society itself appears to enjoy general, if jaggedly uneven prosperity. At the same time, though, it is a society steadily engulfed by economic inequality, social instability and political jeopardy. As such, it is increasingly incumbent on all classes of American society to reflect upon and assess their respective positions with regard to adopting a more viable, alternative economic system, that supports, among other things, the greater wage parity of a 'living wage'.

This essay is not about disparaging the standing of wealth and income, that most essential, personal, and civic of all endowments. It does, however, urge and advocate its' alternative (and more social) allocation, deployment and utilization. Some in the higher echelons of wealth and income accumulation have already decided to protect and extend their position, no matter the social, economic and political consequences to larger society. By the same token, personal reflection and assessment must lead remaining echelons to perceive that certain levels of wealth and income accumulation foster untoward and calamitous economic development, destructive to the unity of society and the democratic values that sustain it; and that something can and must be done about it. The current onslaught of political and economic division produces a correspondent social alienation and alarm. It is not unprecedented.

As the old social- psychologist Erich Fromm pointed out, such alienation can culminate in an "escape from freedom" (Erich Fromm, *Escape from Freedom,* Avon Books, 1965). His urgent analysis, though dated, focuses on the socio-psychological fallout that can attend political and economic upheaval. It is still relevant. As society evolves, the grasp of new freedoms must be accompanied by new social structures and institutions that support growing 'individuation,' orientation, and connection. Otherwise, as Fromm notes, "powerful tendencies arise to escape from this kind of trackless (sic) freedom into submission or some kind of relationship to man (sic) and the world which promises relief from uncertainty, even as it deprives the individual of his/her (sic) freedom" (ibid, p. 52).

In Fromm's case, such tendencies turned negative and helped explain the totalitarian descent into Nazism, which riddled his own experience. There can, alternatively, be positive institutional structures, and more socially affirmative economic policy. It is now a different, but similar time. The binds holding communities together in America are strained. The im-personalization and powerlessness often induced by market relations exert growing pressure on the individual and her sense of freedom. Still, it seems the American capitalist economic ethos continues to thrive. Apparently, it still sustains a broad sentiment that if you put in the work, your rewards will be well and truly deserved, at least for some. This is all well and good, but at the same time, another reality intrudes: certain interests, parties, and institutions have gained an unfair and controlling upper hand, at the expense of other vital and essential social interests – without effective social structures, institutions and wage compensation policies to bolster their standing. Lines of class distinction need to be drawn, and these fall out disproportionately to the advantage and privilege of higher-income cohorts.

Taxation Matters

It should go without saying that America has undergone a great taxation, not to mention wage-compensation swindle over at least the past 40 years. As indicated earlier, the retarded adjustment of tax rates and tax schedules is at the very heart of American political, economic and social dysfunction. How did it happen? As the non-partisan Institute on Taxation and Economic Policy reports, for example, "how is it that in four out of every five states in America (sic), the top 1% are paying a lower tax rate than their middle-class and low-income neighbors?" (Huff Post, *Most States Have Tax Codes that Are Rigged to Benefit the Wealthy: Report,* January 9, 2024). A preponderate majority of states have succumbed to tax mania or been leveraged by their wealthier residents and corporations to adopt "regressive tax codes" (ibid). Through bait and switch write-offs, deductions, and a whole parcel of accounting maneuvers in these states, the middle and lower classes assume proportionately more of the tax burden, and without corresponding higher wages to carry it. And yet it is not a kitchen or dining room, or even nightly news topic. Market capitalist ideology prevails.

In some ways, contemporary America is swamped by materialism without the alloy of critical historical and class perspectives to help understand what's going on. The reserves and ideals of counter-balancing liberal culture appear to run dry. Dynamic market gyrations subdue history and undermine a future of shared prospects. Consumer culture fosters a materialist mentality and narrow self-preoccupation. But materialist history and its class injunctions and wider social claims, can't be eradicated, nor can the prospects of a reborn collective will and collective consciousness. Such prospects linger, biding time until the long undertow of historical legacy takes hold. Materialist History, correctly understood, reveals the causes of systemic exploitation, devolution, and a viable vision of correction.

As Abraham Lincoln said prior to and during America's Civil War, "The dogmas of the quiet past are inadequate to the stormy present. The occasion is piled high with difficulty, and we must rise with the occasion. As our case is new, so we must think anew, and act anew. We must disenthrall ourselves, and then we shall save our country." (www.nps.gov/foth/lincoln-s-legacy-the-eloquent president.htm).

This treatise is an adamant attempt to diagnose and understand contradiction and polarization in contemporary America, especially as a result of economic inequality. It is an appeal to disenthrall ourselves from ingrained economic experiences and attitudes and rise up to embrace an alternative vision, a different way forward, one girded by new analytical clarity. The diagnosis uses the promising lights generated by the under-appreciated and under-reported advances of Europe's social-democratic states. Such lights should help to penetrate conditions vexing the American population, perplexed and in thrall to the central anomaly of our times — vast economic inequality amidst vast material and economic plentitude. By this token, another Lincoln quote is helpful: "If we could first know where we are and whither, we are tending, we could then better judge what to do and how to do it" (ibid).

One way of getting at Lincoln's question of 'what to do, and how to do it', is to re-appraise the massive industrial and technological forces that shape these modern times – as they affect social and economic development. Unprecedented productivity and material abundance lead paradoxically to the disorientation and disruption of social values upon which the entire economic enterprise is based. Though now substantially deposed, certain elements of Marxist analysis are still pertinent for addressing the shifts of human consciousness brought on by the industrialization of society. They apply especially to the differences between European and American economic and social development.

Part III

Historical Materialism

Chapter One:
Historical Materialism

The theory of Historical Materialism is associated with Karl Marx (1818-1883). Not to resurrect his name, whose universal prognostications and prophecies excited false millennial hopes, fostered an ill-conceived revolution in Russia, and the miscarriages of eastern European State Socialism, but he did have some interesting things to say about history and capitalism. It is also impossible to understand the origin and evolution of European social democracy without grasping the salient points of his analysis, one of which is that history is infused by the nature of material relationships. On human historical agency, Marx wrote, "Men, women (sic) make their own history, but they do not make it as they please; they do not make it under self-selected circumstances, but under circumstances existing already, given and transmitted from the past. The tradition of all dead generations weighs like a nightmare on the brains of the living" (Marx, *Eighteenth Brumaire of Louis Bonaparte,* 1852, marxists.org/archive/quotes/index.html).

Marx asserted the capture of people by their economic system, by history, and the dead weight of custom and law against his perhaps exaggerated belief in human capacities for rationality and freedom. But contemporary affairs do indeed appear to leave a narrow gap for a lot of humanity to grasp the potential of their own contemporary agency, beyond the incessant need to just get by.

The comprehensive force and logic of Marx's analysis compelled him to arraign and indict the past and present in no uncertain terms. His putatively scientific method, dialectical materialism, divined collective class interest and exploitation as historically rooted. The systemic economic contradictions between working and capitalist class interests stand in the way of social progress. His prognostications, for better and for worse, took deep, but now attenuated hold these past 150 years in European and world affairs. Marx applied dialectics to the socio-economic world and to its different and evolving historical modes of productive, or industrial relationships - from master and slave, to lord and tenant farmer, to industrial wage relations between owners and workers — each posing one side of dialectic opposition. The differentiation of power in class relations, according to Marx, creates opposed modes of consciousness and the formation of class interest, one against the other. These interests permeate consciousness and generate behavior. He was a materialist, that is, someone who believes that the way we see the world is self-evidently shaped and prejudiced by material conditions, concerns, and relationships.

Dialectic analysis, however, goes beyond economics and politics to include the arts and technology. Though not as spiritually oriented as the Asian 'Yin-Yang' philosophy, the applications of dialectic analysis are similarly ubiquitous; it can be over-extended to the point of intellectual intoxication and/or misapplication. It is one analytical tool. In simple terms, a dialectic relationship exists between theory and practice in which theory asserts a thesis that, when applied in practice, produces a modifying, or contradictory result, an 'antithesis.' When theory and practice are brought into agreement, greater 'syntheses' allow for more advanced application. But dialectic analysis goes beyond basic trial and error experiment. It generally encompasses the interests and processes of opposition and resolution in social and economic affairs, and extends to explaining the direction of historical development. Marx inspected economic class relations between owners/employers and employees in which economic and social tensions are in an ongoing process of conflict and resolution. For him, such processes always favored the systemic power of capitalism and the capitalist class. Dialectic resolution, in his mind, called for a class struggle to overthrow the power of capital. Such an event would signify an unbounded social consciousness, ready to generate and sustain authentic historical progress. For Marx, ultimately, there was no compromise between the economic classes, but only the final synthesis of communism.

Marx's Precursor(s), Ideology & Progress

As preposterous and/or futile as it may appear to address the issue(s) of historical progress at the moment, such conjectures provide essential guideposts. Despite massive economic inequality and social polarization that bedevil current times in America, a social democratic way forward still beckons. The current essay, after all, asserts a "Different Way Forward." This assumes a reference and faith, if not utter conviction, as to at least the possibility of broad, historical progress. Progress is a long trudge and involves what looks like a lot of mucking around. It is multifarious and uneven, but can also be systemic. Its terms are somewhat indefinite and disputable, but it must be about wide, social access to opportunity and material security. Progress is profoundly contingent and never conclusive. It depends on resolute, good faith, not to mention protecting and preserving the natural environment and mother earth as a keepsake for future generations.

Notwithstanding 20th century world wars, the horrors of Auschwitz-Birkenau and the Holocaust, current illiberal entrenchments and encroachments, or a looming oligarchic coup in America, but because of them, the case and cause for social and individual progress can and must still be made. It needs to be re-invigorated. The vast tapestry of a sometimes-brutish history and cacophonous contemporary affairs dims progressive outlooks and prospects. Or, from another perspective, perhaps the progressive flame is subsumed in the magnificent, if ambivalent strides and claims of science and technology. Those impressed with the technological advances represented by AI, among other astounding developments, might claim the case for progress is manifest. AI, in this appraisal, stands in for a collective sense of social progress; but AI, and other assorted innovations, may also pose an invasion, or overthrow of human intelligence and spirit.

It emerges that one of the final measures of AI development, revolves around questions of sentience, or self-awareness. AI systems may not only possess and be able to process vast amounts of data, but also have the ability to perceive, analyze, and understand their own existence." (AI for Social Good, *Artificial Intelligence Self-Awareness: What is the Timeline?* aiforsocialgood.ca, November 1, 2024) "Technological 'singularity' looms, "in which computer programs become so advanced that AI transcends human intelligence, potentially erasing the boundary between humanity and computers, including an increase in technological connectivity with the human body" (*N.*

Barney, A. Zola, *What is Singularity in Technology and AI*, techtarget.com, revised August 2024). AI could even overthrow and control all social communication systems. Transhumanist parties assert that interconnectivity between machines and humans represents a promising avenue of progress – where humans become more physically robust and super self-conscious.

Tellingly, such developments coincide with questions posed and, to an extent, provisionally answered by the foremost and original philosophers of historical progress, Friedrich Hegel (1770-1831) and Karl Marx (1818-1883). Self-consciousness, for both, in different ways, is not only the hallmark of humanity, but also the measure of its evolution and progress. Their convictions were based on the dialectical nature of natural and social evolution. Marx observes the 'self-conscious' trait that most distinguishes the human species: "The animal is immediately identical with its life-activity. It does not distinguish itself from it. It is its life-activity. The human being, on the other hand, (sic) makes her life-activity itself the object of her will and of her consciousness. She has a conscious life-activity. It is not a determination with which she directly merges. Conscious life-activity directly distinguishes the human being from animal life-activity. It is just because of this that the human being is a species-being [Gattungswesen]" (Karen Ng, *Ideology Critique from Hegel and Marx to Critical Theory*, Wiley Online Library, onlinelibrary.wiley.com, 2015). Conscious life-activity, you might say, is the hallmark of our freedom.

Our collective and individual intelligence and spirit, after all, take essential bearing and inspiration from the freedom of the next created moment. AI, in all its majesty, proposes to pre-determine vast realms of the future, and so render the next created moment, day, or week somewhat fixed. It presages the future becoming now, which would stifle some of the vibrant freedom upon which human intelligence and spirit depend.

The philosopher, Ng adds that what constitutes self-consciousness "for both Hegel and Marx, is that it… takes up its life as an object of thinking and willing while at the same time being that life — it is this relation of reflexivity that constitutes self-conscious activity." (ibid) In other words, reflection is necessary about what we do and how to do it. It is not automatic. Before we as a species turn ourselves into automatons, unmoored from our place in, and reverence for the natural order, we would do better to relish and cherish the virtues of our particular form of consciousness, not to mention its spirit.

In their respective, theoretical ways, both Marx and Hegel propose that as the dialectical tensions and conflicts between the material conditions of life and self-consciousness itself are resolved, the collective and individual fortunes of humanity will be fulfilled. They proposed, in their different theoretical ways, fairly reasonable explanations for their beliefs in progress - not for an elite, or for the wealthy, or for some segment of society, but for humanity as a whole.

For Marx, greater self-consciousness would be both reflected and achieved as the means, and/or modes of production are rationalized and come to be collectively owned and managed. The transformation of economic organization would both reflect and generate clarification of individual and collective, consciousness. Progress, for Marx, depends on increasing social consciousness. For Hegel, the expansion of self-consciousness is ineluctably and reflexively drawn by the spirit of reason and freedom in conjunction with natural and social realities. Both views of historical progress are teleological: history has, to one extent or another, an inevitable purpose. Human and social evolution possess the potential of fulfillment. Both views were to a contingent extent, millenarian - that is, that over the millennia humans would work things out and arrive at a 'promised land' on earth, similar in a way to the Christian faith in a 'second coming'.

Hegel could imagine contemporary machine consciousness only in rudimentary terms. It was Marx who witnessed the profound productivity of industrial machinery. He perceived its immense potential – so long as it could be directed by and for the benefit of all social interests. For their time, both Hegel and Marx opened wide domains for rational, critical analysis of historical processes.

They both were inspired by the promise and fulfillment of human rationality; for Marx as noted, this would occur through the resolution and overthrow of systemic economic contradictions; for Hegel, as the resolution over time of contradictions that beset consciousness. That neither of these events looks likely to come about doesn't discredit their analysis. Rather, it puts them into an existential frame of reference, guided not by some future panacea, but by the material and natural, contemporary realities confronting human consciousness.

Today's technological and social advances, though ambiguous, reflect profound social, economic, and individual development, and at least halting progress toward greater historical and contemporary coconsciousness. Social unity and shared material well-being, however, remain elusive. We humans are confined to the age in which we live. Neither Hegel, nor Marx could foresee that their rationalist theories and belief in human progress, would be associated with what could be termed an Age of AI Automaton Hegemony. The case, however, is not completely settled. As Hegelian scholar and author, Jensen Suther points out, it is no secret that human intelligence is challenged by the powers of technology. Nonetheless, he notes, the domains of human consciousness and intelligence remain unsurpassed. These include the intelligence domains of:

"Embodiment, being inhabited by sensible and flexible, physical bodies.

"Situational context" where subtle matters of significance can be detected.

"Need" – where human purposes, needs, and ends are rooted in bodily and situational reality.

"Human purposes, needs, and ends don't exist prior to or somehow independently of either the bodies we are, or have, or the "situation" (Suther, *Hegel Against the Machines, The* New Statesman, July 6, 2023). We are eminently adaptable. In addition, humans are compassionate toward suffering and lovingly procreative. We also dream in our sleep and have access to vast realms of sub-conscious and intuitive insight, all things that thus far, machines are unable to realize. Mastery over the machine is clearly achievable, if we don't let it overtake our sense and belief in the human spirit. Jensen goes on to note, "The task, then, is to rethink artificial intelligence not as a competitor to, but as an inorganic extension of actual intelligence. But putting an end to the ongoing mechanization of human reason is not just a matter of adopting a better theory. It will first require that we "pull the 'emergency brake 'on our runaway mode of production, instead of passively awaiting the mechanical overlords that for anyone paying attention have already arrived." (ibid) Jensen here takes aim, utilizing a Marxist term, at the contemporary market capitalist 'mode of production'. He also offers an invitation to re-consult notions and vistas of human social progress that can provide just the kind of 'emergency-brake' leverage called for, and keep human beings and their communities in the driver's seat. Whatever Souther's theoretical underpinnings, he invokes the very same social will and spiritual self-consciousness envisioned by Marx and Hegel.

Hegel (1770-1831) and his philosophical colleagues first confronted the legacies and capture of Christianity, which posited a more or less static, unchanging world and its spiritual conditions of Good and Evil. These conditions were mediated by morality and faith toward redemption in the life hereafter.

Hegel, especially, was emboldened by the Age of Enlightenment and its worldview – that conditions on earth are, in fact, more dynamic, penetrable and subject to human agency and direction than allowed by antiquated Christian precepts. Situated roughly between England's Glorious Revolution of 1688, the French Revolution of 1789, and the Napoleonic era, which ended in 1815, the formal

Enlightenment marked numerous scientific and philosophical breakthroughs – from Isaac Newton's discovery of physical laws, such as gravity, to Francis Bacon's propagation of the scientific method and Immanuel Kant's categorical delineation of the limits and spheres of reason and morality.

Our sense of and belief in verifiable knowledge would henceforth be attainable, unleashing new confidence and the idea of modern progress. Such developments, among others, gradually supplanted the Age of Faith with the Age of Reason. Hegel caught the wind of these developments and drove them into defining a new, quasi-rationalist philosophy that invested the material world, reason, and freedom with spiritual, idealist, energy. Hegel was, after all, trained as a Lutheran pastor. Though his own Christian views were unorthodox, he was quite the evangelist.

He was a metaphysical idealist, one who believed that humans subjectively construct their own ideas (and ideals) about reality. These are touched by and generative of a universal, unfolding spiritual, metaphysical drama. Our ideas (and ideals) constitute their own primary reality that are necessarily, if not umbilically, attached to the external realities of the material, natural, and social world. A person identifies with and participates in processes that are somewhat larger than life. Philosopher, Samuel Hammond, a neo-Hegelian, informs us that "Hegel identifies freedom and reason with Spirit. For Hegel, this is the essence of his Christianity. However, his revisionist theology does us the favor of purging all the mysticism and paranormal activity from the Genesis story through to the testament of Jesus' life on earth" (Samuel Hammond, *On Hegel's Rational*

Christianity, medium.com, July 18, 2018). Hegel's theology does not locate the Spirit, or God in a remote, heavenly realm of static and eternal omniscience; instead, Spirit is infused with infinite consciousness, seeking to realize itself (right here and now) through reason and freedom, over time and space, in nature and history

Hegel as much as claims that Spirit underwrites the purpose or goal of history: "It is the progress of the consciousness of freedom." — "*Lawrence Evans, Hegel on History*, Philosophy Now, philosophynow.org, 2018) The Spirit comprehends and is infused with a Reason that is implanted in the natural universe. As Hegel writes, "The motion of the solar system proceeds according to immutable laws; these laws are its reason. But neither the sun nor the planets, which according to these laws rotate around it, have any consciousness of it. Thus, the thought that there is reason in nature, that nature is ruled by universal, unchangeable laws, does not surprise us; we are used to it and make very little of it…" *Friedrich Hegel, Reason in History*, from Jack Fox-Williams, *Hegel's Understanding of History,* Philosophy Now, philosophynow.org, 2020).

1. *Footnote* It was just such a doctrine, not incidentally, that inspired American transcendentalists, in a period roughly from 1825 to 1860, including such figures as Ralph Waldo Emerson, Henry David Thoreau, Margaret Fuller, and Louisa May Alcott. American transcendentalism was centered on the individual's self-reliant ability to apprehend spiritual transcendence and empowerment, as an attribute of natural existence – not so much as a result of received doctrine. Spirit is manifest in nature, as much in the moment, as in a heavenly realm. Such insights contributed greatly, among other things, to the abolitionist movement against slavery, and ecological awareness.

Historical Progress: Hegel perceived history in progressive terms. His observations give the human condition metaphysical dimensions. As historian of philosophy, Lawrence Evans notes: "The world, for Hegel, has gone through stages of understanding freedom. At first, only one person, the ruler or despot, is considered free. Then, the Greeks and Romans establish that some persons - the citizens - are free. Finally, the Germanic peoples (that is, Western Europe), through the influence of Christianity, come to understand that all persons, or human beings as such, are free" (or capable, sic, of self-governing reason). (Lawrence Evans, *Hegel on History*, Philosophy Now, philosophynow.org, 2018). Christianity had banished and supplanted the pagan Gods of Rome. This left the world free for the very slow emergence of rational inquiry and investigation. For Hegel, human consciousness of freedom unfolds in tandem with the expansion of a universal Spirit. The extent of human freedom not only increases, but "the concept of freedom itself has fundamentally changed. And if there has been development in the concept of freedom, there will also have been development in the nature of spirit, since spirit is characterized by freedom" (ibid).

Hegel himself was somewhat ambivalent about the role played by Christianity. It served as a catalyst without being a purpose, subject like any 'ideology' to dialectical transformation; that is, it wasn't written in stone. Hegel saw Medieval Christianity as an archetype of what he called "unhappy consciousness," due to what he perceived as the failure of the Church to mediate between individuals and

God." (ibid) The focus in those times was on the Father, Son, and Holy Ghost of scripture, and the requirements of faith. The fallen state of humanity was taken for granted. "It took a particular 'world-historical' moment, namely the French Revolution, for spirit to become truly self-conscious; to escape 'abstract' freedom and realize 'concrete' freedom through the laws as they applied to the people" (ibid). The formation and expression of our ideas and ideals, conditioned and sanctioned by reason, are modal forces of self-consciousness and human progress.

It took the French Revolution to bring about the dismantling of the French feudal economy, along with the overthrow of the monarchy, nobility, and the power of the Church. More importantly, though the revolution itself recoiled and consumed itself, the event brought about a shift in human consciousness. As Hegel wrote, as quoted by the itinerant philosopher, Chris Christensen - "Never since the sun has stood in the firmament and the planets revolved around it had it been perceived that a man's existence centers in his head, i.e., in thought, inspired by which he builds up the world of reality… not until now had man advanced to the recognition of the principle that thought ought to govern spiritual reality. All thinking beings shared in the jubilation of this epoch" (Chris Christensen, *The Trouble with Hegel*, Philosophy Now, philosophynow.org, 2018). Through the growth of understanding and perception, the refinement of values, ideals was made manifest. Yoked together by reason and logic through interaction with the material, social and spiritual world, human capacities for progress were assured. Consciousness expresses itself through the movements and institutions of culture, most particularly, the institution of the state. Consciousness may be the modal force of human existence, but it is the state, for Hegel, that is the modal force of consciousness.

The national state or regime, for Hegel, embodies essential and idealized development. "The state, properly understood, is the highest realization of collective, ethical consciousness, an organic structure that aligns individual freedom with universal rational order." (Simon Gros, *Hegel's Philosophy of Right*, Dover Philosophical Classics, simongros.com, November 4, 2024) "If the state is confused with civil society," as Hegel argues, "and its determination is equated with the security and protection of property and personal freedom, the interest of individuals as such becomes the ultimate end for which they are united; it also follows from this that membership of the state is an optional matter. However, the relationship of the state to the individual is of a different kind. Since the state is an objective spirit, (spirit as manifest), it is only through being a member of the state that the individual himself has objectivity, truth, and ethical life. Union with the state (sic) as such is itself the true content and end, and the destiny of individuals is to lead a universal life" (Friedrich Hegel, *Philosophy of Right*, paragraph 258, from Paul Franco, *Hegel and Liberalism*, JSTOR, *The Review of Politics*, vol. 4, #4, 1997, p. 838). Hegel's was a state, or 'church', seemingly, in which attendance is mandatory. His rationalism was absolute. Such grandiosity presumably supports unlimited state empowerment. There is however, a caveat: only so long as the state embodies rationality in support of individual freedom and vice-versa. For Hegel, then, it is of and through the state, that individuals gain a special sense of self-consciousness.

Human consciousness and self-consciousness for Hegel also unfold through social processes. Progress is seeded in human nature, originating and ever-contested in the evolution of our relations. Consciousness is social. Humans do not develop in isolation, but depend for their development on other people, family, friends, work associates, friend and foe alike. For Hegel, this plays out in primitive terms at the start and continues over the ages as issues of mastery and servitude return to re-assert themselves. Humans are designed to seek recognition from others and to find a mutuality of consciousness. But relationships are always driven by perceptions of domination and subservience. As the cited philosopher, Christensen observes, strife is a component part of "Hegel's Master-Slave dynamic, in which one consciousness contends with the other," until there is mutual recognition. (ibid) This is the basis for a kind of universal, or social consciousness, where the "individual self realizes that it's part of a larger consciousness in a community of others" (ibid). For Hegel, this larger consciousness was an essential human capacity that would progress through history, as society progresses, unto ultimate resolution, and the realization of the "Absolute Mind, or Absolute Spirit" (ibid).

The foregoing offers a glimpse of Hegel's suppositions about historical progress. (nothing has been said of Hegel's *Zeitgeist,* or 'spirit of the times', such as the religious Reformation, the Enlightenment, the aforementioned Age of Reason, or the Atomic Age, which marked out distinct historical periods, when new orders of rationality and the prospects of freedom were expanded (or imperiled); nor of such 'world historical figures', as Jesus Christ of Nazareth, Julius Caesar, Martin Luther, Napoleon, Abraham Lincoln, Madam Curie, Rosa Parks, or Martin Luther King, all of whom (and many more) advanced the social, political and scientific horizons of reason and freedom).

These events and figures notwithstanding, the processes of realizing greater consciousness of freedom and reason in human history are assuredly not walks on the beach. There may be a spirit of reason and a spirit of freedom in the background, but this doesn't prevent the passions of self-and national interest from turning historical processes into self-consuming affairs. As British historian of philosophy, James Fox-Williams sums it up, "Hegel suggests that many stages of human history appear irrational and regressive because society is made up of individuals guided by passions, impulses, and external forces…As a result of the many conflicts, revolutions, and revolts that society endures, humanity attains a greater glimpse of reason" (James Fox-Williams, *Hegel's Understanding of History*, *Philosophy Now*, philosophynow.org, 2020).

This plainly asserts a controversial rationalization of history – that is, all outcomes are to a degree sanctioned. Alternately, you could argue that Hegel's dialectical analysis gave him the view that history is pitiable and tragic. As Hero, writing for The Socratic Method journal notes, "Hegel is suggesting that true tragedy arises when two valid and morally justifiable perspectives clash, leading to an irreconcilable conflict. Genuine tragedies in the world are not conflicts between right and wrong. They are conflicts between two rights" (*The Socratic Method*, Socratic-method.com, January 20). Hegel is concerned with the arduous and 'tragic' conflicts that repeatedly produce resolution in history. His conclusions are not soft sells. As noted, Hegel's dialectic analysis gave him a long view in explaining the course of history - as driven by the progressive evolution of Spirit, Reason, Freedom, and Master-Slave socio-psychological dynamics. These topics are still of great concern today, however modified by our own historical circumstances and debate terms. For some, Hegel's analytical postulates are still persuasive. For so-called 'right Hegelians,' his analysis can be taken to sanction the status quo. If history has yielded the current scenario, or set of economic and political arrangements, they must be sanctioned to a certain extent as inevitable. 'Left Hegelians,' on the other hand, emphasize the utility provided by dialectical analysis for critically interpreting social conditions and evaluating them in rational and progressive terms. Such an approach is adopted by the current essay. Hegelian analysis is "concerned with changes to cultural consciousness, not merely events or occurrences that make the news" (Stanford Encyclopedia of Philosophy, *Hegel's Dialectics*, revised October 2, 2020).

Dialectics are not merely a critical method of analysis; if Hegel is right, dialectics are bound up in the very warp and weave of historical development itself, indistinguishable in some respects, from life itself. Dialectical analysis gives a basis for the critique of what would become social ideologies that, however unjustifiably, govern individual and collective realities. For Hegel, as the philosopher Karen Ng points out, "idealism effectively becomes social philosophy and critique becomes inseparable from social critique…it is clear that ideology critique remains an indispensable resource not only for critical theory, but for anyone attempting to understand the persistent coexistence of reason and unreason in human society" (Karen Ng, *Critique from Hegel and Marx to Critical Theory*, Wiley Library Online, 2022).

Ideology, for better and for worse, plays a role in the formation and expression of consciousness and in the struggles of society. Such 'critiques of ideology' will be utilized in later segments of the current essay to evaluate historic and contemporary regimes, as each accompanies a particular historic mode of production., whether of revolutionary, or antebellum slavery times in America, or of Nazi Germany, or of the social democratic societies of modern Europe. All and each represent particular phases of human consciousness.

Dialectic Processes Without going into intricacies and examples of dialectical analysis, they are governed by three principles or laws: "1) the unity and conflict of opposites, 2) the mutual transformation of quantity into quality, and 3) the negation of the negation" (Allen Gendler, *The Problems with Marx's Dialectic*, Mises Institute, January 5, 2021). These can be summarized as follows: We continually observe and encounter situations in which oppositions and/or conflicts are marginally, or finally resolved. These situations become qualitatively identifiable as they quantitatively multiply, even though they often contain difficult to discern elements. Each side of an opposition houses an internal negation, or weak point that makes it subject to negation, transformation, and/or resolution.

***

As noted earlier, dialectical analysis can lead to over-application, misuse and/or ideological dogma, in which the outcome must conform to pre-given assumptions. This often proved to be the case in the former Soviet Union and under Eastern European state-socialist regimes. Dialectic analysis must be critical, disciplined and restrained. It is but one tool in the analytical tool box. As a Mises Institute commentator notes, "The dialectic explains everything and nothing at the same time." (Allen Gendler, *ibid*) The heights of Hegel's philosophy itself run aground on its 'absolutist' claims and its ladders of progressive causation. Hegel's full-blown, idealized, dialectic outlook is outmoded, if not overrun. The Spanish-American philosopher, George Santayana, for example, insists that Hegel's idealist philosophical outlook is crackpot. "When German idealism (sic) is taught, represented as the rational foundation of science and religion, with neither of which it has any honest sympathy, it becomes positively odious - one of the worst impostures and blights to which a youthful imagination could be subjected." (Ibid, George Santayana, *Winds of Doctrine, IV*)

Though reason, and you might say spirit, have made phenomenal gains in the times since Hegel, partially giving warrant to his theories, common sense alone recognizes that there are limits to self-consciousness. Ultimate resolutions on both spiritual and historical planes, as Hegel stipulates, are not foreordained. Moreover, anyone who has examined his or her interior consciousness knows that the 'thing-in-itself,' supposed to represent self-knowledge and truth, or 'absolute mind,' as Hegel says, is pretty much located in an inaccessible kind of black box. To a certain extent, human consciousness is impenetrable and contingent. Other than perhaps for ecstatic moments, moments of great insight, or the inner equilibrium of the Zen or Swami Master, the fusion of our consciousness with our being escapes practical reach. Most likely, this is the way it is meant to be – and constitutes essential, existential reality, not to mention one of the foundation stones for the human spirit.

The consolation prize for stable human identity, and human prospect, (ameliorating master-slave tendencies) is the recognition and/or love we give and receive from others. We are left to understand our own existence in terms of continuous adaptation, for which we require mostly predictable conditions of 'reasonable 'freedom and compassion, and a safe environment. Since Hegel's time, other theories and goals of progress come to the fore, provided particularly by the evolutionary sciences. Such models, however, are especially contingent and conjectural – "open-ended, local, and non-linear." (Agnes Tam, *Progress,* Stanford Encyclopedia of Philosophy, stanford.edu, revised February 28, 2024) They would have the human species, in evolutionary, biological terms, going nowhere in a hurry. This may be the most that can be hoped for – as long as the evolution and adaptation of evermore affirmative social, economic, and political institutions and settlements can be achieved. Doomsayers, on the other hand, would have us all going to hell in a handbasket.

***

The current essay holds that historical progress (with a small *p*) inheres in the non-violent, ongoing resolution of systemic economic and political contradictions – toward the ends of greater social unity and shared material well-being; toward the greater realization of the twin, not necessarily complimentary aspirations of individual freedom and social equality. The processes of resolution follow uneven, dialectic patterns, which carry promise as long as tethered to positive and inclusive, democratic values. Collective human consciousness, or individual self-consciousness is not about to reach some panacea, but salutary social conditions provide a stable foundation for the development of greater ingenuity, socio-ethical, environmental insight and behavior, and/or creative and spiritual consciousness. The prospect of sustaining open-hearted, affirmative and positive attitudes and outlooks about life and society is manifest. The alternative, that "I'm an 's.o.b.' and I'll spite you and everybody else for it," is equally apparent; as is the imposition of misery-inducing policies and institutions.

As referenced above in the review of Adam Tooze's critical review of European conditions, the social democratic regimes of Europe take this fragility into account and adopt commensurate measures to buffer it; the social stakes of disregard are simply too high. Generally speaking, these societies embody conditioned liberal freedom and social, as opposed to strictly individualist, or private reason. Society holds a certain priority. The social democracies of Europe represent, on their own terms, a historical and dialectical resolution of socialist and capitalist economic approaches. That resolution is grounded to varying degrees by Social Partnership – alliances for and between business, labor, and governmental interests through which social unity, welfare and economic development are, to an impressive extent, mediated and realized.

Despite their limitations and differences, the propositions of Hegel and Marx continue to be instrumental and constructive for their emphasis on self and social consciousness as conduits to human progress. Marx may lend coherence to perceptions that economic systems are ultimately exploitive and unfair. While the grand scope of Hegel's Idealist theory may be invalid, anyone who pursues individual ideals and goals knows that through them, major spurs of human meaning and motivation are summoned. They carry us forth. Both Hegel and Marx provide modern, partial templates, modified and elaborated by innumerable followers, which are still relevant to the critique, management and guidance of human affairs.

The Hegelian State and Liberalism

As rendered above, Hegel's idealized, statist views are averse, if not opposed to liberal and democratic idealism. As he points out, Liberal democratic values, are indeed concerned with the individual's relationship to civil society. Liberalism gives the individual, as she or he is, a certain empirical, precedence. The liberal view holds that social and individual values, principles, and ideals are *liberally* accessible to the mass of humanity, to individuals and groups alike, especially as fostered by humane and effective education. This bequest is vouchsafed more by the birthright of life, than by the state. In democratic terms, the ideals of liberty, equality, and fraternity contain and sustain moral and ethical values – they fundamentally underwrite current and prospective, individual freedom. The liberal view holds that conditions for social, economic and political progress are sufficient, so long as the people's political rights are secure. In this sense, the state is indispensable. So long as people share and are exposed to honest opinions, and accurate information, they'll eventually get around to achieving life-affirming progress.

Such ideals, principles, and conditions can and still do inspire great individual aspiration and social movement. The state is taken down a few notches from its Hegelian, "objective spirit" heights. The state's role may be instrumental, but it is not the driving force by which ideals are propagated or achieved. Instead, they are located in broad individual consciousness, agency and experience, and social interaction. Think, for example, of how ideals are involved in everyday life; or, in historical terms, the role they played in the American Revolution, in the emancipation of enslaved Americans, the advancement of women's voting rights, or in the civil rights movement of the 1960s, not to mention the rights of gay people to be married and raise a family, nor the achievements of European social democracy. True, recalcitrant, or supportive state policy goaded such movements, but they evolved through individual awareness, social activism, and broad, however halting, social support. Historically speaking, states have done at least as much to restrain, if not prevent, the ideals of freedom, as they have to advance their realization.

As all this holds true, however, liberalism itself, at the moment, faces an existential crisis. Its open inclusiveness, and/or permissiveness, generates a certain passivity in the face of social and political challenges. A vacuum of power can thus open that invites the thrusts of illiberal manipulation, currently evident in American and to a more limited degree, European affairs. It is hence essential that liberal policies adapt more robust institutions which assert greater economic social power and connection, that provide modern societies with greater orientation and direction.

Hegel's idealist philosophy, as noted, infuses history with rhyme, reason, and direction. It offers still valid perspective for evaluating the dimensions and standing of human consciousness. As the eminent, American political philosopher, Sheldon Wolin points out, "Marx's conception of progressive dialectics, of a supra-historical reason working itself out in history, a ripening of consciousness, and the master-slave paradigm were all adopted from Hegel, and translated into Marx's own idiom of dialectical materialism and class struggle" (Sheldon Wolin, *Politics and Vision*, Princeton University Press, 2004).

Marx brought the analysis of human affairs back down to earth and the material plane. Though his own theories falter in their hyper-materialist, millenarian dictates, they still offer credible and staunch guidelines for containing systemic, capitalist overreach.

Marxist Class Analysis

Marx believed that human consciousness progressively unfolds as material and social contradictions and conditions are resolved, particularly as a result of socio-economic class confrontation. In contrast to Hegel, Marx was not a statist,' nor was he an idealist. He was a materialist. Ideas and ideology are always and everywhere conditioned by material circumstances and relations. His views were to move legions of people, and influence social transformation, definitively in Russia, but more profoundly, if circumspectly, in Europe.

For Marx, the state was simply an instrument of and for class domination, working against large segments of the population. His famous statement that "the history of all hitherto existing society is the history of class struggles" indicates that socio-economic class, not the idealized state, nor philosophical ideas as such, is the modal force of history (Daniel Bensaïd, *Marx for Our Times*, Verso Publishing, 2002, p. 97). Social classes, after all, are the closest mediators of ongoing material and productive enterprises and processes. They shepherd historical development.

Marx's statement is typically categorical and universal. His proclamation promised to penetrate and explain complex historical processes and customs, whose resolutions are far from inevitable. Though class conditions are ingrained, they are only rarely glaring and antagonistic in the terms Marx proposed. He was impatient to intensify their tendencies and invoke their inevitable dialectic antagonism and resolution. In other ways, Marx's views mirror those of Hegel in their claim of total, exclusive, and "millenarian" resolution of human destiny. (David T. Byrne, *The Victory of the Proletariat is Inevitable: The Millenarian Nature of Marxism*, Kritik, vol. 5, no. 2, December 2011). Both views should be more modestly understood, in liberal terms, to explain human culture. Their apparent opposition should be perceived in a dialectic framework, both valid but needing the other for eventual, though not final, or ultimate, resolution and development.

Marx proposed that material conditions and relations configure consciousness, perception, and behavior. By the same token, Hegel proposed that the ideals and values of consciousness infuse perception, thought, and behavior. They configure the quality and contour of material relations and realities. The question between the two is something like answering which comes first, the chicken or the egg? Consciousness is a mix of perception, thought, and action in both the spiritual/ideal and material world. Marx's' materialist conceptions aimed to clarify economic conditions and so arouse and advance greater social, and hence individual consciousness.

Surplus Value

Marx's materialist insights on the *surplus value of labor* were central to his views on the formation of class. They rocked the world and demonstrated his intent that philosophy should not only speculate about life, but change the world. Once again giving expression to the materialist parameters of his convictions, he wrote, "It is the immediate task of philosophy, which is in the service of history, to unmask self-estrangement in its unholy forms once the holy form of human self-estrangement has been unmasked. Thus, the criticism of Heaven turns into the criticism of Earth, the criticism of religion into the criticism of law, and the criticism of theology into the criticism of politics" (*Karl Marx, Contribution to the Critique of Hegel's Philosophy of Right, The Marx-Engels Reader,* edited by Robert Tucker, New York: Princeton University Press, 1978, p. 54).

Marx was determined to expose the knowable, concrete, and material conditions of actionable reality and experience, over and above the more abstract, theoretical conjectures of Hegel's idealist philosophy. Material reality is immediate, finite and subject to critical analysis. Hence, Marx exposed the phenomenon of *surplus value* as a fundamental component of productive enterprises and industrial relations. Surplus value refers to "Monies extensive of profits, (themselves subdivided into industrial profits, bank profits, commercial profits, etc.), interest, and rent, which are all part of the total surplus product produced by wage labor." (*Ernest Mandel, Marx's Theory of Surplus Value*, part 7, internationalviewpoint.org/spip, article 287, 2003). Surplus value includes profit but extends more to the aggregate of all produced values generated by an economy, after wages have been paid. It is "The additional added value (the difference between total value added (by the market, sic) and wages." (ibid). All those who live off surplus value constitute the socio-economic capitalist class. Thus, Marx drew the battle lines of what he asserted was economic exploitation and the basis of class conflict: "The income of the ruling classes can always be reduced in the final analysis to the product of unpaid labor" (*ibid*).

The toil of the laboring classes was under-compensated and reduced to a market commodity, like any other product. His mention of *unholy* and *holy* forms of self-estrangement in the quote above speaks respectively to the *unholy* alienation of labor from itself as it is often employed in market capitalist production processes. The workers' autonomy and creativity are ostensibly stripped by the rules of employment and the boss's demands. The *holy* forms of self-estrangement refer to the existential, material proneness of the human condition. He assails the system that aggregates and exploits labor power as a "Living production machine of products (sic), in which, taking the production process as a whole, workers exchange their labor (sic) for capital and reproduce the capitalist's money as capital, that is to say, as value-producing surplus value, as self-expanding value" (*Daniel Bensaïd, ibid, p. 120*). Profit is one thing; the financial interest and values added through reinvestment on that profit is another. Marx perceived *surplus value as a kind of usury.*

However bankers and business owners may grapple over loan and deposit interest rates and profit margins, they are in league together in carving up profit and surplus proceeds. Market capitalists do not willingly invite the interests of labor to the table but consigns them to picking up crumbs from the floor. One scholar encapsulates Marx's position as follows: "The antagonism between the two kinds of capitalists, bankers vs. industrialists/merchants (sic) is therefore precisely that which obscures the fact that what both of them earn is a merely quantitative division of the surplus-value. The existence of this antagonism obliterates the social antithesis between capital and labor. Both bank (financial) interest and (business) enterprise profit appear as relationships between two capitalists, not between capitalists and workers" (*Carlo Panico, Marx's Analysis of the Relationship Between the Rate of Interests and the Rate of Profit,* JSTOR, *Cambridge Journal of Economics,* December 1980, vol. 4, p. 367).

The gains produced by *surplus labor,* or *excess of value produced by workers or employees over the wages they are paid* have more than strictly private value (*Oxford Dictionary*). Though putatively privately owned, these gains also have an intrinsic social value that should redound to greater social benefit, including to the benefit of private business itself. Greater purchasing power in the form of more equitable wages, is an essential cornerstone of European social economies, over and against more tight-fisted, market-oriented economies, prevalent especially in

America. At one economic level, the provision of 'living wages', widely manifest in Europe, boosts business formation and overall business activity. This clarifies labor's position and class interest. Capitalists should not have, or be given exclusive dominion over capital. The fundamental traits of capital and labor interests must be continually borne in mind, not in terms of antagonism but in terms of mutual recognition, interdependence, and social partnership resolution.

Beyond their own brawn and brains, all those not owning *means of production,* or capital sufficient to purchase their own productive equipment, property, or land, are compelled to exchange their labor for wages. Wage laborers constitute a class whose ultimate socio-economic interest, for Marx, is irrevocably and irredeemably at odds with capital and/or land or property-owning interests (except that everyone rightfully wants a piece of the action). The extreme contradiction or opposition of interests that dialectical analysis poses may work logically or semantically, but economic and social reality offsets and often mutes these interests. At one level, capital and labor are practically, and inextricably bound together, even if in certain lights, diametrically opposed. Such an observation girds European social democratic reconciliation of capital and labor interests, in particular; it is the basis of social market capitalism.

Material Incentive Matters

Analysis of the reality of economic conditions starts and ends with *'material incentive,'* which compels individuals to seek safety, sustenance, and future prospects in the form of employment. Until that unlikely day when all labor and production are freely organized around public good and social value, people - workers and owners alike- will need to follow material incentives and fend for themselves. The worker surveys the competitive labor field and, depending on ability, availability, and wage levels, enters the labor market. His/her career race begins. Landing a job may induce a certain gratitude and allegiance to the enterprise and the boss who hires her. By the same token, she wouldn't have taken the job if it wasn't necessary or if she had something better to do. Her dependence, or vulnerability in this arrangement, admits that in exchange for wages and opportunity, a certain symptomatic inequality and nominal exploitation will be part of the employment relationship. Marx recognized this but was more interested in the systemic or aggregate exploitation of workers, beyond what occurs at individual or local levels.

The industrial or business capitalist (including entrepreneurs, owners, and employers), for his or her part, surveys market conditions for the most efficient and profitable use of investment capital. This assessment involves a host of factors, from the costs of productive equipment and machinery, and resources involved, to the rates of expected profit, the cost of bank loans, and an estimation of labor costs. Depending on such factors, economic circumstances, and the availability and skill of labor required, wage compensation may be high or low. If it is too high, the owner will not sufficiently profit; if it is too low, suitable employees will not be attracted or will not remain on the job, seeking better employment opportunities elsewhere.

This simple sketch of the private, free labor market highlights the competition involved in the field of employment - both for the worker, in relation to other workers seeking the same job, and for owners competing for efficient and profitable investment to maintain or improve market position. To a certain extent, functional interests between owners/employers and employees in the employment situation appear to coincide, containing a degree of mutuality. Both parties need each other, compelled by material incentives and systemic realities. Further, both parties are motivated by self-interest.

This would certainly be the explanation given by capitalist interests, whose aim is to proclaim the system preordained and to perpetuate it. On such premises, in Hegelian terms, rests capitalist ideology. Marx, however, reserved particular vitriol for the way in which these interests are often concealed behind capitalist veils - to justify and disguise their domination -including all the "legal, religious, artistic, and philosophic doctrines (sic) or ideological forms which are employed to carry out that struggle" (*Dialectical Materialism, an Overview* | ScienceDirect Topics, sciencedirect.com).

The disguises are many and ubiquitous. The one overweening mask presents a sanguine but stern face, suggesting that these economic conditions and relations are all natural and necessary. The economy just needs to be fine-tuned for inflation and unemployment- the less detailed talk about the clefts of income and wealth inequality, the better, even though its fallout is everywhere observable, especially on the other side of town, where wages are low, healthcare is unreliable, and educational opportunities are unaffordable.

The disguise is also visible in all the glossy, idealized production values presented on the evening news and in advertisements. The package of both is designed ultimately to sell products, perpetuate value commodification, and extend the overall hegemony of capitalist ownership, and control of the economy. Its equation of the material and the ideal is complicated and confusing. The real terms and conditions of labor employed in these productions remain hidden.

Network advertising campaigns themselves may be too successful for their own good. Despite the incredible prosperity and material abundance they showcase, a significant portion of the American population reels from a lack of security and prospects that the advertised system promises to provide. Instead, social fallout and polarization create unmanageable, external costs to both people, and the system, both unnecessary and villainous. Worse yet, certain business interests now abandon civic pretense altogether, proclaiming gluttony and greed as natural and necessary. Such interests, in outright confirmation of Piketty's predictions, would defend and perpetuate gross income and wealth inequality as a natural function and outcome of the system.

Class Allegiances

Marx was especially keen on setting out the parameters and real interests of the working class and thereby promoting class consciousness. Of course, working-class interests revolve around wage income and employment conditions, but not reducibly so. These interests also encompass education and healthcare. The standing of labor as a collective interest is also very much at stake. Class definition and class interest aren't solely issues of occupational, or professional categories. Otherwise, the idea of class would be broken down into differences between, for example, doctors, government workers, and house painters — each having different income levels and commensurate stakes in the system. Marx's conception of class "does not draw up socio-professional tables, string together statistics, or labor over borderline cases in the class structure" (Daniel Bensaid, *ibid*, p. 11).

Occupational differences should not obscure the common social and economic conditions produced by surplus-value exploitation. For Marx, these conditions should transform the worker's limited self-interest into broad, if not revolutionary, social interest. "It can indeed be deduced from the logic of Marx's work, *Capital* (sic), that workers in the sphere of circulation (transport, trade, credit, advertising), who yield surplus value to their employer and are subject to conditions of exploitation comparable to those endured by workers in production, fall under the same class determination" (Bensaid, *ibid*, p. 108).

Capitalists, too, as noted, have their divisions. 'Money capitalists' — bankers, for example differ in outlook and purpose from industrial or business capitalists, who depend on bank loans and market-prescribed interest rates to conduct business and calculate wage and profit rates. There are divisions as well in the field of land ownership, for instance, between "vineyard-owners, field-owners, forest owners, mine owners, fishery owners, etc." (*ibid*, p. 110). These divisions, however, do not preclude common interests. For capitalists, their own self-interest and social interest coincide. "We can see that each individual capitalist, just like the totality of all capitalists in each particular sphere of production, participates in the exploitation of the entire working class by capital as a whole and in the level of this exploitation; …we thus have a mathematically exact demonstration (through calculations of interest rates, wage levels, surplus-value, etc. (sic), of why the capitalists, no matter how little love is lost among them in their mutual competition, are nonetheless united by a real freemasonry vis-à-vis the working class as a whole" (Bensaid, *ibid*, p. 108/ Karl Marx, *Capital*, vol. 3, trans. David Fernbach, Penguin, 1981, pp. 298-300).

It was by such assessments, and others, that the social democracies of Europe came to uphold, expand and enjoin the laboring interests of society to take a seat at the table of collectively bargained wage negotiations, and other economic and political venues. However far removed such considerations and realities appear from the current American economic landscape, their adoption may provide a lifeline to current and future generations, and the continuation of democratic society.

Chapter Two:
Ebenezer's Exploitation

In his time, Marx's descriptive characterizations of industrial conditions and relations conveyed a world vastly different from our own. In his world, "the capitalist system's use of… all methods for raising the social productivity of labor are put into effect at the cost of the individual… all means for the development of production undergo a dialectical inversion so that they become means of domination and exploitation of the producer. They deform the conditions under which he works, subject him during the labor process to a despotism the more hateful for its meanness; they transform his lifetime into working time" (Daniel Bensaïd/Marx, ibid, p. 104). The abject rawness of labor conditions in Marx's time was manifest. These conditions featured what other economists described as "the iron law of wages," in which wages fluctuated around the bare minimum. Think, for example, of Ebenezer Scrooge, the character in Charles Dickens's *A Christmas Carol*, whose relentless pursuit of profit squeezed every last ounce of labor from his employee, Bob Cratchit, despite the hardship and poverty it caused. And yet, Bob Cratchit thanks Ebenezer Scrooge at his dinner table prayer. Was Bob Cratchit a class traitor? No. He was caught in the bind of his own private, isolated interests and the ill-defined, unorganized interests of a potential class. He was simply thankful to have a job.

As long as class interest, or awareness remains undefined and unorganized, it remains mostly a dim prospect. Even when, at the individual or factory level, common experiences produce a common interest among the working, wage-earning class, this interest can go unpronounced and unclarified. No matter how far removed and different today's times and living conditions may seem, that common interest still exists. In Marx's time, as workers left hard-scrabble, rural life and sought employment in cities, there was hardly enough work to go around - ideal conditions for exploitation. Now, although materially, there is more than enough to go around, different forms of exploitation persist, albeit based on the same *surplus value* model. The satisfaction of material incentives - so fundamental to the original social contract has reverted to a certain rawness and precariousness for large segments of the American population.

Trade Unions and Purchasing Power

Despite the vast differences between early industrial economic conditions and the tremendous technical and economic advances made since, the social contract is in some ways as endangered now as it was Dickens' time. Just look at President Trump's ongoing efforts to eliminate the collective bargaining rights of federal employees. (Hassan Ali Kanau, *Trump Moves to Strip Unionization from Most Federal Workers,* politico.com, March 28, 2025) Back in the 19th century, thanks in no small part to trade-union movements, fostered both by Marx's analysis and by conditions on the ground, halting progress was achieved in the field of industrial relations. The so-called "iron law of wages" and absolute exploitation turned out to be more flexible than first thought. Marx himself anticipated that competitive, cross-the-board wage increases could counterbalance owners' penny-pinching calculations. Increased labor costs could, in part, be offset by boosting "purchasing power" (International Viewpoint, ibid). Greater purchasing power, in turn, provides grounds for increased capital investment and economic expansion. Not incidentally, as noted above, greater purchasing power provides collective bargaining leverage in European social market capitalist wage negotiations. Greater wage parity benefits the overall economy. This, at least partly accounts for European business support for social market economies. Such leverage, as noted again in **Appendix 2**, is glaringly absent today, for too many sectors of the American working-class population.

Producers and Consumers

Historically, greater wage flexibility and increased purchasing power set the stage not only for more give-and-take in industrial relations between employers and employees but also for the gradual emergence of consumer culture. Workers began to see themselves not only as producers but as consumers. The lines of class identification blur when the purchase of a house, car, or boat symbolize property ownership—a piece of the pie. While not everyone can be a full-fledged capitalist or owner of productive means, individuals can still achieve some gain, if not outright profit. What's to stop a "working-class" person from becoming more property-minded, or bourgeois, in their interests? The question then arises: what, ultimately, is this business of "class" all about? Was Marx selling a bill of goods? He himself struggled to define the precise nature of class and class consciousness. Reading from Marx's analysis of landed classes, the commentator Bensaïd notes, "On the one hand, the peasants constitute a class 'in so far as…' On the other, they do not 'in so far as…' They thus seem to constitute a class objectively (sociologically) but not subjectively (politically)" (Bensaid, ibid, p. 114).

In this context and across-the board, class, and class consciousness seem to depend more on particular conditions and contingencies than on any ongoing, conscious reality. People tend to think individually, more than socially. However vital social relations are to consciousness, they are less ascertainable. Human consciousness is mercurial.

Marx himself was forced to this rueful conclusion in the aftermath of France's 1848 revolutionary upheaval. He expected that newly expanded voting rights and parliamentary processes within France's Constitutional Monarchy would allow for the ascendance of the Socialist Party and a broad alignment of working class and liberal interests. Dialectically speaking, these would provide an 'antitheses to the old feudal "finance aristocracy" in decline and in advance of "bourgeois industry class interest 'thesis'" (Sheldon Wolin, ibid, p. 442).

As it turned out, however, working class and liberal interests were divided. "The lower middle class of shopkeepers, small businessmen, and peasants were social elements with wavering political allegiances and a fervent commitment to small private property" (ibid). It turned out that they were more inclined to support the resumption of a "dictatorship" under Louis-Napoleon III, who seized governmental power by force in 1851, proclaimed himself emperor, and inaugurated the Second Empire in France (Napoleon III, Wikipedia)

In his authoritative, historical account of Western political philosophy, Wolin concludes "The bourgeoisie had turned against its own liberal values in favor of a repressive regime: it denounced party politics as 'socialistic'; the electoral law was cut back sharply, virtually eliminating the proletariat (working class, sic); and forms of popular political action were suppressed in the search for "tranquility" (ibid, p. 444). The rest is history. Marx drew his own theoretical conclusions: "The workers would counter the "bourgeois dictatorship" not by resorting to parliamentary politics or siding with 'social democracy', but by openly embracing their own version of dictatorship," what would come to be known as the 'dictatorship of the proletariat' (ibid, p.443).

Alignment, opposition, and antagonism between class interests can be muted, marginalized, or intensified; class interests can be fickle. As was noted in the analysis of Hegel's philosophy, self-consciousness is ultimately limited. The same can be said, in the Hegelian vein of ideological critique, for Marxist philosophy: there are limits to the fulfillment of social consciousness. This leaves us with the existentialism of becoming. There are limits, but these make it all the more important to prize, protect and extend capacities of social, environmental and individual consciousness that we do have.

Those with wealth and a stable income combine indeed in class-like ways to secure and expand their financial interests. They tend to support the tenets and conditions of market capitalist wage allocation, or distribution. Class interests also exist for those without capital, although their recognition of, and resources to coordinate and advance these interests are more limited. Workers, whether members of the UAW or Starbucks baristas, also struggle to gain better financial, and more secure employment conditions. The system and conditions of life produce struggles for everyone, and the potential for exploitation is ongoing. The point is to reduce the exploitation, while maintaining the legitimate interests of both labor and capital. This constitutes the dialectical resolution of material conditions. It affirms the custodial interests of labor and capital—realized to lesser degrees in America, and to greater, but varying degrees in the Social Democracies and Social Partnerships of Europe.

The galvanization of organized labor was and is a profound development. It represents a quantum social leap in which workers recognize the advantage of joining their own individual interest and orientation to that of a collective, social interest. The trade-union, supported by union dues, allows workers to go on strike. Withheld labor cuts into profit margins and disrupts capital formation and investment. Industrial strikes prevent wages from declining, or even secure wage increases. The power to 'go on strike', albeit limited, balances interests; capital interests, though, still hold the upper hand. Their reserves of capital allow them to withdraw from the labor market, laying off workers until business cycles restore prices to optimize "surplus value"— the amount of profit over and above business investment and labor costs. For Marx, the private advantage of capital over the conditions and interests of the working class represents a fundamental social contradiction - one that in his mind, and that especially of his communist acolytes around the world and in Russia - necessitated the complete overthrow of capitalist systems.

Somehow, the broad public interest needed to be raised to parity with private interests and private ownership. This issue was taken up in different ways by European Social Democrats: working-class economic conditions are existential and universal, and they must be addressed and ameliorated, despite the political complexities of class formation and representation. Hence, the social market was born, advancing provisions for social insurance related to health care, education, and collectively bargained wage parity. This last is essential not only for wage earners, but for maintaining the viability of the broader market. Business interests are thus served, but ongoing issues of cost and investment opportunity must regularly be negotiated. Concessions to the demands of labor for better working conditions and greater wage parity may signal progress, yet capital interests remain at least one step ahead. Wage concessions to labor have an upper limit, controlled by productivity and profitability. However, the so-called "law of motion" holds that in a capitalist system, those in "private" business—capitalists—must constantly increase the rate of "capital accumulation" (*Marx's Theory of Surplus Value*, International Viewpoint, ibid). As Marx himself wrote: "As soon as labor has ceased to be the great wellspring of wealth, labor time ceases to be its measure… On the one side, then, (capital) calls to life all the powers of science and of nature, as of social combination and social intercourse, in order to make the creation of wealth independent (relatively) of the labor time employed on it. On the other side, it wants to use labor time as the measuring rod for the giant social forces thereby created and to confine them within the limits required to maintain the already created value as value" (Bensaïd, ibid, p. 348/Karl Marx, *Grundrisse*, [*Critical Foundations*], pp. 704-705).

A contradiction on top of a contradiction. "This," as the author Bensaïd notes, "is where we are!" (ibid). The industrialized world, particularly in the USA, demonstrates the proliferation of wealth that appears untethered from the labor producing it, even as that labor is underpaid or over-compensated. This is true for the Nanosecond-controlled Amazon line worker as well as for the stock investment broker making money from money. Under such conditions, working class identification and class interest becomes dispersed.

It is for this reason, not incidentally, that Bernie Sanders, along with other U.S. Congressional supporters, proposed the *Tax on Wall Street Speculation Act of 2021*, which calls for imposing "A tax of a fraction of a percent on trades of stocks, bonds, and derivatives. This Wall Street speculation tax, also known as a financial transaction tax, will raise up to $2.4 trillion in revenue over the next decade from wealthy investors that can be used to make public colleges and universities tuition free and debt free. It will also reduce speculation and high-frequency trading that is destabilizing financial markets." *(Senator Bernie Sanders, Tax on Wall Street Speculation Act of 2021, sanders.senate.gov)*

Efforts such as these are underway in America, unsuccessful at the moment, to curb the banditry of modern finance, so imperiling the future of liberal-democratic government. This banditry is thus far more contained by the social democracies of Europe. This difference delineates a more promising way forward.

Chapter Three:
A Glance Backward: Democratic Capitalism

There are many takes on Marx's dialectical interpretation of history, - whether absolutely, or only relatively pre-determined – between total overthrow of the class structure, or class accommodation. Whatever the correct analysis, his philosophy spawned certain "deterministic" followers - adherents who took up his socio-economic analysis in ideological terms and believed unyieldingly that his interpretation of class struggle and exploitation was conclusive and inerrant.

They believed in the possibility -or perhaps the chimera - of a classless society, wherein private property being banished or limited, people would be infused with and supported by social values and the public good. In this vision, personal freedom would coincide with the public interest, "Where nobody has one exclusive sphere of activity but each can become accomplished in any branch he wishes. Society regulates the general production and thus makes it possible for me to do one thing today and another tomorrow, to hunt in the morning, fish in the afternoon, rear cattle in the evening, criticize after dinner, just as I have a mind, without ever becoming hunter, fisherman, herdsman, or critic." *(*Karl Marx, *The German Ideology, Theses on Feuerbach, Introduction to the Critique of Political Economy,* Karl Marx - goodreads.com)

No matter the evident idealism, not to say illusion involved, Marx insisted that such projections were borne out, not only by current conditions, but also by the dialectic development of history. He seconded Hegel's enshrinement of the French Revolution of 1789. For Marx, though, that event illustrated the dialectic of class conflict as a modal historical force of change.

Simply put, what became the new propertied or bourgeois business class of France, alongside the impoverished masses of French society, overthrew the feudal class relations imposed by the monarchy, the landed aristocracy, and the church. The same process occurred earlier, under different terms and conditions in America. The French and American revolutions are pivotal historical events because, over the long term, they ushered in a new era of material and property-class relations, economic distribution, wealth accumulation, and economic power. These events, alongside other historical and economic developments, appeared to validate Marx's contemporary class struggle dialectic projections.

The bourgeois, middle-class triumph over monarchy and aristocracy provided one basis for Marx's deterministic conjecture that, in the next historical phase, the working class would be compelled by economic conditions to throw off its chains of capitalist subjugation. However, that transformation lies in what has turned out to be a distant, if not far-fetched, future. In the meantime, the current paradigm of democratic capitalism still holds substantial, even if at the moment, wavering sway.

As noted in this essay's foreword, while *liberal democracy* or perhaps better said, democratic capitalism - represents significant progress, it still contains certain unresolved and historical "internal contradictions." Perhaps the market conditions it unleashes outstrip and beleaguer the political premises upon which it depends. But democratic capitalism has strong roots.

Liberal, democratic capitalism emerged historically in France, America, Europe and elsewhere. As noted, wealth and power had been concentrated in monarchical, aristocratic, and religious hands in different ways in each country. Yet, both nascent and emergent propertied interests in those societies claimed equal rights and freedom for most classes to pursue and own property. Democratic government was established to advance and protect these rights by law.

In Hegelian and Marxist terms, outlined earlier, democratic capitalism, represents a broadly compatible fusion of ideological and materialist platforms. The ideology and principles of democracy promote equality of rights and equal protection under the law. The capitalist mode of materialist production, on the other hand, offers economic opportunity for all. They fit together, hand in glove. The seams of that glove begin to split, however, when capital, in this global economic day and age, begins to limit, or foreclose economic and political opportunity. Then it is not for everybody, despite the democratic ideology in which it has been embedded, and by which it has been upheld. Henceforth, commentary will take pains to demonstrate the ways in which the hand strains at the glove, or conversely, how the glove strains to contain the hand. American market capitalism, at the moment, portends the overthrow of democratic rights. Its freedom contests the tenets of democratic equality. This strain reveals dialectic contradiction between the ideals, values and processes of democratic governance and those that drive the market capitalist mode of production.

For Wolf as well, and many others, the historic marriage between market capitalism and democratic government is increasingly on the rocks. The breakdown occurs with the growing entanglement of political and economic spheres. Like any marriage, whether personal or governmental/economic, a certain independence is necessary for both partners, or the relationship becomes stifled. As Wolf argues, "There are two main ways in which this delicate balance between politics and market (ideological and mode of production conditions) can be destroyed: state control over the economy and capitalist control over the state" (ibid, p. 29). Historically, state socialism and totalitarian communism, especially in Eastern Europe and the Soviet Union, provide examples where the state took over the economy Conversely, in the west, outright capitalist/oligarchic control over the state has been forestalled, or at least limited. Ideological recognition of democratic rights, processes, and individual economic agency allows for mutual accommodation between democratic and capitalist interests. As Wolf says, "The ability and willingness of oligarchies to create and sustain political coalitions while tolerating genuine democracy is central to the whole story" (ibid, p. 27). Until now, that is.

Conditions in Europe and America offer two variant responses to these circumstances. In Austria and Europe generally, oligarchic-capitalist interests are more restrained and channeled to serve larger social interests. As will later be demonstrated, in ideological and mode of production terms, social market capitalism represents a further, historic, durable fusion of democratic capitalism because, among other things, it has upheld the social democratic interest of labor and thereby extended the dimensions of the market capitalist economy.

Chapter Four:
The Marxist Account Revisited:
A Post-Marxist Perspective

For Marx, as a result of his own historical experience and philosophical suppositions, the oligarchic corruption of bourgeois and capital interests - and the economic system itself - were a foregone conclusion. His survey of history highlighted certain tendencies — regardless of the historical era — toward exploitation, and oppression, of one class by another to the broad society's detriment and peril.

In his own time, Marx argued that the bourgeois interests of capital had run their course and had become malignantly opposed to the broad living-wage interests of labor. His view left no room for dissent. Marx predicted that democrats and liberals would inevitably surrender to market capitalist material interests, reneging on the interests of the working class and society at large. He disparaged and condemned compromise, as would his Russian, axe-grinding, Bolshevik, and international communist followers.

For better or worse, Marx's historical materialist class analysis influenced great numbers of people worldwide over the last 150 years, particularly in Europe. His views on class relations, what came to be known as Historical Materialism, proclaimed that excessive economic inequality was neither inevitable nor justified, but represented a stark systemic contradiction or flaw that should be immediately and entirely overthrown.

This perspective left two particular legacies. The beneficial legacy anchored the labor interest as viable, legitimate, and essential. It established a framework of values at variance with those strictly bound to capitalist markets. The labor interest and trade-union movement, understood and implemented effectively, can prevent both threats to society pinpointed by Wolf: they can prevent state control of the economy and capitalist control over the state.

The other legacy reveals the limitations and corruptibility of ideology. No matter Marx's analytical insights or convictions, the material realities of the present moment, let alone history, are not so easily explained, manipulated, or overcome. Contemporary and historical realities can be assessed and adjusted but not entirely reversed. People need opportunity to eat, clothe themselves, and find housing. These material realties are ongoing and unending. The more social, political, and economic freedom they possess – not to mention free speech and a free press – to make these opportunities real, the better.

Post-Marxism

For these, among other reasons, this essay is post-Marxist. It rejects the ideological and deterministic aspects of classical Marxist analysis—including its strict materialism -and insistence on "economic, historical, and class determinism," and its "anti-humanist" bias (Oxford University Press, *Post-Marxism Quick Reference*, oxfordreference.com, 2024).

At the same time, it staunchly acknowledges and supports labor's role in regulating and reshaping economic and industrial relations. It also employs dialectical analysis and perspective to interpret historical and contemporary economic processes and events, and to understand the unraveling of democratic capitalism and the potential evolution of social democratic capitalism

Further, it argues that the human story – history - is neither predetermined nor random but rather an ongoing, directional endeavor shaped by past and contemporary human agency and association. This association and agency are deeply influenced by certain material and ideological realities, but retain elements of autonomy and freedom. The future is not ordained but upheld by moral and pragmatic commitment, as well as individual, and collective good faith, or not.

At the same time, dialectical analysis of historical and contemporary class conditions is instrumental because, while it recognizes opposition, it also comprehends resolution and a basis for progress. As long as dialectical analysis is not ideologically employed as a weapon against adversaries, it is a practical tool, by which political and economic interests can be measured to foster compromise and resolution and be the basis for social partnership.

The Humanist View

Marxists, if not Marx himself, often insisted that the course of history was predetermined, with the working class ordained to determine it - not just co-determine it. However, human identity, or consciousness cannot be solely reduced to material or class interests, whether capitalist or working-class.

While these interests are significant, fluctuating with circumstances, they are not determinative; humanism (and its many dimensions) prevails over materialism. The human condition depends on the resolution of material inadequacies and contradictions, but extends beyond them, to include our spiritual place in the natural world. The humanist pledge "affirms human ability and responsibility to lead ethical lives of personal fulfillment that aspire to the greater good" (The Humanist Magazine, Definition of Humanism, American Humanist Association, americanhumanist.org, 2024).

It is, therefore, incumbent upon individuals and society to create social, economic and environmental systems that enable and promote individual responsibility and the pursuit of ethical life - connected to the larger tapestry of social, and spiritual existence. Ethical life is composed of and supported by moral ideals and behavior; in America's case, that life is part and parcel of its distinctly liberal-democratic heritage and commitment to the equal rights of life, liberty, and the pursuit of happiness. Historical progress, as noted, depends ultimately on social organization and institutions that permit and support the ongoing, broad development of individual consciousness, in intellectual, social-ethical, environmental, spiritual and creative terms.

In America, at the moment, humanist ideals and democratic values are vexed by the realities of market financialization and commodification, (that all values become monetized) and by hyper-capitalist domination of the economy. These favor the propertied, privileged and the few, at the expense of the many. Looming autocracy threatens self-government and the nominal and substantial freedoms exercised by American citizens. Further, the self-governing freedom of America's judicial, educational, journalistic, and religious institutions is threatened; as are the rule of law and separation of governmental powers, upholding the heritage and future prospects of the American Republic.

Ideology and Marx

Though Karl Marx envisioned a hopeful future for humanity, he was no humanist. A materialist at heart, he argued that the ideological realm, including religious belief and social value systems in general, practically the whole Hegelian realm, was, to all intents and purposes, contained and controlled by society's mode of production and system of industrial relations - its materialist, mode-of-production base. Hence, as is said, 'Marx turned Hegel on his head'.

He referred to the processes taking place in the arts, law, politics, science, and education as belonging to the "ideological superstructure" of society, where social values, ideals, and matters of culture are at play. This contradicts the Hegelian enshrinement of such things, as representing the banners of reflexive human consciousness.

As Marx himself explains, "The ideas of the ruling class are in every (historical, sic) epoch the ruling ideas, i.e. - the class which is the ruling material force of society, is at the same time its ruling intellectual force. The class which has the means of material production at its disposal, has control at the same time over the means of mental production, so that thereby, generally speaking, the ideas of those who lack the means of mental production are subject to it. The ruling ideas are nothing more than the ideal expression of the dominant material relationships, grasped as ideas." (Karl Marx, *The German Ideology*, 1845)

It goes without saying that much of this is fairly self-evident. The American market capitalist system is sustained by particular class interests that control the distribution, deployment and utilization of income and wealth, in increasingly un-democratic terms. Economic ownership interests, for Marx, feed into, and determine all other "ideological" aspects of culture - its laws, education, terms of exchange, media, and the very tempo and pace of productivity and associated social and economic relations. If you feel stressed by the pace of your life, and don't have time to smell the flowers, as it were, (or read long essays like this one), it may partly be explained by the hyper-speed of production required by the capture of hyper-capitalist conditions. The persons controlling the machines of society, for Marx, have a preponderant and unjustified influence on the whole tapestry of social values and ideals. These, in turn, become geared almost exclusively to the requirements of production and capitalist efficiency, at growing expense to the interests of labor, and other social values. Alternative systems, however, can be adopted.

Marxist analysis contributed to the fervor of a revolutionary ideology that proclaimed the complete overthrow of society - not only of its capitalist overlords and their control of the means of production and industrial relations, but of the entire associated realm of capitalist ideological culture. This included its liberal-democratic governments.

For Marx, democratically elected politicians, whether liberal or conservative, were merely the playthings of capitalist corporate barons and oligarchs—libelous traitors to working-class interests. Such vilification and "determinist" assertions are only conditionally valid. In general, they are anathema to the humanist interest and cause.

Contemporary Marxism

Despite these extremities, the Marxist perspective has constructive relevance today, but only in cautionary, not deterministic, terms. Certainly, democratic processes are influenced by capital interests, as well they should be. Capital is essential. But capitalist interests must be restrained and brokered, along with all other social interests.

As Martin Wolf notes, "The delicate balance between the market and politics" must prevent the capitalist overthrow of the state, or democracy, and all the social interests it maintains and represents will fail. *(Ibid.)* This threat is particularly poignant in this second age of Trump, where capital appears to overthrow democracy.

But Marxist determinism is only half-right. Marxist analysis doesn't admit free-associating, democratic variables, ideas, and movements, which emerge to constrain, influence and guide social, political and economic affairs. Such constraints emerged with New Deal legislation under Franklin Roosevelt, the Great Society and Civil Rights movements under John Kennedy and Lyndon Johnson, and in Europe through institutions of Social Partnership. In each instance, and many others, economic, or social conditions had reached such an impasse that thorough reform was required, even, or especially, at the expense of raw-knuckled capital interests.

Capital interests are legitimate and must be recognized, but only in association with other legitimate interests, particularly those of labor, race, gender, or the environment.

Mutual accommodation and resolution - especially between the two dialectic interests of labor and capital - must occur, or the ship of state will eventually founder, bringing about the end of society's evolution and of social unity itself; a dialectic and dystopic dead-end.

The Way Forward

Democratic interests in America appear wholly in flux, both because of the MAGA onslaught and because their own allegiances are over-dispersed. Their constituencies may be broad, but they are insufficiently consolidated.

The guidance of liberalism and the viability of Martin Wolf's "democratic capitalism"—not to mention humanist prospects, are to be restored only by reconstituting industrial relations and prioritizing the material interests of working people. This must be stoked by renewed collective will, social solidarity and an adaptation of institutional structures that support democratic containment of capitalist excesses.

Otherwise, in the parlance of the time, Democrats will keep getting "libbed." Their 'ideology' must be grounded in the transformation of industrial relation.

The European Social market capitalist system and its pragmatic, institutional mediation of business and economic affairs, by contrast, offers a strong alternative adaptation, even against the tides of global hyper-capitalism. Social division, acrimony, and oligarchic takeover are restrained because material conditions are anchored in durable social processes.

This is due, in the main, to the robust social and economic partnerships forged after World War II through social-democratic compromise, and the blending of capital and labor interests, to the sustainable advantage of both.

The humanist project finds horizons of promise in this setting. In the end, the scope of historical progress must, at a minimum, offer the prospect of a hopeful future for a substantial majority of the people. Civic life is thereby ennobled.

The Dialectic Zombie

Dialectic analysis requires the identification of clear frameworks and interests. It is not automatic, or self-evident. Without it, though, the analysis and interpretation of social, and economic affairs become dispersed, or random. They fall to the machinations and control of commercial media, which maintain the superficial, but effective gauze of social unity. Dialectic perspective regresses into somnolence and zombie-like disuse. By the same token, dialectic analysis should not be ideologically driven.

In non-ideological terms, Marx himself at least partially approved of capital interests for driving industrial productivity, economic development, and historical progress. In the end, however, he was so convinced of his final class structure analysis that he, or at least his followers, were misled into thinking that material realities could be overturned by revolutionary vanguards, wielding the right materialist ideology, regardless of the economic and social conditions to which they were applied.

The conservative capitalist interest is not entirely villainous; it is vitally constructive in fostering conditions for material well-being. Its drive to suppress labor costs and hoard profit benefits, including surplus value, has often been extractive, exploitative, and even ruinous for working people and society at large. Its control of the media often distorts and whitewashes social and economic reality, preventing people from coming to satisfactory terms with the modes of production and industrial relations that govern their lives.

But the capital interest is also sanctioned by society: it is tasked with financing the production of goods that society needs—or at least wants—as efficiently and profitably as possible, while reinvesting accumulated capital to spur further economic development and create employment opportunities. Capital, therefore, must be conserved, protected, and perpetuated, even as it is constrained and guided by other social, material, democratic and dialectically identifiable interests. Such recognition of mutuality is the basis of class reconciliation and partnership.

The interests of the working class, on the other side of the dialectical divide, are conflicted by self and social interests, as well as by material and spiritual concerns. Dialectic analysis can only go so far in untangling these intricacies, even when market conditions are largely standardized and legally structured. Both market and working-class conditions appear to constantly shift. It is a challenge to identify and fix definite interests. That is why, (not incidentally), in Austria, among other European states, shop floor-workers councils are elected and maintained, which mediate, in real-time, ongoing labor conditions.

Otherwise, dialectical insight and mediation can become altogether dormant, both at the local level, and in understanding contemporary trends and issues within working-class, or capitalist class cultures - especially when people just want to get on with their lives and avoid the fray of political and economic contest. Nonetheless, class interests are real and instrumental, as are democratic and capitalist interests.

Regardless of employment types or job prospects, particularly in America, working people - without sufficient capital to acquire business equipment and ownership - are mostly excluded from profit and surplus value distribution and the overall direction of how the means of production should be deployed. This defines them as a class in itself.

But how does this class in itself become a class for itself? The same can be said of capitalist class interests. They are perhaps more naked, but still important to identify.

Working class conditions and interests often appear indecipherable amid broader, shifting, social and economic realities. Its dialectic interests are submerged, or disregarded. Correctly applied, dialectic analysis can vivify conditions of alignment, when institutions are established to exercise vigilance on behalf of working people. Maintenance of the social market economy calls out just such dialectic alertness. Sober minds from both sides of the political aisle and cash register must join to work out pragmatic, compromise solutions that will restore and renew the liberal, social-democratic economic paradigm.

Dialectical Issues Today

At the moment in America, however, such resolution appears doubtful, or indeed, appears to go off in wrong-headed directions. Neo-conservative, if not outright reactionary, forces are ascendant, asserting an authority that threatens to roll back the consensus of a more liberal era in which broad social interests were at least nominally validated.

The eclipse of that era can be seen in dialectical terms by the 2024, conservative Supreme Court 'Chevron Deference' ruling that abrogates and reverses the well-established purview and authority of governmental agencies. "The decision will likely have monumental effects on the future of regulatory actions across the entire economy," note authors, Paul Blumenthal and Marita Viachou. "Courts will have wider latitude to strike down everything from climate change regulations issued by the EPA to competition rules from the Federal Trade Commission and net neutrality rules from the FCC" (Paul Blumenthal, Marita Viachou, *Supreme Court Power Grab Overturns 40-Year Precedent in Huge Win for Corporations,* Huffington Post, June 28, 2024). Such changes are borne out by the spate of Trump II executive orders and general judicial acquiescence. What, under these circumstances, happens to the public interest in clean air and water?

The historic shift away from legislative mandate and agency enactment toward judicial fiat is seismic. The commitments of liberal-democratic jurisprudence - separation of powers, and "equality before the law" are overturned. In Hegelian ideological terms, this shift can be seen as a reassertion of McKinley-era conservative values that antedate the welfare state. In Marxist terms, the shift represents the advancement of modern capital and corporate interests over the broader social interest in shared material prosperity, stable government, and social unity. In any case, dialectic transformation, if not resolution, takes place.

The ruling on executive agency and legislative authority is further compounded by the Supreme Court's subsequent decision on presidential immunity, broadly interpreting the president's "official acts" as legally immune. Both decisions challenge traditional securities and assumptions about democratic government. They rival the ancient *Dred Scott* Supreme Court ruling of 1857, which revealed how deeply slavery interests controlled federal governance. Likewise, these 2024 decisions indicate the extent of conservative, reactionary incursion into and control of governmental processes. They make way for a state in which corporations and their minions in government may exercise quasi-feudal control over society.

The approaching challenges may not auger the "irresistible conflict" that William Seward, Lincoln's rival and eventual Secretary of State, warned of before the Civil War, but contention grows. One can even conjecture that the MAGA agenda, incoherent and threatening as it is, might lead to a bizarre and dystopian society. As eerily and plausibly portrayed by Margaret Atwood in her novels Oryx and Crake and The Year of the Flood, such a society features the bi- and tri-furcation of social castes and the random control of corporate-autocratic dictate.

To oppose and overcome the challenges posed by judicial overreach, MAGA populism, and *Project 2025,* it appears that any new public-goods agenda must originate, dialectically speaking, with the Democratic party - even at the cost of its now customary alliance with Wall Street constituents and patrons. The adoption of a greater 'wage-parity' paradigm calls for altering the role and function of government, the realignment of industrial relations, and the coordination and maintenance of social partnerships between business and labor interests. The reconstitution of social insurance, providing universal access to healthcare, technical and higher education, and collective bargaining rights would finally contain and redirect MAGA populism.

Achieving any of this, as unrealistic as it may appear, would require a fundamental transformation of American society, profound leadership and advocacy, and massive economic re-organization. Such are the stakes facing the current and future American electorate, a challenge to test every facet of the democratic process.

Such a transformation would involve a full-throated campaign against the overreach of corporate power in national affairs and against the exploitative elements of market capitalism that harm social unity and shared material well-being. It would demand the fulfillment of New Deal collective bargaining promises to American workers and depend on new ideals of social solidarity. Corporate interests themselves must be re-inducted into a new compact in which the institutions and relationships of social partnership ensure both economic enterprise and labor interest security.

The labor interest becomes all the more salient and necessary to identify. In America, due to a lack of consolidation and social marginalization, labor interests often lack a clear public platform. This stems partly from the history of the American labor movement, but even more from America's particular economic development and recent history. Labor interests are dispersed, divided, and isolated. Recent flashes of trade union strength, as seen at Amazon, the UAW, or Starbucks notwithstanding, consolidation and coordination of the labor interest awaits galvanizing advocacy. The individualist proclivities of the average person must once and for all embrace collective interest and advantage.

Imagine, for instance, labor TV, radio, and internet networks transmitting labor news and perspectives, or Chambers of Labor in each state and region, representing labor interests in ongoing dialogue and negotiation with capital interests, to create a viable social market capitalist market. Imagine workers with the right and duty to form workers' councils on any substantial shop floor where deemed necessary. Such structures would promote the formation and expression of a class not only in itself but for itself, helping American society emerge from the dialectic swamp of submerged, misguided, and destructive polarization and stave off the threat of social dystopia.

To just such an end, imagine the unimaginable - a dialectical paradox. The nation's democratic billionaires collectively perceive the ongoing and urgent threat to democratic society. There are many such billionaires. They outnumbered their Republican counterparts in the recent 2024 federal election. Famous names might include Bill Gates, the founder of Microsoft; investors George and Alex Soros; and media and investment mogul, Michael Bloomberg. Other notable figures include Tom Steyer, a hedge-fund founder; Reid Hoffman, co-founder of LinkedIn; and Pierre Omidyar, who founded eBay. (Thomas Schleifer, *What's a Democratic Billionaire to Do Now?* NYT, Nov. 27, 2024.)

Though customarily prejudiced to advance and protect their own decidedly huge economic interests, they turn their philanthropic attentions to saving Democracy. They realize that the democratic and public interest requires the adoption of different economic modalities, especially concerning structures and scales of wage compensation. They therefore facilitate and underwrite the coordination and consolidation of American organized labor interests. In doing so, they contribute to the emergence of a vital and viable social partnership culture between American governmental, agricultural, business, and labor interests.

Conclusion In foregoing chapters, the practical framework for this essay was established – a survey of contrast and comparison between European and American market conditions. The preliminary survey featured Martin Wolf's analysis of democratic market capitalism, both as to its historic triumphs and struggles in the contemporary age. This was assayed against the adaptations of European social market capitalism. Both economic systems exhibit contexts in which to assess the essay's central thesis, that modern social and political polarization, particularly in America, find root in income and wealth inequality. Economist Thomas Piketty's analysis of historical records and realities underscore the consequences and cataclysms brought about by runaway economic inequality. The contrasting, though complimentary views on human consciousness associated with Friedrich Hegel and Karl Marx establish analytical frameworks through which to understand and assess ongoing social and economic affairs. Such frameworks are also applicable to productive industries, such as the American professional football league.

Part IV
Golden Jocks

Chapter One:
Historical Materialism and the NFL

"Because of its private status, the NFL does not share its finances with the public. However, it was estimated in 2023 to have made about $12 billion in the previous season" (Jakob Epstein, *How the NFL Makes Money*, Investopedia.com, updated February 1, 2024).

The National Football League and affiliated college football leagues, despite their opaque financials, illustrate an anomalous economic model. As another commentator notes, "The NFL is the most profitable sports league in the world" (Nafiz Talks Football, *5 Reasons the NFL is Socialist!* Medium, medium.com, August 9, 2024). At the same time, part of its success, as Nafiz relates, can be attributed to remarkably 'socialist' organizational principles.

For one, the NFL operates under monopoly-cartel conditions. It is practically a state industry. This goes back to the 1960s when Congress extended the *"limited antitrust exemptions"* the NFL had earlier been granted, in addition to giving the league itself nonprofit, tax-exempt status. (Gregg Easterbrook, *How the NFL Fleeces Taxpayers*, The Atlantic, theatlantic.com, October, 2013). Once the NFL and AFL merged in 1970, the new league's status allowed it to negotiate *"as a monopoly regarding television rights"* (ibid). On top of this, league commissioners, established a *'closed league structure,'* fixed at 32 teams, protecting it from undue competition. They wisely adopted *'revenue sharing'* and *'salary-cap'* schemes to ensure parity between large - and small-market teams and longstanding, intra-league competition.

While the league may be organized according to quasi-socialist principles, it operates in a capitalist economy, without excessive regulatory restraint. It is anomalous. The culture that ensues brings to mind a comparison with *The Hunger Games* series, which features state-sponsored megalomania, and socially dystopic entertainment obsession. The glamor of the sport conceals its practically gladiatorial violence and enormous profit incentives and revenues.

To get at the numbers, "The salary cap for the 2024 NFL season is set at $255.4 million per team — an increase of around $30 million per team, or 48% of a team's revenue" (Pro Football Focus, 2024 Salary Cap Tracker: All 32 NFL Teams Ranked by Cap Space, pff.com, March 12, 2024). These caps fluctuate with player movements and contract values. Players' unions push to keep up with the astronomical financial stakes involved. Robert Faurecia and colleagues at ProPublica highlight that "in the past two decades, the average value of basketball, football, baseball, and hockey teams has grown by more than 500%" (R. Faurecia, J. Eliott, E. Simani, *The Billionaire Playbook: How Sports Owners Use Their Teams to Avoid Millions in Taxes*, propublica.org, July 8, 2021). Do team owners really deserve such endowments? This growth redounds to the Minnesota Vikings' owner, Zygi Wilf, who purchased the team in 2005 for $600 million. By 2023, the team's value had soared almost 700% to $4.65 billion (Kurt Badenhausen, *Every NFC Team Sees More Profit Than Any Premier*

League Club, sportico.com, September 10, 2023). Several factors contribute to this surge.

As mentioned, professional sports are an industry anomaly. Its customer base is continually engaged, and the restricted number of teams creates near-monopolistic control. Once in, owners are effectively protected from competition. Leagues do not relegate poorly performing teams (as is the case, not incidentally, in most European soccer leagues). Moreover, team owners control regional markets, profiting from branded media and merchandise without market interference (Shelagh Gupta, Arman Nawaz, ibid). Investment in a team is prestigious and lucrative, explaining why sports teams are so highly sought and coveted.

Lucrative national media and sponsorship revenues add to this. Much of the NFL's income, for instance, comes from the national advertising market, which dwarfs other countries. "National revenue from media and sponsorship partners was $12 billion last year, or 64% of the league's $17.8 billion in total revenue, which meant each team received nearly $375 million before selling a ticket, beer, or local sponsorship. This season, that check is expected to approach $400 million" (Kurt Badenhausen, ibid). Additional revenues from ticket sales, parking, advertising, broadcasting, and merchandising for the Minnesota Vikings reached $540 million in 2022 (Statista, *Minnesota Vikings Revenue from 2001 to 2022*, statista.com, 2024). But fielding a modern professional sports team is costly. After paying players $274 million, taxes, and other expenses, the Vikings ended the 2022 season with $99 million in operating income (ibid). This figure, after considering interest and reinvestment, likely surpassed $100 million — a tidy surplus value for the owners.

Professional sports, particularly the NFL, thus exemplify hyper-capitalist, profit-maximizing tendencies, underscored by high compensation, strict salary caps, and lucrative national revenue streams. The industry's growth appears to reflect the broader economic landscape, which is increasingly dominated by quasi-monopoly control of industries and concentration of wealth and power.

The Roster Depreciation Allowance — RDA

But that's just for starters. Here's where begrudging lament and outrage over such gains should kick in. You see, professional sports team owners are the beneficiaries of particularly generous federal—and often state—tax arrangements. For example, several football teams, such as those in Baltimore and Minneapolis, leveraged extensive public subsidies to construct massive arenas. But what's not to love about owning a team? They have their fans over a barrel, who might balk at seeing their teams and team owners brought before tribunals to exact greater social accountability and curtailment of tax privileges.

At the federal level, under President George Bush — a former Texas Rangers baseball team owner — Congress passed the Roster Depreciation Allowance (RDA) in 2004. Depreciation of physical assets is a standard business tax write-off available to most business entities, and professional sports owners are no exception. However, professional sports team owners now get to write off non-physical assets, too, such as player contract rights and franchise rights for TV revenue. As *Sports Law Today* notes,

"This can generate significant tax value for investors, specifically when amounts are allocated to player contract rights" (Joshua Thomas, *Sports Teams Ownership, Amortization and Depreciation*, Sports Law Today, ropesgray.com, January 2024). Through some pretzel twist of logic, pro-sports lobbyists persuaded lawmakers that such assets lose amortized value over time, even though teams continuously regenerate their rosters and renew their TV contracts. This arrangement is unique. As a *ProPublica* analysis asserts, "in few industries is such tax treatment more detached from economic reality than in professional sports" (ProPublica, ibid).

And sports owners are cashing in on it. Steve Ballmer, the owner of the LA Clippers since 2013, is among them. Team owners across the sports spectrum utilize the RDA to minimize their tax exposure. It's legal, yet by any standard of common sense and fair play, it's highly suspect. According to *ProPublica*, Ballmer deducted amortized values on non-physical assets from his income in 2017, resulting in a tax rate of only 12% on an income of $656 million. He paid $78 million in taxes — a relative pittance compared to the $235.5 million he would have owed at the standard 35.9% rate for his income bracket. "IRS records obtained by ProPublica show the Clippers have reported $700 million in losses for tax purposes in recent years. Not only does Ballmer not have to pay tax on any real-world Clippers profits, he can use the tax write-off to offset his other income" (ProPublica, ibid).

This practice, as noted, is widespread in professional sports. "ProPublica reviewed tax information for dozens of team owners across the four largest American pro sports leagues. Owners frequently report incomes for their teams that are millions below their real-world earnings, according to tax records, leaked team financial records, and interviews with experts." For instance, the Minnesota Vikings' Zygi Wilf "has taken $66 million in losses from his minority stake in the team" (ProPublica, ibid).

Imagine that across 153 professional American sports teams. If each team writes off $100 million a year under the RDA, that's $15.3 billion annually or $153 billion over ten years. Even at $50 million per team, it's still an astronomical sum — an amount that could go a long way toward funding public, vocational, and higher education, healthcare, and an array of other worthy social programs. "Billionaire owners are consistently paying lower tax rates than their millionaire players — and often lower than the rates paid by the workers who staff their stadiums" (ProPublica, ibid). Steve Ballmer isn't alone. His class - within the ownership class- has done exceedingly well for itself. It's no secret that billionaires avoid paying their fair share of taxes. They employ dedicated tax experts and accountants to exploit "exemptions, deductions, credits, and obscure loopholes you've never heard of" to reach the goal of paying as little as possible" (Whizy Kim, *The Billionaire's Guide to Doing Taxes: How the Very Rich Lose Money, Overvalue Art, Buy Expensive Life Insurance and Somehow Profit*, vox.com, March 13, 2024).

The real news is that billionaires pay nothing at all! According to *ProPublica*'s 2021 analysis of leaked federal tax returns, billionaire doyens such as Elon Musk, Jeff Bezos, and Michael Bloomberg paid no federal income tax for several years (Vox, ibid). In this, where is the voice of the IRS, Congress, the Democratic party, the remnants of the Republican party, U.S. trade unions, and all citizen voters in advocating for a public ethos and interest that holds them to account — unless, of course, the goal is to support billionaires at everyone else's expense.

Market capitalism crosses all borders. Recall the refrain cited earlier — there is no limit to the so-called "law of motion," which holds that capitalists must continuously accelerate capital accumulation to maintain and expand their unbridled power. (pp. 55,56, ibid). Unless that is, opposing interests of equal strength arise to counter the juggernaut. The Roster Depreciation Allowance (RDA) signifies the capitalist conquest of yet another arena where public interest once prevailed.

It's no coincidence that pro sports stadiums in America are nearly always named after corporate sponsors rather than municipal entities. When asked to explain or defend U.S. tax policies, a spokesperson for Ballmer declined to answer specific questions but noted, "Steve has always paid the taxes he owes and has publicly stated that he would personally be fine with paying more" (ProPublica, ibid). Well, put your money where your mouth is. "Ballmer's tax advantages reduce revenue flowing to the federal government. Meanwhile, he has publicly criticized a government that spends more than it takes in. He even founded a nonprofit, USA Facts, which provides data on government spending. 'Nobody wants to sacrifice anything in the short term so that we don't leave these huge debts and deficits to our children,' he told Fox Business three years ago. 'That drives me crazy' (ProPublica, ibid).

Quotes like this drive us all crazy for the cognitive dissonance they perpetuate — our beliefs are continually contradicted by such actions and words. So, at present, consolidated interests to challenge and reverse these contradictions remain scattered on the field. The dialectic is a zombie. One day, it will rise again and see to it that those like Steve Ballmer, Zygi Wilf, Elon Musk, Michael Bloomberg, and Donald Trump truly "would be fine with paying more."

Philanthropy

Before moving on to the critical issue of ticket costs, it should be noted that at least some of these owners are not irredeemable scoundrels and pirates; that is, if sharing their wealth to further feather their beds is held virtuous. According to moral inclination and custom, what they take from society, on the one hand, they at least partially give back with the other. Their names and brands are burnished in the very instant they elude, if not evade, tax accountability. Their wealth apparently justifies their selection of worthy causes. Who can dispute the Ballmer Group's investment of hundreds of millions in projects "to grow economic mobility for kids and families in communities across the U.S., especially within communities of color where systemic inequities continue to create barriers"? (*Ballmer Group Invests $175 Million for Strive Together Vision 2030*, ballmergroup.org, September 18, 2023).

Consider the irony (and cognitive dissonance) that the inequities of the larger economic system are, in part, created and perpetuated by the very practices of the Ballmer Group and its numerous counterparts. Failures in the tax system and public policy bear the fingerprints of oligarchic over-accumulation and overreach. It would be far more efficient, though less personally gratifying, if the Ballmer Group redirected its extra millions in support of government-financed universal health care and tuition-free higher technical and university education. That, to a certain extent, is what happens in the social market economies of Europe. In ten of the most prosperous European countries (France, Germany, Italy, Netherlands, Poland, Spain, Sweden, Switzerland, and the UK), citizens collectively donate only one-tenth as much (22.4 billion euros) as United States citizens (224 billion euros).

"Foundations, though, are more numerous (130,000 in Europe compared with 100,000 in the USA), and above all more dynamic: their vitality index, or spending/assets ratio, is 12% in Europe, compared with 7% in the United States" *(Foundations of France, An Overview of Philanthropy in Europe*, foundationfrance.org).

Sure, higher taxes would likely reduce the exceptional range of foundations and philanthropic giving in America, but they would also make the Ballmer Group's 2030 Vision dream a reality more effectively. Instead of the piecemeal, substitute system that now functions to cover over but never mend the growing cracks in the social infrastructure, America could finally establish a viable social state.

Ticket Costs

Football (and all professional sports) pays for itself in all sorts of overt and covert ways. As reported by *USA Today*, "A 30-second Super Bowl commercial in 2024 will cost $7 million for the game airing on CBS" (USA Sports, *How Much Does a Super Bowl Commercial Cost?* usatoday.com, Feb 21, 2024). A large portion of these fees go to finance league and team operations, and they add up quickly. Ticket proceeds, of course, are also instrumental, especially as they continue to grow.

Demand for tickets is a factor in price increases, but rising production costs contribute as well. According to *Ticket News*, the price of an average NFL ticket has jumped "nearly 70% since 2006" (Dave Clark, *NFL Ticket Prices Have Jumped an Average of 70% Since 2006*, ticketnews.com, July 2021). Another source reports the primary ticket average price in 2023 at $377 (TicketSmarter data). Prices vary, depending on the venue and city and whether you can actually see the game or have to watch the Jumbotron from the outer stratosphere of the stadium. But 70%? That's 20% above inflation since 2006. The average single ticket price in 2022 was $151 — hardly affordable for the average family outing (Jakob Eckstein, *How the NFL Makes Money,* investopedia.com, February 1, 2024).

The exploits of the NFL are practically a national obsession. Through television or live attendance, everyone participates. But the cost of participation is high, and getting higher, with pay-per-view fees further throttling access. Individual and social impacts are embedded in those ticket prices. Sure, the stadiums are full and rollicking, but those who can't afford to attend far outnumber those who can. This sends shockwaves through society and signifies the barriers regular people face in trying to access markets in the larger economy. These barriers create zones of exclusion or social class. They produce social fallout and contribute to polarization.

Professional and Division I university leagues generate derivative industries, such as *SportsCenter* replays and rebroadcasts of college games. These amped-up productions sustain viewership and create their own revenue streams, making financial calculations difficult—like following footprints in a blizzard. Revenue levels should determine compensation. Everyone employed in such productions is probably glad to have a job and, for better or worse, accepts the terms offered, even though they may have little idea of how their job cog fits into the larger, professional sport machinery. Transparency is sorely lacking. To some extent, the market defies financial analysis, except for the analysis going on behind closed doors. Presumably, this is exactly how the owners and employers prefer it. They favor an unregulated, loosely controlled market. Private industry, at this level, whether by design or not, is structured to evade comprehensive scrutiny and the application of values (such as social and pay equity) that don't directly originate from or apply to the marketplace. The material reality is rendered fluid and, to a certain degree, incalculable - 'hyper' is the word. Owners have their way, and capital reigns supreme.

But still, the market can be penetrated by analysis and made more accountable. It should be possible, for instance, to examine all accounting records comprehensively. Private ownership entails social obligation. With all the money involved, what if the NFL Players' Union could truly scrutinize those salary caps? Or what if the entire league, along with all American professional sports, were unionized—from concessionaires and referees to the cheerleaders? Maybe even ticket-buying fans could receive a rebate for their role in financing operations.

That's one "what if." Another would be if the American electorate rose up in unison to declare that these billionaire gains are ill-distributed, if not ill-gotten. Everyone would benefit if they paid their fair share of taxes to support public wealth. This kind of scrutiny could be achieved through stronger social partnerships between owners and employers and those they employ. The analysis here is not restricted to NFL and professional sports team owners and respective compensation schemes. The situation in professional sports may be special, but it is, as noted at the outset, particularly emblematic of compensation for large sectors of the American corporate culture. To state it once again, the Economic Policy Institute reports that in 2022, "CEOs in America (sic) were paid 344 times as much as a typical worker in contrast to 1965 when they were paid 21 times as much as a typical worker." (Josh Bivens and Jori Kandra, *CEO pay slightly declined in 2022,* Economic Policy Institute, epi.org, September 21, 2023) The numbers cited are different, according to year and publication, but their size is largely corroborated. Let them sink in. They will be cited again.

Here, the *'ideological,* and *'mode of operation'* or materialist perspectives, as referenced earlier, are more than warranted. The ideology of American professional sport, nowhere more so than in the NFL, grows out of and contributes to the popularity of all the teams, talents, and entertainment they provide. Regarding football, as NYT journalist Jack Reed phrased it way back in 1969, "Football has probably replaced church-going as the number one social function in the South. And it's more than just the favorite sport. It is now a religio-social past-time, a psychic device for the release of tensions, and a vehicle for doing business" (Vann R. Newkirk III, *Football Has Always Been a Battleground in the Culture War,* The Atlantic, atlantic.com, September 27, 2017).

The growth and embrace of professional sports, of the NFL in particular, have increased exponentially since those relatively quaint late 1960s, when Joe Namath and the New York Jets had their heyday. Professional football offers climactic satisfaction and continuous outcome resolution to the viewer. It drapes itself in patriotic, if not nationalistic, garb. It appears relatively harmless. It crosses political borderlines. As Newkirk III further observes, "Football, especially the glossy, packaged form of the NFL, is supposed to be apolitical, but the beer ads, fighter jets, giant flag displays, rigid policing of sexuality and gender roles, and tolerance of violence off the field," offer more than enough confirmation of the social and political status quo (*ibid*). It was this status quo, not incidentally, that Colin Kaepernick's kneel-ins so poignantly interrupted, protesting ongoing and widespread racism, — endemic not only in American sport, but in American society at large. His and other such protests were thoroughly condemned and virtually outlawed.

So much for the powerful ideology represented by the NFL. As noted, its business model, or *'mode of production,'* is unique and anomalous. Its monopoly-cartel status, revenue sharing within the league, and control over the labor pool, among other factors, pretty much guarantee long-term league viability, valuation growth, and ample profit margins.

The ideology, on the other hand, practically consecrates the *'civic religion'* that modern-day professional football has become. It is sometimes a sad spectacle, nonetheless, us entertaining ourselves to death, while other, vast realms of inquiry and spirt-building experiences go unexplored.

Football's popularity enables the stadium venue shakedowns by league teams, of municipalities and their tax-paying citizens, as well as the evasion of tax-payment obligations. Exposing such ideological and materialist - mode of operation, sleights of hand is a good place to start when examining the privileges and overweening wages of corporate ownership in America. Such factors contribute to the manifest realities of income inequality; and lack of market coordination and restraint.

Sports-obsessed Americans rally to support the glory of their teams and athletes. The spectacle of unity conceals deep socio-economic divides without diminishing the larger polarization that weakens society.

Chapter Two:
Historical Materialist Analysis Revisited

It's high time that all partners in production be given access to business information and indices. But such numbers and conditions are neither shared, nor broadcast, the hallmark of private ownership. This is not to depose such ownership, but to transform it.

Historically, there is no doubt that Russian communists and state socialists perverted 'materialist' class-based economic management, not to mention the perpetration of social and political crimes against their societies. 'Materialist' dialectics were raised to the level of dogmatic creed by Communist parties. In fact, Lenin argued that both Hegelian and Marxist dialectics needed to be studied, applied, and promoted because "it must be realized that no natural science and no materialism can hold its own in the struggle against the onslaught of bourgeois ideas and the restoration of the bourgeois world outlook unless it stands on solid philosophical ground. In order to hold his own in this struggle and carry it to a victorious finish, the natural scientist must be a modern materialist, a conscious adherent of the materialism represented by Marx, i.e., he must be a dialectical materialist" (Jason Devine, *From Kautsky and the Bolsheviks, to Hegel and Marx: Dialectics, the triad, triplicity,* Links International Journal of Socialist Renewal Vision, links.org.an, p.12, September 21, 2021). This may have been the intent, but it soon transpired that Soviet ideology was all about state power. An insidious, dialectical ideology subsumed science. It became not only pernicious but also false, ultimately oppressing and corrupting entire societies. It's truly contemptible that the communist-materialist attempt to rid society of false ideologies ended up producing an ideology that was anything but true and objective and which so badly served individual, social, and material needs. The state, in Martin Wolf's words cited above, took "control over the economy."

Effective economic and social analysis should be used by both labor and capital in partnership – the European social-democratic, or social-market capitalist model — to ameliorate class conflict and serve both economic and social justice aspirations. 'Materialist' analysis in the social democracies of Europe departs from strict Marxist ideology in that it reconciles class interests, recognizing each for its essential legitimacy. It balances and restrains both from becoming overly dominant in control of economic development.

One thing Marx got right is that controlling capital interests - like banks, financiers, large corporations, and company owners (NFL league owners being no exception) are, when left to their own devices, more than capable of looking after themselves, often to the detriment of broader society and the prospect of mutual class accommodation. In this hyper-capitalist moment, the competitive mentality and drive for capital and profit in American and other capitalist economies is all-consuming. If unrestrained by greater social consciousness, and associated tax obligations, hyper-acquisitiveness and greed lead to vast income inequality, social polarization and the potential overthrow of democracy.

Not only that, but the capitalist system itself tends toward periodic, if not frequent, breakdown. Consider the Great Recession financial crisis of 2007–2008: "Predatory lending in the form of subprime mortgages targeting low-income homebuyers, excessive risk-taking by global financial institutions, a continuous buildup of toxic assets within banks, and the bursting of the United States housing bubble culminated in a 'perfect storm,' which led to the Great Recession" (*2007–2008 Financial Crisis*, wikipedia.org).

Martin Wolf's commentary further notes that economic transformations since 1980, particularly "deindustrialization, de-unionization, declining participation, liberalization, and the rise of the 'gig economy,' are closely associated with the rise of 'precarious' employment" (Wolf, *ibid*, p. 97) As these changes take hold, as a matter of dialectical necessity, new rhetorical, political, economic, and institutional adaptations must come into play. The system itself must be arraigned.

EU member-state conditions can be generally described in historical- materialist, mode of production, terms. More detailed analysis and assessment will be concentrated on the respective, structural arrangements achieved by Austria and the USA, particularly with regard to the social state and public spending. This assessment will offer a model for resolution, a different path forward to effectively address the era's central conundrum: the rise of economic inequality and social and political polarization amidst material abundance and prosperity. What are the phenomena, causes, and trajectories of this inequality? At what point does such inequality, inherent to any competitive economy - whether market capitalist or social market - become malignant, polarizing, and destructive?

Martin Wolf doesn't discount social and cultural factors like race, immigration, or religion, but he locates the roots of today's crisis of 'democratic capitalism' in the economic turmoil of the 2007-2009 subprime mortgage crisis, and the economic disruption caused by the COVID-19 public health crisis of 2020-2021. "The rise of demagogic nationalism and authoritarianism in high-income democracies -the core of today's political crisis - can be attributed in significant part to economic failures" (*ibid*, p. 106). Each of these events, not incidentally, could be critically analyzed from a dialectic standpoint, identifying their likely origins and interests involved. The recklessness in banking and housing leading up to 2007 may have been hard to perceive, but the political fallout is anything but; it is shocking. The emperors turned out to wear no clothes, but few were held to account, much less the economic system they perpetuated.

"Those in charge had failed to recognize the risks they allowed the financial sector to run. Many members of the public came to believe that these failings were the result not just of stupidity but of the intellectual and moral corruption of decision-makers and opinion leaders at all levels - in the financial sector, regulatory bodies, academia, media, and politics" (*ibid* p. 104). Why were corrective measures and institutions so lax and negligent in restraining profligate practices? The 'ideological superstructure,' or legal system you might say, was driven and overrun by runaway business practices, or 'materialist' modes of production and operation. At the same time, the very ideology of go-go capitalism enabled malfeasance and neglect of broader social obligations. This disjunction needed comprehensive reform, but instead was bailed out and allowed to fester. Such analysis, reform and renewal are essential to ensure the covenant that enables future generations to thrive: the covenant of democratic liberalism, or social democracy, encoded in fair pay for a fair day's work, free enterprise, social solidarity, as well as the legacies of individual liberty, equality before the law, and democratic self-government.

As the saying goes, people must learn from the mistakes of the past or be condemned to repeat them. The alternative is gaining dystopian momentum. The social democracies of Europe and Austria, after the cataclysms of World War II, arrive at a different way forward.

Part V
Austrian Legacies

Describing a people in general terms, as these things go, is a dodgy, if not dubious, undertaking. Generally speaking, however, Austrians — from Vienna in the east to the province of Vorarlberg, bordering Switzerland in the west — are an especially order-loving people, keenly aware of social norms and standards. This is not particularly surprising after centuries of monarchical, military, and religious regimentation. They keep their hedges trimmed and their clothes ironed. For a putatively 'socialist' country, its citizens are remarkably bourgeois. They are property-minded. The old saying is "schaffe schaffe, Hüsle bauen," translated roughly as "toil your ass off and build your own home." They are an industrious people. Before housing prices made the prospect of building and owning a house daunting for the upcoming generation, building your own home was a longstanding social and individual aspiration; it still is, when practical. Otherwise, individual aspiration finds other outlets. Training and educational programs abound, whether for hobbies or in the professions. There is scarcely a skill or trade for which there isn't a training.

Austrians know their customs and manners, and there is a formality to their affairs, starting with the formal "Sie" or "You", when addressing someone you don't know, or have just met. It is rightly said that having too many customs and manners is better than having too few. That, anyway, is how Austrians would have it. Customs keep people together as times change. Austrians have by and large quite successfully moved on from historical convulsions into the modern world. Their sincerity has not been tainted by too much cynicism. They are a conscientious people and, in most instances, give personal responsibility, self-reliance, and individual integrity a good name.

On the ideological - mode of production, materialist spectrum, they are a people committed to social unity and material well-being, best realized when organized and shared collectively, through economic enterprise and individual responsibility.

In more recent times, the social fabric has been frayed to a certain extent. As in the USA and elsewhere, the COVID pandemic *led* to economic and social fallout in Austria. As outlined in the forward, popular resentment toward governmental vaccine and immigration policies, along with a right-wing party ready to exploit the discontent with every breath, has taken its toll on social and political unity. After long negotiations, the 2024 election finally resulted in what looks like a durable coalition between Conservative, Socialist and Neo-Capitalist parties – the agreement stands as an outright confirmation and affirmation of Austria's social state policies and institutions.

Finally, it can't go without saying, Austrians enjoy a good local beer and/or wine, not to mention first-rate bread, cheese, and chocolate.

Chapter One:
A Dive into History

As a nation, Austria has been through the wringer of historic transformation several times. It is no stranger to systemic contradictions. Compelled by circumstance to learn from the misfortunes, mistakes and crimes of its past, it has had to innovate to restore its material, moral- ethical and ideological compass. From the late 19th century alone, Austria experienced a number of wrenching governmental systemic challenges and changes, such, in different ways, as those now confronting the USA.

The Austrian capital of Vienna was once the primary and proud seat of the vast Austro-Hungarian Empire. Budapest, in Hungary, was the other governmental seat. The empire was far-flung, including what is now South Tyrol in Italy, the current Czech Republic and Slovakia, Galicia in what is now southern Poland and western Ukraine, Hungary itself, and the Balkan states of Croatia, Slovenia, Bosnia and Herzegovina, and what was once Transylvania in northern Romania.

Feudal relations and serfdom were slowly curtailed starting in 1789 and finally abolished in 1848. (Wikipedia, *Austrian Empire*, December, 2021)

The dual-monarchy maintained separate control in respective Austrian and Hungarian territories, but asserted united authority through combined foreign and military policy councils. In 1861, a constitutional monarchy was established. The bicameral parliament consisted of an Upper House, whose members were appointed, or held hereditary rights, and a Lower House, whose members were appointed by provincial Diets, themselves mostly under aristocratic control.

Parliamentary influence on imperial governance was limited. Political parties were fledgling, as was the entire electoral system. Universal male suffrage was finally granted in 1896. Executive and effective legislative power were controlled by the imperial ministries and the emperor.

As the economy modernized, a new bourgeois and liberal middle class emerged, as did a self-aware working class. The Socialist Party was formed in 1889. The monarchy relied on a strong military, the authority of the Roman Catholic Church — especially in the countryside — and aristocratic social organization. (Wikipedia, *ibid.*) And then, along with Germany, this ramshackle regime declared war on Serbia in 1914, bringing Russia, France and Great Britain (and ultimately, the USA) into alignment and plunging the western world into destructive conflict.

In defeat as an axis power after World War I, the Austrian Monarchy and Empire were dismantled and dismembered by the terms of the 1919 Treaty of St. Germain-en-Laye - parallel to the Treaty of Versailles signed with, or imposed by, the allied powers on Germany. Austria was reduced in size to its current borders and became a parliamentary democracy. At first glance, it appears almost laughable to compare America with Austria. Today's Austrian population is barely 9 million, comparable in number to the populations in states such as Michigan, or New Jersey. In geographic terms, Austria sizes up with the state of Maine. The geographical and historical circumstances of both countries are also quite different. The Austro-Hungarian Empire developed historically in the furnace of multiple competing European state entities. Perhaps it wasn't a melting pot, but the Austro-Hungarian monarchy did include multiple, contentious nationalities.

American development, on the other hand, has taken place in comparative isolation. There have been no kings (since the revolution), generals, or popes to run its affairs. Austria was a central power surrounded by countries with preening national ambitions. America's open frontiers and the melting pot identity of immigrants who filled its plains, by contrast, give claim to American exceptionalism. Time and space, however, have ways of catching up to 'exceptionalist' pretenses, shaping and redefining them. What continues to be said for the USA, though, that its states are laboratories of democracy — can also now be said of Austria. European borders have come down. Austria is a laboratory of democracy, one of many in the rich tapestry of European Union states. Austria has a long, complex, and quite particular history. Its development warrants serious attention if not emulation for its ability to adapt. Out of polarization and conflict, Austria came to produce enduring political and economic unity. But first, it went through national trauma.

For a long time, governmental convulsions pretty much ruled Austrian history - from the power of the monarch/emperor and aristocracy at the turn of the 20th century, to the broad empowerment of the people and parliamentary democracy in a shorn state after World War I, to the reaction and autocracy of Austro-fascism in the 1930's, to Nazi vassalage and foreign occupation until 1955, to the founding of Austria's modern social democratic state and ultimate inclusion in the confederated states of Europe, the EU. In retrospect, these transformations can be seen to follow dialectical patterns – indicating contradiction within ideological, or material conditions themselves, or between them – giving way to tenuous resolution. Regime change didn't altogether clean the slate, but sublated, or retained certain prior conditions, in Hegelian terms, at the next level. Such radical and rapid transformations as occurred in Austria, however, could only have come about through the scorching privations of two world wars.

Such transformations are not necessarily predictable. Dialectic analysis is canny for interpreting contemporary and historic developments. As Hegel himself noted, however, "The owl of Minerva," (the Roman goddess of Wisdom), spreads its wings only with the falling of the dusk." Though the future can be anticipated, its many variables and possible outcomes resist prescription and prophecy, whether of the fortune-teller, or of dialectal analysis. Hegel was wise to the utility of his dialectic philosophy – it could really only understand a way of life "at dusk," just as it passes away. (Abigail Rosenthal, *The Owl of Minerva Takes Flight,* Medium, medium.com, July 4, 2023) The Hegelian analysis, in other words, leaves ample room for freedom, something categorically foreclosed by the machinations and prognostications of illiberal and autocratic regimes, not to mention the dogmas of Communist doctrine These seek to dictate the terms of the future, while preserving a sphere of lawlessness for the governing clique. Such machinations represent the denial, or antithesis of intellectual, socio-ethical, creative and spiritual freedom.

They foreclose essential avenues for the evolution of individual and social consciousness, and human progress, as such.

Austrian Class Conflict

The partial resolution of class conflict in Austria after 1955 defied Marx's dialectical analysis, which mistakenly underestimated and scorned the prospects for class reconciliation between capitalists and workers. But the road to resolution was long and harrowing, with a particular junction at the end of World War I. At that time in Russia, Soviet Communists took up the cudgel of Marxist ideology and were absolutely and terrifyingly unreconciled to any interest, liberal or otherwise, but their own. They became savage in vilifying and eliminating people who were involved in capitalist enterprise. They became violently, pathologically autocratic.

In 1920, Austrian Socialist adherents of modern economic Marxist analysis were quick to perceive the errors of Soviet Communist, international ideology and its demands for lock-step conformity. In what came to be known as the period of Austro-Marxism, renowned Austrian leaders such as Max Adler and Karl Renner asserted that national conditions should be pre-eminent in determining political strategy. They were not yet themselves *reconciliationist,* but neither were they bloody-minded. Working-class interests, they maintained, had a right to be offended by "the corrupt and evil structure of capitalism" as experienced in Austrian cities like Vienna (*Austro-Marxism,* Wikipedia.com). The equally numerous interests of the landed peasantry in Austria's hinterlands, however, had legitimate claims of their own. Peasants weren't necessarily opposed to capitalist enterprise or to capitalist relations as such. Farming, after all, even tenant-farming, is an essentially entrepreneurial, if not outright capitalist, enterprise. Peasants in Austria had no voracious appetite to dispossess gentry-class farmers of their land. Instead, 'peasant-farmers' at the time were interested in regaining livestock that had been 'requisitioned,' or outright stolen, over the course of World War I. (ibid) Austrian socialists would ignore these landed interests to their own peril.

In addition, Austrian Roman Catholic bishops and priests exerted great influence throughout the country. The Church, as an institution and through its representatives, was loath to cede the authority of God, - much less any authority at all, - to a bunch of secular Marxist socialists.

Such conditions forced Austro-Marxists to seek alternative political strategies and solutions to problems of governmental power and economic development. The times were fevered. The parliamentary democracy of Austria's First Republic, inaugurated after World War I in 1919, lasted until 1933, when social, political, and economic turmoil got the upper hand.

This turmoil itself, reflected strained, economic and material conditions, as well as the dialectical disarray of diverse ideologies and class interests. After the collapse of the Austro-Hungarian monarchy in 1919, political parties of the nascent democracy exercised their newfound rights to the furthest extent of the law - and beyond. It was a time of militant ideological unrest and conflict. Major political parties, most prominently the Conservative People's Party and the Socialist Democratic Party, even fielded their own armed militias! Under such conditions, the prism of ideological-materialist/mode of production interpretation was stretched by multiple variables.

In March 1933, political strife came to a head when the Austrian Parliament was prorogued, and an authoritarian government was imposed under Chancellor Engelbart Dollfuss. Aligned with elements of the military, and those of the Catholic Church clergy, Dollfuss's "Fatherland Front" Party absorbed the Conservative People's Party. Among other policies, the Fatherland Front touted nationalist policies to "protect" Austrian Catholicism from German Protestant influence. Nationalists sought to unite the Austrian people by ruling out political, economic, and social division.

The new proto-fascist government banned labor unions and opposition political parties and erased civil liberties. Nationalism was established by force. A one-month civil war broke out across Austria in February 1934, especially in its major cities. The rebellion was brutally suppressed.

"A thousand men, women, and children lost their lives in Vienna," and thousands more were wounded (*The Rise and Fall of the Third Reich*, William Shirer, Pub. Simon & Schuster, 1959, p. 325).

The *Sound of Music* it was not.

To maintain the government's credibility in upholding Austrian independence and sovereignty, Dollfuss also banned the Austrian Nazi Party. Nazi agents subsequently assassinated him in July 1934, in an unsuccessful coup attempt. His successor, Kurt Schuschnigg, also strove to maintain a semblance of Austrian independence.

The country was rife with Nazi-incited pan-German agitators who called for a union with Germany. Schuschnigg resisted these designs and continued the authoritarian policies of his predecessor in what is widely termed the period of Austro-fascism (1934-1938). The Austro-fascist government adopted a "corporatist" system, not dissimilar to those imposed at the time in fascist Italy and Germany.

Such corporatism attempted to weaken, or even supplant parliamentary processes and instead organize business, industry, and labor as government-dominated unitary interest blocs—from the top down. During this period, Austria's economy was still haunted by post-World War I penury and poverty and was unable to recover from the worldwide economic Depression of 1929.

In 1938, "1/4 of the Austrian working population was still unemployed" (*Austerity in Pre-1938 Fascist Austria*, Social Democracy for the 21st Century, 21stcentury.blogspot.com, September 26, 2018). The Austro-fascist regime pursued deflationary economic policies, imposing high interest rates, freezing wages, and cutting unemployment benefits (*ibid.*). Austro-fascist corporatist ideology forced, or stipulated economic class interests and relations. This impeded and retarded economic reform and adaptation.

To reprise the ideological-materialist/mode of production prism of interpretation outlined earlier, "ideology" is understood as an adoptive belief system, or ethos. Ideology comprises the ideals, morals, and principles by which a people, party, or government justifies and implements programs and policies to improve their lot, or increase power.

In this case, the nationalist Austro-fascist ideology proposed to lead people without taking their broad interests, or participation into account. Civic discourse and debate fell victim to the government's attempt to maintain autocratic control of society. Upon such premises, its management of economic and material conditions was untenable. The bases of social support for its brand of nationalism were too few. Its fusion of ideological interest and material program foundered. By 1938, the people were fed up with its political and economic policies.

Austro-fascism lasted until March 12, 1938. In a February meeting at Hitler's Berchtesgarten alpine retreat in Germany, Schuschnigg was browbeaten. Hitler falsely alleged a host of Austrian violations of German national interests, hectoring that "the whole history of Austria is just one uninterrupted act of high treason" (*ibid.*, p. 326). The so-traduced and humiliated Austrian Chancellor was forced to sign an agreement that would "lift the ban against the Austrian Nazi Party, grant amnesty to all the Nazis in Austrian jails" (including those who had assassinated his predecessor), "and hand over significant ministerial posts to loyal Nazis" (*ibid*, p. 328).

After his appointment with Hitler, Schuschnigg had second thoughts and vainly tried to uphold Austrian independence. He even dared to call a plebiscite so his fellow citizens could decide for themselves on Austrian independence. Such plebiscites, however, being intolerably democratic, prompted the German army to array military divisions on the Austrian border. Schuschnigg backed down from his plebiscite plans. It was too late. The German Army (*Wehrmacht*) overran and occupied Austria, decreeing it *Ostmark*, a province within Nazi Germany. The German occupation was unopposed by the Austrian military, but Austrian nationalists of all political persuasions were identified and subsequently rounded up. In Vienna alone, in the early weeks of the forced annexation, (*Anschluss*), Nazi security forces arrested "79,000" so-called "unreliables" (*ibid*, p. 348). Many of those arrested spent the war imprisoned at the infamous Dachau concentration camp outside Munich, Germany. In the subsequent Nazi-arranged election plebiscite, the outcome of annexation was preordained. After all the confusion and turbulence of the moment, Hitler was greeted by thronging Austrian masses as a liberator.

What a nightmare.

German fascist ideology has undergone extensive analysis. Its massive parameters exceed the purview of this tome. Suffice it to say that it was poisoned by nationalist, racist, autocratic, and demagogic ferocity. These forces fabricated German unity under false and violent pretenses. In contrast to the Austro-fascist model, described above, its corporatist system pursued interventionist Keynesian economic policies in reconstructing the national economy and rebuilding the German military. "German unemployment by 1938 was 3%" (*Austerity in Pre-1938 Fascist Austria, ibid.*, Graph – Unemployment in Austria vs. Germany from 1928–1938).

The fusion of German ideological and materialist/mode of production interests was insidious and formidable—but it went down in flames, on the altar of a psychotic dream to conquer Europe, if not the entire world.

World War II Aftermath

The catastrophe and failure of successive governmental systems in Austria led to a national reckoning after the war. Austrians took lessons from their nation's history. Each regime, for different reasons, had been unable to harness different and divergent ideological and materialist interests. The war's military casualties numbered 261,000 out of a total of 384,700 overall Austrian war-related deaths. Tribunals were established to punish egregious war crimes and criminals. Such tribunals followed the so-called Moscow Declaration issued in 1943 by the United Kingdom, the Soviet Union, and the USA. While confirming victimhood at the hands of Nazi Germany, the Moscow Declaration reminded Austria that "she has a responsibility, which she cannot evade, for participation in the war on the side of Hitlerite Germany, and that in the final settlement, account will inevitably be taken of her own contribution to her liberation" (Wikipedia, *Moscow Declarations, Declaration on Austria*). Efforts to 'de-nazify' the country were, however, limited. Instead, the narrative of German conquest and Austrian victimization in the whole bloody affair broadly took hold. This allowed people to get on with national reconstruction without being crippled by recrimination.

It took until 1991 for Austria to offer official recognition and apology "that many Austrians backed Adolf Hitler's

Third Reich and were instrumental in its crimes" (*Austria Admits Role in Holocaust,* Washington Post, Michael Wise, 7/9/1991). Chancellor Franz Vranitzky addressed Parliament and a national television audience, "acknowledging all of our history and the deeds of all parts of our people — the good as well as the evil. As we lay claim to the good, so must we apologize to the survivors and the descendants of the dead for the evil" (ibid).

In the war's immediate aftermath, it fell to some of the very same Austrian nationalist figures of diverse political stripes, who had been imprisoned by the Nazis in Dachau, to construct a modern, viable Austrian economic and governmental system. Taking somber and sober stock of the several calamities that had befallen their country — not to mention raw economic realities — and drawing on all resources to work in unity, they forged a 'neo-corporatist' democratic governmental-economic system. This system advanced an ideological and materialist/mode of production fusion – based on the imperatives of social unity and shared material well-being – and premised on finally walling off any future prospect of fascist, or communist political domination.

Austrian Neo-Corporatism/Social Partnership

'Neo-corporatism' is a different, not to say foreign concept. It didn't, though, just pop out of a hat. As noted, it has a long, somewhat shadowy lineage. In both Italy and Germany, 'corporatist' alliances of business, labor, and government interests were dictated from the top down. The 'neo-corporatist' system, on the other hand, is supported from the bottom up. It derives its legitimacy and authority from democratic parliamentary party representation and democratically organized representation of business and labor interests. It is the cooperative and voluntary basis of Social Partnership. Despite inevitable and ongoing twists and turns, the Partnership has endured successfully for the past 75 years. It engenders broad economic equality and prosperity and is still widely sustained by business and labor interests, the overall allegiance of the Austrian people themselves, and Europe's social market economy.

The birth throes of neo-corporatism and Social Partnership were considerable and bear extensive commentary; but first, a further note about their composition. Under governmental auspices and mandate, there are today 4 Austrian institutions, or neo-corporatist entities, that bind and represent the functional Austrian economy: 1) the Austrian Economic Chamber (WKÖ), or Chamber of Commerce represents the employer interests of some "517,000 member companies," 2) the Austrian Trade Union Federation, (ÖGB), "comprised of 7 different Trade Unions organized by sector," and 3) the Austrian Chamber of Labor, which upholds the legal representation of approximately "4 million Austrian employees and their rights to equal opportunity, equal treatment and education;" and 4) the Austrian Chamber of Agriculture, representing the farming and forestry interests of some "162,000 business" operations." *(The Social Partnership in Austria*, workinaustria.com/en, November 21, 2022) Chamber of Commerce business representatives are the chief negotiating partners, along with representatives of the Austrian Trade-Union Federation (ÖGB), in the brokering of collective wage levels and employment conditions in Austria. Last, but not least, these institutions partner with Austrian ministries and parliamentary parties, at state, federal and EU levels, in the formation of economic and governmental policies.

In all, the Social Partnership in Austria represents wide-scale and somewhat unprecedented national economic organization – coordinating economic development, that remains both dynamic and socially binding. From an American standpoint, such organization would appear to thwart free enterprise and more-or- less self-regulating markets- even as these become increasingly monopoly-controlled. American markets all too often run an unbridled course, with uneven economic and social outcomes. The Austrian model, by contrast prompts and channels a free enterprise that finds its own efficiency and produces a mostly stable, yet dynamic, social and economic state

As Andreij S. Makovitz's introduction to a compendium study on Austria relates, these social partnership institutions "have rivaled in inclusiveness the sovereignty Austria extends to its citizens, a sovereignty based on participatory concepts of liberal democracy anchored in the individual" (ibid, *Austrian Neo-Corporatism in Comparative Perspective,* Routledge Imprint, Taylor & Francis, 1995/2020, p. 6). They are not top-down, but, to some extent, collaborationist and autonomous organizations. They embody a separate form of representation that is extra-governmental and not always compatible with Austria's liberal democratic parliament or the parties that are in charge.

Though there is extensive membership and policy overlap between the Austrian Chamber of Labor, the national Austrian Trade Union (ÖGB), and the Austrian Socialist Party (SPÖ) in Parliament, the Chambers of Labor and the national trade union are "nominally independent" (ibid, p. 11). Among other reasons, this is essential because Socialist Party parliamentary, electoral fortunes over the years — and to this day — have waxed and waned, but the strength of labor alliances remains relatively robust. This can be attributed to the role played by the Austrian Trade Union Federation - Österreicher Gewerkschaft Bund (ÖGB). The ÖGB is an "all-encompassing umbrella organization" for all other Austrian unions whose interests it represents in the negotiation of collectively bargained contracts (ibid, p. 12). Its continued relevance is vital, amidst all the political vicissitudes of Austrian life.

In general terms, social partnership possesses a number of key attributes or qualities. "It is stable: there is an established system that spans sectors and outlasts any single government. It involves institutionalized cooperation, meaning that in areas such as wage-setting and training, employers and unions work together to solve collective action problems such as ensuring a sufficient supply of trained workers. It also consists of regulated conflict, with particular timetables, forums, and representatives for contesting economic, labor, and other policy decisions, with graded levels of conflict resolution (sic), often with a strike as a last resort" *(Social Partnership, Civil Society, and Health Care,* ibid). The Social Partnership requires, as noted, sophisticated organization — a small but interconnected "number of associations such as trade union confederations or employers' associations that can build up professionalism and trust" (ibid). Organization and coordination of industrial/business and labor interests need not thwart economic enterprise. It can encourage and enhance it.

Social Partnership has a distant, indirect lineage that extends way back to the 'corporatist' "guilds of medieval city-states" (Maskovitz, ibid, p. 6). The 'corporatist' paradigm was revived in the 19th century by Catholic collectivists "in their counterattack against the secular and class-based collectivism of Marxian socialism." These Catholic activists "hoped that the ills of capitalism and the fragmentations of pluralist liberalism might better be countered by a vertically-arranged 'organic' corporation of 'Stände' (alliances) than by the horizontally stratified competition of classes advocated by all versions of Marxism at the time" (ibid).

In addition, various Chambers of Commerce were common, wherein trade, business, and industry could extend their own collective interests. These commerce associations "claimed a certain representational hegemony on behalf of their members and also enjoyed some form of legal recognition on the part of the Austrian state" (ibid).

Then came Austria's raucous interwar years between 1919 and 1934, definitively influenced by the experiences and interests of the social-democratic labor party. Singular among all Central European working-class parties, as Maskovitz notes, recalling Austria's brief Civil War of 1934, the Austrian Social Democrats were the only party that "succumbed to fascism only after an armed struggle" (ibid, p. 9). As much as Austro-Marxists pursued a course independent from Soviet Russia's communist dictates and were more conciliatory to national conditions, their socialist party was fervid in ideological commitment and organizational tenacity. They wore this badge of courage after World War II. It gave them standing in post-war political struggles and negotiations. They represented a coherent socialist legacy in the interest of all types of wage earners.

The Austrian economy was on its knees after the war. The political culture was trashed and broken. It had to be rebuilt from the ground up. The capitalist economic culture, many of whose representatives were tainted by the perfidy of Nazi collaboration, also had to be resuscitated. As noted, many Austrian national patriots who had been rounded up and imprisoned in Dachau's concentration camp after Austria's Nazi occupation, came back to take leading roles in reconstructing Austria's institutional system. As the historian Moskowitz continues, "the cleavages which tore the First Republic apart after 1918, and which led to two fascist regimes in the wake of its demise — 'black,' clerical Austro-fascism from 1934 until 1938 followed by 'brown,' völkisch (folkish) German-dominated National Socialism from 1938 until 1945—had not disappeared by the end of World War II" (ibid, p. 15). In such circumstances, all parties had to pull on the same set of oars. As Moskowitz concludes, "the experiences of the decade between 1934 and 1945 had been so devastating (though often for very different reasons) that — possibly for lack of another alternative — accommodation had become the only venue for future political action. Add to this self-reflective elite realization a completely altered international and European context wherein Austria had become an occupied (and potentially divided) country at the front line between the capitalist West and the communist East, and the politics of pragmatism and accommodation assumed pride of place" (ibid, p. 14).

What these adaptations represent is a shift, if not of Hegelian self-consciousness, then of "self-reflective" historical consciousness that contributed to historical progress. This shift of consciousness was as profound as the one that occurred in America during the revolutionary age and the founding of the American republic, in which political power was removed from a monarch and shared out to the people, through their institutions and the franchise of the vote. And now, new historical conditions prompt new adaptation. Such junctures, using the rubrics of expanded economic opportunity and political representation for all sectors of society, indicate broad historical progress.

You don't have to be John Lennon to 'Imagine' economic, social and political straits in the USA developing to such an extent that people and their leaders are compelled to join together in common cause - to revise and save the American democratic experiment. Just imagine, in addition to the Chambers of Commerce that garner and organize national, state and local business interests in America, there is a Chamber of Agriculture to do the same for farming and forestry interests, a Chamber of Labor to represent the legal interests of employees and a Trade-Union Federation to act as an umbrella organization of individual Trade-Unions organized by sector in the negotiation of collective wage agreements for a majority of American employees. Such an event would pose unimaginable challenges and require the forging of new alliances and wise intervention from all sides of the aisle. It would require the almost, but not quite, unimaginable conversion of American individualist pretense to grasp the potential of greater social organization. The media environment would have to be transformed to safeguard political discourse and make full use of its positive social potential. The interests of labor and capital would have to congeal in new ways. Such a moment of national urgency could presage the adaptation and invention of an American-style Social Partnership.

Wages and Prices in Austria

In the post-war era, Austrians faced unprecedented challenges. Amidst all the rubble and ruins left over from the war and issues of daily survival, they had to establish a new system for wages and prices—something beyond the sole power of parliamentary representation. Starting in 1947, the reconstituted 'neo-corporatist' state, along with business and labor alliances, thrashed out a "series of wage and price agreements" (ibid). These agreements were trial-and-error affairs. In the following five years, through black market distortions, inflationary conditions, industrial strike action, and the exclusion of communist representatives from negotiating processes, these agreements ultimately brought gradual, but significant economic stability and prosperity. The 'neo-corporatist' arrangement required that each party to these negotiations modify its ideological inclinations and interests in the name of national comity and survival. The "Wage and Price Parity Commission," as it came to be known, among other 'neo-corporatist' bodies, would shepherd Austrian economic development over the next 50 years. As Maskowitz observes, the 'neo-corporatist' "arrangement designed to deal with exceptional situations demanding the coalescence of society's major institutions became the norm of government" (ibid, p. 13).

This innovative political and economic adaptation represents the "economization" of politics. As Markovits points out, "much of neo-(sic) corporatism is driven by economic policy." Neo-corporatist business, labor, and state alliances engage in processes of 'concertation' whereby each interest voluntarily adjusts and coordinates wage and price demands amidst marketplace conditions – depending upon productivity and inflation rates. During most of Austria's second republic, dating from 1955 to the present, the government has been proportionately controlled by a Grand Coalition of Austria's two major political parties. The Conservative People's Party still primarily represents business, agricultural, and church interests, while the Socialist Party primarily represents the interests of workers and employees. In the meantime, other parties emerge, such as the market-friendly Neos, the pro-environment Greens and the nationalist Freedom party.

The Social Partnership, as noted, sequesters to some extent political conflict and brinkmanship and moderates social polarization. In more recent years, the Grand Coalition has been interrupted by governments in which power was shared with the right-wing, so-called Freedom Party.

At the end of September 2024, the rightist, so-called Freedom Party, for the first time, outpolled other political parties in national parliamentary elections, winning *28.8%* of the total vote. (Wikipedia, *2024 Austrian Legislative Election*). The populist tide rises in Austria as well, but not to the same extent as in the USA. Austria's governing frameworks have weathered prior storms. The recently formed governmental coalition of 2025, in spite of 'Freedom Party' inroads, indicates, as noted, abiding support for

Austria's social state, Social Partnership and the continuity of its parliamentary democracy.

European and EU Prospects A recent *New York Times* opinion piece observes, in dour terms, that the social market/social partnership system in Europe is losing its grip as a bulwark against illiberal, autocratic movements rumbling across the continent (Anton Jäger, *The One Out of Hell Is Back in Europe, New York Times*, Sept. 26, 2023). States like Hungary and, until recently, Poland have had illiberal governments. Italy, as well, tends in this direction. His report underestimates social partnership and social democratic resilience, but is nonetheless foreboding.

Illiberal movements appear to gain traction across the map. Illiberal-democracy, as it is called, represents a new and different ideological species. It rejects the liberal heritage, which stands for the idea that individuals and political and economic interests in a democracy are capable of sifting through manifold cultural ideas, artifacts, policies, and moral matters, and pretty much lead life by their own lights. They are capable of self-government. Further, illiberalism rejects the legitimacy of free-standing, independent, civic, judicial, educational, religious, and journalistic, institutions. The illiberal cast of mind says that cultural information must be skewed to promote authoritarian, illiberal governmental control. To make matters worse, its form of democracy is bastardized. Democratic representation is circumscribed by less-than-free and fair electoral processes and procedures- things ominously foreshadowed by current developments in the United States.

Since their inception over the past 75 years, the EU's member states have confronted many challenges. As with Austria, it remains to be seen if the EU's social market can hold society together against the current tides of populist agitation. The challenges posed by increased immigration from the Middle East and Africa are no less than those confronting America from Central and South America. The backdrop and contexts, however, are quite different, as are the prospects for successful accommodation and evolution.

Shifting trade policies and their influence on EU state unity, - to say nothing of once-reliable security arrangements, indicate both future challenges and opportunities. As *Social Europe's* Brigid Laffan notes, "If the EU aspires to be a global player, it should act as a pole of attraction in its neighborhood and a hedge for other states faced with the two great powers" (*Brigid Laffan, Europe's Challenge in a New Era of Shift and Shock, Social Europe*, socialeurope.eu, January 13, 2025). Accordingly, Europe extended the Mercosur agreement with Argentina, Brazil, Uruguay, and Paraguay on December 6, 2024, in the aftermath of Trump's re-election. Europe must adjust and anticipate altered relations with the USA. As Laffan notes, Mercosur "is an exemplary instance of hedging US-Sino relations and strengthening multilateralism in the global system" (*ibid*). It is time for the EU to self-advocate.

The Mercosur agreement represents an explicit challenge to the gangster global order Trump seems to envision.

"The goal of the new EU-Mercosur trade deal is to:

183

1. Increase bilateral trade and investment and lower tariff and non-tariff trade barriers, notably for small and medium-sized enterprises.
2. Increase bilateral trade and investment and lower tariff and non-tariff trade barriers, notably for small and medium-sized enterprises.
3. Recast trade and investment rules as they pertain to intellectual property rights, food safety standards, competition, and good regulatory practices.
4. Promote joint values such as sustainable development by strengthening workers' rights, fighting climate change, and increasing environmental protection." (European Commission, EU-Mercosur Agreement, December 2024).

The EU seeks to promote: "the competitive integration of national economies into the international market" (*Laffan, ibid*). This will depend on further integrating and strengthening the EU itself. As Laffan continues, "The EU is now entering a period of significant choices and trade-offs. The power base of the past—values and markets—is insufficient. The Union needs to leverage public finance and collective borrowing to meet its geo-economic and strategic needs." (*ibid*). It needs to uphold and extend the virtues of social market, capitalist economies.

The EU now embarks on the perilous path of militarization. In 2024, recently re-elected EU Commission President Ursula von der Leyen, announced a plan by which European member-states, in conjunction with EU institutional and private investment support, would pursue the development of military industries and capabilities. The plan calls for a build-up supported by *€800 billion* in investments over the next five years (*Emmi Sasipornkarn, EU's von der Leyen Proposes €800 Billion Defense Plan, Deutsche Welle*, dw.com, March 4, 2025).

All this indicates strides toward the kind of greater European coordination and unity, called for in the Adam Tooze article reviewed at the outset of the current essay. The world's political alignments and governing frameworks are shifting rapidly.

Even as 2025 appears to be a watershed moment in history, it remains essential to survey recent political and economic trajectories to understand how we got here in the first place. This should provide further backdrop for understanding the devious path America has taken and the need for course correction toward a different way forward.

Part VI
American Survey II

Chapter One:
Polarization Roots and Realities

Immigration issues are becoming more divisive in Europe. American society, in addition to the immigration issue, is confronted by many other economic and political challenges. Even as wide swaths of the American populace remain prosperous and productive, growing segments of the population are left in functional penury. This includes an increasing number of dispossessed individuals and an even larger group striving to keep up - in what is figuratively a high-stakes poker game -where the ante just keeps getting raised. Such conditions lie at the root of modern-day American polarization.

In materialist terms, the capitalist market economic mode of production, and its associated labor relations, leave many people in the dust. Rather than seeking to change the economic system, many are led to question the value of the democratic process itself; especially when it appears so feeble in containing or softening sharp market conditions and gaping inequalities. This confusion stems from the overarching power and prevalence of American capitalist ideology, making it appear unassailable. The stalemate of the political system simply indicates an inability to change the predispositions of its economic underwriters; an inability to be overcome.

The contradiction between the materialist economic mode of go-go capitalism production – and the ideology of democratic liberalism is complicated. As the author Wolf noted, democracy and capitalism should essentially be compatible. Liberalism endorses economic freedom to the hilt, but only so long as it respects those other cherished liberal values – of social and political freedom. The magnitude of contemporary economic inequality puts the balance of liberal society at risk. It poses unprecedented forms of confrontation and paradox. It produces the odd alignment of over-entitled elements of the American population seeking to protect and extend their wealth, with less well-off individuals who feel great resentment over their perceived betrayal by American society – by some of the very interests with whom they are aligned.

The deceit perpetrated by the oligarchic sponsors of the MAGA movement, whose initiative and policies run counter to the interests of under-served segments of society, often goes undetected. Recently announced Trump II administration plans and policies portend to re-privatize the American economy. Disinvestment in the social, or public goods economy proceeds apace. Where this will leave the 'social contract' is poignantly in question – prospectively with the disenfranchisement of large segments of the American population. The shadows of dialectic polarization grow.

Such sea changes across the American social and economic landscape demand initiative and proposal of a countermanding agenda – the reformulation of an inclusive American 'social contract'. For starters, this requires finally de-bunking the 'trickle-down' argument that somehow the many benefit from the riches of the few. The alternative view, that society is much better off when individuals are supported by social wealth, providing healthcare, education and collective compensation, must find widespread articulation. The conflict over effective, distributive economic justice may not yet be irrepressible. But as Lincoln said prior to another massive conflict — the nation's plunge into Civil War — "the tug has to come. Stand firm" (David Herbert Donald, *Lincoln*, p. 270, Simon & Schuster, 1995). This would implore those currently invested in social and economic justice efforts not only to hold their ground but to move forward.

On what has been the conventional political front, there's incessant talk about compromise and a plague on both houses, but this mistakes the character of the ongoing national impasse and polarization. Bi-partisanship, the American version of European/Austrian social partnership, long accepted as the most practical and aspirational approach to resolve policy differences, now appears defunct. The impasse mostly functions to Republican benefit. It results partly from militant capitalist design and partly from favorable political fortune. These both are an extension of long-standing obstructionist tactics meant to enfeeble the government and the efficacy of the Democratic Party.

The apparent militant Republican design would clear hurdles for a government takeover and coup-like installment of oligarchical, capitalist-corporate interests - to hell with the public interest and liberty and justice for all. It's not a contest between frugal governments vs. expansive government, as the billing went for a long time; it is more an attempt by radicalized capital and its interests to subdue democratic processes and the Democratic Party. Sure, the Democratic Party must share the blame for the breakdown in political affairs. It has made a hash of things trying to be all things to all people, ending up representing too little to too few. Their concessions to capital, particularly on the issue of wage and income distribution, prevented a fuller vision of a viable social state. The void left over presented an opening for Republican-populist militancy. Democrats and reasonable Republicans alike must be prepared to assert a more visionary, counter-mandating agenda of their own.

As seen in the review of Thomas Piketty's analysis, grotesque conditions of income and wealth inequality, now staggering America, are a prelude to such transformations and breakdowns as have occurred over and over again in history (*Capital in the Twenty-First Century,* Thomas Piketty, Translation, Arthur Goldhammer, Belknap Press, 2014). In times such as these, appraisal of other, foreign systems and wider socio-economic analyses can be instrumental. Conditions, of course, on either side of the Atlantic are not replicable, one for the other; historical and cultural, not to mention geographical differences, prevent that. Nonetheless, both worlds share and face common, modern conditions (especially as to income distribution) that provide a basis for comparative analysis. It's not all apples and oranges. Both worlds showcase contrasting cultures, and manners of response to systemic economic developmental challenges. There may be two worlds, after all, but there is only one Earth.

Modern American Economic History

The roots of America's polarizing, capitalist ideology need identification. They lie in the historic soils and irresolution of governmental, capital, and labor relations. These roots help explain the strange phenomenon caused by economic inequality today - in which both those advantaged and disadvantaged by market conditions, somehow find common cause. This especially pertains to the odor emanating from and surrounding the issue of taxation. Relatively recent watershed economic transformations in America, starting in the 1970s, have not been quite as revolutionary as those that engulfed Austria after World Wars I & II, but in some ways, they are just as consequential. The ferment of Republican Party militancy and designs on the economic system moved from nascent to active during the 1970s, in the wake of earlier vexed economic policies. President Lyndon Johnson's decision to fund Great Society governmental welfare programs and America's involvement in the Vietnam War without raising taxes "led to massive inflationary pressures" (Gregory Schneider, *Jimmy Carter & the Malaise Speech*, Emporia State University, Bill of Rights Institute, Google). Such developments, among others, lowered governmental credibility and fragmented the post-World War II welfare state and public interest consensus.

Subsequent congealing events occurred in the aftermath of the Arab Oil Embargo in 1973. The resulting period of hyperinflation stretched from 1974 to 1980 and beyond. Inflation rose to 8.3% in 1974, then to 9.1% in 1975, before falling slightly and rising again to 9.8% in 1979 and 12.4% in 1980. It was also a period accompanied by 'stagflation,' in which both high inflation and high unemployment occurred. Unemployment reached 5.6% in 1974 and 8.5% in 1975, falling a little and then rising to a height of 9.7% and 9.8% in 1983/1984. Gross Domestic Product (GDP) growth occurred during these times, but so did economic recessions in 1974/1975, 1980, and 1982 (*Stagflation in the 1970s*, Barry Nielson, Investopedia.com, 2023). This all amounted to a diminishing and sometimes seething distrust of governmental involvement in the economy. Ronald Reagan capitalized on sentiments of distrust in 1986 with his famous, or infamous, quote: "The nine most terrifying words in the English language are: I'm from the government, and I'm here to help" (*I'm Here to Help News Conference*, Ronald Reagan Presidential Foundation.com, August 12, 1986). This reflects an arcane and outmoded understanding of governmental function.

As a prelude to Reagan's invective, back in the 1970s, the business community in America was arriving at its own conclusions, signaling a titanic shift in economic attitude and policy toward what had been the 'New Deal' social state agenda.

Prior to the 1970s, the analysis of British economist John Maynard Keynes guided economic thinking. He believed government expenditure could stimulate demand in the economy and alleviate capitalist cyclical imbalances. Where his theories translated into greater social investment across Europe, beyond simple welfare support for those left behind by the economy, - in America, his theories were never as widely applied. They were discredited in the 1970s by the American economic mash-up.

But perhaps it was really Johnson's and Nixon's earlier economic policies of the 1960s, which created exceptionally skewed economic conditions. These policies defied incisive analysis and remedy. In any event, according to Evan Osnos, a journalist for *The New Yorker*, the economic downturns of the 1970s and the attendant inability of the Federal Reserve, in particular, to get policies right led to outright "rebellion" in the wealthiest enclaves of American society" (*The Greenwich Rebellion*, May 11, 2020, p. 28).

The rebellion was provoked not only by Federal Reserve inefficacy but by larger governmental policy.

Perhaps it was Jimmy Carter's well-intentioned 'malaise speech' of 1979, in which the President described a national crisis of confidence, that compounded doubts about governmental efficacy (*Malaise Speech*, ibid). More likely, at a time when business was continually unnerved and uncertain about investment prospects, Big Government pursued stringent consumer-protection and environmental protection regulations. This left business executives, Osnos tells us, feeling "besieged" (p. 32, ibid). The rest is history. Osnos cites the book *Reaganland* by Rick Perlstein: "the denizens of America's better boardrooms, who had once comported themselves with such ideological gentility, began behaving themselves like the Jacobins of the French Revolution. They declared war without compromise" (ibid). As previously noted, we know where this all would lead. In 1972, the CEO of General Electric, a Greenwich, Connecticut resident, earned "12 or 13 times" the base employee salary, a little less than the CEO average at the time. An Economic Policy Institute study reveals that "in 1965, the CEO of an average large public company earned about 20 times as much as a front-line worker. Today that figure, (as noted earlier) is between 210 and 278 (sic) times" (ibid, p. 32).

What occurred in Greenwich and other such enclaves across the country in the intervening years was the formation of a new "executive class of the Republican Party" (ibid, p.

31). Such were the origins of what has become, a sharpening 'class war', in which *bipartisan* economic policy is replaced by the goal of outright and impregnable Republican party governmental control. Such were the origins of what would become neo-capitalist policy and the era of illiberal capitalist henchmen, such as Roger Stone, Paul Manafort, Steve Bannon, Roger Ailes, Rupert Murdoch, the Koch Brothers, Sean Hannity, etc. What began as a righteous revulsion toward economic over-regulation in the midst of an oil embargo-induced economic crisis, turned into the practical deification of market goods as the highest, or exclusive social value, whatever the cost to the rest of society.

Attending this convulsive epoch, was the gradual hollowing out of the public ethos and culture that had sustained the American Republic as one of shared interests. E pluribus Unum is out. Maximal profit gain is in. The pro-business capitalist mode of production - and its ideological advance against the liberal, social–interest ideology has made considerable headway, and many of its advocates don't want to look back. Today, being "libbed" is the ultimate, if commonplace, insult, as if professing social values is a form of mental illness. But the liberal paradigm and belief system possess staying power because they are rooted in social reality and human nature. They have been waylaid, in part, because they were insufficiently articulated and implemented

Business transactions have eminent economic and social value, but so do non-economic social values.

Social Values & Public Goods

The place of social values such as friendship, love, tolerance, personal reliability, community trust and environmental awareness, to name but a few, is essential. Being polite and well-mannered and mindful of customs are not only bourgeois virtues, they are the very grain of human interaction and association. Social values at this elemental level are the stuff of life. They are embodied by spiritual and practical inclinations toward community; they are strong and resilient but also challenged by equally compelling values such as those hoisted by the marketplace and politics and by the quest for material security; or by hard times. This is particularly the case in America's over-commodified, market economy, where it seems like just about everything – from healthcare, to education, to material goods - has a (rising) price that kind of shoves the idea of shared social values over into a figurative corner.

Given enough leash, the hyper-competitive, marketplace gradually overtakes the world of internal values. In that world a thing is done or said as a good in itself. It is where such things as healthcare and higher and vocational education are provided more as public, or social goods – rooted in social values - than as private commodities. Telling the truth, let the chips fall where they may, a preeminent moral, internal value since George Washington's time and before, has always vied with external considerations. The truth becomes increasingly difficult to maintain, however, amidst a marketplace and economic mentality run-rampant. The MAGA world's purveyance of 'alternative facts' reflects a contempt not only for the truth, but for a world sustained by community trust. It denudes the basic currency of civic and political discourse. For lack of a common denominator or civic consensus, (long maintained by the apparent marriage of democracy and capitalism) social truth is the first and foremost casualty of polarization, induced by economic inequality. As currently organized, the American market produces a lot of winners, but leaves just as many, if not more people behind. The divide of economic inequality becomes intolerable and the cardinal or premier social value of social unity is expended. The loss of social consensus and unity imperil those other great social values known as freedom, justice, and democracy.

Taxation Doesn't Pay

As noted, the current militant, capitalist class found its modern origins in the so-called supply-side, business-friendly 'Reagan Revolution' of the 1980s. This commenced a historic shift toward what would become neoliberal economic policies on taxation and government spending. They were justified as bolstering investment and economic expansion. Tight money became the byword for Federal Reserve monetary policy. Governmental fiscal investment and so-called welfare spending were demonized. The efficacy of these arguments caused the Democratic Party's virtual retrenchment and failure to envision a more capacious but still affordable, public goods, welfare economy - that could provide universal health care, tuition-free higher and vocational education for all. Under the banner of 'taxation is your enemy', Reaganite Republicans concealed a retrenchment and disinvestment in the provision of living wages for a majority of American workers, not to mention support for trade-union collectively bargained contracts (**See Appendix 2: Collective Bargaining and Wage Inequality**).

As things played out, despite all Republican rhetoric to the contrary, actual U.S. government welfare spending flattened out only a bit during the 1980s. Since then, it has been on a gradual, if not precipitous, rise.

Whatever the actual economic indices, the anathema of high taxes was consecrated in this period and continues to this day. The fiscal contradiction of supporting governmental programs without the taxation to fund them is the main operational cause of an American society in economic and social tumult. That contradiction is now presumably solved by the Trump administration's policy to defund the government and lower taxes, especially for the already well-off, damn the dystopian consequences for the rest of society.

It's true, a review of tax history shows that taxes have only stingily risen from $175 billion of non-defense spending in 1980 to $751 billion in 2022 (Chart 1: Stef W. Wright, *How U.S. Government Spending Has Ballooned Since 1980*, Axios, March 10, 2023). Over that time, from 1980 to 2022, when the Republicans were in power, they were not quite ready to defund the government in such a way as to offend the electorate.

What they did was cut taxes, relative to GDP growth, consequent federal budget deficits and inflationary pressures be damned. The resulting economic growth, they held, would "trickle down" more than enough to support all economic classes and make up for reduced Welfare State outlays.

And the Democrats went along with it!

There would have been more than enough money to support investments in public healthcare and education, not to mention greater wage parity, but tax rates were kept punitively low. The American public was - and is - bamboozled.

Meager taxation didn't trickle down. It enabled a massive wealth transfer in reverse, toward business corporations, industries, and their executives, and to the higher-income and wealth echelons of society.

It's the crime of the century!

It may be that Trump administration economic and tariff policies, including decimating the power of organized labor, will bring hordes of money and investment in off the sidelines to reinvigorate America's manufacturing sector, and provide greater living wages for larger sectors of the populace – a greater sharing of the wealth. His restoration of more laissez-faire economic conditions, however, runs roughshod over historic and economic experience. The market gyrations of such an economy are prone to the mania which led to, among other economic disasters, the Great Depression and the Great Recession. His tariff policies are a gamble in which the domestic and international economic and political cohesion of the modern world is at stake. May it work out, but the prospect grows that these policies will only re-commit and compound the crime of widening economic inequality and social polarization.

The contradiction between governmental outlays and insufficient taxation can only truly be solved by realigning the American welfare state toward up-front social investment supported by commensurate increases in taxation – so that people really get something tangible for their tax dollars. Instead, the wealth transfer in reverse will continue. The campaign finance system virtually guarantees it.

Campaign Finance As is generally recognized, corporations financially support both political parties: "Republicans spent roughly $4.2 billion, and Democrats spent about $4 billion when money spent by candidates, political parties, and outside groups are totaled for the 2021-2022 election cycle" (Quorum Blog, *Which Party Receives More Corporate Donations?,* quorum.us/blog, 2022).

It's quite a racket. Corporations make out rather well. Their lobbyists argue that lower corporate taxes increase corporate revenue, which can support more efficient and productive investment in the economy. Over time, this argument has effectively prevailed to further ingrain market capitalist assumptions and prejudices in the American psyche. The market capitalist parameters of the American economic mode of production become clear.

But the 'corporate investment' argument, as already demonstrated, is a shibboleth, an outmoded, and invalid argument. As former Secretary of Labor Robert Reich cogently pointed out in Senate Budget Committee testimony, "U.S. corporations generally used the tax windfall they received in the 2017 Republican taxation overhaul not to reinvest in the American economy. Many corporations bought back stock to augment share price for their shareholders" (*Robert Reich's Full Testimony Regarding Corporate Profits and Inflation*, YouTube, April 2022). Reich's testimony, among other evidence, amply demonstrates that corporate power in America has been augmented by lower corporate taxes, but without redounding to the benefit of the American people, at-large.

Corporate Income Taxes The U.S. corporate income tax rate, at the moment, is not high by historic standards. According to the IRS, "the current corporate tax rate in the United States stands at 21 percent." In the 1950s, the statutory corporate tax rate was 50%. In 2013, it was 35% (Thomas Hungerford, *Corporate Tax Rates and Economic Growth Since 1947*, Economic Policy Institute, Google, June 9, 2013). Evidenced nowadays by all the corporate-named stadiums across the land, corporations have practically arrogated to themselves the role of sole sponsor and custodian of American economic development. They had to do something with all their newfound, ill-gotten wealth, other than share it for the general betterment of American society. While this reverse transfer may have produced great wealth for some and transformed economies worldwide through economic globalization, it has created a legacy of ominous economic inequality and social/ political polarization in America. As noted in the Wolf podcast quote above, "the market system" and its political agents "recreated an oligarchy" (Edsall, NYT, ibid). Lenient corporate and upper-end tax policy is not only the furnace of inequality and polarization; it forecloses viable and sustainable remediation that would get the country out of its quagmire.

Tax Policy

Reciting the arcane history of income tax policy since 1980 is mind-numbing but instructive for those trying to keep account. Successive taxation regimes have gone a little back and forth during this time period, but overwhelmingly in favor of businesses and corporations, higher-earning individuals, and stockholders. Since 2001, income taxes have risen most for the top 1%, from 33.2% to 37.5%. For the next bracket, however, between the top 1% and the top 5%, taxes have risen just 1% over that time. Tax rates are flat or have fallen for all other brackets. (Erica York, *Chart: Top 1% Share of Taxes* (those earning over $540,000 a year) *Has Increased Over Time — Shares of Income Taxes by Income Group 2001-2020*, Tax Foundation, Google, January 26, 2023). For a supposedly progressive tax system, you would think significant tax increases would be fair — at least for the top 1-10% of the most prosperous sectors of the population. But here's the rub. Market capitalist advocates have apparently convinced a majority of American people, that this largesse is necessary as an incentive and that prosperity at the top means prosperity for the economy as a whole; trickle down revisited.

In general, as a token of the not-so-glorious Reagan Revolution, income taxes are held in check, are quite high enough, thank you, for upper-end incomes to grow. In a report issued by the Center for Public Integrity, "income for the top 10% of households in America since 1980 has gone up 135.6%" and counting. Since 1980, though, "the middle 40% of households saw their incomes rise just 35.7%," and "the bottom 50% of households saw an income rise of just 21.4%" (James Steele, *How 4 Decades of Tax Cuts Fueled Inequality*, Center for Public Integrity, November 29, 2022). Keep in mind, two things: first, the economic GDP has increased close to 13 times and second, inflation has increased 132% during that time period. It doesn't take much arithmetic or insight to perceive how these numbers send tremors up and down the economic and social ladder. Market values indeed.

So, drive through the small towns of the northern Atlantic states, from Rhode Island, Massachusetts, and Maine to New Hampshire and Vermont, clear through upstate New York. Besides some great scenery, you will see a good share of house and building dilapidation. Purchasing power for townspeople doesn't appear to allow for much restoration or renovation, not to mention renewal. These towns, instead, appear to be stuck in time, going back at least 50 years. The economic growth and expansion otherwise touted have passed them by, seeding stagnation and frustration. And this is not the only region so affected.

The flip side of this coin exhibits many 'tax breaks' to cushion tax exposure — for estates, for capital gains, for dividends — for those who already have money, but not so much for everybody else. The tax code is a thicket with more variables than the alphabet. It gets wrangled over. Some claim the tax system remains sufficiently progressive, meaning that ever since tax progressivity was introduced in 1913, the rich have paid sufficiently more in taxes than the poor. The Tax Foundation makes the authoritative-sounding claim that "contrary to common perceptions, the CBO (Congressional Budget Office, sic) data indicate that: (1) income earned after taxes and transfers has increased over the past several decades for all income groups, (2) the federal tax system is progressive and has become more progressive over the past three decades, and (3) the federal system relies heavily on higher earners to raise revenue for government services and means-tested transfers. Policymakers should remember such facts when considering proposals to increase tax burdens or reshape the distribution of existing taxes" (Alex Muresianu, *Yes, the US Tax Code Is Progressive*, Tax Foundation, 9/17/2021).

Here, you see the liturgy of high capitalism, more than suggesting that tax rates on the wealthy are quite high enough, and tut-tutting the very idea of something more progressive. And so, the prevailing tax imprint of the last 40 years gets reinforced. But as the Center for Public Integrity shows, the wealthy have made out like bandits over the past 40 years compared to the rest of the population. They have been able to keep up with rising costs and put some money aside. It is indeed a fact, provided by the U.S. Census Bureau, that in 2018, the "highest earning 20% of families in America made 52% of all U.S. income." Roll that around in your mouth for a while. It means that the rest of the population, 80% of families, made do with the remaining 48% of total income – and beside this, you can imagine how little wealth these 'quintiles' were able to accumulate. One has to wonder how middle- and bottom-income households manage. As related above by the podcaster Martin Wolf, income and wealth inequality make many of those at the top nervous that they'll fall behind. What about the nervousness in the lower ranks that they are able to keep up at all? A large number in the well-to-do ranks, in any case, seek to make permanent the great Reagan years' tax swindle.

For them, it appears that economic inequality is an ordained outcome, confirming their talent, hard work, and financial thrift. Each of these is of course a laudable trait, but at the moment in America, they increasingly contribute to the self-serving conceit of entitlement. This large coterie of people now brandishes their own, increasingly exclusive moral belief system. They have earned their good fortune, and those less fortunate have earned their lesser fortune. Economic inequality of this magnitude is a natural outcome. It should be hard-baked into policy and law. If anything, the tax burden they carry should be reduced. Again, what you see here is the consolidation of an economic class with its own growing, quite belligerent interests. This is the paradigm that must be overthrown. French economist Thomas Piketty's observations about labor market inequities, cited earlier, are amplified. These "are not natural phenomena, but outcomes of unequal power relations, political choice, and ideologies that justify inequality" (Marten Keune, *Inequality Between Capital and Labor and Among Wage Earners: The Role of Collective Bargaining and Trade Unions*, Sage Journals, May 24, 2021). In addition, these labor market and income/wealth-inequities maddeningly generate conditions for more welfare income redistribution - the very bane of Republican ideology. The need for a thorough overhaul of America's tax code and financial and economic system becomes self-evident.

Piketty is right.

What all these amounts to is a striking exposure and indictment of the gaudy ideological, fig leaves that market capitalist proponents used to justify their policies. Neither "trickle down - corporate investment," nor lower taxes on corporations, or high-end earners, redound to any effective, broader public good. These are components of an ideology meant to serve private interests, plain and simple.

The materialist class basis of this argument is further demonstrated by the tax code, which indicates - sure enough- an underinvestment in the public economy, by which public goods are secured. Militant capitalists and their political foils have indeed achieved a fusion between ideological and materialist interests. But that fusion, as in all such cases, must be judged by its outcomes.

The table below shows how taxes range for joint-filing couples/households in 2022/23, from 10% for the lowest-earning couples to 37% for the highest-earning households. You have to pay a certain graduated amount of taxes on the first amount and then the marginal tax rate — 10%, 12%, 22%, etc. — on anything over that, up to the next bracket (2022-2023 Tax Brackets and Federal Income Tax Rates, NerdWallet, April 2023).

Tax Rate	Taxable Income Brackets	Taxes Owed
10%	$0 to $20,550	10% of taxable income
12%	$20,551 to $83,550	$2,055 + 12% over $20,550
22%	$83,551 to $178,150	$9,615 + 22% over $83,550
24%	$178,151 to $340,100	$30,427 + 24% over $178,150
32%	$340,101 to $431,900	$69,295 + 32% over $340,100
35%	$431,901 to $647,850	$98,671 + 35% over $431,900
37%	$647,851 and above	$174,253.50 + 37% over $647,850

Other models, however, show how constructive, social institutional design can reduce class conflict and promote public good.

The whole tax rate discussion is dauntingly arcane. You need to be an accountant to completely understand it. But that doesn't foreclose common sense criticism, summary, and dispute. As the cited Center for Public Integrity article concludes, "taxes have been a principal engine of worsening economic inequality simply because the wealthy, thanks to their success in Congress, now have more money - to buy stocks, invest in real estate, build mega yachts, blast off into space, and make campaign contributions to politicians so the cycle isn't interrupted" (*How 4 Decades of Tax Cuts Fueled Inequality,* Center for Public Integrity, 2022).

Political Process Impact

Now, the analysis moves to further unravel how market capitalist interests control the political process. This unraveling largely validates the Marxist "ideological superstructure" argument presented earlier. There is now little recourse, but to conclude that the social, political, and legal values that support society at large, the liberal democratic social-state, are being overthrown by the market capitalist mode of production, ownership, and organization of industrial relations.

To illustrate, it is enough to amplify *QuorumBlog*'s note, cited above, on 2022 congressional campaign contributions. This is simply par for the course: "Over the past six election cycles, both Democrats and Republicans each received $7 billion in corporate donations" (*OpenSecrets*, non-partisan contribution tracker).

On taxation policy, this corporate money largesse was apparently enough to induce sleepiness, if not outright catatonic somnolence, among Democrats who should, in particular, know better. Instead, we see how an economic system, the American economic system, is bought and perpetuated; and at what cost. Just to cite a couple of gnawing factors, consider the extent of contemporary income and wealth inequality and the current melee of American politics. It appears more than evident that conditions would be vastly improved if that $14 billion of political contributions over the past 24 years had instead gone to supporting universal healthcare, higher and technical educational opportunity and collectively bargained salaries.

Nonetheless, claims upholding the social and economic benefits of American market capitalism keep rolling in. Citing a published *Economist* magazine report, *NYT* commentator David Brooks reminds us that "over the past 30 years, far from declining, American capitalism is dominant and accelerating... Capitalism, like a great river, just keeps rolling on" (David Brooks, *The Power of American Capitalism*, *NYT*, April 20, 2023).

Two cheers for capitalism. Bravo. Brooks' remarks belie the inequality of the system at a time when the MAGA-militant, Republican overthrow of the whole economic system becomes more manifest with each passing day. Certain benefits have accrued on the capitalist ledger - but at enormous expense to the financial solvency, civic comity, public interest, and future welfare of the rest of American society.

Get over to that other part of town, on the other side of the tracks. Witness the insolvency. This is the real balance-sheet.

Part VII
Modern Austria

Compared to other countries, such as Austria, the American tax system is relatively flat; it's not all that progressive. As the table below shows, there are also seven tax rate categories in Austria, calculated in euros. The American joint filing household rates were considered above. This table shows the rough equivalent in Austria. The current American spread between lower and higher income tax rates is 37%. In contrast, the spread in the Austrian rate is a very progressive 55%. Notice the rate and the extremely wide spread for individuals earning between €93,121 and €1,000,000, and compare it to the American ledger. Americans earning more than $93,000 pay only 22%.

Austria Personal Income Tax Rates (in Euros)[1]

Tax Rates (%)	Taxable Income Range (€)
0%	11,693 and below
20%	11,964 to 19,134
30%	19,135 to 32,975
40%	32,076 to 62,080
48%	62,081 to 93,120
50%	93,121 to 1,000,000
55%	above 1,000,000

One can almost hear the American chortle among higher financial cohorts: 'What fools those Austrians are!' There

---

[1] Austria Individual — Taxes on personal income.
Last reviewed — 03 March 2023 taxsummaries.pwc.com.

are Austrian political parties that would have it otherwise, too — but so far, they haven't held government power long enough, or exclusively enough to breach longstanding taxation policy consensus: higher taxes are okay as long as they are shared alike by individuals and businesses. This is the basis of the social market, not socialist economy. Austrians might well respond to this chortle by saying, 'Yeah, the rich here may not be quite so rich, but the poor aren't quite so poor. Our society is not riven by economic inequality, lack of opportunity, and polarization. We may be taxed more, but we also have higher across-the-board salaries. Higher salaries provide greater purchasing power, which support, somewhat counter-intuitively, greater business formation - every right-minded capitalist's desire. There's more money to go around to support more enterprise. This may be the chief difference between market capitalist and social market capitalist systems.

Such differences reflect historical trajectory, and decisions about the public goods of health, education, and relative income parity. In Austria, and elsewhere in Europe, with comparable tax rates, and higher relative salaries, they calculate the advantage not only to consumers, but to businesses themselves. Profit is assured, but so too is greater sharing of surplus value, to the social benefit of all concerned.

The Austrian economy thrives because of a larger service sector of businesses in tourism, sales, banking and finance, education, and health care, comprising "70.7% of its GDP" (sic). The manufacturing and construction sectors of the economy are also vital, producing "28.1% of GDP" (sic) through machinery, steel, chemicals, electronics technology, and automotive engine and transmission concerns. Agricultural, forestry, and fishing industries comprise a small but comparatively robust "2.5% of economic production" (sic) (*Austrian Federal Economic Chamber, This Is Austria, Facts & Figures,* wko.at, Sept 2018). The relatively high rate of taxation in Austria is rewarded by all sorts of social, medical, and educational benefits—a fair mix of welfare and pre-distribution amenities. Austrians receive a lot in return for their taxes. These include Social Security welfare-state amenities for unemployment, health, pensions, education, maternity/paternity/parental benefits, as well as disability/work accident/survivor benefits.

To specify just a couple of social insurance provisions: "maternity leave in Austria is 16 weeks, 8 weeks prior to and 8 weeks after a child's birth… After 16 weeks, the mother is entitled to unpaid maternity leave until the child is 2 years old, during which time the mother/family receives childcare pay under the Child Care Payment Act" (Astrid Pennersdorfer, Brigitte Zierer, *Country Profile Austria: Social Policy, Social Economy and Social Work: Principles of the Austrian Welfare State,* Social.net, October 2018). The childcare payment is not a tax credit but a cash-in-hand benefit, an extension of principle and policy that supports family status in the provision of social benefits; extensive of social democracy. The same goes for child support payments, which continue up to the age of 18 or 24 for children who pursue higher academic degrees (we know such payments in America as the now-discontinued Child Tax Credit provisions, part of the pandemic-related American Rescue Plan). It is the in-kind pre-distributive transfers from the social and employment system, however, that really make the difference. Over the years, the Social

Partner chambers representing business, labor, agriculture, and government ministries have cobbled together a system of benefits that is anchored in employment and payroll taxes. Here we see the alignment of income and tax systems that support social unity and shared material prosperity. World-wide income shares, in this respect are illustrative (**See Appendix 4, World-wide Income Shares**).

You will note, in cursory fashion, respective income distributive differences between American and Austrian economies. In 2023, the "top 10% of Austrian households took 34.4% of distributed income," while "the bottom 50% took 23.7%." In America, by contrast, in 2023, the top 10% took 46.8% of distributed income," while the bottom 50% took just 13.4%" (World Income Inequality Database, wid.world, 2023). Extrapolating further, you will notice that this leaves 41.9% of distributed income in Austria for the middle 40% of the population. In America, by contrast, the middle 40% takes home 39.8% of distributed income. The numbers and spreads are significant in their differences. The Austrian economy shares income to the broader benefit not only of its recipients, but to the broader benefit of the Austrian economy.

You might observe that any income distribution advantage Austrian lower economic classes enjoy, is offset by higher rates of taxation. But this income and the taxes it supports goes right back into the economy, countering inflationary pressures, to purchase and provide outstanding educational and medical goods and services.

Health Care Employer payroll tax contributions in support of employees (in addition to taxes on revenue) amount to 21.8% of every paycheck, covering health, accident, old age pension, and unemployment insurance. These contributions are complemented by employee payments into the system for health, old-age pension, and unemployment insurance, which amount to 17.12% of their wages (*Austria: Mandatory Benefits, Payroll & Taxes,* PapayaGlobal.com, November 2022). Statutory, universal public health care is financed in this manner, serving as the first pillar of Austria's 'pre-distribution' system. Coverage comes with getting a job. (The unemployed are covered by a different fund) The employed (including spouses and dependents) are registered in the health care insurance system (the Krankenkasse/Illness Fund) through their employer. The insured receives a so-called e-card to present at the hospital or doctor's office — no questions asked, no forms to fill out. Maternity care, medical treatments, hospitalization, check-ups, and highly supported co-pay medications are covered. There are no deductibles.

Obviously, this provides great security, equality, and solidarity. It placates the muted but ever-present social tension and insecurity characteristic of individual pay-as-you-go health insurance systems, such as in the USA, where those who can pay on their own, through work or otherwise, might think, "I can do it. Why can't you?" In such circumstances, the uninsured might well feel inadequate, status-wise, and intolerable insecurity. Not incidentally, the World Health Organization ranked Austria 9th worldwide in the provision of health care in 2015. It spent "11.2% of GDP on health care" (5th highest in Europe) against the 18% of GDP which the USA spent (highest in the OECD—Organization for Economic Cooperation and Development)

(Statista.com 2021). This raises clear questions and dismay about the overweening, privatized health insurance system in the USA.

Austrian Trade-Union Milestones

Labor Conditions The (ÖGB) Austrian trade union federation, representing unions across the country in seven sectors of industry and business, together with their partners from the Chamber of Commerce, negotiate annual collective bargaining wage agreements that cover "around 98% of all Austrian workers" (sic) (Vera Glassner and Julia Hofmann, *Collective Bargaining in Europe, Austria: From Gradual Change to an Unknown Future,* 2018). After near-universal health care, this is the second pillar of the 'pre-distribution' economy. The benefits of these collective contracts extend to all employees, union members, and non-union members alike. They include not only fair baseline pay, below which it is illegal to go, but also level out the reaches of high pay. To once again give context as to compensation, according to *The Economic Times*, "CEOs in the USA 'earn' on average 265 times more than the typical worker. The Austrian CEO to typical worker salary ratio is 49 times more" *(Global CEO Pay-to-Average Income Ratio*, Bloomberg, International Monetary Fund, December 2017).

Austrian contract provisions include several benefits, many if not most of which were negotiated by the ÖGB, along with its affiliated Union of Private Employees, over the course of the past 70 years. Agreements with counterparts in the Austrian Chamber of Commerce for business and industry interests emerged out of a combination of: 1) historic conditions, 2) union density (the percentage of workers who are union members), and 3) decisive strike actions. Business interests agreed to concessions because all businesses alike share in them to level the economic landscape and because stable industrial relations enable consistent productivity and business growth. Social investment is good for the economy. Business interests accede to these benefits, perhaps somewhat grudgingly, and to the shared prosperity they produce.

Strikes in the 1950s induced the General Social Security Act, whose template defined the terms of compulsory health, accident, and pension insurance, and sanctioned the formation of Social Partnership alliances and procedures in 1957. The 1960s brought about enforcement of the 40-hour work week and a minimum of three weeks of vacation. The 1970s produced the Equal Treatment Act, which eliminates wage inequality between men and women; the Youth Consultative Councils Act, which established the apprenticeship system for youth employment; and the Labor Constitution Act, which further defines the rights and roles of worker representation in company work councils and their relationship with representative trade unions. Not incidentally, Austrian trade union membership density in 1960 was right around 60%. (GPA — Meine Gewerkschaft (*Union of Private Employees: Milestones in Our History*, gpa.at, 2024). It now stands at roughly "28%." (European Trade Union Institute, etui, Industrial Relations in Austria: Background Summary, etui.org, October 2016). This indicates systemic integration of labor interests and is a testament to Social Partnership viability. The moral of the story is that trade union membership density probably needs to grow at a high rate in multiple sectors of the economy for the labor interest to gain effective leverage.

The 1980s brought about a reduction in the work week to 38.5 hours and a Solidarity Wage Increase in collective agreements for low-wage groups; wage gains for this group, thereafter, would be proportionately higher than wage increases for higher-wage groups. The 1990s created a baseline nominal minimum monthly wage, which currently stands at 1,500 euros ($1,600), plus benefits. Technically, the minimum wage is unsanctioned, but it was passed to bring about wage uniformity in all industries across Austria (ibid). The last general strike took place in 2003. Of short duration, it arose in response to neo-liberal and conservative parties taking coalition control of the government and threatening to dismantle the terms and conditions of the social state. To protect these conditions, the administration of social insurance was removed from state purview and invested by law, as a matter of 'self-administration,' in Social Partnership business and labor institutions. Protection of pension coverage and employment conditions for part-time and independent contractors was also mandated and extended. In the 2010s, the Wage and Social Dumping Act was negotiated and passed. The Act stipulates penalties for companies that don't comply with Social Partnership employment conditions and seek to gain competitive advantage by underpaying (often immigrant) employees. In this era, fathers gained the right to take a month off with pay to be with a newborn child (ibid).

Other negotiated labor conditions include a standard 13th and 14th salary paid in June (for summer vacation) and November (for upcoming holidays), maternity leave (already described), 25 days (5 weeks) of holidays, 6 to 12 weeks of sick days (depending on years of employment), strict conditions for contract termination, and severance pay, "calculated as a multiple of the remuneration payable to the employee before termination" (*Austria: Mandatory Benefits, Payroll & Taxes,* ibid).

Not incidentally, after all these developments, Austria stands out for its relatively low number of work days lost due to industrial strike actions. As cited by the European Trade Union Institute (ETUI) "Compared with other countries, Austria has an extremely low level of strike action: per 1,000 workers, there were 2 days lost per year (in the period 2008-2016. This is due to the social partnership system whose informal rules and principles provide consensual ways of reconciling interests" (Strikes in Austria: Background Summary, updated March 2019). This record was maintained in the intervening years until 2023. (Duration of Austrian Industrial Strikes, 1950-2023, Austrian Chamber of Commerce, Austria Chamber of Labor, Austrian Trade Union Federation, updated 2024).

The Austrian fusion of ideological and materialist-productive mode conditions achieves a striking balance of the many social and economic interests involved. As indicated by brief survey of its tax structure, pre-distributive provision of educational and medical access and collective bargaining wage system, Austria's 'materialist' productive mode is tied to the social solidarity values of its "ideological superstructure." These are the mainstays of social democratic market capitalism, representing the dialectic transformation of its democratic capitalist antecedent. Whatever the grandiose claims about human and historical progress made by Hegel, on the one hand, and Marx on the other, Austrian society, has at least advanced the local time horizons and prospects of equality and freedom, by which social progress can be gauged.

With the Austrian paradigm, social values aren't simply ideas, or ideals; they are integrated into economic function and actual industrial relations. Material and ideological modes are functionally fused to take account of labor and capital economic interests. You can imagine the bargaining complexity and heat involved in social partnership negotiations. The interplay involved must be intense, despite well-worn analytic formulas, in calibrating the many factors of wage, cost, and price pressures to ensure both livable incomes and sufficient investment and productivity rewards.

Austrian Business Status — Pre-distribution

Despite all these costs and benefits, it pays to do business in Austria. As Wikipedia states, "The economy of Austria is a developed social market economy, with the country being one of the 14 richest in the world in 2022, in terms of GDP per capita—$52,026 (sic)." But it is also very true that you have to pay to do business in Austria. The 'coordinated market economy' established as part of the social market in Europe and in Austria includes many pre-profit social costs as simple costs of doing business. This reflects a deep understanding and commitment to equally apportion public and private goods. So far, Austrian business has adapted to globalization and remains competitive despite its relatively high costs. General prosperity abides, among other reasons, because business conditions are equal for each sector-level industry and company involved. Competitive advantage is sought and found elsewhere in product quality and innovation. The business class also generally recognizes the economic advantages of collective bargaining and the system of income distribution/remuneration it underwrites. It provides broad consumer buying power, one of the hallmarks of Austria's social economy – over and against strictly capitalist market conditions.

Education Tuition costs for education, up to and including university and vocational training, are covered by the state. Besides near-universal health insurance and collectively bargained contracts, this is the third pillar of pre-distribution in the economy. Students in higher education pay a nominal fee in tuition and must cover housing costs themselves. However, general educational access is provided for all. Additionally, an extensive optional system starts in high school that supports apprentice training in all trades. In the words of the country profile cited above, "Considering comparatively low unemployment, low poverty risk rates, as well as relatively equal distribution of household income, the Austrian welfare state is relatively effective" (ibid). But it is a welfare-state of different design, on another plane altogether than the one being steadily overthrown in the USA.

The pre-distribution components of Austria's economic system, as noted, make the difference. They provide an example, par excellence, of stakeholder capitalism. Health care, collective contracts, and education give people a leg up in the race of life. In most cases, what is pre-distributed up front doesn't have to be given at the back-end in redistributive welfare terms, as remediation for personal misfortune or market inequity. It is efficient.

In fact, the thorough study cited above by the authoritative American Economic Association of 26 European countries from 1980 to 2017 reveals that "inequality grew in nearly all European countries, but much less than in the US" (Thom Blanchet, Lucas Chancel, Amory Gethin, *Why Is Europe More Equal Than the United States?* American Economic Journal: Applied Economics, Vol. 14, No. 4, October 2022). The article indicates that "contrary to a widespread view, we demonstrate that Europe's lower inequality levels cannot be explained by more equalizing tax and transfer systems. After accounting for indirect taxes and in-kind transfers, the US redistributes a greater share of national income to low-income groups than any European country. 'Pre-distribution,' not 'redistribution,' explains why 'Europe is less unequal than the United States'" (ibid).

All this notwithstanding, the EU and its member-states are now under acute pressure to further integrate state and economic operations and to rally around a greater sense of European unity and identity.

Mario Draghi's report to the EU Commission on the need to reform Europe's economic model in September 2024, has gained increased volume. The MIT-trained economist and head of Europe's Central Bank (ECB) during the worst years of the sovereign debt crisis in Europe (2011-2019), and later Italian prime minister (2021-2022), Draghi's analysis admonishes the loose, confederated status of EU economic arrangements – and amplify those of Adam Tooze, cited earlier in this essay. The hour may be passing in which individual European states can continue to assert national priority and privilege. As Draghi warns: "The obstacles that European Union members impose against each other do much more economic harm than the U.S. could with tariffs" (*Jason Ma, Europe is already sabotaging its own economy far more than U.S. tariffs could, former ECB president says*, *Fortune*, fortune.com, February 16, 2025).

The European Union was originally established to promote free trade between its members. It provides one of the greatest incentives for ongoing EU member-state support. As noted earlier in the section on the latest Mercosur Trade Agreement, the EU continues to support open and free, international trade. But within Europe, according to Draghi, too many barriers still remain. "Europe's internal barriers are equivalent to a 45% tariff on manufactured goods" (*ibid*). This shows that national markets still enjoy what Draghi views as intolerable protections. "Trade between EU members is less than half what occurs between U.S. states." (*ibid.* Additionally, Draghi criticizes the EU and the ECB for their strict monetary management. The European economy, he argues, suffers from a lack of federal public investment. "From 2009 to 2024, measured in 2024 euros, the U.S. governments injected over five times more funds into the economy via primary deficits, €14 trillion to €2.5 trillion in the Eurozone" (*ibid*) Primary deficits highlight the "underlying structural imbalance between the amount of money that the federal government brings in each year (primarily through taxes) and how much it costs to provide government goods and services" (*What is the Primary Deficit,* Peter G. Peterson Foundation, pgfg.org, updated February 3, 2025) These numbers reflect various institutional, organizational and political differences and priorities between the American and European economic systems. They also throw the notes above on member-state "pre-distribution" commitments into new relief. The numbers reveal the imbalance between European federal and individual member-state investment and the extent to which those states attempt to keep the federal state on a tight, financial leash. In addition to primary deficits, America and Americans, after all, pay a lot of money to service the interest on these primary deficits, without commensurate tax increases: funny money, indeed.

Still, according to Draghi, Europe's still somewhat fledgling Union needs to catch-up to fast-changing world economic and political conditions. As he concludes: "Europe has focused on either single or national goals without counting their collective cost. Conserving public money supported the goal of debt sustainability. The spread of regulation was designed to protect citizens from new technology risks. Internal barriers are a legacy of times when the nation-state was the natural frame for action. But it is now clear that acting in this way has delivered neither welfare for Europeans, nor healthy public finances, nor even national autonomy, which is threatened by pressure from abroad. That is why radical change is needed" (*Mario Draghi, Forget the US — Europe has successfully put tariffs on itself, Financial Times*, ft.com, February 14, 2025).

Such issues, especially investing in and coordinating common military defense capacities and perhaps establishing an integrated capital market similar to the NYSE, call on the nations and peoples of Europe to recognize a stronger supranational identification. It appears what Draghi calls for is something along the lines of a United States of Europe.

It is an open question whether, in this process, Europeans will be able to retain customary affinities for their deep-rooted social states. The many benefits of these systems, Draghi's comments notwithstanding, do indeed provide great welfare and civic unity. As *Social Europe* authors, Hemerijck, Bagadirov, and Wilson amply demonstrate in their study of European state competitive capacities, public goods-welfare state systems are not luxuries, or superfluous. They provide essential services and investments for democratic societies to flourish: "Far from being a drag on economic performance, for [European] welfare states, the opposite is the case: there is a positive correlation between welfare expenditure and per capita gross domestic product, with the universal Nordic welfare states and the developed social-insurance models of mainland northern Europe in the van in both cases) (See graph) (A. Hemerijck, A. Bagadirov, R. Wilson, *Capacity to Compete - Rethinking the Welfare State, Social Europe*, socialeurope.eu, January 8, 2025

Austria, for example, in this study, spent an average of 35% of its GDP on health, education, and welfare between 2012 and 2022 and ranks in the upper 25% on the Global Competitiveness Index (2017-2019). "What makes the difference is that high social investment in each citizen — from quality childcare through to universal health care, comprehensive public education to post-school education or training for all and lifelong learning — allows people to develop their capacities and effectively use them throughout their lives." (*ibid.*)

The Tax Accountant and the Social Worker

The positive gloss given thus far to European and Austrian economic and political arrangements is both real and substantial. But Europe and Austria are not utopic. Headwinds in both political and economic spheres gain momentum. The fusion of material and ideological interests in Europe and Austria, extolled above, may be wearing thin. There is another side of the story.

Even though he expresses personal and professional satisfaction with his life in Austria's Vorarlberg province, small and medium business tax accountant/ advisor, Ulrich Nosko, gives voice to growing alarm that the Social Partnership currently fosters a debilitating, over-regulated and over-taxed economic environment. He readily concedes the Social Partnership's historic role for creating conditions of general prosperity, but the Austrian economy is now in the midst of a three-year recession, "the longest since the beginning of Austria's Second Republic, (sic) dating back to 1945" (Austria is in its Third Year of Recession, Austrian Institution for Economic Research, wifo.org, March 27, 2025). Nosko believes the recession at least in part stems from and is extended by Social Partnership conditions. His views harken back to the Reaganaut era and express contemporary neo-liberal economic sentiments. Over-taxation, he points out, has led to a burgeoning 'black market, or underground economy' in which many business transactions "take place off the books." (Nosko interview, May 30, 2025) Cleaning ladies, for example, only will come to work if their services go untaxed. Building trade receipts, likewise, often include only partial account of services rendered. Businesses are hobbled by employment, building, tax and social security regulations. All combine "to constrict the entrepreneurial spirit, pursuit of business opportunity and market expansion." (ibid)

He likens the Social Partnership to a "shadow government" that leads Austrian citizens to become partially illiterate when it comes to economic and political affairs. He notes that "Austrian citizens (sic) don't even fill out their own income taxes." If Austrians but knew the realities of their economic circumstances, Nosko maintains, "they would support Social Partnership reform." (ibid) In any case, he further argues, the system is profligate. Even though the cleaning ladies mentioned above may want to work 'under the table' during their working careers, when they turn 60 and it comes time to retire, they still expect full pension benefits. And, according to Nosko, these they receive even though they haven't paid into the system. Likewise, the health insurance system encourages over-use. No deductibles, co-pays, or even nominal fees lead people to exploit medical services for 'every headache, or cut finger'. Healthcare budgets and outlays are over-stretched. Such views are echoed by others. Karl Pokorny, erstwhile Vorarlberg Social Worker and Works Council representative, not pre-disposed to any political party or ideology, but also a proponent of the Social Partnership, believes the system has grown too fat, and that "the public discourse in Austria and management of its economic affairs must urgently become more realistic." (Karl Pokorny interview trans., May 28, 2025)

It may be that the system of governance and economic management upheld by the Social Partnership has succeeded too well. Nosko virtually throws his hands up in the air when challenged to explain why there is not more vocal and political opposition to the Social Partnership. The system coddles people, he suggests, and placates popular agitation. Political parties and representatives, of whatever stripe, are so entwined in Social Partnership organizational processes that they become complicit in their execution. Even the Conservative Party, normally attuned to upholding business interests, refrains from advocating wide-ranging Social Partnership reform. The Neos, Austria's pro-market political party, polled 9.1% of the vote in the last national election. (PolitPro, Latest Polling Data and Election Polls for Neos, politpro.eu, May 2025) Nosko could foresee the Neos advocating stiff reform of the Social Partnership, but doubts even they would sustain their opposition if once they came to hold greater power.

In sum, Austria faces more than the perennial budget challenges that concern all states at the moment – of keeping a balance between revenues and expenditures. The Recession is perhaps rooted in excessive Covid Pandemic outlays, but also reflects the financial commitments and economic processes of the Social Partnership system. Nosko believes the system as it stands is unsustainable, not only in Austria, but in Europe at large. In the absence of greater budgetary discipline, he could foresee the eventual, radical de-valuation of Europe's currency, the Euro.

European commitments to social unity and shared material prosperity may prove economically unfeasible over the near-to-medium term. Austria's economy has seen excessive deficit: GDP levels over the past three years. At "3.5%" over that period, well less than the "6% average" recorded in the USA, Austria still needs to manage and reconfigure. This, the current government strives to accomplish. (*Austrian Gov't Budget*, tradingeconomics.com, June 2025/*What is the Deficit as % of GDP*, usgovernmentspending.com, August 10,2025) In conjunction with EU economic authorities, it must now implement a deficit reduction plan over the next four years.

In such ways are EU member states obliged to train and discipline economic management. Deficit reduction procedures facilitate more-or-less non-political navigation through sometimes harsh economic and political headwinds, and the accommodation of both social justice and economic enterprise imperatives. Despite Nosko's prognostications, the Austrian business community appears to accede to Social Partnership-guidance, presumably because it fosters adequate, if not favorable economic and business conditions. Political and economic awareness among Austrian citizens may not be so much submerged by the Social Partnership, as Nosko argues, as it is sublimated. The economy doesn't yet provoke political agitation. Austrians are astute about economic bottom lines and personal finance. Until everyday economic experience indicates otherwise, popular acquiescence signals more than tentative approval of Social Partnership arrangements. It signals support for the effective and durable frameworks that the Social Partnership provides in the maintenance of shared material prosperity and social unity.

Part VIII
American Survey III

Chapter One:
The Welfare State & Slavery

To rejoin the analysis of deviant American economic and political conditions, on top of the tax advantage that upper-earning classes and corporate enterprises feel entitled to, there's also the longstanding effort to defund and limit the American welfare-state, including, as of February 2025, access to affordable health care, particularly for the aged and lower-income segments of society.

These are two sides of the same coin.

As alluded to earlier, "In 2023, federal and state governments spent $1.3 trillion on public welfare for Food & Nutrition, Housing, Income Security, Medicaid/Medicare, and Unemployment benefits." (Candace Begoody, *50 Important Welfare Statistics for 2023*, LexingtonLaw.com, 2023).

Commensurately, as the conservative Heritage Foundation notes, "the share of income taxes for the top two income brackets in America (earning respectively over $218,000 and $540,000) was 60%." (Adam Michel, *In Chart 1, How Much the Rich Pay in Taxes*, The Heritage Foundation, March 3, 2021). A large portion of that money (60% of $1.3 trillion is $780 billion) goes to support welfare programs and their recipients. And militant Republicans and their militant capitalist voter base are increasingly and militantly unhappy about it.

Now, after the onset of DOGE, all bets are off. It's no longer a question of whether, or to what extent, the welfare state should be reformed, but rather whether the issues and conditions of welfare will be addressed at all. In any case, the writing has long been on the wall.

On healthcare, for example, then House Speaker Kevin McCarthy proposed "taking Medicaid coverage away from people who do not meet new work-reporting requirements. The McCarthy proposal would apply to all states, but in practice, it would heavily impact people covered by the Affordable Care Act (ACA) Medicaid expansion." (*Center on Budget and Policy Priorities*, April 20, 2023). Under the now U.S. House approved so-called 'Big Beautiful Bill, such provisions come closer to going into effect.

Given the unsettling, freaky, and media-magnified events and conditions that often characterize American society, it's no wonder people of all dispositions begin to doubt the efficacy of the American welfare system. The soft underbelly of American liberalism may be that it underwrites civic profligacy.

For militant Republicans and their relatively higher-taxed, but higher-income cohorts, such profligacy enflames indignation and gives pretext and shield for what is essentially raw economic, class interest. It's true, higher-income earners pay a higher (but still inadequate) share of taxes, a large proportion of which supports a larger share of welfare costs. And most welfare recipients don't even vote Republican. "Damn high taxes and damn the welfare state!" the embittered class cries.

In rebuttal, when an economic system creates such great welfare need, then it is high time to create an alternative system that produces and allocates more widespread prosperity. That starts with reconceiving a different public goods paradigm and agenda and reconfigured systems of taxation. Of course, these self-serving cohorts carry relatively more tax burden. But this results from false and misguided financial calculation. The burden would have been shared more equitably and efficiently if, in the first place, the system afforded higher wages to the lower-earning 50% of the population. More people paying into the system reduces costs for everybody and provides greater services. This is an actuarial reality. But now, higher earning cohorts want to slough off their tax burden while still enjoying their higher skewed incomes. This is the stuff on which historical and national destinies turn.

Thankfully, neither a different public goods paradigm, nor a system which produces and allocates broader prosperity have to be invented out of whole cloth. The Austrian and European social market economies present different tax and income actuarial models which produce greater systems of 'pre-distributed' public welfare. These have been ignored and/or bypassed by American policymakers, political parties, and the American electorate for far too long, and now at increasing hazard. It is not only, however, models of pre-distribution that need to be perceived. The wisdom behind sharing the wealth produced by the economy to the greater benefit of all social sectors involved also demands inspection. This calls into question bedrock assumptions about the American market capitalist economy, whose militant proponents now take aim at dismantling the welfare state.

The welfare system debate in America gets falsely framed. It is allegedly about dollars and cents and economic efficiency, and apparent profligacy, but the strategy for dismantling social welfare investment has always depended on racist aspersions.

Long before Reagan trotted out his famous (Black) 'Welfare Queen' (sic) to stereotype welfare recipients, and continuing right up to the contemporary false hysteria over Critical Race Theory, racist tropes have served to prevent the realization of a united society, that depends on and serves all social echelons and classes. The welfare debate in America has been exploited and controlled by American capital interests and racist customs. This serves to deprive all Americans of an effective social state – one that embraces not only well-conceived welfare provisions but also universal access to medical care, higher education, vocational training, and fair labor compensation, not to mention coordinated free market enterprise.

These benefits have their distributive origin and administration in social agency and negotiation, especially between business and labor interests, requiring only governmental sanction and protection for their execution.

American economic policy took an untoward, regrettable detour after the market meltdowns of the 1970s. Capital interests took advantage of the impasse, as noted, and propagated nebulous and discredited 'trickle-down' policies to justify tax cuts. To further the economic case, welfare was vilified in racial terms. As former Demos think-tank president Heather McGhee argues in her groundbreaking analysis, *The Sum of Us*: "In railing against welfare and the war on poverty, conservatives like President Reagan told white voters that government was the enemy because it favored Black and brown people over them, but their real agenda was to blunt government's ability to challenge concentrated wealth and corporate power." (Heather McGhee, *The Sum of Us: What Racism Costs Everyone and How We Can Prosper Together*, Random House-One World, 2021).

Actual evidence proving the reach and distribution of who actually receives welfare support doesn't seem to touch the scales of the welfare debate. A Pew Research study, for example, reverses common assumptions that black-skinned people are the largest group of welfare beneficiaries. The study found in 2020 that "Non-Hispanic White-skinned people accounted for 44.6% of adult Supplemental Nutrition Assistance Program Food Stamp/SNAP recipients and 31.5% of child recipients. About 27% of both adult and child recipients were people with black skin. Hispanic people, who can be of any race, accounted for 21.9% of adult recipients and 35.8% of child recipients." (Drew Desilver, *What the Data Says About Food Stamps in the U.S.*, Pew Research Center, July 2023).

These numbers are similar to those reported in a 2013 Agriculture Department study, cited by accredited Quora.com commentator, Chris Joose.

Both studies, then, contradict the stereotype implanted through the media and political rhetoric, not to mention social bias, which promotes "the notion," as Joose observes, "that SNAP (Food Stamp) recipients are either people of color, non-working, or undeserving in some way." (Chris Joose, *A Large Share of SNAP Recipients Are White*, Quora.com, *Huffington Post*, 2013).

American Slavery The system and heritage of American slavery deserves review here because, in some ways, its influence on economic and social conditions remains somewhat indelible. The ideological component of slavery clearly validates Hegel's view that master-slave propensities are not only implicit in human consciousness, but can become manifest. The master's total economic and political freedom is predicated on the idea of total subjugation, or subordination of the enslaved.

This distortion of freedom and equality, essential counterpoints, — skews conditions Hegel thought necessary for the evolution of human self-consciousness. Hegel notes in his *Encyclopedia* (§ 539) "that freedom and equality are indeed the fundamental determinations of a modern rational constitution and are indeed even the final ends, the ultimate purpose of any such "constitution" (Terry Pinkard, *Hegelian Equality as Inseparable from Freedom, Polemos Journal,* 2018).

Moreover, you don't have to be any kind of Marxist to perceive the interlink between the ideology of slavery and its *mode of production* — "the enslavement and forced labor of blacks by a white master class" (Dinesh D'Souza, *We the Slave Owners,* Hoover Institute, hoover.org, September 1, 1995). It wasn't only the total exploitation and subjugation of their labor that prefigured slavery's *mode of production*, but also the reduction of the Black race to chattel-status. Slaves were bought and sold like any other commodity on the market.

As D'Souza points out, this brought in its train the rationalization, or ideology, of "racial superiority." The subsequent denial of Black humanity, as issued in the infamous Supreme Court *Dred Scott* decision of 1857, "invoked Black inferiority to exclude slaves from constitutional protection, and pronounced slave ownership as a fundamental property right." (ibid). The injustice of the labor system forced all sorts of logical contortions, particularly against the backdrop of the Republic's founding principles.

"After all, if Blacks are men, and all men are created equal, then Blacks are entitled to the same rights as whites, including the right not to be held in captivity. Fortified by racism from the beginning, American slavery itself fostered an institutionalized bigotry." (ibid).

Bigotry, in turn, spawned a perversion of manners, a distorted culture of gentility among slaveholders that served to cauterize their bestiality toward and dehumanization of human property. The slavery economy was an enforced fusion, of a *materialist- mode of production* and ideological interests, or attitudes. It was irrational. In Hegelian terms, you might say, the perverse and contorted ideology of freedom that slavery advanced could not sustain its 'mode of production.' The proposition that my freedom is predicated on your enslavement makes the idea of freedom itself pathologically illogical. Moreover, you might shackle bodies, but the mind and spirit remain to some degree autonomous. Such internal contradictions, as noted earlier, feature the dialectic "negation of a negation."

The inhumanity of the system proved to be unsustainably efficient. It was dragooned by American abolitionists and broad public opinion in the American

North. These invoked the inviolability of individual rights and an alternative *mode of production* based on free labor, upheld by the staunch leadership of Abraham Lincoln and the newly founded Republican Party. The Republicans under Lincoln forbade slavery's territorial expansion, and the issue culminated in the Civil War.

But the legacy of slavery, the failed Reconstruction of the South, and subsequent Jim Crow laws of discrimination and segregation, left deep mental scars, and a kind of social retardation in their wake. As D'Souza concludes, "racism is a peculiar reflection of the moral conscience of America and of the West. Racism reflects the oppressor's need to account for the betrayal of his highest ideals" (ibid).

This detour into America's history of slavery provides a backdrop to understand the evolution of American labor relations and the irresolution of its welfare state. Both increasingly play right into the hands of militant Republican cohorts. These cohorts protest that they can't be held accountable for the legacies of racism, and to be so impugned insults their dignity.

At the same time, however, that dignity sustains an economic system that, to a certain degree, hides behind a market-sanctioned exploitation of labor, - a legacy of long-tendrilled slavery – which so disabused the culture of American labor relations.

The unstable shambles, economic inequality, and polarization that characterize too much of contemporary American society can't be understood without taking racial and racist conditions into account. Racial polarization is the most enduring and persistent social and economic cleft, among all contemporary divides in American society - between MAGA/militant, rogue Republicans and 'socialist' Democrats, between economically advantaged and disadvantaged, and between any number of other social identifications. It has prevented the reconstitution of America's economic system and the formation of an effective social state.

As thus far argued, the relationship between social and political polarization and economic inequality is reflexive—that is, they drive each other like a push-me-pull-you cart. The most constructive means to address both is to reconstitute the economic system toward greater shared wealth, premised on an overhaul of industrial relations between capital and labor; only in this manner can the instrumental legacies of racism and discrimination be overcome.

Racism

In *The Sum of Us*, noted above, Heather McGhee dissects the legacy and resurgence of racism. It is the prevalent wedge preventing the full development of an American social state—one based on greater partnership between social and economic interests, rather than their division. Her book ultimately projects and prompts new thinking about social solidarity. But first, the polarizing forces that racism unleashes require review. The undertow of persistent racism in the form of longstanding regressive economic and political policies holds back forward movement, as do racial attitudes of disassociation, indifference, and outright racial animosity.

One such attitude, current even among more informed and open-minded white observers, is that blacks in general don't rise to the opportunities afforded them through the promulgation of their voting and civil rights in the 1960s. This assessment is vaguely supported by perceived persistent violence in some black communities, by overblown cries of racial victimhood, and especially by the perceived disproportionate poverty that continues to plague many black communities. In actual fact, numbers reported by the Center for Disease Control and the Pew Research Foundation reveal that such assessments are false. Progress is being made, under regressive, not to say close-fisted conditions. Between 1970 and 2010, life expectancy for black people "rose from 64 years to 74 years." In that time span, black household median adjusted income (that is, the exact middle between higher and lower income households) "rose from $23,000 in 1967 to $39,760 in 2011." "21% of black adults over 25 years had a completed college education in 2012 as against 5% in 1964" (Habib F., *Are Black Americans Actually Worse Off than in the 60s?* Quora.com, 2012).

While encouraging, these gains are insufficient to counteract what appears to be a resurgence of racial/racist attitudes and policies. In fact, they may excite them. The disclosure, cited above, that black people are less reliant on food stamps than white people also appears insufficient to the task of reversing and re-directing racial backlash. Instead, the other side of the coin gets burnished. Perceived shortfalls in communities of color, especially black communities, get amplified to perpetuate racist stereotypes—not only to denigrate the progress of black-skinned people but to distract from the real issues driving economic inequality and insecurity. For example, "17.1% of all black-skinned Americans fell below the poverty level—$29,678 for a family of four—in 2022, as against 8.6% of all white-skinned people" (sic) (*Data on Poverty in the United States*, Center for American Progress/US Census Bureau Statistics, 2022). Heather McGhee points out that "white-skinned (sic) people have 13x the median household wealth of black-skinned (sic) Americans" (ibid, p.6). Such numbers are used to reinforce the opinion that "poverty is primarily a black problem" (ibid, p.34). The accelerated incarceration rate of black-skinned people also reinforces such prejudice. Since 1960, the incarceration of black people has increased 3.5x (per 100,000 residents) from 1,313 to 4,347 in 2010 (ibid, p. 6).

Such numbers beleaguer and are used by both sides of the racial divide: on the one hand, to confirm the perception of some kind of racial deficit, bolstering further discrimination; on the other, these numbers are upheld to confront continued racial persecution, the injustice of economic conditions, and the need for remediation. Racial attitudes and conditions are difficult to specify. With regard to integration, they can be contradictory. In summing up developments on this front, the 2005 book *Failures of Integration* states that "the civil rights revolution put in place laws that attempted to guarantee that no one should be restricted in their access to education, jobs, travel, public accommodations, or housing because of race. For most people, this was what integration meant. Blacks, whites, Latinos, Asians, and Native Americans might not share social space, but our public institutions, our workplaces, and our schools were no longer to be divided into separate domains…" (Sheryll Cashin, *The Failures of Integration*, AmericanProgress.org, June 2005).

As other studies purport to show, most people are for an inclusive society and equal opportunity, but as Cashin points out, "Americans seem to have come to a tacit, unspoken understanding: State-ordered segregation has rightly been eliminated, but voluntary separation is acceptable, natural, sometimes even preferable" (ibid). What was true in Cashin's 2005 analysis appears even truer now. The suggested ambivalence toward integration among all parties involved produced a certain vacuum, stasis, and even regression among distinct elements of the white-skinned population.

Racism again rears its ugly head. Extremist groups, according to a Southern Poverty Law *Hate Map*—from anti-immigrant, LGBTQ, Muslim, Semitic, to neo-Nazi, white nationalists, and neo-Confederate groups—sprout up by the dozen like toxic mushrooms across the land (*Hate Map*, splc.org, by ideology, 2022). Such developments only confirm the urgency of reigniting movements of solidarity. Other studies indicate that a practical majority of white-skinned people think racial relations are generally good. It is uncertain, though, if this reflects support for and recognition of gains made by parts of the black-skinned population, or only registers a certain obtuseness or 'disassociation,' mentioned earlier, about actual, broader racial conditions.

The demonstrations and riots that erupted after a police officer's murder of George Floyd in Minneapolis in May of 2020 were certainly concerned with police brutality. They were also an outcry against the structural racism that creates inescapable economic conditions that hold back a significant portion of the American population and the whole of American society itself. The racial and economic conditions that most black people encounter are not exclusive to them. They hold back all racial groups, including whites. It's racism, though, encountered by black-skinned people on a daily basis in manifold situations, that really sticks, and augurs social and economic regression. It should go without saying that ideologically-correct speech efforts to reverse, or ameliorate this reality, misdirected as they may be, have provoked the Trump administration ban on DEI initiatives. Critical Race Theory exposes the depth of racism in American society and how it retards the expansion of material opportunity and prosperity.

The Tenets of Critical Race Theory

CRT tenets aren't far-fetched at all, but palpable to anyone with their eyes open. One can't help but notice skin color and all the personal and social associations that go along with it. Impressions can be positive or negative. But in the main, according to the first CRT tenet, it is indisputable that certain attitudes and associations prevail—" that have been created and maintained by dominant groups (especially white people in the USA) to justify their oppression and exploitation of other groups on the basis of the latter's supposed inferiority, immorality, or capacity for self-rule" *(Critical Race Theory,* Encyclopedia Britannica, Brian Duignan, editor, 2023). This references the insidious tendrils of slavery still influencing attitudes, mentioned earlier, but also the authority and institutions in society that consistently confront people of color and sustain ingrained racist attitudes and policies. You might object and say that the progress and opportunities afforded by university programs such as Affirmative Action were all about integration. Progress, within the constrained frameworks of liberal market capitalism, was certainly achieved for individuals and communities of color, but not enough over time to withstand the backlash of 'reverse racism,' inadvertently bred by Affirmative Action. The racial relations conundrum in America continues. CRT is a reasoned outcry against the persistence of structural, racial, and economic conditions.

A second CRT tenet holds that encounters with racist attitudes and treatment "are normal, not aberrational for most people of color" (ibid). Put in quantitative terms, a 2019 Pew Research report reveals a glaring discrepancy between white-skinned and black-skinned experiences. Affirmative responses to the statement, "People see racial discrimination where it really does NOT exist," are shared by 52% of white-skinned people. Black-skinned people answered 14% in the affirmative (Julia Horowitz, Anna Brown, *How Americans See the State of Race Relations*, Pew Research Center, April 2019). The statement, "People DO NOT see racial discrimination where it really does exist," drew an affirmative response from 48% of white-skinned people, as against 84% of black-skinned people. Similar, though not quite as high, were responses from Hispanic and Asian respondents. Such views reflect interactions and experiences in the real world, with regard to having a job or loan application denied, paying more for products and services than their white-skinned peers, being unduly suspected of criminal behavior, or being more subjected to police brutality and/or the use of lethal force. (ibid)

These conditions may not be as systemic and codified as they were in the Jim Crow South until the end of the 1960s, but CRT holds that they are structural, or built into daily reality; that is, they are stubbornly intractable and systemic. Black-skinned people are more often than not subject to forms of 'housing,' 'education,' and 'medical care' discrimination and disadvantage (ibid). These, along with employment frameworks that support income inequality, are issues that inflict hardship on all racial communities. They thwart, if not throttle, social solidarity and the formation of social partnership agencies and institutions that would reverse them. Some believe Critical Race Theory to be invalid because it dares to explain the causes of inequality in racial terms. It dares to assert that gains of racial integration were not fulsome enough but served other "convergent interests"—such as America's public image on the global stage—of dominant groups and institutions (ibid). CRT argues that the Brown v. Board of Education decision against school segregation and other civil rights measures didn't materially affect "the racial hierarchy that generally characterizes American society" (ibid). The more things changed, in other words, the more they stayed the same. The extra burden of racial identity doubles the weight of existence.

Suppose that you're a black-skinned person and you want to get, or re-negotiate a loan. Imagine such circumstances in a tight economy. And when hasn't the economy been tight, especially for those earning at or below the average income levels of $63,442 in 2022? (Annual Social and Economic Supplement, US Census Bureau Current Population Survey of 75,000 households). The winner-take-all mentality manifest in that tight economy prevails. The tightness of economic conditions is held against you as a person of color, even if you've got collateral and some assets. But your racial reputation, however personally undeserved, is also a liability. Under such circumstances, it is at least twice as hard to get ahead. Sorry, your loan is denied. Civil Rights progress obviously changed the composition of classrooms and reversed discriminatory Jim Crow laws. These advances finally allowed the country to partially come to terms with the legacy of slavery, 100 years after the Emancipation Proclamation.

CRT goes on to raise other aspects of racial reality; how important it is, for example, that black voices be admitted and take part in any social, economic, or political dialogue. At the same time, CRT emphasizes the importance of deracializing said discourse and social relations. They want it justifiably to go both ways, neither more nor less than white-skinned people or any other racial group would expect, were the tables turned. It is not on their account that the system should be reconstituted, but on account of everybody in society. Racial identity should be only one narrow aspect of broader identity affiliations. This "intersectionality," as it is termed, clearly indicates that CRT is not a racist statement. To the contrary, it is an anti-racist statement, seeking to diagnose and protest deep-rooted racial conditions in America. Indeed, it issues a possible roadmap past the old roadblocks toward a more open country and healthy racial relations. So, what is all the fuss about?

As it stands, rhetoric and policies to outright ban the teaching of CRT at whatever level—even when its language is clearly aimed at graduate-level classrooms—aim to suppress racial discourse. Racism wouldn't exist, according to this conceit, if people would just stop talking about it. Apparently, black-skinned people should just get along, play more by the rules stacked against them, and let conditions for greater equality quietly evolve over time. Black-skinned people just need to try harder. This itself is reminiscent of the white priests in Birmingham, Alabama, in 1963, who counseled black civil rights leaders to forebear and find a better time for protest. In his *Letter from a Jail in Birmingham*, Martin Luther King rejected such placation: "For years now, I have heard the word 'wait.' It rings in the ear of every Negro with a piercing familiarity... His 'wait' has almost always meant 'never.' We must come to see with one of our distinguished jurists of yesterday that 'justice too long delayed is justice denied.'" (Martin Luther King Jr., *Letter from a Jail in Birmingham*, California State University, Chico, August 1963, p. 2)

The false hysteria over CRT is only the most recent 'dog whistle' employed by 'dominant groups' in the media and in some governmental chambers to reinforce racial discrimination and whip up a newly mobilized constituent base. The 'dog whistle' finds only too much resonance. A near-majority of the American voting public supported MAGA messaging and its racist/ethnic undertones in the 2020 presidential election. And now, in 2024, that inferred support is redoubled. Critical Race Theory represents a coherent challenge to the mentality and manipulations of white-centered American culture. Therefore, it must be suppressed and resisted along with any other expansive governmental social or economic policy that would reduce racial inequality. The dog must be kept on its leash. But make no mistake. The racial dog whistle gets blown and exploited, not only to enforce anti-social mentality, but also as a means to distract attention from the more fundamental realities of income and wealth inequality, where racism really gets enacted. Racism will not be attenuated or solved by moral injunction—" Thou shalt not be racist." There is, however, a good chance of reducing its corrosive power by postulating and advocating an economic agenda that will serve every racial group.

The Sum of Us

This observation is bolstered by Heather McGhee in her treatise on racial and economic relations, *The Sum of Us*. The couched, if not outright intentional, racism involved in banning CRT in some states, is a weapon not only against greater racial tolerance, but most particularly, to maintain the exploitation of the economic system. McGhee spells out the historic legacies that have compounded racial disadvantage and foreclosed systemic overhaul. You don't have to recall the gruesome murder and desecration of Emmett Till, emblematic of countless other racial crimes, or be a card-carrying Black Lives Matter member, or ascribe to Critical Race Theory to perceive the truth of McGhee's rather normative and objective observations and analysis. They strike an informative and intuitive chord. First, she cites historical experience bequeathed to people with black skin. "The New Deal of the 1930s transformed the lives of workers with minimum wage and overtime laws – but compromises with southern Democrats excluded the job categories most black people held, in domestic and agricultural work. Then the GI Bill of 1944 paid the college tuition of hundreds of thousands of veterans… but few black servicemen benefited, as local administrators funneled most black servicemen to segregated vocational schools." (Heather McGhee, ibid, p. 22)

The litany and legacy go on. Housing mortgage benefits were also part of the GI Bill. "Federally sanctioned housing discrimination" severely curtailed the ability of people of color to become homeowners and thus gain an equity stake in the economy. In later decades, such sanctions were widely, if not systemically, extended by 'redlining,' wherein realtors and banks connived to refuse black people loans who sought to live in white neighborhoods and districts. Then there was redlining in reverse, wherein banks imposed higher, predatory interest rates on loans to black people who were/are interested in starting a business or purchasing a home. This practice was particularly useful during the subprime mortgage crisis: "Numerous reports backed up the allegations in these lawsuits that predatory mortgage lenders were targeting minority neighborhoods and that these lenders had an unusually large share of lending in African-American and Hispanic neighborhoods." *(Reverse Redlining, Discrimination, and For-Profit Education,* Student Loan Borrowing Assoc., National Consumer Law Center, Aug. 2011) All such marketing devices, and others, extend structural, if not systemic, roadblocks to the social and economic advancement of minority racial groups, particularly people with black skin. They turn a blind eye to the racial/racist implications involved, or perhaps actually depend on deeper racial ignorance, indifference, or even animus for their application.

McGhee's primary aim is to get at the zero-sum deeper-rooted nature of such beliefs and attitudes. The "sum of us," heralded in the book's title, can only be achieved by expunging the so-called "zero-sum." As the director of Demos Research Institute, dedicated to scientific analysis of American economic, educational, and medical conditions, McGhee posed the question of, "What if racism is actually driving (economic, sic) inequality for everyone?" (ibid, XIX). The "zero-sum" attitude is better understood as "cutting off your nose to spite your face." It goes a long way toward explaining the legacy and reality of a racism that undercuts the interests of its own purveyors. The "zero-sum" sentiment and mentality also come to the fore in the results of a Harvard Business School economic survey of white-skinned respondents. (ibid, p. 5) Essentially, "zero-sum" amounts to thinking that "if things are getting better for black people, it must be at the expense of white people." (Michael Norton and Samuel Sommers, *Whites See Racism as a Zero-Sum Game That They Are Now Losing*, Perspectives on Psychological Science 6, 2011, pp. 215-218)

Incredible as it appears, given the obvious "reality of continued white dominance in U.S. life, from banks to business corporations to government," (McGhee, ibid) a large number of respondents surveyed actually believe that "whites are now the subjugated race in America." (Norton & Sommers, ibid) Such sentiments can be latent or outspoken. They came to a head with the Tea Party movement of 2010 (after black-skinned Obama's election as President) and later proved more widespread than at first suspected, as noted above, with the emergence and re-emergence of Donald Trump and the MAGA movement. Today's media echo chamber features greater racial belligerence and innuendo, restoking old and, one hoped, worn-out prejudices. In fact, as certain black-skinned individuals and communities have gained prosperity, a backlash of resentment among some white-skinned people takes place. Black-skinned Yale Sociology Professor Elijah Anderson reports going out for a jog in a prosperous Cape Cod town and being jeered at to just "Go home." He could only infer that his assailant meant he should return to the ghetto. (Black Success, White Backlash, *The Atlantic*, p. 9, November 2023) Such incidents are not isolated. They lead him to reflect on a "recurring cultural phenomenon" (ibid, p. 10) in America, where backlash kicks in when black-skinned populations advance. Advancement occurred for a brief moment after the Civil War until 1877, when the long rule of apartheid-like Jim Crow decrees was commenced, following the withdrawal from southern states of the federal union army. Advancement occurred again to an extent in the American Labor Movement but was throttled, especially in the South, by racial discrimination.

And it is happening today. After advances afforded by the Civil Rights era and the successes of Affirmative Action and the diligent efforts of many in black (and white) communities, the "largest black middle class in American history" has come into being. (ibid, p. 11) This success, as Professor Anderson notes, "has inflamed" what he calls "the inevitable white backlash." Due to job displacement for many white people resulting from globalization and deindustrialization, good jobs for black people are the very "embodiment of what's wrong with America." (ibid) This rhymes with earlier observations as to the social/economic vulnerabilities of white-skinned populations in America. Heather McGhee offers this assessment: "Decade after decade, threats of job competition between men and women, immigrants and native-born, black and white have perennially revived the fear of loss at another's gain." (*The Sum of Us*, ibid, p. 14). This points to an economic system that remains stuck in time, unable to equally accommodate all sectors of the population at the same time. Instead of disarming the fear of race through reform of the economic system, in which all segments can gain security, the narrative continues in which "white people should see the well-being of people of color as a threat to their own. It (sic) is, McGhee notes, "one of the most powerful subterranean stories in America." (ibid, p. 15)

The "zero-sum" reality is riddled with the "cut your nose to save your face" anomaly. According to polls, the American electorate widely favors reforms to gain universal health care, access to universal higher education/vocational training, and trade union collective bargaining. McGhee can't explain the defeat of such reforms and the anomaly it represents, except by referring to issues of "belonging, competition, and status, questions that in this country keep returning to race." (ibid, XVII) Oddly, status concerns appear mercurial and stable at almost the same time. They assume many guises—social, material, financial, gender, marital, and, of course, racial—each fixed and somewhat fluid. "Convergence of interests," noted above, can also apply to status. Material and financial status achieved within the current rules of the system translates for some into a sense of entitlement..." whatever I get, I deserve." This is a salutary, self-serving convergence. It follows that if "you don't get it, you don't deserve to get it." This attitude 'converges' for many white-skinned people with racial prejudice. It appears invincible and stands as a sentry against all policies that propose alteration of the 'status quo.' Changing the 'status quo' of economic conditions to re-orient racial attitudes and realities has thus far proven extremely difficult, especially with regard to wage parity, health care insurance, and educational opportunity. The main premise of the current essay holds that if these hallmarks of a social state were accessible to all classes, races, and ethnicities, rather than withheld by the market, race relations would dramatically improve – not to mention the yawning disparities of income and wealth inequality that drive polarization.

Trade unions and collective bargaining have a checkered legacy in America, owing in the main to the effective resistance of 'capital' interests. Significant organizing gains have been offset by sharp reversals. As McGhee notes, "There's been no greater tool against collective bargaining than employers' ability to divide workers by gender, race, or origin, stoking suspicion and competition across groups." (ibid, p. 109) The only solution historically to one group, ethnicity, or race being played off against another was for workers "to bargain collectively: to band together across divisions and demand improvements that lifted the floor for everybody." (ibid, p. 109) Gains for all groups of workers—women, immigrants, and people of color—made in the 1880s under the "Knights of Labor" Union were reversed when Jim Crow discriminatory laws were mandated across the South in the 1890s. In the early 20th century, the exclusion of black workers by the American Federation of Labor (AFL) "was so prevalent that whites in early unions saw black people as synonymous with strikebreakers. Because (sic) unions rejected black workers, employers routinely brought them in as substitute workers to cross picket lines." (ibid, p. 110)

During World War II, because of labor shortages, exclusion on the basis of race, gender, and origin declined. The Congress of Industrial Organizations (CIO) expressly committed organizing efforts to interracial unity for entire industries "regardless of 'craft' or job title." (ibid) The role of trade unions and collective bargaining in the economy expanded by leaps and bounds. As McGhee notes, "The 40-hour workweek, overtime pay, employer health insurance and retirement benefits, worker compensation—all these components of a 'good job' came from collective bargaining and union advocacy with governments in the late 1940s and 50s." (ibid) And then came another decline. "After the 1950s peak, the share of workers covered by collective bargaining has fallen every decade." (ibid, p. 112) (in 2019, it stood at 11.6%, OECD. Stat) It is axiomatic that broader collective bargaining and attendant higher employment standards "compels employers to compete upward for labor." (ibid, p. 113), promoting broader wage parity (**See Appendix 2: Collective Bargaining and Wage Inequality**). But something else got in the way.

Unions had their own internal problems. Their embattled history in America, as will be seen, can partly be explained by their assuming and being assigned adversarial status. Partnership doesn't come into the question. Unions have been cordoned off and left to battle for position among themselves. Such marginalization contributed, in part, to trade-union racketeering and involvement with the mafia, as became emblematic under Teamsters President Jimmy

Hoffa between 1958-1971. Such activities put trade union organizing back on its heels. The titans of government and capital, and tighter economies, restricted union power as well. In general, though, it is proven that broad unionization boosts wages and working conditions in all industries. This leads McGhee to inquire, "Why would any worker hoping to better her lot in life oppose a union in a vote?" (ibid) The short answer is racial prejudice. In the intervening years, economic vicissitudes prompted by recession, trade agreements, such as NAFTA, or globalization have certainly influenced market and labor conditions. But in labor union votes, the issue of race re-emerged as decisive, particularly in the South. McGhee cites a culminating, if anecdotal, moment in Canton, Mississippi, in 2017, when the Nissan car company prevailed against efforts to unionize workers. The company employed every trick in the book to persuade white workers of their preferred position in the company without a union. Recounting a discussion with one of the workers involved, she asked how unions are perceived in Canton. His response was flat: "The people we see, as soon as they see UAW, and even if you bring union, they just think color. They think that unions, period—not just UAW—they just think unions are for lazy black people and a lot of 'em, even though they want the union, their racism, that hatred is keeping them from joining.'" (ibid, p. 117)

Labor leaders up and down the block, and for a long time, see the South as the movement's "Achilles' heel." (ibid) White people in the South generally just haven't been able to expand their conceptions, mentioned above, of 'belonging, competition, and status.' And it isn't limited just to the South. As McGhee, in conclusion, notes, "The low-wage southern labor model is no longer contained to the geographic South nor to manufacturing… As Walmart expanded from Arkansas, it brought its fiercely low wage and anti-union ethos with it… the difference between workers in the industrial Midwest and the South was nearly seven dollars an hour in 2008; three years later, wage cuts in the Midwest had slashed the regional difference in half." (ibid, p. 119) The anomaly of zero-sum calculations persists. Many white-skinned people opt for apparent racial advantage and the inequality which it extends, over the real material gains that would be achieved if they shared them with black-skinned people and other communities of color. In this, they hold onto the anchor and security of racial status against the ostensibly far greater financial and material status they would gain through trade union membership and negotiated collective bargaining. Social custom and tribal prejudice are reflected here, as is the prevalence of dog-whistle racist policy and propaganda. But the absence and failure of clear-sighted political and economic 'solidarity' advocacy is also at play. The potentials involved in greater union organization and effective social partnership between government, business, and labor, based on a thorough re-conception of distribution, deployment and utilization of economic resources go untapped.

Chapter Two:
Legacies of Racism Continued — Health Care Insurance

Barack Obama's campaign and election inspired all sorts of hope and opportunity for reform. He was immediately confronted by countervailing economic and political realities. The banking crisis forced his administration to adopt emergency policies to save a sinking economy. His election also prompted racist responses and revealed the realities of the racial divide. McGhee reports that "numerous social science studies have shown that racial resentment among white people spiked" as Obama assumed office (ibid, p. 52). His room for maneuver was limited not only by economic conditions on the ground, but also by the challenge of proving himself and his race in a crisis as a new President. It was evident from the beginning that, despite his ingenuity, great popularity, and oratorical gifts, Obama would conduct his office in conventional, presidential manner. He eschewed the populist opportunities the political moment might otherwise have afforded.

Intense political wrangling preceded the passage of what would become the Affordable Care Act. In an alternative political universe, in the 6-7-month window that existed prior to the votes, imagine President Obama taking the case for the Health Insurance Public Option to 8 or 10 corners of the country. His argument went like this: the "public option" puts all Americans into a "national pool" to lower insurance actuaries and reduce premiums. It allows "collective bargaining to lower prescription drug costs"

(McGhee, ibid). In conducting these immense rallies, Obama could have roused public opinion and pressured Congress to break free from constraints against the Public Option imposed by the mammoth and monolithic Health Insurance industry. The case against the healthcare insurance industry was and is ready-made. Its usurious exploitation of people's health and healthcare—through high premiums, deductibles, co-pays, and erratic, inconsistent coverage—is universally abhorred. Solidarity is summoned by calling out negative realities as well as by articulating positive solutions.

In this alternative scenario, Obama's campaign against the current health insurance system would have ruffled a lot of feathers and upset very large economic interests. It would have rocked the system and tested all of his considerable political and rhetorical skills. He would have promoted adoption of the "public option" in free-market terms that would not only improve medical care insurance, care, and services but also be a boon to the competitive economic system. The private health insurance industry would simply have had to compete with the terms and conditions offered by a Public Option program. Health care, after all, is not only a private good but also a social one. Reform would change the playing field monopolized by the healthcare industry. The outcry against such a "socialist" alternative by defenders of private enterprise would have been deafening but nothing compared to the aroused will of the people.

This is but one conceivable, and not entirely far-fetched, scenario by which politics can change the system. But it was not to be. Because of its half-measures, among other lost legislative opportunities, healthcare reform didn't contain the brewing populist tide. It didn't take long before a negative populism threatened to take over the political landscape. As it was, the Affordable Care Act passed by a squeak. It got rid of some hateful insurance industry practices—like denying coverage because of "pre-existing" medical conditions, "dropping customers when they got sick" (sic), or "requiring young adults to leave their parent's insurance before age 26" (ibid)—but it came up short in many ways. In the end, perhaps, the rationalist Obama and his team underestimated racist resistance as a factor undermining the passage of the more promising "public option." McGhee cites a study conducted by Brown University political scientist, Michael Tessler, "on the way race (sic) and racial attitudes impacted Americans' views of the Affordable Care Act in 2010: whites with higher levels of racial resentment and more anti-black stereotypes grew more opposed to healthcare reform after it became associated with President Obama" (ibid).

Another study, conducted by Stanford University researchers, confirms this finding. The experimental study attributed Obama's health care plan "to Bill Clinton and found that the link between healthcare opinion and racial (sic) prejudice dissolved" (ibid, p. 53). In parallel, speaking to a presumably white majority audience, Rush Limbaugh characterized Obama's ACA as a "civil rights bill, this is reparations, whatever you want to call it" (ibid). Racist factors play a volatile, but not insurmountable, role in American politics. McGhee's analysis recommends confronting racist undertows by over-accentuating all the benefits and advantages that white folks would enjoy, not incidentally aided and abetted by advocacy of solidarity. The status of your healthcare concerns can be wedded to collective interest and are of far more consequence than those of race.

Education

Education is another domain where racial prejudice, rationalized in the name of economic frugality and profitability, constricts access and opportunity to what is clearly a social good. "Drastic cuts" in state funding for public higher education institutions since 1980 led, in 2017, to a "majority of state colleges relying on student tuition dollars for the majority of their expenses" (McGhee, ibid, p. 42). This development coincided, not coincidentally, with increased enrollment of students of color, now and then taking advantage of the expansion of their civil rights. Enrollment of students of color grew from "just one in six in 1980, to over four in ten" in 2020. In its heyday, public investment in state college and university education registered an efficient "$3-4 return on every $1 invested" (ibid). In 1976, public support for state university and college tuition "provided $6 out of every $10" (ibid). Actual tuition at many public educational institutions was minimal, or even tuition-free. That tradition has been overthrown. "Since 1991, tuition has nearly tripled, helping bring its counterpart, skyrocketing student debt, to the level of $1.5 trillion in 2020. This represents an alarming stealth privatization of America's public colleges" (ibid, p. 42).

You can bet that the portion of educational debt held by people of color is disproportionate. This represents the legacy of racially biased policies that leave black-skinned and other families of color without enough wealth to pay for college. As McGhee notes, "Eight out of ten black graduates have to borrow and at higher levels than any other group" (ibid, p. 43). The glaring anomaly of the evolved "debt-for-diploma system" is that onerous student debt is owed by large portions of white-skinned people as well. "Student debt is most acute among black families," as McGhee reports, "but has now reached 65% of white public college graduates as well" (ibid). Compounding interest rates "means they must pay at least 33% more on average than the amount borrowed." Stealth privatization indeed. Where is the outcry? More generous outlays for education were once affordable and efficient in the post-World War II period up to 1980 for white-skinned college students. Suddenly such outlays became unaffordable with the emergence of black-skinned and colored student populations in the post-Civil Rights era. The successful propaganda campaign that portrayed taxes as welfare for people with different skin colors culminates now in a higher educational system that is unsustainable, "unexplained and apparently unavoidable" (ibid).

The society of white enfranchisement is hoisted by its own petard. Until the entire population gets over its taxation/racial prejudice, overhaul of such an exploitative, inefficient, and unaffordable system will not take place. Anomaly once again rears its ugly head.

It is one of the anomalies of the economic system that its rewards and benefits imbue the holders with a certain presumption of moral standing. But if the system ain't right, how can those so privileged stand by in moral indifference? This is the question that confronts sectors of the American populace that proclaim an interest and commitment to social justice. Cognitive dissonance comes to the fore.

Status and the American Ethos

Conservative, Republican, and capital interests may have won the intervening economic and social debate by successfully leveraging racial prejudice, as McGhee argues, but issues of access to education, medical care, and employment compensation summon their own conditions, relations, and media campaigns. They require correct formulation, context, and a new "convergence of interests." The liberal argument thus far has been too weak, articulated by those in the ranks who have greater social and financial assurance and who can afford high-minded principles about greater racial equality. But such sentiments of greater fellow feeling haven't thus far extended toward systemic overhaul of the economy—something that might put their economic status at risk. The aim must be to drive such sentiments toward policies and programs that support greater material security for all people, regardless of skin color. There is a case to be made: greater material security for people, after all, redounds to the greater benefit of society, as McGhee says, to "the sum of us." (ibid)

The idea, or vision, of creating an economic system that ensures greater financial and social status for broader shares of the population, a social economy, has largely fallen by the wayside. The efficacy of liberal programs was overtaken by economic contortions, conservative rhetoric, and the promulgation of the "winner-take-all" mentality—the notion that status must be individually earned, as if it isn't or can't be earned in a system that provides baseline security for all. The country is left with an over-glorified market capitalist system that simultaneously fosters deep wedges of economic inequality and insecurity. Liberal platform initiatives of the

1960s and 70s, and ever since, couldn't prove their efficacy enough to escape the brand, or epithet of "tax and spend." Liberal initiatives didn't go much beyond well-known welfare state provisions—health insurance for the poor and aged, unemployment compensation, etc. A broader social vision was not extended, with which people could perceive the tangible benefits of higher taxation—employer-supported affordable health care, state-supported tuition-free higher and vocational educational access as an investment in the broad prospects of all citizens. (but they did get a lot of military expenditure)

The conditions, in what was otherwise the heyday for liberal sentiment, weren't right for such initiatives and programs. Markets still appeared unlimited. Republicans won the economic debate with the charge that government spending was profligate and eroded the basic incentive structures and profit reaches of the system. For lack of a forceful alternative argument, in the overheated Cold War moment, most Democrats either colluded with or accommodated the retrenchment of a broader social policy and public goods agenda. Capital formation and investment won the day.

The straits into which the country has been driven by these policies are now clearly visible. Militant Republicans and their oligarchic underwriters want to achieve authoritarian supremacy. They seek to demobilize the dialectic between democracy and capitalism and freeze historical evolution. The utility of various racial "dog whistles" was - and still is - instrumental in maintaining the winner-take-all ideology of American market capitalism. These whistles allow many at the high end of the economic spectrum to protect and extend their status, no matter the cost to the larger society. They also beckon those at the lower end of the economic spectrum to overlook their own interests as long as the system permits them a nominal sense of racial status and prospect. In both cases, racial prejudice is operative.

And so, the country lands in a condition of lopsided tax policies, out of step with broad social developments, and an outmoded and confused social ethos, vulnerable to the exploitation and rhetoric of division.

The case to remedy the "racial wealth gap," in McGhee's words, is compelling - not only because it involves longstanding injury and disadvantage, but because it points the way to reducing economic inequality. The cause for remedy is made especially in the case of homeownership. Here, in particular for communities of Black-skinned people, as noted, "redlining" and "reverse redlining," among other policies, have left a dearth of homeownership and a consequent deficit of assets that could be passed on. As McGhee notes, "The ability of white families to count on inheritance from previous generations is the biggest contributor to today's massive racial wealth gap." (ibid, p. 276)

"If the U.S. adopted policy interventions to close the racial disparities in health, education, incarceration, and jobs, the U.S. economy would be $8 trillion larger in 2050." (ibid) Such interventions would represent the realization of what McGhee terms the "social-solidarity dividend." (The Sum of Us, ibid, p. 271) Great debate, discourse and pointed advocacy driving the case for reform of employment-industrial relations, universal healthcare and tuition-free higher and vocational education, must arise. Such an economic and political movement would blow right by enduring legacies and realities of racism – their vestiges transfigured and overcome by social partnership. In the same breath, the Janus-face of political polarization must be confronted.

Chapter Three:
Political Polarization- Roots and Realities

Political conditions in America suffer from a blizzard of commentary, now compounded by the confusion and consternation inaugurated by a re-installed Trump administration. This makes it all the more important to review the history of the current moment, to survey the field and grasp a clear way forward. Get out the snowplow.

Dialectically speaking, unresolved contradictions in the political field reinforce polarization that leaves the government prone to overthrow. Trump administration, 'autocratic' initiatives thus far threaten to regress political processes and remove them from democratic purview and resolution. And now, economic processes are threatened with the overthrow of the Federal Reserve Bank governance. This conflict between a politics sanctioned by law and tradition and a politics driven by autocratic fiat is the first and most immediate consequence posed by polarization in the American political sphere. It overthrows conventional political opposition and is largely unprecedented in American experience.

The authoritarian movement brandishes belligerent, often false rhetoric and tactics, whose threat is muted only by the remaining norms of democratic process and perception. Among other plain indicators of political overthrow, the illiberal autocracy threatens ethnic, electoral, and reproductive minority rights essential to individual liberty. The overthrow of these rights would establish what commentator Thomas Edsall cited as "minority authoritarian" rule and control. (The Republican Strategists Who Have Carefully Planned All of This, *NYT*, April 12, 2023.) Since November 5, 2024, that minority has suddenly morphed into a majority.

Edsall, the commentator, was not then, nor is he now, given to false alarm. His appraisal of the convulsions of the modern 'conservative movement' was spot on. The worst is probably yet to be seen, but it has been a long time coming. Many warnings were issued in what now appears an almost quaint immediate past.

Harvard professor of Political Science and Sociology, Theda Skocpol contended, for example, "that many of the developments in states controlled by Republicans are a result of careful long-term planning by conservative strategists, particularly those in the Federalist Society, who 'are' developing tools to build 'minority (majority, sic) authoritarianism' within the context of a nominally democratic system of government" (ibid).

The veracity of this prognosis, as noted, can be traced back at least to the 1990s, when Newt Gingrich's *Contract for America* and Grover Norquist's taunt to "shrink the size of the US government so small that it could be drowned in a bathtub" were thrown down like a gauntlet. These were opening legislative and rhetorical salvos in a long-ranging campaign, going even further back to the 1970s and the Reagan years. They extend now to the overthrow of America's liberal-democratic state and culture.

The Federalist Society, a conservative lawyers' organization that is highly networked and influential, carries on that campaign. Its presence has grown since the early

1980s through judicial system appointments and in state and national ranks of the Republican Party. Currently, six justices of the U.S. Supreme Court are erstwhile or former members of the Society. Its agenda is property-centered, nationalist, and 'exceptionalist' in nature, - meaning that rules and conditions that apply elsewhere in the world don't apply to America. In spite of this, since Trump's re-inauguration, it appears the Supreme Court and broader judicial system is the last, if thin, line in defense of American liberal-jurisprudence and democratic processes.

America's surge toward illiberal authoritarianism didn't just appear out of nowhere. Its path forward appears increasingly unencumbered. Its roots are many and go beyond being animated by a cult figure, tapping into broad strands of social and economic insecurity to aggrandize himself and his class.

Authoritarianism is abetted by the viral, multifarious nature of contemporary mass media, anti-democratic demagoguery, and the steady drumbeat of rancorous talk-show hosts. These fill discourse voids and vacuums left open by largely supine democratic policy and the breakdown of liberal idealism. But issues of class interest and financial avarice are the main driving forces. Many of the very rich and very powerful, have concluded they just don't have time for democratic values and processes anymore. These are but trifles that serve only to limit the expansion of their own economic, social, and political power. Their ideological justification is self-serving and anti-democratic.

And it isn't only the plutocrats. This burgeoning crowd of militant capitalists and militant Republican leaders has perceived the clock running out on their era of entitlement for some time. The privileged position that wealth has gained, particularly in the past 40 years, is clearly indefensible. And for that very reason, and in a way more coordinated and organized than supposed, vast swaths of this cohort appear ready to defend it until the last.

As Edsall defines it in another opinion piece, this is a watershed moment for the American polity. He quotes a February 13, 2023, *Financial Times* podcast from the already cited Martin Wolf, "Economic changes and the performance of the economy interacting produced quite a large number of people who feared they were becoming losers. They feared that they risked falling into the condition of people who really were at the bottom." (*Thomas Edsall, What Republicans Are Doing Is 'One of the Odd and Scary Things About American Politics,' NYT, April 18, 2023.*)

Such an observation lines up well with analyses of what happens in society when economic inequality reaches a certain magnitude. It increases a broad social tendency to see the world primarily "through the lens of wealth as the main conduit for determining one's own place in it" *(*Jolanda Letter, Kim Peters et al, *Consequences of Economic Inequality for the Social and Political Vitality of Society: A Social Identity Analysis, International Society of Political Psychology, 2021*).

When a certain cohort of the population really makes it, or gets away with making too much, not only do they become nervous, but it makes other cohorts down the ladder insecure.

Edsall's podcast goes on to say, "The immense growth of the financial sector and the dominance of the financial sector in management generated some simply staggering fortunes at the top. The market system recreated an oligarchy. Those who suffered felt the parties of the center-left had largely abandoned them and were no longer really interested in their fate" (Edsall, ibid).

In the meantime, the militant Republican Party and their militant capitalist cohort align themselves with forces of populist agitation whose targets, among others, are the liberal mindset, ethnic/racial minorities, public education, libraries, gun laws, and the public's interest in a healthy environment.

The turbulence thus generated destabilizes society and conveniently serves to augment claims that wealth, property, and the market capitalist paradigm itself are under assault.

Opposed to these brewing alignments, on the other end of dialectic contradiction, stands broad, democratic human solidarity in all its forms. Despite all material challenges, this solidarity remains a testament to non-material social values. And it can be re-enacted through systemic economic re-alignment.

The scale of political polarization defies conventional analysis. It is ill-constituted. The Republican side enacts economic piracy, unrestrained by conventional norms and rules of political discourse and debate, not to mention any ledger that includes public goods and social welfare. They advocate for the disintegration of economic and political systems that serve social equality, equal opportunity, and social unity.

Meanwhile, the Democratic Party and its supporters, represent the heritage and ideology of equality and social justice. They still contest political power in more customary terms. Democrats are in a street fight, wielding policy paper swords against opponents armed with the knives of class interest. The only remedy is to call out the bully's plan and tactics with more forceful political and economic rhetoric and programmatic coherence.

The democratic interest or belief system generated the Civil Rights Movement, the Great Society legislation of the 1960s, and the economic policies of the New Deal in the 1930s. It sustained the country in wars against fascism and totalitarianism and remains a great well of social identity — in dire need of renewal. It has been forged by transformative events on our own shores, including the Civil War, which ended slavery, and the founding War of Independence from Great Britain.

The democratic heritage of representation, equal rights, and the rule of law is heralded and embedded in the U.S. Constitution. It still stands as a beacon to the world, shining until recently in the name of democratic sovereignty and the outlay of American funds, weaponry, and popular support for embattled Ukraine.

At the moment, however, and in contrast to the immediate authoritarian upsurge, the Democratic party agenda is dogged by a certain incoherence. It appears mostly unable to articulate and renew a compelling economic agenda, one that assures capital interests while upholding economic justice and social solidarity. It too, is captive to outworn, and obsolete market capitalist precepts.

It is still possible to counteract oligarchic interests and the malignant ascendancy of globalized, multinational capitalism. But since the defeat of the Harris-Walz Democratic Party presidential ticket, time appears to run short.

A survey of recent political history accounts, in part, for the setback of the democratic agenda, but it is also useful to invoke Hegel's standards of freedom and equality, as measures of self-consciousness and ideological orientation. It is plain that the old balance between freedom and equality, the counterpoints of modern consciousness, has grown skewed and confused.

That balance is based on the recognition that freedom respects equality, and equality respects freedom. Either without the other stultifies the spirit, or leads to massive polarization. In the collapse of that balance, the "master-slave" dynamic comes to the fore again in almost naked terms. Authoritarian government represents a breakdown of civic freedom and the equality of democratic rights. It poses, instead, the assertion of autocratic party domination and mastery.

At this point, it is important to recall Martin Wolf's observation, cited earlier, that despite the inequalities of economic outcome, necessary in any competitive economic system, the "Ideal of equality of status among all adult citizens is one of the great moral and practical achievements of democratic modernity" (ibid, p. 25). This echoes Hegelian standards, mentioned earlier, and invokes the great balance between equality and freedom achieved by democratic capitalism. That balance now teeters. To recall: "There are two main ways in which this delicate balance between politics and market (ideological and materialist conditions) can be destroyed: state control over the economy and capitalist control over the state" (ibid, p. 29). This sizes up the contemporary crux of polarization. Polarization is dogged by systemic contradiction and the truncation, and distortion of political and economic discourse.

Recent Political History

The backdrop to this truncation involves recent political history. Ever since the landslide defeat of George McGovern to Richard Nixon in the 1972 presidential election, the Democratic Party has faltered in upholding the interests of its core constituency—the interests of Labor. As Joshua Mound points out in a 2016 *New Republic* article, "Following McGovern's defeat, Democrats began running toward the center and haven't looked back, even though that center seems to have moved further and further to the right with each passing election" (*What Democrats Still Don't Get About George McGovern*, The New Republic, 2/29/2016). All political parties, over the decades, understandably adjust their agenda to changes in the marketplace, moods of the electorate, and historical national conditions. Such adaptations occurred during the hyperinflation and oil embargo of the 1970s, the purported austerity and low taxes of the 80s, the triangulation of the 90s, and, after 9/11, the neoliberal policies of the 2000s, and so on. In acceding to the Republican argument over taxation in the 1980s and 90s, however, and not fighting instead for worker wage parity or bolstering the progressive tax system, the Democratic Party lost its political orientation and standing. They mistook the historical moment and forsook their historical mission.

The interests of labor, ever at risk of becoming subordinate or unequal to those of capital, were overrun by claims - especially after the hyperinflation of the 1970s - that the capitalist system was endangered. Ever since then, the Democratic Party has attempted to straddle the line between Capital and Labor. It couldn't, or didn't, extend its policies beyond the stamp of "welfare-state tax and spend," by which it would be branded and to which it has partially succumbed. It has supported an alleged meritocratic, market-based conception of income distribution, instead of advocating that all labor has merit and should be compensated accordingly, beyond what the market, narrowly construed, might stingily offer. There are, however, other kinds of markets - the European Social Market, for one - where the interests of labor are sanctioned by law and custom and are a central variable in most economic equations. This is the lodestar for ideological and policy reformation.

Back in the 1990s, it may have appeared politically advantageous for the Clinton administration to "triangulate" ideas from the political left and political right to create a new electoral base. But the strategy, as the Wolf quote above attests, ultimately left the working poor and legions of underpaid workers stranded. Currently, the Democratic party's putative electoral advantage is at risk. Now it has to surmount redoubled threats of economic exclusion and inequality, which its policies indirectly enabled. Hence, as Mound further notes in the *New Republic* article, "Democrats are unable (sic) to effectively counter the expanding extremism of the GOP or the increasing income and wealth inequality and persistent racism that Republican radicalism (sic) has facilitated." (ibid) These political realities have only intensified since 2016, when Mound first made his observations. The divided allegiances of the Democratic quandary still abide.

At this point, somewhat ironically, it is the Democratic Party and Democrats across the country who appear to be the primary curators or conservators of the national heritage. Militant Republican, authoritarian interests foreseeably plan to extinguish or overthrow that heritage. Their legitimate disagreements with tax-and-spend policies over the years have morphed and metastasized into non-negotiable dogma. The dogma has been transfigured into a coordinated and planned assault on liberal- democracy, and the freedoms of its civic, judicial, journalistic, religious and educational heritage - the bedrocks, that underpin the identity and future of the American republic. Usually, after electoral defeat or disappointment, political parties realign toward the political center. But since the Trump election and the introduction of "alternative facts" into the American political discourse, Republicans have abandoned such course corrections. As the Edsall article further relates, public policy Professor Jack Goldstone of George Mason University points out that, "When the Republicans lost the presidential election in 2020 and did much worse than expected in 2022 (even worse than in a normal midterm contest), they did not abandon the leaders and policies that produced these results. Instead, they have doubled down on even more extreme and broadly unpopular leaders and policies, from Trump, to abortion and guns." *(What Republicans Are Doing Is 'One of the Odd and Scary Things about American Politics'*, ibid) This surely reflects the determination of the militant capitalist economic class.

The mendacity of their route to asserting authoritarian control is now nakedly visible. It lies in removing "vertical accountability" through extensive gerrymandering and voter suppression. Democrats' loss of "horizontal accountability" resulting in control over legislative, executive, and judicial branches of government since 2024 is an accomplished fact. (Thomas Edsall, ibid) The mounting challenge to democratic ideals and processes must be confronted in all its guises, especially by a renewed liberal democratic vision.

Congressional deadlock, as noted, provides further evidence of the long-standing Republican campaign to make government serve capital. It is a campaign that is contingent, as always, on the twists and turns of contemporary times. The threatened shutdown by House Speaker Kevin McCarthy in 2023 over raising the governmental debt ceiling is only the latest in a long line reaching back at least 30 years. Such political machinations are made strictly at the behest of bloated and distorted capitalist economic interests.

Shutdowns in 1995-96, in 2013, and again in 2018-19 extended tactics to provoke governmental dysfunction. Again, under the guise of democratic procedure and alleged fiscal prudence, militant Republicans threw down a gauntlet to undermine the social and political compact. These events were not aberrations, but part of a long-term strategy to divest federal and state governmental interest and financial control over business and corporate affairs. Such brinksmanship, as with other obstructionist tactics mostly of benefit to Republican interests, has damaged trust in governmental function. On a bipartisan basis, Congress approved massive expenditures for infrastructure and health care under the Biden administration. Now, however, the tables have turned. The current Republican majority, in concert with large corporate interests, seeks to undermine the long-standing pluralist system of democratic interest-group advocacy and representation.

As Robert Reich, the former Secretary of Labor, points out, the "corporate takeover of American politics" began with a strategy of corporate lobbying to take control of federal and state government business policy. *(How the Corporate Takeover of American Politics Began,* Robert Reich, YouTube, December 2022) Pro-business lobbyists are funded over public interests' groups, especially in election years, at a ratio of 6:1 - that is, $6 billion to $1 billion dollars. (ibid) This means that pluralist advocacy carried out by such entities as consumer, environmental, and labor interest groups are increasingly overwhelmed by highly financed business and industrial special-interest lobbies. Through hefty financial contributions, lobbies for gun rights, pharmaceuticals, medical insurance, the US Chamber of Commerce, or the Business Roundtable have come to exert lock-like political influence and constraint on state and national political processes.

The consensus and compromise supposed to be generated by interest group plurality and the voting public is overthrown by lopsided corporate influence. Consensus and compromise—and the social compact it represents—have disintegrated into zero-sum, stalemate politics. The Filibuster Rule in the US Senate, which has always protected property interests and prevented wholesale systemic reform, only enforces and augments corporate power and control over the economy. In such ways, is the 'ideological superstructure' controlled. Short-sighted corporate behavior and monopolization of the economy is manifest to the point of being self-evident. As such, it is utterly assailable. Its iron grip on American affairs can still be assailed and reversed. The contradictions must be confronted, head-on.

Citizens United

Another aspect of the rigged political process exacerbating polarization plays out in the political campaign finance system. This was fomented by the Citizens United Supreme Court decision of 2011. In the words of legal analyst Tim Lau, "The ruling has ushered in massive increases in political spending from outside groups, dramatically expanding the already outsized political influence of wealthy donors, corporations, and special interest groups." *(Citizens United Explained, Brennan Center for Justice,* Google, 12/12/2019) Incessant, virtually unlimited campaign fundraising, no matter how stellar the candidate, produces commodity politics and distrust as to the viability and honesty of the system. The contradiction violates broad interest and participation in the political process. The Citizens United decision enables Super-PAC "dark money" outside groups unprecedented and anonymous political influence. Private interest, in short, has overtaken the public interest. Policy, in this context, appears to be up for sale. The voice and equal participation of the vast un-monied American electorate is choked, if not vanquished. The Citizens United decision, not incidentally, was supported and defended, if not initiated, by the very same Federalist Society, cited earlier, as being behind efforts to establish a 'minority authoritarian' regime.

Public interest perspectives and principles are degraded and ridiculed. As militant Republican forerunner, Glenn Beck, informed the world, *"Progressivism - the idea of a common good—is a disease,"* (Katherine Seelye, *Progressivism Is Disease, Say Conservatives, Seattle Times*, February 20, 2010).

Beck's bombastic rhetoric beats down the idea that social consensus about public goods is even possible, leading to a society of stranded, atomized individuals, unable to resist moneyed and corporate interests. Beck needs to be told that the common good is as obvious as going out your front door and enjoying a certain amount of trust with the people you meet on the street.

Beck's solipsistic views echoed Rush Limbaugh's talk radio diatribes, which likewise disparaged social unity. At first, Beck's and Limbaugh's harangues appeared innocuous, consigned to AM radio dials. Turns out, these were but Trojan horses breaching the gates of the American political landscape.

The resulting cacophony of views endangers support and understanding for the overall political system. You might say that the democratic process must include all voices – even militant Republican ones. This would be true, except for voices that are patently anti-democratic and intend to repress or cancel the broad participation and representation of the American electorate. At such a time, it is imperative to examine and consider systemic change that serves all the people and a greater social contract.

Schedule F

In fact, efforts are newly reinvigorated since Trump's re-election to outright overthrow the political order.

Republican U.S. Congressman Jodey Arrington of Texas has enjoined "the archivist of the U.S. to tally applications for a convention from state legislatures and compel Congress to schedule a gathering when enough states have petitioned for one." (Carl Hulse, *A Second Constitutional Convention? Some Republicans Want to Force One,* NYT, September 4, 2022) So, they call for a constitutional convention. Given the current political landscape and environment, such a prospect is not so far-fetched. Article V of the U.S. Constitution contains language in support of such a motion. Though fraught with procedural hurdles and questions of ultimate design, many Republican-controlled state legislatures have already applied or indicated intent to apply, to finally restrain and restrict federal power and overreach. Only 34, or two-thirds of states, are required for such designs to move forward.

Project 2025, as now widely recognized, is a 1,000-page handbook assembled by the Republican Party think-tank, the Heritage Foundation. It spells out in harrowing detail, plans to dismantle, if not overthrow, the liberal state. *Project 2025* delineates the ongoing plan of execution. "The idea is to have the civic infrastructure in place on Day One (of a new Republican administration) to commandeer, reshape, and do away with what Republicans deride as the deep-state bureaucracy by firing 50,000 federal workers." (Lisa Mascaro, *Conservatives Plot to Dismantle U.S. Gov't, Replace with Trump's Vision, AP, Huffington Post*, August 29, 2023) This would extend a "Schedule F" Executive Order issued by Trump during his first term, which "reclassified tens of thousands of the 2 million federal employees as essentially at-will workers who could be more easily fired." (ibid) Upon taking office, the 'Schedule F' order was rescinded in 2021 by President Biden. Schedule F, brutishly implemented by Elon Musk in 2025, among others, is now patently revived. It involves reverting federal employment to what Public Administration Professor Mary Guy of the University terms the "political spoils patronage system of the 1900s." (ibid)

Such developments confirm what is termed the Unitary View of Executive Power, also promulgated by the Heritage Foundation, which would cede "autonomous power" to the U.S. President. This defies and upends the "checks and balances" tradition and design of the U.S. Constitution in which the powers and duties of each governmental branch are defined in such a way as to contain and balance their function. Remember, the Founding Fathers who framed the Constitution had just escaped Britain's imperial government. They were determined to restrain governmental power. In 2024, the U.S. Supreme Court's ruling in favor of presidential autonomy and unspecified immunity presages a radical break and departure from the American heritage of democratic government. It can only be hoped that the Supreme Court's earlier 2023 decision to deny the applicability of the "Independent State Legislature Theory" will not now be overturned by executive fiat. An affirmative interpretation of the theory would have "given states wide authority to gerrymander election maps and pass voter suppression laws," not excluding the power to overturn the results of otherwise free and fair elections. (Ethan Herenstein, Thomas Wolf, *The 'Independent State Legislature Theory' Explained,* Brennan Center for Justice, 6/30/2022)

Such is only a partial account of stalemate, contradiction, and conflict in the American political sphere—resulting from and contributing to national polarization. Further contradictions in economic and socio-psychological spheres need attending as well. For the present, if you want, shout into a well. Maybe you'll raise an echo. Or better yet, give your consternation a more constructive outlet. Your representative would love to hear your protest. Or better yet, check your dialectics and organize friends around a democratic cause. The materialist moment raises a distorted authoritarian, illiberal ideology that trammels all over the freedoms of association, discourse and speech upon which personal sanity depends. In any case, acting as though nothing were amiss is no longer tenable. The redcoats are not only coming; they have arrived.

Class War and Politics

Class war is typically associated with the downtrodden masses rising up to overthrow an unjust system and class oppression.

The ongoing class war in America demonstrates a fairly unprecedented reactionary campaign to overthrow the democratic welfare state and its rule-of-law, from the top - social solidarity dividends be damned. The ascendency of reactionary capital in the last 43 years, in whose league you will find figures like the Koch Brothers, Peter Thiel, and a host of other financial and corporate interests, threatens an oligopolistic takeover.

Kleptocracy, if you can believe it, is not too strong a word, or description for the designs of the ongoing regime, in which *"a society or system is ruled by people who use their power to steal their country's resources."* (*Kleptocracy*, Wikipedia.org).

Not that there is anything necessarily wrong, or bad, about capital, but it is only one side of a coin minted by labor. Capital and the capitalist market system are indispensable as long as each function and is committed to a larger social ethos. But that commitment is now threadbare. Capital interests become increasingly bare-knuckled and audacious. Currently, capital and its representatives have a stranglehold on tax policy. Democrats have to kick and scratch to restore some semblance of tax equity in the system. Joe Biden was unsuccessful in raising the top tax rates for individuals up to 39.6% and on corporations from 21% to 28% (Investopedia). But Democrats and the Democratic Party are not helpless. They must change the script to envision and re-articulate a new ethos of American capitalism. Democrats and fair-minded capitalists of all stripes are left to uphold democratic norms and a reconstituted welfare state. That state has forestalled mass poverty, but it now must be extended through new institutions that invigorate social interest alignments in the name of greater shared material well-being and social unity. As it stands, the Democratic Party struggles to garner enough popular support for its time-worn social and economic agenda. Welfare state constituencies are scattered and atomized. Many just manage to scrape by. Liberal support is strong but thin. These constituencies and others were enough to hold the line in the 2020 national election, but not in 2024.

Starting in the 1990s, the Democratic Party increasingly aligned itself with the interests of finance, business, and capital. It compromised its long-standing support of and allegiance to the interests of labor. It relinquished an economic vision by which mobility could be realized for all classes of wealth - a devil's bargain indeed. It exchanged its own short-term political prospects without resolving the one economic contradiction or problem that all societies must eventually come to terms with – the tension between capital and labor. The Democratic Party seemed to escape the 'materialist dialectic' moment or reckoning that Austria confronted, but that moment has returned with a vengeance, heralded by economic inequality, wide-ranging poverty, polarity, and division in American society. The contest between American capital and labor, once epic, has been distorted and contrived in the past decades. It has been eviscerated by successful advertising, public relations, political ineptitude, the virtual atomization of the workforce, and the concomitant breakdown of the American labor movement.

Reagan Revisited

The protracted and lamentable downfall of the American labor movement was decades in the making. One of the more poignant chapters unfolded during the Reagan years. A strike for higher wages conducted by 11,000 unionized Air Traffic Controllers was broken. The upward wage pressure exerted by organized labor represented not only a threat to profits, but to the status and prospects of capital. Maintaining unwarranted, huge, profit margins, fighting inflation, and thwarting its organized power meant unions had to be subdued. To this effect, as pointed out in a recent *NYT Opinion* piece, Bryce Covert cites the 1980s Federal Reserve Chairman Paul Volcker's efforts to tame economic inflation and recession. Volcker stated, "It was very clear that what he was doing required getting negotiated wage settlements down." *(The Fed's War on Inflation is a Class War,* 3/31/2023). To tame inflation, Volcker raised interest rates to a shocking "20-21.5% in 1981," (Paul Volcker, *interest rates*—Wikipedia), an all-time high in the modern era. Get a load of that. This, of course, prompted the recession from 1980-1982, "in which the national unemployment rate rose to over 10%" (ibid). Reagan had won a great victory, at least for the interests of business and finance, at a decades-long cost to the laboring public.

Despite a setback here or there and even some recent signs of labor revival, the campaign opposing labor and trade unions has been very successful. In 2021, only 10.3% of American workers belonged to a union, compared to 20.1% in 1983 and 33% in 1955. Currently, also according to Robert Reich's Senate testimony, "only 6% of American workers in private enterprises are unionized" (ibid). Given the still-powerful "go-go gone-berserk capitalism" cultural imprint that high taxes are all that ail the American economy and not low wages, labor interests appear truly submerged. Indeed, the militant Republican "right-to-work" doctrine, as it did in Scott Walker's Wisconsin, now prevails in many states to outright thwart union organizing and influence. To regain its stature, the Democratic party and labor advocates will have to assert a different agenda in restructuring labor relations and contesting the arrangements by which finance is organized and managed.

Fascism The entire foregoing commentary borrows on conventional assumptions and analysis. These may themselves be outmoded and subdued by contemporary American political developments. Fascism may not be too strong a word to describe current Trump administration machinations. All conventional bets may be off. From his overthrow of the Republican Party, to his unilateral and erratic tariff decrees, to debilitating democratic direction of the government and the rule of law, to enforcing ICE actions with military intervention, (and now ominously funded to allow the construction of 'detention centers') the prospect grows of fascist encroachment. Words like authoritarian, or autocratic may be too weak.

The Trump administration, as with any authoritarian system, appears intent on amassing and exercising unitary governmental control and power. Fascist control, however, goes right off the ideological spectrum by insinuating and forcing itself into the proceedings and customs of society. In this, it is served by putatively nationalist and racist agendas, to be implemented by incalculable threat and the brazen edicts of a charismatic leader to control entire populations.

This gives an outline of fascist ideological characteristics. To achieve effective and enduring power, ideology must also achieve fusion with police and military forces, and the class, or material elements of society. Rogue elements of American society appear ready to fuse. The military must face itself as it is called upon to occupy and control civilian population centers. But other elements, especially business interests, must also fall in line with regime designs, however errant, irrational, or unethical they come to be. Business interests may themselves resist, and form new alliances. The extent of submission depends on the exercise, direction and force of regime control. Perhaps Trump will work out febrile compromises with American business interests. A pretense of economic normalcy will be important to maintain. On the other hand, to escape governmental persecution, business elements may enter into a devil's bargain and surrender their autonomy, in order to subsist and gain party, governmental, or economic advantage.

At the onset of this second Trump era, both ideological and material conditions for fascism are prospective and formative. The wells and resources of liberal democratic tradition and culture run deep. Social and historic conditions inject contingency and chance into the proceedings; further, the ongoing political crisis (except for the crisis of polarization), is not mirrored by comparable calamity, or unrest in society. In any case, economic enticements of accommodating fascist power must exceed expected sacrifices of moral purview and autonomy. American business and economic interests weigh their prospects, but a sense of decency, pride and their own significant power may re-assert the prospects and advantages of social, economic and political convention, and perhaps even democratic transformation. And so, to convention (and transformation) the narrative returns.

Economics Reconsidered-Collective Bargaining

In the opinion piece cited above, *"The Fed's War on Inflation is a Class War,"* Covert also inveighs against the campaign to restrict collective bargaining. He argued in 2023 that recent Federal Reserve interest rate hikes take place on the backs of American workers. In charge of monetary policy and the money supply, the Federal Reserve is mandated to mediate and arbitrate Capital and Labor economic interests in America – 'to keep inflation low and employment up'. When the labor market gets tight, when demand for labor exceeds supply, wages tend to rise, and these lead, among other things, to product price increases (inflation).

By now, it is almost axiomatic that if the economy gets overheated and prices rise too much, interest rates are hiked. This curtails lending and business expansion, which leads to unemployment. As Covert points out, the Federal Reserve inevitably resolves the "power imbalance (between Capital and Labor)" in favor of employers over their workers. (ibid) This again reflects social decision and priority. Higher wages can also be compensated for, as Covert notes, by "lowering profit ratios, (leveling the playing field, sic) or increasing productivity." The Federal Reserve is institutionally predisposed to align itself with the interests of banks and capital. Rates of inflation and productivity are decisive gauges of economic activity, which can be equally accessed and utilized by both labor and capital interests.

Were it only true that enough trade-union strength existed to include its interests and those of its members as significant stakeholders in collectively bargained wage and employment negotiations. Instead, the labor interest is semi-shackled to the roller coaster of the market economy and the calculations of market managers. Had labor interests in 1981 been strong enough to press for wage parity against the rise of prices—not in winner-take-all negotiations, but as legitimate economic partners - they could have maintained, or even expanded income capacities. They might also have changed the metrics and power dynamics of the economic system. Working people, then and now, however, have lost a clear sense of class identification and consciousness over their collective economic (and political) role—at enormous cost to the collective labor and social interest. "Collective bargaining increases and equalizes wages for union workers and nonunion workers in unionized occupations and sectors." (Lawrence Mishel, *The Enormous Impact of Eroded Collective Bargaining on Wages*, Economic Policy Institute, April 8, 2021, p. 2) (**See Appendix 2: Collective Bargaining and Wage Inequality**) Economic Policy Institute research further shows "that unionization has typically boosted wages for low-wage workers in these settings the most, and these union wage boosts have been larger at the middle than at the highest wage levels, larger for Black and Hispanic workers…and for those with lower levels of education. This pattern of wage increases narrows wage inequalities." (ibid) The current fraught status of affairs results from practical, criminal negligence of these basic social, economic and political realities. The root cause of polarization in the country, as demonstrated, has racial underpinnings. But racial/ethnic rivalry or animosity doesn't drive polarization as much as income and wealth inequality. The question facing the American polity is whether it can reach and resolve this root cause, in the name of the democratic republic, to achieve new systemic balance, without undergoing, as was the case in pre-World War Austria, massive social and political catastrophe and conflict.

America's hyper-capitalist market economy remains impressively productive, but at terrible cost to at least 1/3 of the working population and to social unity. Low-end wages are inadequate to maintain a decent standard of living, much less keep pace with high-end earners. Such concentrations of high and low wealth are a dead-weight on the economy. In his Chartbook, Adam Tooze points to "broad wage gains outpacing price increases for the past 13 months." (Adam Tooze, *Wage Growth in America*, Chartbook, link 412, April 27, 2024) Perhaps, after all, the market rights itself in allocating and distributing income. The people just have to be patient over what looks like almost 40 years. They should not have had to wait.

The damage done in the meantime appears irrevocable. Society is riven by polarization and insecurity of such proportions that systemic change is inevitable, whether desired and planned, or brought on by multiple crises. A revival of collective bargaining initiatives gives hope for greater social unity and progress. Will Starbucks Coffee stifle demand for unionized contracts at individual stores, or finally allow nationalized, collectively bargained contracts? Will the UAW be able to extend its organizing reach to other car manufacturing companies beyond the Big 3? (Ford, GM, Stellantis) Recent gains may be portentous. Maybe the UAW will finally extend union reach to manufacturing plants in the American South. The point to remember is that wages should not be exclusively dependent on market gyrations; instead, the market should be designed to support livable wages. Economic transformation should not solely rely on the revival of trade union strength, but on broad social recognition of its dire necessity. European and Austrian 'partnership' collective bargaining experiences are instructive, if not exemplary.

Part IX
European Social Market Capitalism

Chapter One:
Austrian Echoes

As earlier noted, Austria had been thoroughly absorbed, if not completely willingly, into an alliance with Nazi Germany as an Axis partner in World War II. Its economy had been overhauled and industrialized to support war efforts on all fronts. At its defeat in 1945, Austria was occupied by the four triumphant, Allied powers - France, the UK, America, and the Soviet Union. Starvation and misery were widespread on the land. Austria's cities lay in rubble and ruin. Supply and demand were crushed. Black markets flourished. Shortages of every sort were rife, as was inflation. Productive capacities in the economy, whether in agriculture or industry, were reduced to one-third, to half of pre-war levels. The newly established United Nations Relief and Rehabilitation Administration provided broad assistance. Materially speaking, the country was on the floor.

Austria also found itself caught right in the middle of nascent, but growing Cold War rivalries. The Allied countries sought to keep Austria in the fold of capitalist Western economies against what appeared to be the possible expansion of communist control. The Marshall Plan for European Recovery came to the fore in Austria, where a significant portion of its' aid was allocated. Receipts from the sales of American-produced goods went into a fund against which Austrian entrepreneurs and industrialists could take out loans to rebuild the Austrian economy. According to a 1959 article in the Indian Economic Review, by contrast, the Soviet Union perceived American/Western assistance as an outgrowth of imperialist interest. In their sector of occupation, in eastern Austria, the Soviets were far more interested in seizing the assets, - so-called "German Property" -that had sustained the Nazi war effort. As war reparations, they expropriated the resources of over "420 industrial and trade enterprises" and "millions of tons of oil" without payment (*The Development of Austria's Economy and Export Trade in the Post-War Years*, JSTOR, p.70). The Western nations weren't interested in confiscation; they were focused on investment.

To defend itself from economic depredation, and protect what remained of its industry, the fledgling government of Austria's Second Republic "nationalized important basic industries in 1946/1947, as well as the sectors of banking and hydroelectric and electric power generation." (ibid, p. 72). It pursued the development of heavy industry in metal processing, textiles, chemicals, iron ore, and tourism. There was a meteoric rise in foreign trade" (ibid, p. 73). In this case, industrial nationalization saved the country. The role of government was instrumental, as was the burgeoning revival of the Trade-Union Federation and the Business Chamber of Commerce. Combined, these entities determined and defined, in fledgling partnership, the nature of post-war Austrian industrial relations – particularly the relationship between employer and employee. A further article on that period, entitled *Austrian Economic Growth and Governmental Policy: A Country Study* (Google, Washington GPO, Library of Congress, 1994), makes clear that the "occupation (of Allied forces) encouraged Austrian people into a more cooperative attitude toward each other and toward their leaders" (p. 1). Austria responded to the incentives of the Marshall Plan and produced what many observers describe as an "economic miracle in economic rehabilitation" (ibid). To finally usher out occupation forces of whatever national stripe, and reassert long-standing national pride and dignity, Austrians had to demonstrate unequivocal social, political, and economic unity and viability.

For reasons previously noted in the chapter on neo-corporatism, the lion, so to speak, lay down with the lamb. But the period was not without contest and rancor. The largely nationalized economy, labor and business councils, commissions, and the national Parliament thrashed out agreements that laid the groundwork for the equitable, yet productive political-economic system of Social Partnership. Social Partnership takes many forms in Europe and elsewhere. The Austrian form is distinct, if not unique, wherein the "organizations representing the economic partners are integrated to a considerable extent in the whole process of national policy formation" (Joan Traub, *Co-determination and the New Austrian Labor Code: A Multi-Channel System of Employee Participation*, JSTOR, *The International Lawyer*, Vol. 14, No. 4, Fall 1980, pp. 613-635).

And it does so to this day. It continues to share definable, common Partnership characteristics that "involve coordinating the collaboration of key interests, freeing the state from deep involvement in organizing work and wages while overcoming economic distortions and solving collective action problems such as training" (Scott L. Greer and Michelle Falkenbach, *National Library of Medicine - National Center for Biotechnology Information, Social partnership, civil society, and health care*, ncbi.nlm.nih.gov/books/NBK). In Austria today, packages of collective wage bargaining continue to be thrashed out by the Social Partners on an annual basis. The partners, as indicated above, include the Austrian Trade Union Federation (ÖGB), representing unions across the country, and spanning seven sectors of industry and business, along with their counterparts from the Chamber of Commerce, which negotiates on behalf of the entire, diverse field of business and industry. Their negotiations yield collectively bargained wage agreements that cover "around 98% of all Austrian workers" (Vera Glassner and Julia Hofmann, *Collective Bargaining in Europe, Austria: from gradual change to an unknown future*, 2018). It is one of the highest rates in the world, not to mention Europe. Wage floors are established and top-end salaries are restrained. Flattened pay scales and sectoral bargaining establish a level playing field for business and industry. To repeat, according to *The Economic Times* "CEO'S in the USA 'earn on average 265 times more than the typical worker. The Austrian CEO: Typical Worker salary ratio is 49 times more (*Global CEO Pay-to-Average Income Ratio*, Bloomberg, International Monetary Fund, December 2017). General prosperity abides. Greater wage parity puts more money into more pockets and this is seen to support the economy. Decisively, this garners general, if ever-watchful business interest support. These are the foundation stones of Austria's social market economy.

Chapter Two:
Social Partnership Origins and Development

In the beginning of this era, many breakthroughs had to occur. The "economic royalist" perspective, not to mention conventional economic thinking, was overturned when labor agreements were achieved almost unbelievably on a nationwide basis!" Charles Gulick, *Collective Bargaining or Legal Enactment: The Austrian Development,* International Review of Social History, vol. 2, pp351-370).

At the same time, nationalized agreements created a level playing field for all businesses concerned and permitted competitive market coordination. To this day, though ever-contested, forthright and enduring Social Partnership arrangements and negotiations resolve knotty business and labor economic concerns.

With Finland and Sweden, Austria joined the European Economic Community (EEC) in 1995. The EU commenced in 1957 to promote broad European economic integration, - first with six, then nine, then twelve, then fifteen countries, until the formation of the European Union Social Market in 2000. Austria was an original member and adopted the Euro as its national currency.

After close to forty years in which important sectors were nationalized, the Austrian economy was mostly re-privatized in 1992. The government still holds market interest shares in these enterprises, but private interests are again allowed to dominate. In the meantime, economic globalization has created new and different economic challenges and opportunities. The bonds of Austria's Social Partnership have been tested, but remain steadfast.

Inflation pressures also test the Social Partnership bond. Well -organized labor interests exert ongoing demands for wages to keep up with inflation. Their interests are consulted and included, not ignored, or overridden. Concessions must be calibrated, not to contribute to inflation, while maintaining business profit incentives. Especially in the current Ukrainian War economic environment, however, capital and business interests are strained to meet these demands. But the maintenance of wage and price parity is the lodestone of Social Partnership viability. As noted above, consumer purchasing power flows back into the production of goods and services, keeping inflation at bay.

Social Polarization and Immigration

Social polarization also comes to the fore in Austria around the issue of immigration. There is a longstanding Turkish immigrant population that dates back at least to the 1960s and the years of original economic expansion. Now in its third generation, this population has largely been integrated.

Additional arrivals, however, pose new social assimilation challenges, as does an ongoing influx of immigrants from the Middle East and Africa. This excites nationalist, if not racist, resistance, which gains political momentum and further tests national and provincial political equilibrium.

So far, Austria's coordinated market economy, within Europe's Social Market provides economic and social ballast and security. The stability of Austria's coordinated market contains polarization and extreme social conflict, but critical challenges remain. Many people question why the benefits of the social state should be afforded to new populations who haven't contributed to its upkeep. Such observations lose track of the potential contributions these populations will make to future economic development. Social solidarity is tested.

The Austrian School of Economics and Social Market Capitalism

The roots of Social Partnership in Austria and elsewhere in Europe lie as much in historic socialist aspirations and ideology as in the realities and conditions of market capitalism. The heritage of Austrian market capitalist enterprise goes way back.

The *"Austrian School of Economics" (Wikipedia)* fostered some of the greatest champions of capitalist economic philosophy in the 20th century. Figures such as Friedrich Hayek and Ludwig von Mises were lion-hearted free-market advocates, with a streak of libertarianism. They were staunch opponents of "planned economy" doctrines and promulgated the textbook primacy of *"individualism, the concept that social phenomena result exclusively from the motivations and actions of individuals" (ibid)*.

They rejected, in other words, the Marxist emphasis on economic or social class as a primary means of explaining social and economic developmental phenomena. Only through analysis of individual consumer, entrepreneur, business, and corporate behavior, these free-market advocates maintained, could stable conclusions be formed about market development.

Only through strict calculations of supply and demand that business entities make can scarce material and capital resources be most efficiently employed. On this basis alone, they argued, are such issues as cost, price, and wages adequately and economically settled. Those active in the market - shop owners, businesspeople, and investors, not to mention consumers, - are the best judges of its tendencies.

To operate properly, the competitive market must be made as free as possible from external state interference. Only then could the market optimally and efficiently produce and allocate goods and services.

The Social Market Economy and its Origins

Of course, this is a far cry from market realities today, when state intervention across the world, to one degree or another, is more of a norm. Still, the capitalist character of European and Austrian Social Market economies is important to emphasize because, from American perspectives, they are so often branded as *"socialist"*- that is, economic systems that are state-planned and dictated.

The origins of the European Social Market idea are also important to recall. It has a historic pedigree that went through the wringer of economic philosophical contention and debate.

The European Social Market emerged from historical calamity. Germany had undergone the cataclysm and horror of World War II and fascist dictatorship. It had witnessed firsthand the criminal excesses of *"corporatist"* state economic planning. It was desperate to rebuild itself and bid adieu to Allied occupation forces.

West Germany was in an existential struggle not only to outperform the alleged *"communist"* state being set up by former fellow citizens in East Germany, but to do so while providing and maintaining social and economic security and justice. Such conditions and capitalist views, as described above, were instrumental in the formation of both German and Austrian post-war economies and in the development of Europe's Social Market economy.

After the destruction and devastation of World War II, it was incumbent on those who followed to create a stable economic model that borrowed from, - but transcended, - economic systems of the past. In Hegelian terms, this represents in profound dialectical resolution of capitalist and socialist approaches. "The Social Market Economy was the creation of the German Ordoliberal (Ordered Market) Freiburg School and, in particular, of the economists Walter Eucken, Alfred Müller-Armack, Wilhelm Röpke, and the former German Chancellor Ludwig Erhard. "It was in 1946 that, for the first time, Müller-Armack proposed adopting a new economic system, a third way between laissez-faire and state-planned economies - the Social Market Economy. Doing so required following a 'market freedom with social 'balance,' that combines the productive prosperity of a capitalist-driven economy with institutions and regulations guided by the pursuance of social justice as a new style of economic policy." (Ignacio Herrera Anchustegui, *The Social Market Economy and the European Union,* Social Science Research Network, Maastricht University, p. 75 January 2016).

Their theories developed and deployed the productive and competitive capacities of capitalism, but within a *'social'* regulatory framework that would contain its exploitative and monopolistic excesses. This could be termed *'social market capitalism'*, but times being what they were back in the early post-war years, the social emphasis took priority.

They invoked the pursuit of social justice, upheld as much by the state as by *"individualist ethics"* - the ethic that each individual is responsible for his or her actions (or inaction).

To the greatest extent possible "in this crazy world" *(Humphrey Bogart/Rick Blaine, Casablanca)*, it's up to each person to look out for his or her own welfare. There's no free ride. Social justice resides, and must be cultivated, in each citizen. This, as noted before, is resonant with the humanist outlook.

Social Market Capitalism

The Social Market Economy, born of profound political and economic insight, was the brainchild of German statesmen and economists. It helped not only to reconstitute the German state but also to influence subsequent treaties and the formation of supranational policies and institutions in Europe. The implementation of Social Market principles has been revised many times, most recently in the major 2009 treaty agreement, the Treaty on the Functioning of the European Union (TFEU). It is a treaty that guides European economic and political development without, however, being a constitution.

Thus far, the states of the European Union and their citizens have mostly (and strikingly) defeated constitutional referenda. Despite EU membership, national pride still holds the states and their citizens back from ceding too much national authority to the EU, or maybe they're just waiting for the right plan. At present, in any case, the bonds of a treaty are less onerous and perpetual than those of a constitution. What you get is a legally defined and bound confederation of states, not quite a United States of Europe.

Article 3.3 of the Treaty on European Union nonetheless forthrightly states: "The Union shall establish an internal market. It shall work for the sustainable development of Europe based on balanced economic growth and price stability, a highly competitive social market economy, aiming at full employment and social progress, and a high level of protection and improvement of the quality of the environment." (Ignatio Herrera Anchustegui *The Social Market Economy and the European Union,* Social Science Research Network, p. 74 Maastricht University, January, 2016).

The phrase *"highly competitive social market economy"* is noteworthy. It is indeed market competition that is at the crux of economic development. It provides incentive and unleashes productive enterprise that underwrites the bounty of a prosperous economy. It serves a social interest.

As the cited article asserts, "Competition is indispensable as an instrument for social organization, economic function, and private and public welfare." But it needs guardrails. "Competition should be protected by not letting the market be totally self-regulated, which may lead to abuses of economic power. Instead, the social market order seeks to set legal rules to the economic game to protect competition as such and the efficient outcome of the market economy." *(Ibid, p.76).*

Competition should be protected. Competitive markets, as noted, allocate scarce material and capital resources productively and efficiently. But unfettered competition regularly results in boom-bust business cycles, vast economic inequality, worker exploitation, and monopoly power conditions that are not self-correcting. It is not only the state that can distort competition but the competitors themselves.

The longstanding debate ensues, - ongoing in all advanced economies of the world, as to what kinds of state intervention are legitimate and justified in the name of what social interest The European social market adopts solutions predicated on conceptions and principles of economic competition, social unity, and shared material prosperity.

Walter Eucken (1891-1950), the Freiburg School of Economics Director during the 1930s and after the war, enunciated principles that define the social interest of a market economy. It is not, as American neo-liberals would have it, synonymous with, or the same as economic interest.

Eucken rejected the Marxist view that "Historical development follows and is dictated by certain self-fulfilling laws or processes," but also the view of classical economic liberalism that "Societies automatically converge to the best economic and societal order (natural order)." (Klaus Dieter Johns, Ph.D, *The German Social Market Economy - Still a Model for the European Union?,* Chemnitz Technical University, Germany, Theoretical and Applied Economics Journal, 2007,p. 6).

Society needs *"constitutive"* social principles which, however adaptable, require abiding commitment from the citizenry and the state. These constitute the central social-contract between citizens and the state. Social principles are primary.

But markets are pre-eminently pragmatic affairs. Their most basic *practical* principle, or condition is to create a functioning price system, "Unmanipulated by government-decreed price ceilings and/or price floors and simultaneously the development of institutions which impede the manipulation of prices by the private sector regarding the market economy, by such things as monopolies and cartels." *(Ibid)*.

The ideological and materialist conditions of social market capitalism come into view. It sets up practical, social parameters, beyond those given by market capitalism, to serve the efficacy and stability of the market itself, to restrain monopoly and cartel formation in the first place. The ideological commitment is practical – to maintain material relations, such as collective bargaining, (or, for that matter, higher social insurance costs) that allow ongoing maintenance of social unity and shared material well-being. *Democratic processes and extra-state institutions* are indispensable to insure the durable fusion of ideological and mode-of-production, materialist concerns.

Chapter Three:
Competitive Economy — Ludwig von Mises Revisited

It is only fair, in this context, to recall the penetrating assessments of Ludwig von Mises (1881-1973), referred to earlier as an "Austrian School" lion-hearted, free-market proponent. His views provided a fountainhead for such American advocates of capitalism as Milton Friedman and libertarian Rand Paul, and they still influence the neo-liberal free market agenda of the University of Chicago School of Economics.

Von Mises defended the market as the sole and only reliable arbiter of economic development and welfare: "It is a fact that with many commodities in many countries, monopoly prices prevail, and moreover, some articles are sold at monopoly prices on the world market. However, almost all of these instances of monopoly prices are the outgrowth of government interference with business. They were not created by the interplay of the factors operating on a free market. They are not products of capitalism.... it is a distortion of fact to speak of monopoly capitalism. It would be more appropriate to speak of monopoly interventionism or of monopoly statism" (*Human Action: A Treatise on Economics,* vol. 2 (LF ed., oll.libertyfund.org).

Von Mises and his ilk rejected the entire analytical framework of those such as Eucken and John Maynard Keynes, noted earlier, who believed the free-market incapable and inadequate in maintaining economic equilibrium. The free-market economy cannot be divorced from the uncertain social world in which it exists. No, that social world is pre-eminent.

After such economic catastrophes and destitutions as the Great Depression, not to mention the Great Recession, the need for government intervention in the name of social unity and survival was and is paramount. As part of society, business interests are always prone to disruptive social and market forces. The free-enterprise market, engendered by classic economic theory, does not function in a vacuum. It requires a social market to operate consistently, and to preserve the democratic interest.

The fire-eaters of the contemporary neo-liberal conservative market reject this diagnosis. Instead, they are inflamed by the orthodoxy of von Mises' analysis. It is their only claim to ideological coherence. "Manufacturing and commercial monopolies," von Mises goes on, "owe their origin not to a tendency imminent in a capitalist economy but to governmental interventionist policy directed against free trade and laissez-faire" (Ludwig von Mises, *BrainyQuote*).

The fire-eaters, with von Mises, would have us arrive at some sort of non-existent free-market Garden of Eden. Alternately, they might argue that the social and economic costs, or 'externalities' of a "free market" are necessary for its long-term viability. In their way, this is as much a fantasy as the utopia promised by high-water socialists in the 19th and 20th centuries.

The free marketeer utopia is a devolved position that can hardly conceal naked class interest in defense of grotesque accumulations of wealth and at least, a tacit acceptance of widespread destitution and extreme economic inequality. It is a position that now stokes militant capitalists in America.

Monopoly Control

This issue of monopoly or quasi-cartel control is quite prominent today in the USA. Former Labor Secretary, Robert Reich testifies that too many "corporations in America can raise prices simply because they can" (*Robert Reich's Full Testimony...to US Senate Budget Committee, YouTube, 2022,* ibid).

Reich goes on to note that "two-thirds of American industry since the 1980s have become more consolidated." In many instances, such corporations and industries don't face meaningful competition. Therefore, they can "raise prices without risking the possibility of losing customers who have no other choice" (*ibid*).

In this context, Reich cites several industries/corporations in the meatpacking, oil, and pharmaceutical sectors, among others, that enjoy virtual monopoly or quasi-cartel control. Such industries could have absorbed upticks in cost during the pandemic and the Ukraine conflict. Instead, they raised prices only to declare enormous quarterly and annual profits, which they then used to buy back stock, enhancing stock value for their shareholders.

The curse of monopoly control rears its ugly head.

Profits largely were and are not reinvested in the economy. Moreover, since the *Tax Cuts and Jobs Act* of 2017, the economy has been trickle-up, decidedly not a trickle-down affair - a detriment not only to social unity and solidarity but to economic function itself.

Reich prescribes a few remedies for these maladies: stricter enforcement of anti-trust laws, assessing windfall profit taxes on exorbitant profits to penalize price-gouging corporations and discourage profiteering in the future, and, most controversially, setting price controls. This last measure invokes government intervention in the economy. It is a last resort to restrict anti-competitive, monopolistic market behavior.

In other contexts, Reich invokes the lack of trade union involvement in the economy. In the European social market model, trade unions, to some extent, advance economic stake-holding claims that restrain and offset the primacy of shareholder avarice.

Europe's Social Market Revisited

Of Europe's social market origins, Eucken went on to declare other "constitutive" social market principles in support of

- Open markets
- Private ownership
- Freedom of contract
- The complete liability of property owners
- The importance of stable, if not permanent, state economic policy (Klaus Dieter Johns, *p. 7, ibid*)

Such things are generally accepted as essential to business enterprise, planning, and the calculation of supply and demand.

Eucken's support for the private sector is thus indicated. At the same time, he recognizes that competitive market orders "might lead to results which are socially not acceptable." (*p. 7, ibi*d) In a work posthumously published in 1952, Eucken invokes "regulating principles." (*ibid*) These include, as mentioned, the state's most important task - "the control of monopolies." (*ibid*)

Another is the redistribution of income, where the market's income distribution, "though fairer than other possible distribution schemes… does not take care of the social needs of society." He recommends, therefore, "a progressive income tax." (*ibid*) This is also characteristic of social market economies.

In the context of income distribution, the role of trade-unions and collective bargaining is essential. Here, income is regulated by both social and market interests, embedded in economic processes, and not by state dictate.

These and other "regulative principles" settled templates for the adoption of policy and for debate and adaptation over the ensuing decades. The extent and reach of the welfare state remain a central issue in how basic social conditions of need and want, unmet by the competitive market, should be addressed. These include such things as food, housing, and medical care. Through broadly shared, collectively-bargained wages, and company supported social insurance, including health insurance, these matters are effectively addressed as functions of the market.

This all represents a stern evaluation of competitive market shortfalls and compensatory responses that invoke the social interest.

Eucken and the founding fathers of the European social market economy devised a modern conception of social thought in the context of competitive economies. The give-and-take debate as to balancing the virtues of both is ongoing.

Original social market proponents insisted, for example, that the social market is never only a welfare state. In fact, orthodox social market thought is invoked to this day. EU Commissioner Mario Monti, who served in the EU Commission Directorate for Internal Market, Services, Customs, and Treaties in the early 2000s, before becoming Italy's Prime Minister in the early 2010s, put it quite plainly: "The Social Market Economy calls for a maximum of free market, for reliance on competition, wherever possible" (Vaclav Smejkal, *Competition Law Corporatism and the Social Market Economy Goal of the European Union*, International Comparative Jurisprudence, p. 36, Nov. 201).

This echoes the attitude of a Social Market founder, Ludwig Erhard, who argued in 1957, against the collectivist welfare state and the prospect of a "social order under which everyone has one hand in the pocket of another" (ibid). It is to be a social, not a socialist, market economy, in which economic incentive and initiative remain the primary spurs of economic activity and development. Welfare-state policies should never be considered ends in themselves, but as a means of balancing economic gyrations and social interest.

The EU and most of its states put forth a firm, socially affirmative agenda that holds the line against competitive market depredations. This, of course, means ensuring the supply of public services that would be too costly for customers, or not profitable enough for the private sector to provide - such as public transportation, care for the elderly, postal services, and the maintenance of prisons. Such services are justified in economic, not purely social, terms and are termed - "Services of General Economic Interest (SGEI)" (*The Social Market Economy and the European Union*, ibid). These are hallmarks of any social state economy, which the current Trump administration, not incidentally, appears intent to dismantle.

Over time, in Europe, more specific and detailed treaty law was necessary to define not only the principled "what" but also the "how" of service implementation in the original EU treaty. The already noted second *Treaty on the Functioning of the EU* (TFEU) extended provisions of the *Maastricht Treaty* of 1992, the first European Union treaty. The TFEU enumerates and clarifies federative EU institutional powers in relation to member states. It entitles "member states to define which services they consider to be SGEIs and intervene in the market to guarantee the universal provision of these social services, for instance by entrusting private or public undertakings… to render these services, sometimes by granting them exclusive rights over the activity" (p. 77, ibid).

The language suggests public monopolies, but note that services may also be provided by private undertakings. In the Social Market scheme of things, either entity must fulfill market efficiency standards.

"Both the Union and Member States shall take care that such services operate on the basis of principles and conditions, particularly economic and financial conditions which enable them to fulfill their missions. (p.78, ibid).

In all, such statements define a social interest or sphere that is compatible with, but not synonymous with, the competitive marketplace. Economic activity, again, is not a *sine qua non* for social interest. As the European market has grown and changed over time, it has had to adapt ideas and principles related to the *Services of General Economic Interest (SGEI)*.

How have original Social Market principles, goals, and commitments fared? How has the talk been walked - particularly with regard to the adjudication of complex monopoly/cartel conditions, policies, and laws? This is critical because it reveals the extent to which the social market overcomes market capitalist contradictions and inefficiencies.

Europe's Competition Law

The EU Commission is Europe's premier executive authority. At the same time, in contrast to American governmental design, it is also Europe's premier legislative authority. It is comprised of the 26 European heads of state, or their appointees and governed by a President nominated by its members and approved by the European Parliament.

Originally, the EU Commission assumed powers of overall economic analysis, interpretation, and adjudication of anti-trust affairs, including the enforcement of the EU's "*Competition Law*" defining and stipulating anti-trust policy. The duly delegated Commission was soon overrun with cases and challenges to its judgments.

So, as Vaclav Smejkal's *Competition Law* article cited above states, it became necessary for the federal authority to delegate and share authority with member-states related to "monopoly/cartel controls, mergers oversight, state economic aid guidelines, and market dominance abuses" (p. 34, ibid).

The EU is developing a federal-confederated system. Delegation of authority was formalized through the *Treaty on the Functioning of the EU* (TFEU). The TFEU authorized the "*European Competitive Network*," and its 27 "*National Competition Authorities*", first established in 2004, to regulate *Competition Law* compliance at national levels" (*Wikipedia, EU Competition Law*). The arrangement *"maintains coherence and integrity of the system"* (ibid). As noted earlier, EU organizational, if not constitutional development now faces imminent demands to accelerate the tempo of both.

Among other broad reforms of the TFEU, the *Lisbon Treaty*, adopted in 2007- 2008, amidst the economic crisis, was a *"reversal of neo-liberal emphasis on deregulation"* (Smejkal, p. 34, ibid).

While banks were failing in the USA and then being re-liquidated, the European Union revamped anti-trust policy.

The EU anti-trust system must maintain "coherence and integrity." As one would expect, however, there is an ongoing tug-of-war between federal and state authorities as to how and when legal prohibitions against cartels/monopolies and abuses of dominant market positions should be enforced.

EU member states, for example, often resist strict enforcement of Competition Law "on behalf of their most salient national companies" (*Wikipedia - EU Competition Law*).

By the same token, Treaty Law strictly controls amounts of "direct and indirect monetary aid" member states can give "to companies to enhance their competitive position" (ibid).

This is an especially sensitive topic, given the varied regions of the European Union, where different economic standards and conditions exist. It is an ongoing effort to maintain harmony, unity, and balance between the wealthier European regions of the north and west with those of the south and east, to ensure fair market practices.

The *National Competition Authority* offices, mentioned above, have plenty of work to do. Anti-trust law and policy on behalf of maintaining a free (competitive) market continue to be adapted and applied, as stipulated by the *Competition Law* at both federal and state levels.

Under Articles 101 and 102 of the TFEU, infringements such as price-fixing and the abuse of market position dominance are prohibited. These "cause concrete harm to direct and indirect customers and end-consumers in the form of higher prices and/or loss of profits" (*Antitrust damages actions in Europe*, europa.eu, Competition Policy").

Long-established *European Court of Justice* case law already entitled "any individual, citizen or business, to claim full compensation for the harm caused to them by such infringements of EU antitrust rules."

But a lot of individuals and small - and medium-sized enterprises were denied their claims by often conflicting rules and conditions of the different member states.

So, in 2013, "the Commission proposed a Directive, which would remove the main obstacles to effective compensation, and guarantee minimum protection for citizens and enterprises, everywhere in the EU" (ibid). The *European* Parliament, which exercises power of review and approval of legislation initiated by the Commission, adopted the law. All member states of Europe implemented the "Anti-trust Damages Directive" into their legal systems by 2018.

This implementation is noteworthy because it reveals a commitment to smaller stakeholders who are entitled to sue for infringement and abuse of their positions by corporate interests. Certainly, not all claims are equal, and some don't merit a hearing. But such conditions provide a contrast to those in America, decried by Reich, among others, in which the shareholder is prioritized and has first claim not only on corporate policy and management but also on profit allocation.

American Anti-Trust Enforcement

Anti-trust adjudication in America takes place between the Federal Trade Commission and state anti-trust jurisdictions. State Attorneys General oversee state anti-trust law divisions. Just as in Europe, adjudication of anti-trust laws is an ongoing challenge, particularly influenced by administrative priorities, economic policy, and the economic environment.

In America, over the past 40 years, pro-business, pro-market attitudes have created a negative anti-trust law enforcement climate. It's not, though, for want of laws on the books. Constantine/Cannon law blogger Ethan Litwin puts it this way: "Despite a statutory regime supposedly designed to protect competition and protect consumer welfare, public antitrust enforcers have failed to achieve either goal. Responsibility for this gross dereliction of duty is decidedly non-partisan: For more than 20 years, enforcers loosely associated with both political parties have boasted of general political agreement on anti-trust policy, which has been largely influenced by the Chicago School's hands-off approach to the market. Dissent was cabined at the margins, and no one questioned the orthodoxy, much to the detriment of our democracy. For the political and economic health of our society, an antitrust revival at both the federal and state level is long past due." (Constantine/Cannon, *Antitrust Has Failed, Ethan Litwin, Sept. 2021)*

Such a view is particularly poignant, recalling Robert Reich's diatribe, cited above, bewailing U.S. corporate price gouging and profiteering.

"Corporations and industries don't face meaningful competition. They raise prices without risking the possibility of losing customers who have no other choice." *(Robert Reich Full Testimony…, ibid)* Reich's plaintive question, *"Do* we have a corporate-centered economics, or a people-centered economics?" - gives a decisive nod to the former: "We have policies in Washington D.C. that continue to improve the well-being of American corporations." *(ibid)*

The climate for anti-trust law enforcement in America, as Litwin declares and as Reich's testimony demonstrates, is due for a change. But it is about more than anti-trust law enforcement. The American market economy lacks built-in restraints, such as widespread collective bargaining agreements, mentioned above, which share the wealth and limit monopoly-forming combines. In a competitive market, there is no guarantee on the limits of competition. In Europe, it is a contest between its EU legislated Competition Law and EU Court of Justice rulings "those collective agreements, especially those between management and labor, and those aimed at improving working conditions, are generally exempt from EU competition law." (Shaun Bradshaw, *Collective Agreements and EU Competition Law, Do We Need Exemptions?* University of East Anglia, April 2019) The tentative outcome of such contests still finds that "while collective bargaining in Europe doesn't directly prevent monopolization, it can play a role in mitigating its effects and promoting a fairer, more inclusive market economy. Collective agreements, which are the result of collective bargaining, can help ensure decent working conditions and wages, potentially preventing businesses from competing solely on labor costs, which could lead to lower wages and potentially stronger monopolies." (Isabelle Schömann, *Collective Agreements and the Limits of Competition Law,* European Trade Union Institute, (ETUI) 2022

Social Market/Austrian Anti-Trust Review

Any EU, or Austrian review of Anti-Trust compliance, in actual terms, must consult EU Competition Law extensions. The handoff and sharing of authority between federal and state authorities are distinctly influenced by the longstanding legal traditions of each European state. Austria is no exception. It builds on tradition, but also must adjust to market expansion and competition brought about by participation in the EU and the more globalized economy.

Many issues treated in the Austrian Competition Act align with EU Directives, and Austrian legislators have properly amended the country's internal laws to meet EU requirements *(Competition Law in Austria*, LawyersAustria.com, March, 2023). Though arcane, Article 101 of the Treaty on the Functioning of the European Union (TFEU) prohibits agreements between companies that prevent, restrict, or distort competition in the EU, or between member states. It prohibits price-fixing, in other words, and market-closing cartels.

As indicated, however, interpretation and enforcement depend on the reading of the law, national conditions, and the attitudes of member states. Austria, for example, appears to have lightened its enforcement of *restrictive agreements*. These occur when companies arrange to contain costs or prices *vertically* within the supply and distribution chain of their business, or *horizontally* when companies in the same business arrange the same prices across the market. Such arrangements restrict competition and arouse suspicion.

Austria has seen fit to make horizontal company agreements exempt from prohibition, if:

> 1. The agreement contributes to improving the production or distribution of goods or to promoting technical or economic progress.

2. It allows consumers a fair share of the resulting benefit.
3. It does not impose disproportionate restrictions.
4. It does not eliminate competition concerning a substantial part of the products in question. (ibid)

Such adjustments appear to grant businesses more elbow room and signal adaptation to market expansion. When viewed through the lens of globalization, competition and market position take on very different dimensions. The economic playing field becomes enormous. Laws are adapted accordingly.

The Austrian Cartel and Competition Law Amendment Act of 2021 was amended to raise thresholds by which mergers are required to notify the Austrian Federal Competition Authority *(Austrian Federal Competition Authority,* globalcompetitionreview.com, enforcer-hub, 2022). This reduces merger caseloads and simultaneously signals that Austria is open for business.

At the same time, however, safeguards to protect Austrian business autonomy have also been reinforced. On recommendation from the Austrian Competition Authority, the Austrian Parliament adopted the Investment Control Act in 2020 to implement EU regulation and strengthen Foreign Direct Investment (FDI) screening.

"The definition of 'foreign investment' in the new legislation encompasses the direct or indirect acquisition of a company, of voting rights (10%, 25%, 50%), and controlling influence, or essential assets of a company. The 'controlling influence' does not only refer to voting rights, but covers any "possibility of influencing the activities of the target company through rights, contracts, or other means individually or together, in particular through rights of ownership or use of all or substantial assets" (*Austria: New Investment Control Act Widens Scope of FDI Screening,* United Nations Conference on Trade and Development (UNCTAD), Investment Policy-Hub).

Plainly, Austria's economy is comparatively small. It has, for example, only 1,090 businesses that employ more than 250 workers *(Statista.com)*. Nonetheless, many of these businesses are attractive to foreign investors. In response, Austria has risen to protect against undue foreign control: "Foreign investments are assessed as to whether they pose a threat to security or public order, including crisis preparedness and the provision of public services." *(New Investment Control Act,* (*ibid*)

The Austrian Federal Competition Authority oversees all such matters. It is an independent investigative institution whose annual reports are submitted for Austrian parliamentary review. The authority includes five regulatory agencies in the fields of energy, electricity and gas, broadcasting and telecommunication, railroads, and financial market supervision.

Where infringements of competition law are found, applications for adjudication are submitted to the Austrian Cartel Court or, on appeal, to the Austrian Supreme Cartel Court. Funding and staffing are authorized by the Federal Ministry for Digital and Economic Affairs, but otherwise, the Competition Authority appears to exercise independence and autonomy, beyond the reach of political agendas. This stands in contrast to what are often politicized Attorney General Arrangements in the USA.

In all, it appears that the EU and Austria maintain anti-trust monopoly oversight and enforcement in line with original Social Market principles, which identify monopoly practices as anathema to open, free enterprise markets. Europe's social market economy exceeds in size America's market economy, making upkeep of anti-trust oversight a gargantuan task. It depends very much on federal-member state coordination.

The thumbnail sketch offered here of European and Austrian Social Market *competition* policy demonstrates a commitment to maintaining market dynamism, while at the same time restraining monopoly forces – which can so exacerbate political, economic, and social polarization. Social Partnership, trade-off conditions restrain monopoly formation. As cited above, business tax accountant/advisor, Ulrich Nosko, notes. "Austria doesn't currently have any monopolies." (Nosko interview, May 30, 2025) But, in another vein, he decries untaxed inundation of foreign products from Amazon, for example, or China, which has shut down many home-grown businesses. He advocates a 20% value added tax (VAT) for all such imports to protect all European markets. Such global interests, in this analysis, come to exercise virtual monopoly power and hence invite more stringent free-market regulation.

Part X
American Survey IV

Chapter One:
Socio-Psychological Polarization

At the outset of this essay, particular attention was given to the polarization that divides American political and economic affairs. Polarization is rooted in an essential economic contradiction between business and labor interests. The lock hold of business interests has long driven the design and allocation of income distribution. Defense of this position results in political deadlock, stalemate and the mounting machinations of militant capitalists and their Republican cohorts. Bi-partisan compromise gives way to zero-sum calculation, dysfunction and the menace of authoritarian agitation.

Political polarization, producing loggerheads in Congress and state legislatures, is exacerbated by campaign finance and voter suppression issues. Economic contradictions, producing inflexibility on issues of taxation and welfare, result in theatrical fulmination rather than constructive compromise. The apparent failure of America's social welfare state doesn't consist so much in spending, or delivery, but in both sides inability to create a system that serves the social and economic interests of all parties concerned. Both parties, in different ways, lack inclusive, social and economic vision.

Actors on the Democratic side are only able or willing to support incremental policy changes that don't approach the actual requirements of systemic renovation and reconstitution. Republican actors, on the other side, are apparently intent on bringing the political system down. The legacies of Grover Norquist and Newt Gingrich live on. Nero fiddles.

Such positions leave the government unable to resolve the conundrum, in a land of plenty, of income and wealth inequality. As noted, social realities related to race, racial prejudice, and discrimination further vex resolution. Racism is exploited and used as a tool to prevent further political evolution and the achievement of a solidarity society, wherein wage parity, medical health insurance, and educational opportunity, among other social investments, can be afforded to and by all.

Opposed interests and agendas along all these lines strain civic comity and, at the extreme, conceivably threaten civil war. The analysis of polarization takes political and economic factors into account, but it must also consider socio-psychological factors and how these are manifest among populations in American society at-large.

Polarization can only be stemmed and peaceably resolved by policies that effectively recognize and reintegrate affected populations-where the unity of compromise overthrows polarization. Dialectical resolution, as noted earlier, occurs only when dominant interests identify and represent themselves in clear contention with intent to arrive at a common understanding of conditions, or conflicts, and reach consequent solution. Thus far, the Democratic Party is straddled by a rear-guard retreat, unable to contest and counteract militant Republican designs with an effective political agenda of its own.

It is incumbent on Democrats and of what remain constructive elements in the Republican Party to wrestle with the phenomenon of polarization in society, before it is too late. Economic inequality must be systematically addressed. At the moment, the socio-psychological fallout of polarization particularly concerns people marginalized by the economic system and stuck in generational cycles of poverty. Democrats must get over seeing this segment as a potential aggrieved constituency and instead change the system in ways that these millions can again find the tide of social and economic prospect and prosperity. Republicans must likewise get over their smug attitudes of expectation and privilege and work to create a system where employment provides adequate compensation with which to rise out of poverty- a system that, in the end, will fundamentally serve all economic interests.

Chapter Two:
Straits of Poverty

At the outset of this text, citing numbers and observations rendered by Princeton sociologist, Matthew Desmond and Thomas Piketty, poverty levels and divides of wealth were surveyed as matters of historical proportion and extents of economic inequality. It matters how poverty is measured and defined.

The American Official Poverty Measure (OPM) employs three standards: pre-tax income, that income compared to a threshold set at three times the cost of a minimum food diet in 1963 (inflation-adjusted), and family size. In 2021, the OPM counted 37.9 million people in poverty, or 11.6% of the population. By this standard, "a family of three would be poor if their pre-tax cash income was below $20,780 in the United States in 2018" (David Brady, *American Poverty Should Be Measured Relative to the Prevailing Standards of Our Time*, April 27, 2021).

But this so-called "absolute" measure of need is contested by both American and European economists and sociologists. On the face of it, for a family of three to get by on an income of $20,780 is a grueling, if not absurd, prospect. The inflation-adjusted cost of a minimum food diet in 1963, multiplied by three, is an insufficient indicator. Other needs have arisen for families in the meantime that are not being measured. The OPM is hence outmoded.

"Most poverty researchers agree it sets the poverty line far too low" (*ibid*).

Of course, poverty can also be a matter of perspective. Friends say nobody should complain. Compared to prior times, the vast majority of people in America, with all their devices, TVs, and other appliances, are living like kings. Still, economic insecurity can be overwhelming. It enervates. Well-being isn't just measured in material terms, but generally, it does depend on being able to make ends meet, at the end of the month and feeling adequate economic and social security.

European economists adopt a more "relative" measure of impoverishment, "as a shortage of resources relative to needs defined by the prevailing standards of time and place." Incomes, as Brady further finds, "confer status in communities and society, and status is always relative to that of others" (*ibid*). Status is an objective, if subjectively assessed, factor. Who is to say what an absolute list of needs would look like today, considering manifold and growing internet and cell phone communication costs, for example, and/or costs associated with transportation?

The European measure thus tends to adopt a more "relative," elastic measure of "income that is below 50% of the median." Using this measure, "a family of three would be poor if their income was below roughly $34,000 in the United States in 2018" (after incorporating all taxes, tax credits, and welfare transfers).

"Absolute" and "relative" measures produce different assessments and estimates of poverty. According to the *OECD, Government at a Glance Fact Sheet*, more precisely, "17.8% of the U.S. population lived below the poverty line in 2018" (*Relative Poverty Rate (comparison) after taxes and transfers,* Figure 13.9, OECD Better Policies for Better Lives, USA Fact Sheet, 2021). "The U.S. population in 2018 was 326.8 million" (*U.S. Census Bureau*).

This renders the number of Americans living in poverty in 2018 at roughly 58 million. The size and shape of poverty are crucial to understanding both economic inequality and polarization. The polarization effect is grasped when lower/poverty income levels are compared with upper-income sectors of the population.

In 2020, "14% of the U.S. population earned $219,572" (Rakesh Kochar, Stella Sechopoulos, *How the American Middle Class Has Changed in the Past Five Decades,* Pew Research Center, pewresearch.org, April 20, 2022). As noted above, stark income distribution differences between those in the upper 10% and those in the lower 50%, in America, disclose what appear untenable levels of income and wealth inequality.

The economic cleft between upper- and lower-income levels reveals the deep social and psychological strains of polarization. In a competitive economy, you might say, a certain level of inequality and even poverty are inevitable. Perceived need and disadvantage can be a great spur to redouble industry and training. Such numbers, however, indicate the difficulty of finally getting ahead in America. Entrenched or indigent poverty becomes cyclical and throttles social and economic dynamism, not to mention social and human well-being.

Austria's relative poverty rate in 2024, using the European metric, is measured at "3.7%" for people who experience "severe material and social deprivation."

(*Poverty,* Statistics Austria, statisik.at, March 27, 2025) (The U.S. Census Bureau, by contrast, using the Supplemental Poverty Measure, calculates the 2023 American poverty rate at 11.1%(Emily Shrider, *Poverty in the U.S.: 2023,* census.gov, September 10, 2024) In both America and the EU, there are local income disparities, but systemic responses are different. For one, a prevailing American attitude might hold that while poverty may be ameliorated, it is essentially intractable. In Europe, and Austria, on the other hand, the governing consensus is that poverty must not be allowed to become intractable.

The Poor and Indigent Poor

In a March, 2023 *NYT Opinion* piece, entitled *'American-Style Deprivation' Doesn't Have to Be Our Reality,* Matthew Desmond further frames his analysis around people in American society who are poor and indigent. He reports that "1/3 of American households make less than $50,000 a year." This is a critical mass going well beyond, as noted, the official poverty boundary. Desmond cites a Hamilton Project study, showing that while housing assistance and food stamp provisions are effective and essential, "the U.S. devotes far fewer resources to these programs as a share of GDP than other rich democracies."

This coincides with an OECD report published in 2019. The resources dedicated do not fill the gap left by "relatively low wages at the bottom of the income distribution scale*"* (*OECD Data, Confronting Poverty, America's Poor Are Worse-off Than Elsewhere,* confrontingpoverty.org, 2023). This American-style deprivation, or enforced marginalization, has many cultural and historical roots.

Forget the culture wars for a moment - the attitude continues that poor people are responsible for their poverty. America is a big country. Opportunity abides. This attitude reflects and reinforces the perspective that social hardship is avoidable and expendable.

Social mobility is a vital component of social viability. It is also a significant factor in the study of poverty, as should be the case for any society that purports to be democratic, where all social groups deserve a seat at the table. Where social mobility is at play, economic performance improves, as measured by GDP, as does social cohesion.

Social mobility is thwarted by high levels of poverty and income inequality, particularly when "the distance between the poor's average income and the poverty line" is so large - not to mention the divides between rich and poor. This "poverty gap" is defined as "the percentage by which the average income of the poor falls below the poverty line." The distance between the poor's average income and the poverty line is nearly 40 percent," (ibid), among the highest of all OECD countries. This is a harrowing and troubling measurement of the fate confronted not only by millions in America, but by society at-large. Marginalization produces polarization. This segment of the population is not only marginalized; it appears to be forgotten. This is an outcome that results from long-standing, conscious and willful market capitalist override and its multiple doyens.

"The federal minimum hourly wage, as earlier cited, is just $7.25 and has not increased since 2009" (Ben Zipperer, *The Impact of the Raise the Wage Act of 2023*, Economic Policy Institute, July 2023.) Help, though, was reportedly, if belatedly on the way. In 2023, legislation was introduced in both houses of Congress to raise the "federal minimum wage to $17 an hour by 2028. The bill would also gradually raise and then eliminate subminimum wages for tipped workers, workers with disabilities, and youth workers, so that all workers covered by the Fair Labor Standards Act (FLSA) would be at the same wage level" (ibid). Federal uniformity is essential to overcome jerry-rigged and uneven state initiatives. The legislation would have impacted "27,858,000 workers across the country, or 19% of the US workforce." (ibid) It would have represented a first step toward achieving greater wage parity.

To address the issue of wage parity, Trump's sop to remove taxes on tips and on overtime hours, part of the recently passed so-called 'big, beautiful bill' legislation, extends limited relief to only "8% of hourly and 4% of salaried workers who regularly work overtime." (Natalie Wu, *Trump's 'Big Beautiful Bill' Promises No Tax on Tips and Overtime, but There's a Limit—Here's Who Qualifies*, cnbc.com, July 9, 2025). "Tipped workers comprise only 2.5% of the U.S. workforce." (ibid.) Deductions allowed apply only to federal income taxes. The legislation does nothing to address the 'sub-minimum' wages for servers, which diners are increasingly expected to subsidize with tips, on top of often exorbitant menu prices.

Minimum wage provisions are but one way to address income disparity and inequality. Austria also wrestles with the issue. In the main, it is resolved by the system of collective bargaining, which sets wages more in line with prevailing economic conditions in each sector of the economy. However, negotiating gaps produce uncertainty, such that an informal minimum wage of pre-tax €30,072, or $34,265 provides a negotiating baseline.

It is worth recalling, as cited earlier, the status of economic classes in America and Austria. "Since the Great Recession (2007-2008) in America, U.S. adults identifying as working, or lower class (with household incomes between $30,000 and $58,000) have increased from an average of 37%, pre-recession, to 45% since." (Megan Brenan, *Steady 54% of Americans Identify as Middle Class*, Gallup Poll, May 23, 2024.)

This compares with Austrian numbers, which indicate greater class stability and concomitant social unity. 'Lower-class' Austrians, earning 60% or less than the current median income of $35,183, rose to 15% of the population in 2023, from 13% in 2013. Middle-class Austrians, earning from 60% to less than 180% of equivalized median income, comprised between 76% and 78% of the population from 2013 to 2023. (Martin Mahr, *Distribution of Income Groups in Austria from 2013 to 2023*, (trans.), Statista.com, December 16, 2024.) The status of America's economic class and social unity is comparably more fluid, and currently prone to fallout, if not outright regression.

. According to Pew Research Center and its analysis of government data, in contrast to cited Gallup poll numbers, the middle class in America comprised 61% of the population in 1971, but just 50% in 2021. (R. Kochar, S. Sechopoulos, ibid.)

World Economic Forum Measures

Comparative studies are revealing. The World Economic Forum, the one that meets every year in Davos,

Switzerland, published a *Global Social Mobility Index 2020, Why Economies Benefit from Fixing Inequality.* The index ranks the USA 27th out of 82 economies measured - behind most European countries, Canada, Japan, and Australia (ranked 14th-16th), but ahead of others such as the Russian Federation (39th), China (45th), and Mexico (58th).

The scores are measured by access to healthcare, education, technology, work opportunities, work conditions and wages, social protection, and inclusive institutions. The USA stands at 70.4 on a 100-point scale, scoring higher on work opportunities, employment rate, and access to technology, with scores between 83 and 90.2. In the category of work conditions and wages, however, it scores a regional low of 43.8. The USA has the highest share of low-paid workers, with most earning less than two-thirds of the median wage - which, in America, (depending on the study), ranges from $65,000 (Global Data) to an impressive $88,610 (Statista). The half of the country earning above the median line is presumably able to handle the high costs of the economy, but these costs, as alluded to earlier, prey on social security. The upper half can't help but notice the other half below the median, for whom the disparity is painfully obvious.

This analysis has so far only focused on income levels. In socio-psychological terms, "wealth inequality in America (including investments, property holdings, etc.) is even more harrowing." This refers especially to inter-generational wealth. Indeed, the *Mobility Index* referred to above, further analyze data to estimate the number of generations it would take a low-income family to approach the mean or average national income level. It indicates that economic and educational resources available to people in the Nordic countries of Denmark, Sweden, Norway, and Finland would enable a 2-3 generation transition.

The USA estimate, shared with countries like Italy, Korea, Portugal, the UK, and Ireland, is that such mobility would take five generations. This analysis demonstrates the likelihood, by country, that parental income determines the future income prospects of their offspring. Low-income floors are sticky, as, at the other end, are high-income ceilings.

"Intergenerational income elasticity" numbers, as they are termed, provide striking indicators related to the fairness or future viability of economic systems and how they distribute income and wealth. You might say that is exactly the point. Intergenerational well-being acts as a vital incentive to remain productive and provide for succeeding generations. It is an essential component sustaining the energy of capitalist enterprise. Inequality is built into any system; it acts as a lever. However, gross inequality acts as a cudgel of entitlement, with which those below are kept down

Entitlement, one might argue, is but a reward for productivity. But gross entitlement, as the earlier review of Tom Piketty's analysis of economic history demonstrates, is unsustainable, and augurs the breakdown of civilization and/or social dystopia.

Stakeholder Capitalism

As mentioned earlier, the World Economic Forum endorses stakeholder capitalism. This aspirational paradigm, declares that corporations should be more responsible to all stakeholders in an economy - customers, suppliers, employees, and shareholders alike - and not simply dedicated to increasing shareholder value (and bloated CEO paychecks).

The Economic Forum report asserts that "if countries were to increase their Social Mobility Index score by 10 points, there would result in an additional 4.41% GDP growth by 2030" (p.5). Such growth benefits everybody and belies the claim, heard from a growing number of the well-to-do that pronounced inequality is not only necessary, but fair.

These different GDP growth numbers may account for the wide disparity between European and American prosperity. The trip across the northern Atlantic states in America, alluded to earlier, features general small-town dilapidation, where the American Dream is running on fumes. In Europe, conversely, where wealth is more evenly shared, rural populations still manage the upkeep, if not the renovation and renewal, of property holdings and infrastructure.

European countries and Canada, to a certain extent, appear to have more successfully resolved the social and political conundrum posed by economic inequality. In these countries, incentives remain without causing entrenched inequality. These countries have reversed the prevalent American attitude or argument that inequality is an incentive, and somehow efficient.

As the seams of the American social fabric burst, however, such tropes increasingly end up only sanctioning ever-greater profits and salaries alongside broader, collateral social insecurity.

Chapter Three:
The Bicycle Reaction

The World Economic Forum's Global Social Mobility Index ranking of American performance provides insight. As earlier cited, America's relatively low score on the Work Conditions and Wages metric reflects a relatively aggressive system of wage compensation and industrial relations between employers and employees. It is not only the poor who suffer economic insecurity; it permeates the whole system and undermines social solidarity. Sociological analysis penetrates the involved socio-psychological dynamics.

In his book, *"The Impact of Inequality,"* Richard Wilkinson demonstrates the social repercussions of increased inequality: „Those who have been most humiliated, who have their sense of selfhood most reduced by low social status… try to regain it by asserting their superiority over any weaker or more vulnerable groups" (*The Impact of Inequality*, Richard Wilkinson, p. 225, New Press, New York, 2005).

It is easy to see manifestations of such behavior in current antagonisms erupting across the American social landscape.

"Your status is just as much a matter of whom you place yourself above as it is of whom you find yourself below," Wilkinson continues, "and asserting your superiority over others is an attempt to enhance your own status." (*ibid.*)

Has America really become such a psycho-sociological hothouse? You can say with probable assurance that the unmitigated, grotesque financial separation occurring in the American economy is a chief cause and exacerbation of social aggression. As noted above, it fosters dialectic force, both at the upper and lower income ends.

Such assertions of superiority, likened to a *"bicycle reaction,"* bring us right back to the jungle, where non-human primates (apes, chimpanzees, etc.) "show their backs to the top (the high-earners) while kicking toward the bottom" (*ibid., p. 224*). Thank goodness for the human neocortex, which helps to mediate and moderate outright aggression. The neocortex, however, loses energy when social and economic tensions become particularly acute and longstanding.

"Bicycling reactions include the tendency for racial discrimination and racist attacks to be most frequent in times of high unemployment and economic hardship - when more people feel their dignity and status are threatened by relative poverty. In the United States, racial prejudice has been shown to be worst in the states where income differences are greatest" (*Kennedy et al, 1997, ibid.*)

And that was way back in 1997. Since then, income differences, social status, and racial and ethnic tension in certain social quarters, have commensurately and dialectically grown more acute. As noted earlier, the acuity of income, status, and racial factors, characteristic of the hyper-capitalist age, - results from "a broad social tendency to see the world primarily through the lens of wealth as the main conduit for determining one's own place in it"

(*Consequences of Economic Inequality for the Social and Political Vitality of Society:* A Social Identity Analysis, ibid.)

Such conditions are only exacerbated by the two-faced, militant capitalist and Republican rhetorical tactic, which exploits and leverages racist and status aggression to create populist upheaval and antagonism - against conditions that their attitudes and policies largely foster.

It is also noteworthy of the *"bicycle reaction"* that people and groups tend to kick downward instead of toward those higher up the economic ladder. This reflects the overall capture of an economic system and the validation of its outcomes. Its legitimacy is maintained by ubiquitous market reinforcers - from the still-prevailing ideology of market capitalism, to commercial advertising, to lavish entertainment spectacles. By certain measures, the system produces fantastic wealth. By others, it produces ever-more threatening amounts of *"displaced aggression"* (*ibid*).

But citing statistics and income class analysis is still too sterile a way of conveying the realities of poverty and racism, which grip all strata of society. Everybody perceives the premier value and position of income, no matter how discreet, or invisible its manifestations. Everybody feels the bite of high costs, none more so than the poor or racially marginalized, and how it launches not only ambition, but deep privation and constant anxiety to stay afloat.

Leaving the current market alone to allocate income is a primary driver of economic inequality and its many social repercussions. It becomes the unavoidable lens of economic, social, and personal assessment. It is the enemy of broad social solidarity and the driving cause of pervasive polarization. Despite the *individualist mentality* so ingrained and reinforced in American social and commercial culture, recognition of common conditions can forge a transformative collective identity.

This transformation has indeed occurred in certain reaches of the MAGA movement, spurred on by a demagogue, but it is febrile, misplaced and manipulated, askew to actual economic conditions and causes. More stable collective identity formation awaits further developments, events, and existential definitions of economic interest, not to mention barnstorming campaigns, such as recently launched in 2025 by, among others, Bernie Sanders and Alexandria O. Cortez.

The times demand resolve, confrontation, and resolution, yet glaring and increasing economic inequality - at the heart of polarization persists, and goes largely unaddressed. The increasingly militant Republican side appears to herald the prizes of inequality as deserved fruits, refusing to acknowledge their threat to social unity. The Democratic side, wary of attenuating the position of wealth, addresses inequality indirectly through indeterminate welfare-state programs, or identity politics.

It defers to the market and its lopsided industrial labor relations as the main arbiters of wage and employment conditions. It lacks a truly coherent alternative vision of economic renewal and comprehensive social good. That vision should almost exclusively focus on the nemesis of economic inequality, the one basic divide that can only be bridged through:

1. The regeneration of the trade-union labor movement
2. Thoroughgoing social partnership advocacy
3. The achievement of universal healthcare
4. Greater vocational and higher education opportunities

Part XI
European Overview

Chapter One:
European Social Partnership Appraisal

The contours and functions of the Austrian Social Partners -including the national Chamber of Commerce, the national Trade Union, the regional Chambers of Labor, the Chamber of Agriculture, and Worker Councils at the company shop level - promote social cohesion and prosperity. The Social Partnership provides economic frameworks and political order without squelching economic dynamism. It resolves the dialectic impasse between overblown hyper-capitalist developments and outmoded, liberal, welfare-state, paradigms, by being integrated into the operations of the broad Austrian economy.

Austria is only part of a wider European Social Market, likewise dedicated to fostering cohesion and prosperity. The ancillary effect of these social market enterprises is to head off the iniquities and divisions of polarization, especially those resulting from income and wealth inequality. As already noted, the social market adopts certain social and economic parameters to "coordinate" what are essentially market-driven economies. These parameters were (and are) established in full recognition of historic shortfalls and calamities produced by unrestrained market capitalism. Hence, the modern welfare state was established, but it needed additional elaboration to provide greater political stability and wider prosperity.

As the earlier cited, historian, Tony Judt, points out, the relationship between the citizen and the state in Western

Europe since 1945, "became increasingly characterized by a dense tissue of social benefits and economic strategies in which it was the state that served its subjects, rather than the other way around" *(Postwar - A History of Europe Since 1945,* Tony Judt, p. 360, ibid).

This illustrates a stark contrast in the governing ethos, or belief system, between Europe and America, especially since 1980. But European economies are not simply welfare states, along lines similar to and familiar with the American welfare state. The original and influential European social market precepts admitted the necessity of welfare, but insisted that social economies must go beyond welfare provision and be integrated, as noted in the case of Austria, into the workings of private economic enterprise and initiative.

The private interest was inducted into the public interest, and not, as in America, the other way around. Both public and private interests in Europe, in dialectical resolution, combine to serve the social interest. Capitalism, as noted, is seen as instrumental, but not as an end in itself. Indeed, after the cataclysms of the Depression and World War II, capitalism was generally identified as a culprit cause of both catastrophes. But it was not to be overthrown - leading Social Democratic parties and affiliated Trade-Unions across Europe were no longer interested in such revolutionary visions.

Judt further explains that, "as a solution to the injustice and inefficiency of industrial capitalism, the 19th-century paradigm of violent urban upheaval was not only undesirable and impractical, it was also redundant. The task was to use the resources of the state to eliminate the social pathologies attendant on capitalist forms of production and the unrestricted workings of a market economy: to build not economic utopias but good societies." *(ibid, p. 363).*

Even before World War II, some European states experimented with one form or another of Social Partnership between government, business, and labor interests. Partnerships in Italy and Austria, as noted, were fascist, forced, and dictated from above - a result of respective, bitter and violent civic conflict.

Sweden also knew conflict. In 1931, the shortages and privations of the Depression led to a paper-mill strike and confrontation that was "suppressed by the army" *(ibid, p. 364)*. Such disturbances continued to prevail in Sweden until 1938 when, in the town of Saltsjöbaden, "representatives of Swedish employers and organized labor signed a Pact that was to form the basis of the country's future social relations" *(ibid, p. 364)*. Sweden's example provided a model for "neo-corporatist" democratic partnership after the war, particularly in reconstructed Austria, and to varying degrees across the continent. Not incidentally, Austrian statesman Bruno Kreisky (1911-1990), spent the pre-World War II years in Sweden, exiled from Austria, working alongside prominent Swedish Social Democrat, Olaf Palme. He absorbed a variety of social democratic-social-partnership experiences and would forge many Social Partnership innovations when he served as Austria's Chancellor, from 1970 -1982

Could America ever have a Saltsjöbaden moment? It is not only imaginable but foreseeable; it depends, however, on the extent to which Americans can revive the tenets of their democracy. This requires the identification, representation, and organization of effective democratic interests, especially those of organized labor. It depends on effective and inspirational political rhetoric. These would collaborate with comparably organized business interests to work out cross-the-board resolutions of their differences and disputes. Such a moment, unfortunately, is most likely to occur in the midst of, or after an economic, or political crisis, such as the one now occurring in America. The government would serve as the broker and ombudsman of an American-style social partnership.

Chapter Two:
European Collective Bargaining

The ground for post-war collective bargaining developments in Europe was fertile. It provided widespread traction under the guise, in many instances, of Social Partnership between organized labor and business. These didn't just arise out of thin air - they resulted from a history of longstanding, widespread, and varied trade-union and labor struggles.

Class interest and class conflict, promulgated in many cases by Marxist analysis, were vehemently defined and prosecuted in many, if not all, European countries. It caused division and polarized society. This was about to change, especially after the ravages of World War II.

Broad, coordinated collective bargaining between labor and business interests became normalized and provided redress to class division and conflict. Historically speaking, it appears that class division and conflict are preambles to social and economic progress. Threading the needle of that progress requires sustained, visionary, non-violent rhetoric that assigns social remedy for on-the-ground, untenable economic conditions and circumstances.

As it played out in Europe in succeeding years, the visionary, yet viable programs of Social Partnership and collective bargaining were significant for abridging and staving off renewed polarization. Collectively bargained agreements achieved through Social Partnership negotiations provided transparency, orientation, and standing for the working careers of millions of people in countless occupations.

Aside from the financial benefits that collective bargaining achieves, (to be scrutinized in a later chapter), it also produces socio-psychological benefits. It counteracts the anonymity and im-personalization that attend mass democratic society – not to mention the 'bicycle reaction', alluded to earlier of inter-class aggression - maladies increasingly exploited by the forces and interests of negative and polarizing politics.

What is the current nature and scope of collective bargaining in Europe? It is difficult to give a precise answer. Late and recent market conditions in each region and country are always somewhat in flux. According to a European Commission staff document, based on the OECD, *Institutional Characteristics of Trade Unions, Wage Setting, State Intervention, and Social Pacts* (ICTWSS) database, collective bargaining coverage fell from an estimated EU average of about 66% in 2000 to around 56% in 2018, with particularly strong declines in Central and Eastern Europe" *(Eurofound, Collective Bargaining Coverage, December 2022)*.

This is one estimate, among others, that reflects not only ever-changing market conditions, despite efforts at coordination, but also how the economies of Central and Eastern Europe, now in the EU, need to recalibrate their once state-planned economies. Partnership in these regions is fledgling, if at all present.

It is again necessary to emphasize the contrast between social market and capital market economies. The capital market ethos, now mutating in America, wants regulation of economic affairs left to the market, despite the unruly inequality and social and political polarization it produces. The regulatory state, the bane particularly of militant capitalists in America, is to be reversed, if not completely vanquished.

The social markets of Europe, by contrast, uphold an economic ethos that restrains the market from running roughshod over political, economic, and social conditions. The mechanics of that restraint are as much grounded in market operation as governmental regulation, through Social Partnership.

European Social Dialogue

Europe's advances with regard to collective bargaining are homegrown and distinct in each country. But they are also the result of broader, longstanding social market commitments to the European project.

In 1985, then-European Commission President Jacques Delors, initiated what became known as the European Social Dialogue between European supranational trade union confederations and "two employers' organizations, the Union of Industrialists of the European Community and the European Center for Public Enterprise" *(Fact Sheets on European Union, European Parliament, Social Dialogue)*.

Such dialogue was meant to follow up on and pursue social partnership trends in each of the member states and Europe, at-large. The dialogue contributed to meaningful treaty clauses, beginning with the Maastricht Treaty of 1992.

Levels and kinds of collective bargaining received particular attention in this ongoing dialogue, such that in the Lisbon Treaty, or *Treaty for the Functioning of the European Union* (TFEU, 2009), Article 152 became part of the basic law of the EU. It states: "The EU recognizes and promotes the role of Social Partnership at its level, considering the diversity of national institutions. It shall foster dialogue while respecting autonomy between the social partners" *(ibid)*. This statement is significant.

First, it finalizes, by treaty, federal EU support of Social Partnership as a vital component of the social economic market system. It culminates long and arduous EU Commission efforts to harness sometimes balking business and industry participation in Social Partnership processes.

Second, the statement recognizes both boundaries of federal and state power and the autonomy of Social Partnership arrangements. Neither the EU (executive) Commission nor member states should overreach and dominate these arrangements. This would exert too much top-down "corporatist" influence and deplete the democratic and adaptive energy that makes partnerships -and the many involved labor and business interests, sustainable.

Third, the statement recognizes the variety with which Social Partnership may occur at the member state level, both as to extent and mode of collective bargaining coverage. This ranges from countries like Poland (16% coverage) and Hungary (9%), where agreements are chiefly achieved at the company level, at the low end, to countries such as Romania (65%) and Croatia (46%), which are east European outliers that have higher rates, despite lower Social Partnership coordination. (Eurofound, *Moving with the times: Emerging practices and provisions in collective bargaining,* Publications Office of the European Union, Luxembourg, Contributors: multiple, 2022)

Chapter Three:
Social Partnership Status Survey

The United Kingdom is its own case. During the Margaret Thatcher era in the 1980s, social partnership industrial relations were severely curtailed, if not banished. The Anglo-economic model is simply more exclusively market-oriented than the social markets of Europe. Bargaining for collective contracts "predominantly takes place at the local or company level" in the United Kingdom. "26.9% of the workforce in Great Britain was covered by collectively bargained contracts in 2019" (OECD, United Kingdom: Main Indicators and Characteristics of Collective Bargaining, oecd.org, 2019).

In this context, it should be noted, that of all European social democratic parties, Britain's was the last to renounce the Marxist goal of proletarian overthrow of the capitalist system. This precluded the potential of Social Partnership reconciliation and adaptation that took place in other European countries; history and the fortunes of people pivot around such developments.

Collective bargaining coverage rates are highest where regional, industrial-business sector, or higher-level agreements are reached in combination with company-level agreements. This includes countries such as Germany (45%), the Netherlands (76%), Austria (94%), Spain (94%), and Italy (80%). Such combinations between sectoral and company-level agreements are highest in Sweden (92%), France (94%), and Denmark (70%). (ibid)

All of these countries have longstanding Social Partnership traditions. Some partnerships, such as in Germany, Spain, and Sweden, are more *bi-partite* in composition, where business and labor confederations (without much governmental involvement, or interference) are more exclusively involved. Sweden, Denmark, and Finland, in different ways, and for different reasons, are wary of too much governmental influence, involvement, and domination. The *bi-partite* business-labor partnerships in these countries insist on the autonomy of their dialogues and the implementation of agreements.

Others, such as Austria and France, maintain *tri-partite* partnerships involving not only the interests of business and labor, but also the ministerial and legislative interests of the government.

In France, "officials must consult with the Social Partners on any legislative or policy proposals related to individual and collective labor rights, employment, and vocational training" (Stefan Berger and Hugh Compston, *Policy Concertation and Social Partnership in Western Europe: Lessons for the Twenty-First Century*, 2002, Edition: 1, Published by: Berghahn Books)

Italy remains a Social Partnership outlier. It extends partnership and solidarity in national, universal healthcare and toward defraying most costs for higher public education colleges. (International Citizens Insurance, Italian Healthcare System, internationalinsurance.com. *Beyond the States, Going to College in Italy as an American Student*, April 2023) However, industrial relations in Italy are characterized more by opposition, or adversity, than by partnership. Business, government, and labor interests have yet to form frameworks for mutual accommodation. Governmental instability, business inflexibility, and frequent trade union strikes hobble both the economy and the unity of the country.

Social Partnership frameworks lead to different public policy processes. Social partnerships are meant to be voluntary and must be beneficial to the parties involved.

In the USA, current lock-step Republican party obeisance aside, market development is supposed to be guided and restrained by the formation and implementation of public policy. These processes are described as *pluralist*, where multiple interests contribute to what ultimately becomes governmental policy. It is a process grown deeply distorted in the aftermath of the Citizens United Supreme Court ruling, which allows, in some cases, unlimited manipulation of the political process by deep-pocketed business lobbies By contrast, in European countries where Social Partnership holds sway, public policy is formed through a process of *concertation* (ibid), reflecting the coordinated, consolidated, and negotiated interests of business and labor bodies, in some cases independent of, and aside from governmental involvement.

The European and American approaches enact two different forms of interest group representation and policy formation. On the face of it, "pluralist public policy formation appears to be more representative and inclusive, but it is also a more disparate and random approach - one that ultimately gains governmental sanction. Public policy *concertation* on the other hand, is closer to the actual economic and social operations of society, not so much brokered by the calculations of political representation. Policies generated represent more the consolidated or *concerted* interests of the economic parties involved. Conclusive analysis as to the efficiency and efficacy of either model must be left to further study, but on the face of it, the frameworks and processes of concertation are more orderly and effective in controlling the mayhem of economic development.

The fortunes of Social Partnerships wax and wane accordingly, but generally, they have proven durable and are now deeply embedded in economic cultures across the European social and political landscapes. Not incidentally, it is worth pondering what course economic affairs would have taken had Social Partnership frameworks been more involved in the management of American economic policy, during and after the Great Recession, near-total collapse of the global economic system. One terrible miscarriage at the time, a result of errant economic policy, actually foreclosed on thousands of homeowners who had been issued ill-produced bank mortgages. They lost their homes. For the most part, the banks got off scot-free.

Social Partnership and collective bargaining temper and thus far supersede many polarizing trends in Europe. Its financial benefits will be scrutinized later, as will other aspects, including facets of its educational and healthcare insurance.

The viability and scope of Social Partnership invite thorough examination, not only for its collective bargaining advantages, but also as a model for overall economic organization and development. The social partnerships girding Europe's social market augment productivity and efficiency and possess collective power that mitigates, or staves off forces of polarization, - now running loose and rampant in the USA.

Chapter Four:
Social Market Economy Law

All this being said, and as addressed in the Tooze article review, the EU and its member states must still vie with contemporary market conditions. As long as humans walk the earth, their governing institutions are obliged to find a balance between the demands for economic freedom and development and those for social and economic justice, in Europe no less than in the USA. Recognition of this manifest, social reality is the essential alloy for achieving balanced social outcomes. Acceptance of this basic human condition forms the foundation of social partnership - the North Star guiding a way forward out of social and civilizational impasse.

The injunction toward social and economic justice pertains specifically and profoundly in Europe and the EU to the rights of labor, which are enshrined in treaties and the aspirations of its member-state governments.

"Work is central to the human experience, and labor law as such, be it at EU or national level, is much more directly central to the peoples of Europe than the regulation of capital movements, financial services, takeovers and mergers, international trade, or customs duties or other barriers to free movement of goods and services, which absorbs most of the attention of (EU) lawyers" (Michael Doherty, *Whither Social Europe? –Labor Rights in a Social Market Economy*, p. 87, Chapter 5, The EU Social Market Economy and the Law, editors D. Ferri & Fulvio Cortese, Routledge

Publishers, 2019). Karl Marx, himself, couldn't have said it better.

Positive recognition of the rights and role of labor is essential to the fabric of European social and economic activity. "The EU has long recognized the key role that autonomous social partners play in labor regulation, at both the EU and national level" (ibid, p. 90). This commitment, however, is continually tested by the practical demands and realities of managing competitive market economies. This is especially borne out in the field of European labor law, "where the market and the social meet" (ibid).

Court of Justice of the European Union (CJEU)

EU and member-state commitments to the "autonomy, scope, and function of labor law and the inclusion of labor rights as fundamental human rights" are paramount:

"From the 1980s, the social partners at the EU level—the workers' representative organization, the European Trade-Union Confederation, and the employer groups BusinessEurope (private sector) and public sector employer equivalent have been given a unique role in relation to policy - and lawmaking in the EU" (ibid, p. 90).

Europe's Supreme Court, the Court of Justice of the European Union (CJEU), is nonetheless constantly called on to adjudicate economic claims that can uphold, but by the same token, narrow, impinge, and impair the rights and interests of organized labor.

In the field of labor law, as with the European Central Bank (ECB) and national government financial management described earlier, the EU combines a mixture of countervailing, if not contradictory, interests and authorities. Many authorities are involved — between the EU Commission, Parliament, and judicial authority; between federal and member-state legislative realms, and, most tellingly, between social commitments regarding labor and those upholding the mechanisms of a market economy.

The EU member-states tentatively checks federal authority. Member-states may opt out of taking part "in a particular field of EU policy," (including Court of Justice EU directives) in order to avoid stalemate collisions between federal and state interests. (*Opting Out, EUR-Lex.europa.eu*). Member-states also have leeway in interpreting and implementing EU directives. However, and as the Draghi quote given above relates, EU market integration increasingly demands cross-border European legal harmony and uniformity.

The Court of Justice for the EU, for its part, feels compelled to harmonize the overall function of the European economic system, to keep the machine well-oiled. "It tends to move, albeit not definitively, in the direction of (indirectly) undercutting labor rights at the national, member-state level" (ibid, p. 88).

From the outset of the Common Market in the late 1950s and through all the European treaty agreements, *"Social objectives,"* including those protecting labor interests, were to be "achieved only in an intergovernmental fashion, with Member States in the driver seat, and were to be achieved primarily via market mechanisms and not legislative action" (ibid, p. 88).

***

Social progress in the realm of labor law can't be mandated by legislation alone, nor can it be left entirely to market integration. The Single European Act (SEA) circumvents single Member State veto power and invokes the Qualified Majority Voting (QMV) rule. Both measures were subsequently adopted by treaty agreement. They allowed successive EU legislative enlargement of labor protections, first in the realm of "health and safety" (such as the Occupational Safety and Health Act – OSHA - in the USA) and then including "working conditions," equal opportunity, and wages for men and women, "and information and consultation of workers." (ibid, p. 90)

But what the Single European Act giveth, can also be taken away. The Court of Justice for the EU may adjudicate in favor of Single European Act provisions that limit or curtail labor conditions or rights. There are at least two sides to the story. Labor interests were further mandated in the TFEU Treaty of 1989 with the adoption of the "Charter of Fundamental Social Rights of Workers:" "From the 1980s, the social partners at the EU level—the workers' representative organization, the European Trade-Union Confederation (ETUC), and the employer groups BusinessEurope (private sector) and public sector employer equivalent — have been given a unique role in relation to policy and lawmaking in the EU — EU Charter of Fundamental Rights (EU CFR) in 2000." (ibid)

These charters, augmenting EU treaty commitments and acts, confirm federal support of labor interests. They help to bind the Member State confederation, but they arise from prior treaty agreements which reserve to the member-states authority in the areas of "pay, the right of association, the right to strike or the right to impose lock-outs." Member-state institutions, traditions, and customs of "social partnership and social dialogue with regard to labor conditions" have precedence. (ibid)

These arrangements do not, however, altogether preclude enforcement and extension of EU Competition Law, whose injunctions, as noted above in the discussion of anti-trust law, regulate "anti-competitive conduct by companies to ensure that they do not create cartels and monopolies that would damage the interests of society" (Wikipedia, European Union *Competition Law*, 2015).

"TFEU Article 102 explicitly prevents firms with a dominant market position from abusing it." (*EU Competition Law: Article 101, Article 102* | StudySmarter) But economic interest and "freedom to conduct business" involve conduct beyond monopoly and cartel. Freedom to conduct business is persistent and as much a part of the lifeblood of an economy as the conditions of labor.

Prior to the adoption of the 2007 Lisbon Treaty on the Functioning of the European Union, the CJEU "managed to avoid conflicts between internal market norms and national labor laws, by supporting a certain autonomy for labor law." (ibid, p.91) But the enlargement of the EU sphere and the 2007 economic crisis introduced new complexity and challenges. Here, the CJEU showed new colors. In court cases of the time, Europe's Supreme Court "destroyed any cozy assumptions that labor law may in some way be insulated from the internal market case law of the Court." (ibid)

More than this, in a case that involved the "freedom to provide services" vs. labor's right to strike, the court indicated that "economic freedom was considered 'the rule' and the collective labor right was identified as 'the exception'." (ibid) The 2007 economic crisis brought about a change in judicial weather. The CJEU overrode treaty restrictions barring EU intrusion into labor law areas reserved for the member states. As the author states, "so much for the 'autonomous nature' of labor law." (ibid, p. 92)

So now, there's an increased tug-of-war going on - regarding overall market conditions between federal-executive- legislative/judicial and Member State authority. Perhaps this tug-of-war between business and labor interests is dialectically inevitable. If so, the labor interest must be compelled to press its own case and standing in social partnership negotiations in ever more vivid, resolute, and renewed terms.

The tug-of-war between federal executive-legislative-judicial and business interests is presumably straightened out by the newly founded federated Economics and Finance Council (Ecofin), made up of economics and finance ministers of the Member States. Ecofin's "Country Specific Recommendations" (CFRs) "become ever more intrusive in the area of labor law, focusing increasingly on wage-setting mechanisms." (ibid)

Such developments render the commitments and clarity of EU treaties and charters somewhat ambiguous. Now that "national collective bargaining and wage-setting" barriers have been breached, as the author notes, "the role for the social partners, in the 'social market economy' is somewhat opaque." (ibid, p. 93)

The free market wants to be free to unleash productive, economic energies. "Market logic increasingly supersedes labor law's protective functions." (ibid) The struggle to maintain balance between market freedoms and public interest regulation is ongoing.

Here again, and especially after Brexit, which created systemic tremors, the EU's supranational Commission re-invoked high-sounding principles to reassure member states as to economic designs and commitments. It issued a new statement, the "European Pillar of Social Rights" (EPSR) in 2017, which mandates: "Adequate minimum wages shall be ensured... All wages shall be set in a transparent and predictable way according to national practices and respecting the autonomy of the social partners." (ibid, p.98) As constituted, EU federal law and respective enforcement powers are limited, as the quote notes, by member-state and social partner autonomy. The European Pillar of Social Rights is a "political, rather than a legal instrument." (ibid, p. 99)

Nonetheless, the document shores up consensus and confirms continued EU support for member-state collective bargaining traditions and processes.

Notwithstanding other labor right abridgements, the Court of Justice of the European Union (CJEU), issued a similar signal. It affirmatively defended the right of collective bargaining against the charge that it poses a kind of "wage cartel." This kind of cartel is not aberrant, the Court found, but "is perfectly legitimate, if one accepts the necessity for employees to combine in order to overcome structural market imbalance; indeed, the "whole process of collective bargaining is based on combining employees in order to alleviate the pressure to undercut the price of each other's labor." (ibid, p.94)

Part XII
American Survey V

Chapter One:
Polarization Profiles Continued…

As described earlier, impoverishment and concomitant marginalization - as tokens of polarization - affect a large sector of the American population. A second social group in the scheme of American polarization, perhaps overlapping with the first, includes those who have more or less completely withdrawn in disinterest, frustration, and/or despair from political and economic involvement.

Unresolved civic disharmonies leave many feeling despondent at the intractability of problems and the inefficacy of political attempts to solve them. The World Economic Forum report, cited above, somewhat self-evidently observes: "When people believe income and opportunity distribution is unfair, they disengage from social and economic life. This, in turn, may contribute to societal polarization, the weakening of social fabric, and a rise in extremist sentiment." (p. 12)

Such observations confirm the central thesis of the current analysis. This second group can be afflicted by an understandable strategic passivity. When manure hits the fan, in other words, the best thing to do is duck. This results from the enforced, yet controlled mayhem of economic conditions in America.

Additionally, conditions of economic and income inequality can also activate an aggressive nihilism - an attitude that finds all the market reinforcers, ideologies, entertainments, and endless story narratives - as empty as broken promises. The social contract becomes counterfeit.

This aggressive nihilism accounts for growing incidences of drug abuse, but also for growing resentment against any and all liberal pretensions, ideas, principles, and policies. These are seen as balderdash, impotent in addressing prevalent aspects of material reality and lived experience.

A third group, also perhaps overlapping with the first two, includes self-identified MAGA supporters. Some in this group respond with evident belligerence and fury to current political and economic conditions. It is an empirical fact that a majority of the voting population, 49.9% in the 2024 presidential election, about 77.3 million people, (according to Wikipedia) - expressed more trust in those who egregiously and repeatedly lie about the public trust, than in those elected or appointed to uphold it.

This propensity, as noted, is augmented by working-class resentment, along with a Republican political party prepared to exploit all who come aboard. Moreover, an extremely strange attitude takes hold – one that appears narcissistic and almost pathologically empiricist. It is as if social phenomena can't or don't exist unless they can be immediately seen, heard, tasted, or touched. This reflects a kind of social solipsism, which constitutes and portends an alarming breakdown of social trust and civic discourse. Commentary that tries to parse or understand social and economic phenomena in theoretical or analytical terms - the present essay not excluded - is simply too abstract or ideational to warrant attention.

The reported world is perceived as too complicated, nuanced, and challenging to make sense of. It doesn't correspond in any way to lived experience. *The news is fake*

- the reasoning goes, *so why not support a fearmonger who makes up the news just as it suits him?* This apparently corresponds more closely to the lived reality of Trump's supporters than all the "liberal" explanations in the world.

A significant part of this group has finally had enough of the current system; it is simply too hard and complicated to keep up with the American market-capitalist world. Paradoxically, their vote favors more of it. Trump becomes the mouthpiece for this exhausted discontent. Too bad that what his autocratic pronouncements portend, in the name of self-serving, oligarchic interests, will only make things worse.

But anyway, the people have voted and chosen a potentially autocratic President. Rational explanations are many, but they don't entirely capture the phenomenal, somewhat irrational hold of Trump's personality, around which - quite alarmingly - a practical cult has formed.

Chapter Two:
Authoritarian Personality/Cult

The numbers only give a rough idea of dimension. However they shake out, large swaths of people, - presumably from Groups 2 and 3, the disaffected, disempowered, and those roguishly activated, and most instrumentally, the militant capitalist group yet to be described, who substantially bankrolled his campaign - appear to be caught up in a kind of reverence and obedience to Donald Trump. They're animated by what seems to be a personality cult.

In his rhetoric, manner, and policies, Trump personifies an anti-authority authoritarianism that captures the mood of many people. It is a persona that corresponds or appeals to the mindset of what is described as an "authoritarian personality type" (William Bergquist, *The Authoritarian Personality: Contemporary Appraisals and Implications for the Crisis of Expertise*, libraryofprofessionalcoaching.com, Feb. 6, 2023, p. 1). Trump has summoned a practical cult around his personality, inciting people who, by nature, or nurture, suffer a want of status, or, as it is termed, "status anxiety" (ibid).

Alternatively, such anxiety also captures people whose sense of status is exaggerated and who therefore seek extra aggrandizement. High "status anxiety" is the keystone for the authoritarian personality theory, which builds on earlier socio-psychodynamic analysis. Supported by questionnaire surveys, such analysis was first conceived and tested in the aftermath of World War II in an attempt to understand why people were prone to follow fascist political leaders and enact their agendas.

The original theory, adopted by Theodor Adorno among others, utilized Freudian nomenclature to describe an imbalance between the "id," "ego," and "superego" facets of the human psyche. The theory explains the socio-interactive-psychological dynamic involved. It has since been updated with the more accessible and understandable concept of "status anxiety."

Obviously, every time we walk out the door, each of us has a care or slight anxiety about status and a particular and/or general sense of authority by which status is assessed and enforced. Status has to do with the interplay between external, social sources of identity - found in the community and family - and our internal, associated sense of self-esteem, or how we feel about ourselves.

To appreciate the centrality and power of status concerns, consider the "status benefits" of having a secure and adequately compensated job, a faithful marriage, and stable mental health, or the corresponding absence of these things. Envy, after all, is a component part of human nature. The interplay between external and internal status influences is fairly febrile and fluid in our formative years. This helps explain why adolescents and young adults, for whom connection with larger groups can be tentative and vulnerable, are sometimes subject to rampant alienation, if not paranoia. Each of us is concerned with how things will turn out and how or whether we will be judged. It is built into our social being.

The "authoritarian personality" scheme surveyed here applies to adults. It would place each of us on a continuum with regard to status anxiety and how we relate to authority. It measures such things as:

- Preference for uniformity
- Generalized prejudice
- Group authority to coerce behavior
- Cognitive rigidity
- Aggression and punitiveness toward perceived enemies
- An outsized concern for hierarchy
- Moral absolutism

In some ways, such measures don't seem to correspond to behavioral types associated with the Trump following. As mentioned, he seems to appeal to anti-authoritarians. But at the core of such dispositions is deep-seated disappointment at the fallout of standard norms and rules and yearning for the reinstatement of social order, whatever the cost to other people's interests.

Status anxiety can also be applied to information filtering and fake news, as well as to the quasi-pathological empiricism described earlier. If information can't be immediately sensed, according to this perspective, it must not exist. All such information is counted as alien, bewildering, or fake, leaving only room for the authoritarian source. The "authoritarian" mindset comes closer into view.

In extreme cases, as described by the renowned psychoanalyst, Erich Fromm, cited earlier, the "authoritarian character" can be *sado-masochistic,* someone who derives sexual gratification from harming others or oneself. *Sadism* applies to someone who seeks to have total control over others. Alternately, a *masochist* is someone who totally submits oneself in identification with a stronger other, giving up self-responsibility. (*Erich Fromm, Psychoanalyze des Faschismus. Über Faschismus und Autoritären Charakter - The Psychoanalysis of Fascism – About Fascism and the Authoritarian Character, Erich Fromm Study Center Berlin, YouTube*).

Obviously, such authoritarian personality traits can be found on either end of the ideological or political spectrum. They are typical of a relatively small number of people (thank God) who, unfortunately, can have an "outsized impact" (sic, ibid) on social and political affairs. They are most visible, however, where authoritarian movements prevail and are magnified - especially in current times - by social media and the internet.

But the phenomenon should not be over-dramatized. Authoritarian personalities are not necessarily raving lunatics. They can also include competent, highly functional individuals who, as noted, just don't want to put up with all the nuance, and waywardness of society, as well as the indecision of the democratic process. They've had it.

Better to let somebody (like Trump), who seems to exude personal strength, take control of the system, whatever the cost to legal boundaries and norms, or the risk to governmental legitimacy. For some folks, frustration about confusing social, political, and economic processes translates into real anxiety about status. They don't find their place.

Status anxiety compels them to compensate for disorientation and/or frustrated grandiosity and submit their allegiance to an external authority figure or system. This is not to excuse their behavior, but to understand it. Submission not only brings relief to such people, but enhanced esteem. According to the theory, they get caught up in a socio-psychological dynamic that enacts "prejudice and ideology" (ibid).

The gist of the argument is that "status anxiety produces authoritarian discipline, which 'allows' both repression of one's own faults/anxieties, and an outlet for aggression against authority," which is then "projected onto minorities and outsiders" (Brown, 1965, p. 504).

One of the central insights of this theoretical perspective, which has received a great deal of empirical support, is that "a man or woman (sic) who is hostile toward one minority group is very likely to be hostile against a wide variety of others" (Adorno, et al., 1950, p. 9).

In other words, "The authoritarian is an individual for whom generalized prejudice has become a structured aspect of his or her personality." (John Jost, Johanna Sterling, *Authoritarian Personality*, General Overview, Oxford Bibliographies.com, 2015)

It may sound a bit complex, as does any general analysis of personality and behavior. (The original Adorno American survey sample and analysis of college students, professionals, and union members in 1950 ran to 1,000 pages.)

For purposes of the present analysis, however, the proof is in the pudding. Allegiance to Trump is observable. His anti-establishment authoritarian stance is somewhat incoherent as an ideology, until now, but nonetheless clearly communicable. The message is joined to the messenger.

His apparent ability to escape the consequences of his own behavior, in defiance of political and social rules/norms, compounds his authority. It is confirmed by the discipline or devotion of his followers and extended through their prejudicial, - at times racist, and other times nationalist - behavior. As Bergquist notes, "Status anxiety to this degree is created in a collective manner, but contained by collective action." (ibid)

We probably haven't seen half of the incitements to collective action likely to come. Take, for example, Ohio U.S. Republican Representative Jim Jordan. On Trump's latest federal and classified document misuse indictment, Jordan blessed the former president, - "by God."

What an incitement!

Jordan appears to be a driven man, highly adrenalized. Perhaps he finds the commotion of society intolerable. He seeks absolutes. His record in Congress appears more than replete with "aggression and punitive rancor" and "collective action" (sic) toward perceived enemies.

As his blessing indicates, he is a disciplined and devoted follower of Donald Trump, no matter the proof demonstrating Trump's legal calumny. And Jordan is just the tip of the iceberg of devoted followers.

Each of us carries different levels of "status anxiety" in our daily lives. Each of us seeks and maintains status balance, not only in private but also in relation to the community and the larger public.

Strong political leaders elicit support, which provides their followers with a sense of social security, or status confirmation. Barack Obama had his following, as did Ronald Reagan, John Kennedy, and Franklin Roosevelt. But none inspired a cult response of comparable, populist allegiance as Donald Trump has done.

Trump's emergence elicits a widespread, almost electric response among people who experience and recognize similar conditions, - as observed at sports bars on Sunday afternoons or just driving through the country.

In whatever matter, Trump seeks to preserve his freedom of initiative, impulse and 'instinct.' His supporters outright identify with these traits, perhaps because they are patently human, and also under apparent duress. It doesn't seem to matter that, at the same time, their President is prone to sometimes egregious, erratic, and dishonest behavior that threatens the nation's security and undermines the social contract.

As political geographer, Natalie Koch observes, while driving through upstate New York, "I didn't do interviews with the people putting up Trump signs, flying Trump flags from their cars, or painting their sheds with "TRUMP**,**" but I started to have the sense that they were trying to outdo their neighbors." (Natalie Koch, *Natalie Koch on Authoritarianism and Cults of Personality,* Illiberalism.org, October 12, 2022)

This cult-like response is clearly associated with Trump's brand of authority and personality. Besides personal identification, these trade on the portrayed corruption of political, economic, and social arrangements, the so-called "carnage" of society.

Only Trump, presumably, will set things to rights. His diatribes prompt a "grassroots curation of the cult, whereby ordinary people socialize one another into the cult, and perpetuate it through their mutual surveillance. This is an intrinsic element of how cults function." (ibid)

The authoritarian personality description also helps explain the virulent outcry and resistance to the public health crisis posed by the spread of the Covid-19 virus. Many of those who cast aspersions on government health officials, and resented measures designed to protect public health, reacted because the sickness was diagnosed by an alien, and distrusted government-sponsored medical authority.

The diagnosis assigned status. The prospect of mass inoculation (against a scientifically proven virus) threatened many individuals who were, you might say, hypersensitive or unstable in their status orientation. Or maybe they were simply being hyper-vigilant.

Status and Inequality

The "status anxiety" response may be provoked or elicited by an authority figure, but it is also rooted in these very polarized times. Generally, and particularly speaking, status concerns are quite magnified - even commodified - when it comes to attaining such things as decent healthcare, adequate education, and a livable income - matters of social survival.

It's also known as keeping up with the Joneses. Not surprisingly, it is in these areas that the terrible spread of income and wealth inequality in the USA plays out most visibly. The world looks quite different between those who have secure health plans, educational training, a well-paid job, and stocks in the market - and the status each confers - and those who are insecure and feel themselves disadvantaged or victimized, in this day and age, by how to attain such things.

Again, lower-end income conditions are somewhat ameliorated by a functional welfare system. It is rather the grotesque inequality between upper- and lower-income strata that injects so much uncertainty and insecurity into the system. How much more unequal will the spread become? Welfare only goes so far. Status security gets thrown into the air.

For those adopting authoritarian personality traits, the solution is quite straightforward: invest practical, total allegiance in an authority figure who represents the prospect of rescue, or deliverance. Strangely, such an investment apparently yields more effective and immediate results than the pursuit of democratic transformation - a dodgy prospect full of self-initiative and commitment, apparently too daunting and complicated, even to contemplate. Throwing one's allegiance to an authoritarian figure appears, irrationally, to provide more immediate gratification. This recalls Erich Fromm's 'escape from freedom'.

This is all very contrary to the portrayed and assumed American national characteristic of "ultra-independent thinking." Trump captures this temper in his bloody-minded statements and manner. But such independence is betrayed by blind allegiance. It reveals that Americans are not so exceptional after all. They are simply human - just as prone to extreme herd-like responses in hard times as any other people in this world.

Staunch individualism is certainly a strong American characteristic. But, as the brief survey of authoritarian personality demonstrates, individuality is always imbued with social reference and standing.

Austrian Parallels

As an illustrative coda to these observations, compare them with the Austrian experience of authoritarianism. Examination of the Austrian case demonstrates not only the durability of authoritarian personality characteristics but also tortured attempts to evade and bury the past - despite convulsive evidence to the contrary. The bloodlust of crime is not easily redeemed.

Directly after World War II, in 1946, Austrians were surveyed with the question: "Do you believe the whole Austrian people share guilt for the war because it let a government come to power that plunged the world into war?" Only between 4-15% of those interviewed answered in the affirmative or partial affirmative. Seventy-one percent saw no shared guilt at all. (Gerhard Weinberg, *The Anschluss in the Rearview Mirror, 1938-2008: Historical Memories between Debate and Transformation"*, Victim Doctrine" chapter, 2008).

This response illustrates many things: possible ignorance, denial, patriotism but also the seeds of the "Victim Doctrine," referred to earlier, which endured as a narrative in Austria for at least the next 50 years. Authoritarian personality characteristics are rampant as well, especially the denial of individual responsibility and the tendency to slough it off onto higher, external authority.

But this also goes to the heart of the vagaries between collective and individual responsibility in mass society. The individual sphere is at times overwhelmed by collective events which, as indicated, challenge status. Authoritarians attempt to forcibly close the disjunction between collective and individual experience and perception. They interpose themselves as the sole arbiter of public interest, dictating individual choice. In this, they engender and prey negatively on human ignorance and vulnerability.

This makes them - and especially the current MAGA leadership - especially contemptible, if not criminal. By the same token, the disjunction between collective and individual experience frustrates liberal ideals and hopes for social reform and/or remedy. This disjunction must be seen and accepted as an existential condition and an ongoing challenge to political progress.

Later in Austria, subsequent interviews confirmed the longevity or endurance of authoritarian mindsets and outlooks. Even in 1978, long after Holocaust events were widely disclosed and reported, a wide spectrum of Austrians in both "left" and "right" political camps (19%) agreed that: "Worse things than the emergence of another Hitler can happen." *(ibid)* Additionally, Twenty-one percent of respondents accepted the proposition that: "Obviously, there were aberrations in the Third Reich, but it is certainly not true that six million Jews were killed."

In both cases, interestingly, these numbers are similar to those who supported Trump's Big Lie campaign after his loss at the polls in 2020. (Phillip Bump, *MAGA Supporter Survey,* Washington Post, September 2, 2022.)

The process of contrition in Austria for participation in Nazi war crimes, as noted above, took a long time. "The (Kurt) Waldheim affair of 1986 proved to be the turning point in giving the lie to the 'Victim Doctrine' (sic), i.e. Austria's existential lie of non-complicity" (Gunther Bischof, *Victims? Perpetrators? Punching Bag of European Historical Memory? The Austrians and the WWII Legacies,* German Studies Review, p. 22, JStor, vol. 27, February 2024).

Waldheim was a former UN Secretary General (1972-1981) and Austrian President (1986-1992). His denial of war crimes committed in war theaters where he had served in a relatively high-ranking capacity just didn't hold up anymore. His many subterfuges "all combined to expose a prominent Austrian demonstrating the absurdity of Austria's post-1945 victim-perpetrator reversal." *(ibid, p. 23)*

His presidency (in Austria, mostly a symbolic head-of-state position) was besmirched, but continued until 1992. Austrian Socialist Party Chancellor Franz Vranitzky's statement acknowledging Austrian war crimes, reported above, came just at the conclusion of Waldheim's term.

In 2000, Austrian Conservative Party Chancellor Wolfgang Schüssel "unleashed a flurry of restitution initiatives to get back into the good graces of the EU and to demonstrate to the international community that Austrians are serious about making amends for past misdeeds." *(ibid)*

Austria put some of its money where its mouth was. "By the end of 2000, a $400 million fund was set up to compensate an estimated 150,000 Eastern Europeans forced into virtual slave labor, who had been exploited in the Ostmark (Austrian) economy."

Such are the terms of restitution on earth. But the crimes — enslavement, executions, massacres — still stink to high heaven.

The foregoing gives only a flavor of authoritarian criminal entanglements in Austrian history. They provide a cautionary tale for Americans now involved in what looks like their own authoritarian jeopardy.

Chapter Three:
The New Executive Class

Returning to the socio-psychological analysis of American polarization, another group comes to the fore: the militant Republican cohort. Besides people without financial resources, the poor, and those disheartened and disengaged from civic involvement, the rogue and substantial cohort supporting MAGA, militant capitalist Republicans should also be included in the polarization scheme.

Militant capitalist Republicans observe the powerful social unrest and dynamics unleashed by Trump's populist rhetoric and constituency. They ensure that the movement so generated, serves the ends of uncontested political and economic power. The dovetailing of populist and more militant Republican elements comprises another aspect of the so-called MAGA movement.

The authoritarian personality type involves more than those anxious about status. It also includes those not content with mere success and moderate social standing – but those driven by hyper self-aggrandizement - Trump clones. Another element of this MAGA constituency is gathered by financial and monied interests, cited earlier as the "new executive class."

This class of individuals has now invested in the MAGA bandwagon as a means to augment and perpetuate their entitlement. The *New Yorker* reporter Osnos relates the outcome of this transaction: "The story of Trump's rise is often told as a hostile takeover. In truth, it is something closer to a joint venture, in which members of America's elite accepted the terms of Trumpism as the price of power." *(ibid)*

Taking up Osnos' article again, *The Greenwich Rebellion-* "traditional commitment to thrift and general economic prosperity lost currency after the economic turbulence of the 1970s and early '80s. By 1999, the rules had changed, the big banks had become public companies, and investors expected large returns... Instead of directing most of their capital to funding businesses that hired people and made things, the financiers in New York and Connecticut had become an economy unto themselves." *(ibid, p. 35)*

The wheels came off a system ostensibly committed to balanced economic investment and shared financial gain. Greenwich Associates financial consulting firm manager, William Wechsler, observes, "Every year that goes by, more and more of the added value in our society goes toward capital and less toward labor. What you end up with is a very unstable society." *(ibid)*

This speaks to the formation of an economic class in and for itself, which preens itself in righteous resistance to taxes and to government "as a matter of moral principle." *(ibid)* Attempts to intervene and contain the graft are condemned with wholesale scorn. When then - New York Democratic Governor Andrew Cuomo proposed raising taxes on hedge funds, he was outright condemned by one such hedge fund stock market '*casinoist*' as "a flat-out lying demagogue, who was trying to run a gulag, not a state." *(ibid)*

Such is the facade of economic greed and narcissism, which should end in ultimate social condemnation and isolation. In sum, Osnos quotes the Dartmouth economic sociologist Brooke Harrington, who observes, "The underlying massive change is that wealth no longer needs to justify itself - it is self-justifying... I look back, and I think, that's when the society gave up on being a 'we'" *(ibid)*.

The longstanding over-insistence on individuality in American culture has metastasized. It is perhaps the perfect token of polarization caused by - and further exacerbating - economic inequality. May a chorus of Andrew Cuomos come to the fore and be joined and supported by legions of middle-class Americans who are able to disentangle their property interests from the hyper-capitalist juggernaut.

It is no wonder that Trump supporters in 2016 earned an average of $72,000 annually or that two-thirds of his supporters in that year "had incomes higher than the national median." *(p. 30, ibid)* In 2020, 54% of voters who earned more than $100,000 voted for Trump, as opposed to 42% for Biden. *(ibid)* Many who enter the game feel compelled to favor policies that benefit wealth accumulation. The writing was on the wall for such people, no matter the lies, authoritarian conceits, or resultant breakdown of social cohesion.

The 2017 Tax Cut was a no-brainer when seen from the perspective of Trump's monied constituency. Now, of course, the militant capitalists in the Trump throng are flush with governmental power. They declare their support for so-called conservative causes, the vilification of social groups, for example, or immigration reform, or putting the right people on the Supreme Court. But these are just props for actual business operations in the backroom.

By anomalous contrast, in 2024, "the number of points that voters who make less than $100,000 a year shifted in Trump's favor" (Domenico Montanaro, A Wild Year in Politics, by the Numbers, npr.org, December 27, 2024). The ravages of the COVID-induced inflation surge cut deeply into electorate sentiments. The Democratic Party lost its customary hold on 'working class' constituencies. "Four years ago, Biden won voters who make less than $100,000 a year, 56%-43%, but Trump won them 51%-47% in this election. On the flip side, in 2020, Trump won those making $100,000 a year by 12 points, and Harris won them this time by 4." This reveals a dramatic reversal on the American political landscape and demonstrates, for Democrats, that to regain their traditional constituencies, their "work is cut out for them."

The operations become more visible despite themselves, for the sheer nakedness of their interest and the conditions of social disharmony they provoke. It may be, as David Brooks opines, that there are "more oligarchs in America who are Democrats," but the militant oligarchic interest is definitely aligned with Trump's MAGA re-ascendance. (PBS NewsHour, *Brooks and Capehart on Biden's Legacy and What to Expect from Trump's 2nd Term*, youtube.com, Jan. 17, 2025). They are pushing and bankrolling the movement. The Democratic oligarchs have thus far been unsuccessful in mounting an effective resistance. Their financial interest is, anyway, tied up with perpetuating the market capitalist system.

As noted earlier, however, it may be time for democratic billionaires to stand Marx on his head, put their money where their mouth is, and rescue American democracy by underwriting - the cultivation of an American-style social partnership with American organized labor. Now, wouldn't that be one for the history books?

The fourth, ultra-capitalist group in the polarization scheme should perhaps be the first. As the prior chapter on the "*Greenwich Rebellion* noted, the group has long aimed to overturn the liberal welfare-state.

The effort has many components, but none more tellingly - as will be elaborated in later chapters - than their assault on organized labor. In her book, *A Collective Bargain: Unions, Organizing, and the Fight for Democracy*, Jane McAlevey documents the litany of "conservative" efforts over the years to unseat and disenthrall democratic interests that impede and threaten the designs of advanced capital. The campaigns of Elon Musk and the Koch Brothers only scratch the surface, however engraved their efforts may be. "Right-wing corporate leaders understood the power structure of the United States far better than liberals, social do-gooders, and the Democratic Party. To take down government regulation, control the electoral system, and destroy the earth with impunity, they had to first destroy the most important corporate power-balancing force this country ever had: unions." *(ibid, HarperCollins Publishers, 2020)*

The ultra-capitalist group found their champion in Trump, one who could arouse and exploit populist gullibility, and discontent for all its worth. In certain terms, it's no wonder that MAGA followers identify with capital interests over and beyond their own rattled and dispersed, experiences. This is not to excuse their plight, but to understand it.

Corporate and finance chieftains represent mastery of the only economic system rogue MAGA followers have ever known, whatever the deficits of its performance. Tycoon success is pronounced and profound – maybe, such followers appear to conclude, the tycoons should lead the way. They don't have pretentious scruples. They are prepared to co-opt Christian nationalist, white-identity groups, and any other interest, especially those ready to upend the nostrums of the current economic system - liberal-democratic safeguards of the Republic included. It may be that the rights of free speech, free assembly, and equal protection under the law are mere historic conceits. The prospect of kleptocratic, oligarchic, autocratic rule waits in the wings.

It remains to be seen how far the second Trump administration will roll back the New Deal liberal, democratic heritage of the past 90 years or so, not to mention the principles of the American constitutional Republic. There are indeed foreseeable limits. The stock market, of all things, may curb Trump's policy designs. His tariff initiatives notwithstanding, he may not want to really drag down the domestic market economy. The 2025 Republican majority in the House has thus far been effective, but its numerical advantage and mandate is thin and may be unable to pass additional elements of Trump's legislative agenda. The Supreme Court may not be as ready to deny impending legal challenges to Trump's executive orders, as it was to grant impeachable immunity to presidential "official acts."

There is always the hope and prospect that the American people themselves will organize to oppose draconian, and/or unconstitutional policies that threaten their democratic rights. These and other political and social impediments could disorder Trump administration priorities and plans. Disorganization hindered Trump's first term. Despite the *Project 2025* agenda, it may undermine his second term too.

An ancillary part of the fourth 'militant capitalist group', also could include normal Republicans. Their worldview is fully legitimate, and associated with more normal economic business conditions. These Republicans cherish capitalism because it prompts and rewards productive behavior. It promises that anybody can prosper if they set goals and keep their nose to the grindstone. Free enterprise opens the door of opportunity for all and primes individual initiative and responsibility - each trait possessing great moral and social utility.

This embattled and increasingly marginalized Republican cohort supports stringent and accountable fiscal and monetary policy. But their views and policies don't appear to hold much water anymore against the juggernaut of the MAGA movement. Hence, we hear the resentment and vitriol voiced by Steve Schmidt, among others, on YouTube 'Lincoln Project' video segments. Many in this cohort, however, appear to submit to the force rendered by the putative electoral mandate and its looming power. Alarmingly, their former scruples seem to disappear.

In fact, normal economic conditions may be bygone. Unrestrained, global capitalism and the unfathomable wealth and power it has created, may outstrip traditional economic and political assumptions. The unsustainable, economic inequality it leaves in its wake appears unassailable, even as it effectively closes the door of opportunity to so many stretches of society. It threatens to disintegrate the manifest and indispensable marriage, described earlier, between capitalism and democracy.

The speed and power of developments seem to have overtaken this more reasonable Republican cohort. How are these more normal Republicans to keep up with the populist nihilism now afoot, which their preferred economic system, despite its benign promises, is fundamentally responsible for producing?

Finally, the MAGA movement must be arrayed and arraigned as a dialectical force. Its virulent propensity and potential are in fact, riven with internal contradiction, especially between its militant capitalist, oligarchic wings and those wings marginalized by the economy. Trump's attempts to re-privatize the economy and restore domestic manufacturing at least possess ideological coherence. This coherence, however, is undercut by what appears a monstrous, hyper-capitalist-class agenda that would leave those who benefit from more stable employment beholden to unbounded corporate and oligarchic control. Far be it for Trump, though, to actually pronounce a measurable economic plan or program. This would leave him accountable, the last thing he appears to want. As noted, Trump's popularity is partly premised on his ostentatious ability to exercise freedom of initiative, impulse and 'instinct' – that finds resonance with many renegade sectors of his constituency.

As noted earlier, however a counteracting economic agenda, such as the 'social partnership' one outlined in this essay, may find foothold and attraction among economic classes from across the spectrum, as it renders more tangible and realistic benefits, not only for their prospects, but for their democratic republic.

Democrats

Last but not least, this leads to the fifth group in the polarization scheme -the earnest but now seemingly hapless Democratic Party and its constituency, who still try to maintain the integrity of America's conventional economic and political systems.

They tinker at the edges of economic redistribution and/or ameliorating working conditions, and at issues such as gun control, electoral reform, minority rights, and the rights of women to abortion. They are unevenly, but understandably inducted into the strictures of "woke" idealism. The list is familiar.

But other than a mostly valiant presidential campaign and diffuse, defiant statements made against the MAGA movement, or against economic inequality in general, the Democratic Party hasn't marshalled a united thrust to confront the polarization and economic system that produces it. Having in large part forsaken or forgotten the interests of labor, Democratic Party operatives, and representatives are now holding up a pretty tattered banner, still beholden to the raw interests of capital.

Democratic leaders continue to maintain the fast-fading belief that their interests and those of capital, as currently constituted, can reach accommodation. But customary belief that consensus could be achieved by competing economic interests has been repealed. The other side quit the game and now wants to drive the remnants of such bipartisan "partnership" into the ground.

For all the arguments, reasons, and forays given above, among which:

That unresolved economic contradiction between business and labor interests and resultant economic inequality drives polarization;

That political stalemate, or obstruction is not an accidental outcome, but a purposed strategy and coordinated machination;

That corporate and economic class-war drives Republican militancy;

That provision of 'living wages' for America's working classes is antithetical to the design and function of market capitalism;

That authoritarianism strikes deep social and psychological roots in the population, it is time to follow a different (and promising) way forward.

The polarization described and the forces that drive it must be surmounted. In Tolkien terms, another ring must be found to bind them all together anew.

It is time for the Democratic Party, or another worthy party amalgam, - to forthrightly and consistently make a new socio-economic case for all sectors and groups of the American populace. The alternative of not doing so, appears increasingly grim.

Dystopian Interlude

Start such a case with Trump's first inaugural denunciation of "carnage in America." How dare he excoriate carnage when it is more than partially caused by the austere, neo-liberal economic policy and militant capitalist class of his own Republican Party?

Then, turn Trump's carnage on its head. His portrayal and perception of the country are utterly negative. As Duluth, MN citizen commentator David Sorenson put it in a Letter to the Editor, the MAGA movement Trump leads (in its many manifestations) sees the democratic polity as anathema. "Social justice movements are a threat, the press is a threat; fair elections are a threat, the judicial system is a threat; libraries, schools, and universities are a threat; and people of different races, religions, sexual preferences, or gender identities are a threat." (David Sorenson, *Judicial System Has Slowed Insurrectionists*, Duluth News Tribune, Letter to the Editor, June 7, 2023). For want of positive vision, wholesale negativity somehow caught the majority's fancy.

And this was prior to the 2024 presidential election. All these things are telling of an authoritarian, even a fascist, outlook and rhetorical blackmail. Either you, the listener, submit, or you are part of the carnage.

Sorenson goes on to relate the historian Tim Snyder's assessment: "Legal institutions which permit the succession of power allow citizens to envision a future where leaders change but states remain. A fascist presents institutions and laws as the corrupt barriers…that must be circumvented or destroyed" (*ibid*).

The MAGA view exploits social fallibility and flaws to further polarize society in the name of a self-entitled, growing righteous minority. It is the antithesis, in dialectic terms, of the "We the People" united, democratic creed. The MAGA assault on democracy aims to overthrow its unity and divide society. It heralds a dystopic age.

Practical Idealism Reborn

Turning Trump's view of carnage on its head advances positive evaluation, remedy, and reform. It requires a message so clear and strong that it breaks through the worst dissociative features of mass communication and social media.

Yes, the crime rate in America is high by world standards. The perpetrators are to blame, but so is the system, which cultivates frustration, if not failure, and doesn't offer enough educational, vocational, and financial range for people to succeed. The carnage that apparently engulfs American society is a result as much of the, too thin liberal-democratic paradigm as it is the overreach of capitalistic and corporate interests over at least the past 40 years.

In that time, the Democratic Party has taken on every viable social interest or social identity cause at hand to achieve justice, so to speak, through the back door. But the one true social interest in a fair economy is left stranded and bays like a wolf. Democrats have come up short in advancing a vision that embraces the whole polity and laboring workforce in firmly confronting and defining the position and role of capital in society.

This involves confronting the limits and deficits of the market economy and finally embracing, and fully articulating an alternative, social economy.

It is a wonder that so many people function effectively and independently despite all the tormenting hooks and ladders of the system. These hooks and ladders impede social function and unity. They need to be straightened out.

The diagnosis is clear. Rampant economic inequality and the polarization it drives are untenable. It doesn't need more proof. People feel it in their bones -the authoritarian, so adept at exploiting grief and misfortune, picks up on the vibe. As the troubadour, Leonard Cohen sings: "Everybody knows the dice are loaded. Everybody rolls with their fingers crossed. Everybody knows the war is over. Everybody knows the good guys lost. Everybody knows the fight was fixed, the poor stay poor and the rich get rich. That's how it goes. Everybody knows." (Leonard Cohen & Sharon Robinson, *Everybody Knows,* from the album, *I'm Your Man, 1988)*

The black cynicism chimes with the apparent intractability of the social, if not human, condition. It seems to surrender to injustice and concede the authoritarian claim that corruption and injustice are endemic to society.

Another, more persuasive response is possible because it is practical, comprehensive, and socially responsible. It is the still robust response of the Social Market Partnership in Austria and elsewhere in Europe, - not to be replicated, but used as a model. It is possible to confront the beast of this historic moment with a stout heart and a laser-like focus on the three pillars, alluded to earlier, of economic pre-distribution.

It involves investing in people up-front before the race of life begins, providing secure conditions for incentive and productivity, and reducing the need for redistribution. It requires confronting entrenched interests in education, medicine, and business - no small order - not to mention reversing the culture of minimal taxation. No small order, either; higher taxes, it must be shown, will produce tangible benefits for everyone.

Vocational and technical education, as well as higher education, should be accessible and mostly tuition-free for all. The medical insurance industry monopoly needs to be unseated to allow at least for public-option, medical coverage plans, restoring at least a semblance of actual competition and ultimately bringing down costs, not to mention eliminating co-pays and deductibles.

Business and industry interests need to be harnessed in horizontal partnership so that collective wage bargaining and uniform employment conditions are shared. Such consolidation of interest can only be leveraged by greater trade-union representation and empowerment.

There is a ring that may bind them all anew: one that creates more opportunity and wage compensation for the poor, marginalized and vast, underpaid sectors of American society, that tames MAGA dissent, and that overthrows the false and threatening pretenses of militant Republicans. It is a ring encompassing the prospect of social democracy and historical progress – binding the strata of political, economic and socio-psychological polarization, elucidated thus far, in a restored and durable social compact – even those strata enmeshed in the legacies and realities of racism; a ring forged in the advancements of social market capitalist economic enterprise. Enough with the negative, disruptive, and disorganized mayhem of the contemporary American market capitalist economy.

These are the social, not socialist, remedies that will restore more trust and hope, and help to elude Leonard Cohen's prognostications of despair and the wholesale cynical mindset.

At the heart of it all, of course, is retraining and redirecting the power of capital. Capital formation, investment, and profit are each of quintessential social interest, alongside, but not exceeding, other social interests in the environment, education, health care, and in equitable distributions of income.

Additionally, providing secure conditions for economic pre-distribution clears the way for broad incentive and productivity — every capitalist's dream — while at the same time broadening, securing, and advancing all democratic interests in a New, New Deal. This could be the foundation of a new American social partnership.

Status anxiety will never be fully eradicated. As conservative creeds never fail to remind, the attainment of status is grounded in positive individual incentive and effort. Overcoming anxiety is part of the deal.

But status attainment requires a stout reckoning with social, and, economic vulnerabilities, so much a part of modern, industrial economies, not to mention the greater human condition. Positive recognition of these vulnerabilities leads to positive social and economic resolution, as opposed to submitting to their dominance - expressed in ever more threatening forms of aggressive status aggrandizement, status insecurity, and/or status defeat.

Of all things to contend with, it is perhaps the virulent self-aggrandizement currently flouted by militant Republican cadres – in defiance of social norms, values, and ordinary standards of truth and objectivity that is most telling of systemic and cultural errancy. It is a self-aggrandizement that appears to validate and depend upon narcissism, uncoupled from and antagonistic toward what it contends is an outmoded, if not corrupt, public goods and social values heritage. Any affirmative social heritage is better than the nihilism that such narcissism portends. Democrats have to conceive and communicate a new public goods agenda that converts this inverted and malignant self-interest into a new understanding of social interest; one that resides in personal identification with the prospects of revived social prosperity and unity. Such were the challenges that Europe confronted at the end of World War II.

Part XIII
Post-War European Treaties

Before examining the design and extent of Social Partnership in Europe generally, and Austria, in particular, it's instructive to review the evolution of European treaties since World War II. These treaties provide insight into the broad inter-national, institutional network that supports social partnership in individual countries. Aside from this, the treaty convocations themselves are noteworthy. Each resembles a practical, constitutional convention, held every ten years or so, prior to - and perhaps instead of - the writing and confirmation of an actual constitution. These treaties are great examples of collective design, adaptation and achievement.

The Treaty of Paris (1951)

The original treaty setting Europe on a course toward eventual union after World War II was the Treaty of Paris, signed in 1951 by France, Italy, Germany, and the Benelux countries Belgium, Luxembourg, and the Netherlands. (Treaty of Paris, Wikipedia)

This treaty set the stage for the eventual creation of Europe's single monetary market. It removed trade barriers and customs duties for the undersigned countries for many goods, but especially for coal and steel. The treaty established the groundbreaking terms for The European Coal and Steel Community (ECSC). (European Coal and Steel Community, Wikipedia)

There were many more Treaty steps to follow in creating legal frameworks for greater integration of

European state economies and, eventually, for greater political integration.

The Treaty of Rome (1957)

The Treaty of Rome (1957) brought about the European Economic Community (EEC), one of the institutional forerunners to the creation of the European Union. (Treaty of Rome, Wikipedia) It further expanded single market frameworks for free trade in goods, labor, services and capital management for member states. It also "proposed the creation of a Common Agriculture Policy, a Common Transport Policy, and a European Social Fund. The treaty established the European Commission." (ibid)

The Commission and the newly constituted Parliamentary Assembly were comprised of representatives elected and/or appointed by the member states. The Commission and Parliament were consultative and deliberative bodies. Their proposals were taken up by the European Council, comprised again of state leaders, or their appointed representatives, who enacted the proposed policy, or legislation, or not. The European Court of Justice was also established.

The Merger Treaties/The Treaty of Belgium (1965)

Further advances toward integration were accomplished by the Merger Treaty of 1965, also known as the Treaty of Brussels. The treaty unified "the executive institutions (formerly separate), of the European Coal and Steel Community, the European Atomic Energy Community, and the European Economic Community." (Merger Treaty, Wikipedia) The treaty reconstituted the Commission to have oversight over all three bodies. It was this treaty that inaugurated the "real beginning of the modern European Union." (ibid)

The successes of economic integration in subsequent years and decades finally led to the adoption of the Maastricht Treaty of 1992.

The Maastricht Treaty (1992)

This treaty officially established the European Union and increased the number of member states to include Denmark, Ireland, Greece, Portugal, Spain, and the United Kingdom. Each member state was called on to ratify the treaty, either through referendum or parliamentary act.

The treaty did many things. It defined "provisions for shared European citizenship." (European Central Bank, (*5 Things You Need to Know about the Maastricht Treaty*, www) It decreed the introduction of a single European currency and "increased cooperation between national central banks and the increased alignment of Member States' economic policies." (ibid)

Further, the Maastricht Treaty specified "Compliance Rules" (ibid) for joining the currency union. The old concern of inflation was a primary target – "a country's average inflation rate should not exceed the inflation rate of the three best-performing EU Member States by more than 1.5% during a one-year observation period." (ibid)

As many states, including Austria are currently reminded, the treaty was equally stringent regarding "annual fiscal debt, interest rates, and exchange rates," specifying strict percentage limits in each case. (ibid) Such provisions demonstrated the seriousness with which the fledgling union would keep its economic house in order.

GATT Negotiations (1994)

The Maastricht Treaty enabled Europe to negotiate as a unified entity in matters of international trade. Hence, it took part in the final General Agreement on Trade and Tariffs (GATT) negotiations in 1994, known as the Uruguay Round, which cleared the way for the formation of the World Trade Organization (WTO) in 1995. Each European state under the European Union (EU) banner became a founding member.

The GATT Treaty had been re-negotiated eight different times since its inception in 1947. The World Trade Organization, which GATT fostered, now includes "164 members" (GATT, Wikipedia), all of whom are obligated to uphold standards of fair and free trade, particularly by maintaining low tariffs. Say what you will about the USA's preferred position in world trade - the role of the dollar as the world's reserve trade currency remains controversial - but the reduction of trade tariffs has been a boon (and now a Trump administration bane) for global commerce.

Starting in 1947, when "tariff levels for the major GATT participants were about 22%," by 1995, "after the Uruguay Round, tariffs were under 5%." (ibid)

For better or worse, the globalization of world trade has continued to expand ever since. Europe, as a unified trading entity, GATT and the WTO, is a primary partner in this process. As Dartmouth College economic historian Douglas Irwin points out, "the growth of world trade has contributed a great deal to the prosperity of the world economy over the past half-century." (ibid)

In sum, the European states involved each went to great lengths to form and join an expanded and unified market - not only within Europe but also in relation to the rest of the world. In so doing, they determined that such a move was in the best interest of their people and the most effective way to maintain limited national autonomy.

Chapter One:
The Eurozone

But the work was and still is far from complete. Many internal matters remain unresolved, particularly the sensitive issue of a federal constitution.

The European Union, as noted, is a broad 'confederation' The Eurozone, however, is a separate entity and should not be confused with the EU itself. The Eurozone comprises 20 countries "that adopted the Euro as their primary currency and implement the policies of the Economic and Monetary Union (EMU)." (Eurozone, Wikipedia)

The Eurozone members are: Austria, Belgium, Croatia, Cyprus, Estonia, Finland, France, Germany, Greece, Ireland, Italy, Latvia, Lithuania, Luxembourg, Malta, the Netherlands, Portugal, Slovakia, Slovenia, and Spain. (ibid)

However, affiliated non-Eurozone members within the European Union also figure in the matrix. These seven countries - Bulgaria, the Czech Republic, Denmark, Hungary, Poland, Romania, and Sweden - continue to use their own national currencies. "However, all but Denmark are obliged to join once they meet the euro convergence criteria." (sic) (ibid)

The Eurozone countries are legally and financially bound together in a federation. The monetary authority of this zone is, however, coordinated informally by member state finance ministers and the "European System of Central Banks. This body ensures and coordinates "cooperation between Eurozone and non-Eurozone EU members," in conjunction with the European Central Bank. (ibid)

This provides only a simple overview of the financial organization; its procedures and processes are highly complex. Among various measures, for example, since the financial crisis of 2007-2008, the Eurozone has established and used provisions for granting emergency loans to member states in return for enacting economic reforms." (ibid)

As addressed at the beginning of this essay in Adam Tooze's Chartbook article, the EU remains a confederated system. "There is no single institution responsible for economic policy. Instead, the responsibility is divided between Member States and the EU institutions." (Economic and Monetary Union, Wikipedia)

Member states still exercise significant economic and legal authority. They "set their national budgets within agreed limits for deficit and debt and determine their own structural policies involving labor, pensions, and capital markets." (ibid)

That said, great benefits, incentives, and interests exist for abiding by the conditions of a unified market.

The Lisbon Treaty (TFEU) 2007-2009

Such interests propelled the member states of the EU to adopt the Lisbon Treaty, or Treaty on the Functioning of the European Union (TFEU), which defined internal EU regulations and established a unitary legal code. This treaty is particularly instructive as it demonstrates the design and viability of the European Union. It exemplifies the variability of (quasi) constitutional arrangements.

The Lisbon Treaty - Treaty on European Union (2007-2009) updated the Maastricht Treaty (1992. The Treaty of Rome (1957) was similarly updated by the Treaty on the Functioning of the European Union. (TFEU - Lisbon Treaty, Wikipedia) It established the EU's Bill of Rights - the "Charter of Fundamental Rights", legally binding for all member states. It also clarified the procedure by which member states could "leave the EU" (so arduously and recently carried out during Brexit) (ibid)

Both treaties further settled questions about governing authority by designating new executive and foreign policy offices. They also granted the European Parliament co-equal power with the European Union Council Ministers in matters of EU policy and financial appropriations. Together, in an almost bicameral fashion, the Parliament and the Council of the EU constitute the EU's Legislative Branch.

The EU's 705 parliament members are individually elected by the citizens of each member state and hold the power of legislative approval alongside the Council of the EU. The Council does not have fixed members, but is composed of national ministers who meet in "10 different configurations, each corresponding to the policy area being discussed." (*Council of the European Union - Overview*, european-union.europa.eu/institutions, 2023) Together with the European Parliament, the Council negotiates and adopts laws, "based on proposals from the European Commission" a college of commissioners nominated by state leaders. (ibid)

Interestingly, and in contrast to the American political system, the EU legislative branch does not initiate legislation. In this respect, it is perhaps less driven by political calculation and partisanship.

The Lisbon Treaty was designed to enhance "the efficiency and democratic legitimacy of the European Union." *(TFEU - Lisbon Treaty,* Wikipedia) However, it was controversial. Danish representatives, for example, argued that the treaty "would centralize the EU and weaken democracy by moving power away from national electorates." (ibid)

This claim was countered by the argument that the treaty "brings more checks and balances into the EU system with stronger Parliamentary powers and a new role for national parliaments." (ibid)

Article 18 of the Treaty on the Functioning of the European Union (TFEU) establishes binding social laws and principles. It outlaws "discrimination on the basis of nationality." It also enumerates Executive Branch powers.

As stipulated by Article 19 of the TFEU – executive power still depends on the consent of the EU Parliament.

"Articles 20 to 24 establish EU citizenship and accord rights to it; free movement, consular protection from other states, the right to vote and stand in local and European elections, the right to petition Parliament, European Ombudsman powers, and the right to contact and receive a reply from EU institutions in their own language"

Article 25 of the TFEU "requires the EU Commission to report on the implementation of these rights every three years." (*TFEU,* Wikipedia). Such articles are standard, but essential, constitutional fare for established Western democracies. Such rights are imperiled in authoritarian countries or outright erased for minorities and other vulnerable groups. They have special relevance in these times of American constitutional turmoil.

As noted, the European Union governmental structure is uniquely designed. Veto power is reserved for the 27 heads of state who constitute the European Council - executive power, indeed. It is carried out, however, not by a single president but by a "prevailing majority" of Council members. The head of the EU Commission, its President, is nominated and "elected by a qualified majority of fellow heads of state to a 30-month term," which may be extended to a second term. His or her election must be approved by a parliamentary majority. The Commission's legislative proposals are vetted or checked by either the Parliament or the Council of the EU and its 27 nationally appointed ministers.

There are internal, built-in checks and balances. Both executive and legislative branches are quasi-bicameral. "The ordinary legislative procedure gives the same weight to the European Parliament and the Council of the European Union on a wide range of areas (for example, economic governance, immigration, energy, transport, the environment, and consumer protection). The vast majority of European laws are adopted jointly by the European Parliament and the Council." (*About Parliament - Legislative Powers - How does the legislative process work, European Parliament,* europarl.europa.eu, 2023)

The procedure of "co-decision" or co-approval applies to the majority of legislative business. On matters of taxation, however, the European Parliament exercises only a "consultative" function. It must be informed on taxation issues and its opinion heard, but its approval is not required. This indicates the persistent control of EU member states over the power of the purse.

Other than Parliament, however, Council and Commission members are not directly elected by the people, even if subject to parliamentary approval. In all, the design exhibits the tight control and influence exerted by each European member state and its nominated or appointed representatives in formulating EU policy. The EU has more administrative than executive federal power. The member states, all erstwhile proud nations, hence maintain not only influence and control but also limited autonomy (*Institutions and Bodies of the EU - Austrians in EU Institutions*, Federal Ministry Republic of Austria, bmeia.gv.at).

EU Courts Revisited

As noted earlier, the status of the EU's judicial system and its authority is in evolutionary flux, particularly regarding its role in mediating between business interests and those of labor and between federal and state power. Spheres of authority in Europe remain somewhat unresolved. The EU's structural design at the federal level appears complicated and unwieldy, reflecting the institutional and political youth of the EU project.

As stipulated by the Treaty on the Functioning of the European Union (TFEU), member-state influence and control are further elaborated in the design and composition of the EU Court of Justice. The CJEU consists of 27 judges, one from each member state, "who are appointed by common accord of the home governments and hold office for a renewable term of six years" (*European Court of Justice,* Wikipedia). They are assisted in their duties by 11 "advocates general," who are likewise appointed by member-state representatives seated on the Council of the EU.

The European Court of Justice, (CJEU) is Europe's Supreme Court, tasked with "interpreting EU law and ensuring its uniform application across all EU member states. It deals with requests from national courts, much as state courts in the USA appeal to the US Supreme Court, especially on questions that involve constitutional interpretation.

Interestingly, and illustrative of member-state authority, the CJEU is the highest court in matters of "Union law" but not national law. It is not possible to appeal against the decisions of national courts in the CJEU. Furthermore, it is ultimately for the national court "to apply the resulting interpretation to the facts of any given case" (*ibid*).

The other EU court, the General Court, takes on individual and business cases "against acts of the institutions, bodies, or agencies of the European Union" on matters of "competition law, state aid, trade, agriculture, and trademarks" (*ibid*).

In terms similar or parallel to conditions in the USA, the foregoing illustrates the ongoing accommodation and strain between federal and state power. European states appear to hold more prerogative and precedence, than do the American states

The EU states draw mostly on their own legal and political traditions to maintain and achieve legal and social harmony. Each state asserts a distinct historic national identity as a counterweight to overriding federal power. Each state in Europe has been through the historical mill (materialist/industrial relations and otherwise) many times over, and evolution on such issues as social security and social protection reaches its own national, albeit still-contested, accommodation. Austria's political and economic systems are no exception. These reflect accommodations made to Austria's particular history, and attendant experiences of polarization.

Conclusion

Bearing the lopsided strains and realities of federal and state authority in mind, it is remarkable that the EU holds together as well as it does. The treaties, apparently, did their work well. Confederation within the broad terms of the Social Market, outlined and explained earlier, provides enough constitutional framework for unity, even without a constitution.

As also noted, the Eurozone economic framework provides a mighty incentive for all EU member states to maintain the Union. The EU retains and exerts budgetary and some legal leverage to restrain illiberal policies, such as those pursued at the moment by states like Hungary and Italy and perhaps now, even the Netherlands. There, in 2023, a right-wing party gained a 24% majority share of the vote in the Dutch multi-party democratic system.

The campaign to recognize and extend "the efficiency and democratic legitimacy of the European Union" is not immune from ethnic divisive pressures. However, the Union's gravitational pull is anchored by Social Market prosperity and the social justice it provides.

The 'European house', so to speak, is mostly in order; a phenomenal historic accomplishment. With the advent of Trump's proposed tariff policies, however, that House will be shaken. Trump's contention that the parameters, or conditions of global trade are unfair to the United States, perhaps reflects the extent of European economic development. Perhaps in his eyes, this development has been shielded by the U.S. (and NATO) for long enough. It is now time to take the gloves off. Perhaps the U.S. has ceded too much of its industrial and manufacturing base to the international trade order, which in many ways it authored. It is a daring, if not monomaniacal proposition: The controlled competition of global trade (including the controlled and regulated economies of the EU), in this view, should be subject to more robust economic competition – as a function of greater economic development and progress. The dialectical picture is clarified. Trump's contention is rife with risk. The potential for international conflict is palpable. Europe must rally. It is ready to compete on its own terms in the global economic world.

Part XIV
Social Partnership Over Polarization

Chapter One:
European and American Contrasts

As referenced now in multiple contexts and instances, Social Partnership manifests itself in diverse alignments. It formalizes and extends mere political, bi-partisanship, customary to American political affairs, to a whole different level. For some countries, such as Austria, it involves tri-partisan government, business and labor interests in the management of political, economic and social relations. Its particular post-WWII origins shape and inform Europe's widespread Social Market compact and economic ethos.

Social Partnership is rooted in commitment to economic capitalism, but within given social parameters. These parameters provide the basis for what are termed "coordinated market economies." The free market, however, still prevails. Anti-competitive, monopolistic business practices, as indicated, are counteracted at both the federal EU level and, as exemplified by Austria, at European state levels - though it often amounts to a game of catch-up, or whack-a-mole.

The review of post-war European treaties highlights respect for commonality and variety among member states. The balance between state autonomy and wider European integration and unity demands continuous maintenance. This process is similar to the American states' rights issue and points of contention between the states themselves and federal power. The American complaint that federal power exceeds its rightful bounds has been cacophonous. However, it often ignores or forgets that federal power increased because states themselves were slack in upholding creeds and constitutional principles that define national economic, political, and social order.

No better recent example exists than the inconsistent and degrading state enforcement of the Voting Rights Act. This was enabled when the Supreme Court negligently declined federal jurisdiction and enforcement of the Act, failing to uphold a unified electoral system.

Europe, by contrast, features states with profound historical identities, experiences, and evolution. These states responded to the civilizational catastrophes unleashed by World Wars I and II by fostering new Social Partnership templates. The ongoing European Social Dialogue, as noted, contributed to the adoption of Article 152 of the TFEU federal treaty, which expressly and officially sanctions the advancement of Social Partnership industrial relations throughout the continent. This sanction itself is an outgrowth of the new social realities that predominated both before and after the world wars in many countries.

Social Partnership has local roots, abetted at the federal level as a commitment to human welfare and social justice. This commitment reflects a novel and sober recognition of the human condition in mass industrial societies. As witnessed above, status maintenance in modern society is a somewhat febrile and fragile matter. It is subject to many impersonal and anonymous forces that often outrun the binding influences of traditional family, community, and individual determination - as well as the putative security provided by the rule of law and an independent judiciary.

Individual status is challenged and sometimes overwhelmed by the sheer dimensions of the mass market enterprise.

At the same time, the mass industrial organization of society bestows palpable, though unequally distributed benefits of material plenty and security. To maintain the overall balance of this gargantuan, somewhat astounding, and unprecedented enterprise - and to ward off divisive polarization - systemic organization and solidarity become imperative. Partnership extends across and includes wide-ranging business interests, paralleled similarly across and including broad labor interests.

It is not only solidarity, however, that compels businesses and labor to negotiate and share prosperity through collective bargaining as partners. Indeed, solidarity in the rough-and-tumble world may only be nominal. It must also be practical. Where industrial relation and wage compensation costs are relatively equivalent, the playing field of enterprise is level. Competitive markets are sustained and grown by broad consumer and social investment. When more people have more disposable income, it is positively good for business and economic development, not to mention greater social unity.

An impressive result of this social evolution is that most European states share a common commitment not only to collective bargaining, but also to the broad provision of health care insurance and access to higher education and/or vocational-technical training. These universal private and personal goods are simply recognized as social goods. This conception of social or public good leads to different organizational and systemic modalities.

In contrast, America's blind reliance on individual incentive and a competitive, but often anti-competitive, monopolized model has led to systemic irregularity, gross disparities in educational, medical, and wage-compensation coverage – and to social and economic inequality. This results in weakened solidarity and heightened polarization - not to mention huge and intolerable out-of-pocket expenses, student debt, and exploitative employment relations.

To put a finer point on it, the attitude that 'America's Business is Business' still retains a stranglehold on social policy. Though it's social welfare outlays and commitments are vast, these are viewed more as incidental or accidental than consequential to the function of the economic system. The state retains an asocial attitude toward populations—whether racial or financial—that are marginalized by the economy. This ambiguity or indifference renders both state and society vulnerable to the anti-social predations of Trump's second administration (under DOGE, in particular), and its plans to re-privatize the American economy. The prospects of a 'social state,' in which no populations are marginalized, is thereby nullified.

The question arises: Can America escape from the capture of its historical experience and turn a new page, or will it be ground into the dirt by ever-widening civil division and governmental repression? In this context, the virtues and advantages of Social Partnership are evident not only on their own account, but also as a system to ward off, if not completely contain, the ominous threats posed to democracy by polarization.

Chapter Two:
Compare European/American Market Conditions

Again, it is important to stress the importance of collective bargaining – and the equitable wages it produces – at the foundation of Europe's social economies, reaching beyond the more strictly market economies in America and elsewhere. Earlier, the origins, nature and scope of European collective bargaining were described, as were the mechanisms of its' oversight and implementation, exercised through social dialogue and social partnership. The conjunction of collective bargaining and Social Partnership negotiation, in particular, is essential.

Widespread European collective bargaining takes place in different configurations and at different levels. "Across the EU as a whole, six out of ten employees (60%) are covered by collective bargaining, although there are important variations between countries" *(Collective Bargaining Coverage,* worker.participation.eu, European Trade Union Institute (ETUI), 2023).

France and Belgium have collective bargaining coverage at *"98% and 96%,"* respectively. France pursues collective bargaining predominantly at the *"industrial or company"* level, though governmental oversight and coordination are also involved. In Belgium, the government sets a *"national framework."* (ibid)

Collectively bargained contracts in Austria, as noted, cover an estimated *95%* of employees, predominantly negotiated at the sectoral, or *"industrial"* level. At the other end of the spectrum, with *26%, 16%, and 10%*, respectively, are the UK, Poland, and Greece, where collective contracts are primarily negotiated at the "*company*" level." *(ibid)*

Again, these numbers reflect each state's historical evolution, "*legal frameworks*", and various approaches to industrial policy. *(ibid)* The Trade Union Institute article cited above observes that many countries with "*very high levels of collective bargaining coverage at around 80% or above*" significantly outreach levels of "*union density*." *(ibid)* These levels reflect legacies of union density and legal custom that reflect systemic development. In all European countries, there is a strong correlation between historic levels of union density and contemporary collective bargaining coverage.

In Austria, for example, collective bargaining coverage is between *95-98%* of the workforce - while *trade-union density is currently around 28%*." (ETUI, *Industrial Relations in Austria:* Background Summary, etui.org, 2016) In 1960, Austrian union density was *60.1%*. (OECD Statistics, *Union Density in Austria and Other Selected OECD Countries -1960-2020*). Of many things, such numbers indicate the deep integration and custom of Austria's industrial relations system – anchored in Social Partnership.

Among other things, to be seen later in detail, the strength of collective bargaining in Austria reflects its' *one-big-union* industrial relations organizational approach. Here, "Seven affiliated, industrial sector, and professional unions" *(sic)* are represented in negotiations on a yearly basis by "One umbrella organization, the Austrian Trade-Union

Federation," which negotiates with an equally organized national Chamber of Commerce. *(ibid)*

At the federal EU level, in addition to the social dialogue mentioned above, collective bargaining is monitored and promoted by the EU's *Eurofound*. This agency conducts a "European Company Survey (ECS)" to establish levels and types of coverage across the continent and the extent and "influence of employee representation and social dialogue at company level." *(Collective Bargaining, Survey Data, EU Context*, eurofound.europa.eu, January 2023). This ECS survey provides a basis for *Country-specific recommendations (CSRs) on matters of alignment between pay developments and productivity, minimum wage-setting, and pay indexation systems*," as well as the degree of conformity with "EU Labor legislation" *(sic) (ibid)*.

The social good of collective bargaining is thus woven into the cultural, economic, and political fabric at both state and federal levels. In many respects, collective bargaining issues are removed from the political fray, and are resolved as a normal fixture of business affairs. The structures and institutions of the coordinated market system are mature and reflect long historical development, both prior to and after World War II.

The tide of their evolution was advanced by far-reaching trade-union organization and interest, reaching such critical mass that the interests of business and industry were compelled to recognize and accept their partnership. More than this, however, business interests were convinced of the economic utility of the social market.

American Trade-Unions

The trade union movement in America is far from reaching critical mass. As noted above, however, the cause of trade union collective bargaining undergoes tenuous regeneration. New agreements achieved by automobile manufacturers and the United Auto Workers (UAW) in 2023 demonstrate the power of collective negotiation to reach better wages and conditions, but also industrial accommodation and re-alignment. It remains to be seen if non-unionized automakers will also be compelled to unionize simply to stay competitive in the labor market. Employees at Tesla, VW, Hyundai, Nissan, and Toyota, numbering "150,000 workers combined" (sic), equal to those employed by GM, Ford, and Stellantis, must be weighing their options. (David Shepardson, *UAW Launches Bid to Organize Tesla and Entire Non-Union Auto Sector in US*, Reuters.com, Nov. 30, 2023)

UAW's organizing campaign attempts to strike now, while the iron is hot. But resistance is strong. "Several foreign automakers have announced significant pay and other compensation improvements in response to the UAW contracts in a move many analysts and industry officials saw as an effort to keep the UAW out of their plants" (ibid). The strategy here appears to 'buy off' workers in the short-term to forestall long-term systemic accommodation and integration of their interests.

Either way, to the benefit of all associated workers, the auto production playing field gets leveled. To ensure the benefits of consistency and progress going forward, though, the UAW aims to 'sectorize' as much of the auto industry as it can. This would be a giant step toward creating a wider trade-union movement in other sectors as well.

Such a development, however, presupposes that the benefits of unionization outweigh the status of individual initiative and incentive, which continue to define American employment attitudes. The social incentive of a greater trade-union movement in America must be seen to compliment individual attitudes. Greater unionization also depends on the overthrow of racist calculations - described earlier - which crippled past union organizing efforts in some regions, particularly the South. Most of all, eventual partnership presupposes a transformation of American industrial relations in which both the interests of capital and labor see accommodation as ultimately more productive and profitable than adversarial stalemate. Cooperation, at the heart of partnership, must preempt zero-sum competitive calculations.

Collective bargaining in Europe, as noted, is anchored and negotiated by a panoply of social partnerships. Business, labor, and state interests involved in these partnerships take on various guises in the different European states. This reflects the principle of 'subsidiarity,' essential to the whole social market enterprise. Subsidiarity respects regional and national differences and recognizes a certain autonomy in the design and maintenance of individual systems. It balances, or compliments centralization. This interplay between federal and state interests is a hallmark of American democracy. Systemic change can also be state-generated.

Health Insurance

Comparisons of European and American market conditions also extend to the provision of health insurance. Here, state-level subsidiarity is also at play in Europe. Each state features different healthcare delivery designs, but partnership and solidarity are common in each case. In Austria, as has been noted, businesses, as well as individual taxpayers, pay into a common healthcare fund, the *Krankenkasse*. Similar arrangements exist in most European countries. Health insurance is provided as a social good and not simply as a private market commodity.

In his comparative study, political scientist Frederico Toth reports: "Out of the 28 European countries examined in this work, 13 ensure universal coverage, 5 have what we can call 'quasi-universal' coverage, and 10 countries do not have universal coverage. The 13 countries with universal coverage (where 100% of the population is thereby covered) include Croatia, Czech Republic, Denmark, Finland, Ireland, Italy, Latvia, Lithuania, Malta, Portugal, Slovenia, Sweden, and the United Kingdom." (Frederico Toth, *Prevalence and Generosity of Health Insurance Coverage: A Comparison of EU Member States,* Journal of Comparative Policy Analysis: Research and Practice, Volume 21, 2019, p. 4).

But 'quasi-universal' in five countries is quite extensive. In 2015, Austria's system of 'quasi-universal' coverage provided healthcare insurance to "99.9%" of the population. (ibid, p. 5) Austrians are covered 'universally' through employment. The unemployed are 'quasi' covered through different taxation streams.

Whether universal, quasi, or not, the EU-28 healthcare insurance coverage in 2015 was an impressive "98%." (ibid) Only 2%, or about 9 million of 448 million people, are uninsured.

Comparatively, the private/public insurance system in the U.S. is a long way from universal. The U.S. Census Bureau reports: "In 2022, 26 million people - or 7.9 percent of the population - were uninsured." (*The Share of Americans without Health Insurance in 2022 Matched a Record Low,* Peter G. Peterson Foundation, November 9, 2023)

While much higher than the numbers in Europe, the American uninsured rate — reflecting healthcare COVID-19 pandemic investments… "was the lowest since 2017." (ibid) In 2016, 8.6% of Americans were uninsured. Prior to the passage of the Affordable Care Act under President Obama in 2010, "15.5%," or some 51.5 million Americans, were uninsured. (*ibid,* U.S. Census Bureau)

This brief description outlines the 'prevalence' of healthcare coverage in Europe and the USA. It should go without saying that healthcare security is a great benefit, not only for the sake of physical and mental health, but to advance social equality and a sense of belonging. Efficient healthcare provision is an antidote to polarization.

'Prevalence' is one thing; the 'generosity' of healthcare coverage is another. In the cited Toth article, 'generosity' relates to the extent of coverage, to what "is guaranteed by insurance coverage." (ibid) He finds a correlation between countries with 'universal', or 'quasi-universal' coverage and lower "out-of-pocket expenditures and self-reported "unmet medical needs." In countries without universal coverage, the out-of-pocket expenditure averages 23.4%, whereas in countries with universal or quasi-universal coverage, the out-of-pocket spending averages 13.2%. (ibid, p. 8) Here, 'actuarily' speaking, the more people are enrolled, the greater delivery efficiencies can be achieved.

In Europe generally, it is clear that socially supported universal health insurance coverage constrains market forces that, in America, at least, exploit consumer vulnerability for the sake of market position and profit maximization. Health care insurance providers compete with each other not to provide the best, most affordable service to customers, it would seem, but to deliver a product that garners the most profit.

Under this system: "The United States has one of the highest costs of healthcare in the world. In 2021, U.S. healthcare spending reached $4.3 trillion, which averages to about $12,900 per person. By comparison, the average cost of healthcare per person in other wealthy countries is only about half as much." (*Why Are Americans Paying More for Healthcare?* Peter G. Peterson Foundation, July 14, 2023)

In Europe, by contrast, and broadly speaking, the social organization of healthcare provision contains costs more efficiently, but still within a market framework. As the *Atlantic* magazine's Olga Khazan reports: "Several European countries have health insurance just like America does. The difference is that their governments regulate what insurance must cover and what hospitals and doctors are allowed to charge much more aggressively than the United

States does." (Olga Khazan, *Why Europeans Don't Get Huge Medical Bills,* The Atlantic, April 11, 2019)

So, in Europe, the insurance industry maintains business profitability, but within boundaries negotiated in partnership by the government and insurance industry representatives. 'Neo-corporatist' organization between the involved interest blocks contains market pressures. The same applies to doctors. They are "not allowed to charge more than the payment rates negotiated (sic) between the tax-paid public (sic) illness funds and the doctor's associations." Markets for private health care delivery also exist across Europe. In Germany, for example, "a very small number of the country's physicians are private and don't accept payments from the public (sic) illness funds, but they have to tell patients how much they'll charge before a patient is treated." (ibid) This removes the sometimes-shocking element of surprise with which medical bills in America arrive – after the fact.

The United States struggles to provide equitable, efficient, and effective healthcare insurance within the overriding framework of a competitive marketplace. It is a marketplace dominated by private healthcare insurance companies. The Affordable Care Act notwithstanding, healthcare costs continue to rise, as do out-of-pocket healthcare payments and incidences of unmet medical needs.

In the U.S, "relative to the size of the economy, healthcare costs have increased over the past few decades, from 5 percent of GDP in 1960 to 18 percent in 2021" (*Why Are Americans Paying More for Healthcare*, ibid).

Alongside the salutary increase in healthcare insurance coverage in the U.S. over the past 10 years, there has been a regrettable and concomitant increase in adults who are underinsured. According to Statista surveys, "the percentage of adults who were insured all year but still paid high (sic) out-of-pocket costs or deductibles (relative to their income) has increased from 9% in 2003 to 23% in 2022" (Statista, Health, *Pharma & Medtech: Health System Percentage of Adults with Health Insurance in the U.S. 2003-2022*, published by Preeti Vankar, Oct 27, 2022).

In another survey, Statista estimates that "total out-of-pocket health care payments in the U.S. continue to increase, surpassing (sic) $433 billion in 2021" (StatistaTotal *Out-of-Pocket Health Care Payments in the U.S.*, July 2023). With such high out-of-pocket expenses, it is no wonder that people are not meeting their own medical treatment needs. The survey reports that "out-of-pocket costs are rising at much faster rates than workers' wages in the United States. (sic) This is one reason why so many people who have health insurance find themselves in medical debt.

According to a 2021 survey, nearly 40 percent of U.S. adults have medical-related debt. Due to all of the financial challenges, decisions regarding a visit to a doctor or receiving specialist care can come down to cost, leaving many people without the care they need.

"Since 2014, the percentage of U.S. adults who go without healthcare due to cost has been around 35 percent" (ibid).

With such numbers and conditions in mind, it is indeed remarkable how much financial weight the average

American citizen, or household has to carry. Rising costs become unsustainable, as does the fostered inequality. Yet the system persists. This reflects the monolithic capture and control of the system, as if alternatives didn't exist. Instead of adopting an alternative system in which making a profit off people's health - or lack thereof - is constrained, Americans submit to an exploitative and inefficient healthcare system that produces growing inequality.

American Higher Education Conditions

Unrestrained, hyper-capitalist market conditions in America are now demonstrably over the top in producing or providing goods and services that are less and less affordable. Cyclical inflation is only partially at fault. The whole system seems to depend on rising costs to raise profits, to finance itself. The number of people who can afford such costs becomes prohibitive.

This phenomenon widely applies - to Vikings football tickets, new cars, healthcare, etc. - and also to the realm of higher education in the United States. Summing up the situation in what is otherwise a positive assessment, Penn State's professor of education, Andrzej Gapinski, perceives "looming dark clouds over the horizon (sic) of American higher education" (Andrzej J. Gapinski, Ph.D., *Higher Education: Europe vs. USA,* Penn State University-Fayette, Pennsylvania, USA, 2010).

The article issues a siren call that "the dramatic rise of costs in the form of university tuition fees, well above inflation rates, caused by a decrease in public funding, may jeopardize university access for ordinary citizens. The financial burden of the cost of education, combined with growing income disparity among socio-economic strata of society, puts heavy brakes on social mobility" (ibid).

Typically, state funding for higher education is prone to cyclical economic recessions. This was particularly true after the Great Recession of 2008-2009. National emergencies, such as the 9/11 attacks in 200, or the recent pandemic-induced economic downturn, also put a strain on state budgets. State funding shortfalls resulting from lower business and individual tax receipts lead to cuts in services. These shortfalls affect higher education budgets.

In a majority of states, shortfalls are offset by increasing tuition costs. Subsequent and current studies indicate that "the average cost of one year at a public university for an in-state student is $30,090 (college board statistic, sic)" (Per, son of Jürgen, B. Sc, journalism, U of Kansas, *Why Is College Free in a Lot of European Countries but So Expensive in the U.S.,* Quora.com, 2020).

This contributes to a burgeoning student debt load. According to a Federal Reserve study, the current median student debt is in the mid-$20,000 range - the median (again) being the number in the middle between those students owing higher and lower debt levels for a bachelor's degree. Debt amounts vary between different degrees, such as Psychology/Sociology, Architecture, or Computer & Information Systems" (Marcus Lu, *Ranked: Median Student Debt for a U.S. College Degree,* visualcapitalist.com, October 23, 2023).

Overall, the current median figure represents a "40% increase" from 2013 (ibid). According to Education Data Initiative numbers, "20% of all-American adults with undergraduate degrees have outstanding student debt; 24% of postgraduate degree holders report outstanding student loans" (Melanie Hanson, *Student Loan Debt Statistics,* educationdata.org, August 20, 2023). Of course, owed amounts are much higher for private college and master's degrees.

The economic and educational environment, though, appears different. "With this (Pandemic, sic) recession, enrollment had already been decreasing in many parts of the country, and was predicted to continue for some years. Without an increase in enrollment to cover the reduction in state funding, higher education institutions may continue to lose the tuition revenue they rely on" (Quad C - *Leadership in Higher Education, How the Recession Will Affect Higher Education Institutions,* August 22, 2023).

Unless states step up again to support higher education and push down tuition costs, enrollment will suffer, as will the extent and quality of available educational opportunities. State investment would require raising taxes - anathema to the current, tax-manic, hyper-capitalist mode of thinking. Raising taxes, though, may lead to public demand that monies be more efficiently and equitably deployed.

Broadly carried, high student federal-debt, which "alone has tripled since 2000," self-evidently exerts a "negative impact on worker economic mobility, the labor market, and racial wealth inequality," not to mention economic inequality in general. (Oluwasekemi Odumoso, *The Impact of Student Debt on the Low-Wage Workforce,* Workrise, Sept. 23, 2023)

Student debt puts a crimp, if not a vice on post-college graduation plans, whether it means not being able to purchase a home, or a car, having to "postpone or opt out of enrolling in graduate or professional school," or simply managing to get by. (ibid) It places a bitter dead weight on the accomplishment of a degree. Large debt at the beginning of a career inhibits the ability to fully participate in and contribute to the economy.

You might say this is the *American Pay Your Own Way* — bills received and paid as a measure and matter of individual initiative and responsibility, whatever the cost to social stability and development. Republicans amplified this view in 2023. They supported the Supreme Court's rejection of the Biden Administration's proposed $400 billion student debt cancellation plan. Then House Speaker Kevin McCarthy applauded the decision, contending that "the 87% of Americans without student loans are no longer forced to pay for the 13% who do." (Adam Liptak, *Supreme Court Rejects Biden's Student Loan Forgiveness Plan,* NYT, June 30, 2023)

As demonstrated above, McCarthy's number underestimates, obfuscates, and minimizes both the scale and importance of actual social and educational higher education conditions in America. This is par for the current Republican course: Do not believe in, or depend on scientifically researched and vetted economic, or sociological data.

American Student Debt Relief

The debt relief story needs to be retold. The factors cited above prompted an effective response from the Biden Administration. To get at the burden of debt, it invoked language from the *HEROES ACT*, designed to provide student debt relief in the aftermath of "war, or other military operation or national emergency." (Adam Liptak, *Supreme Court Rejects Biden's Student Loan Forgiveness Plan*, NYT, June 30, 2023) The act was passed in response to the attacks of September 11, 2001. The pandemic, so the Biden administration argued, interrupted all sorts of income flows and payment capacities and, therefore, constituted a national emergency.

Supreme Court Chief Justice Roberts rejected this argument. The Biden plan's overhaul of higher education finance provisions effectively "abolished them and supplanted them with a new regime entirely." (ibid) Whatever the legal ramifications, the administration tried in wholesale terms to counteract the scale of untenable higher educational conditions. The Biden administration vainly attempted to extend 'social state' amenities to promote a social good.

Debt relief offers a potential off-ramp to lighten one set of educational and economic burdens. While pandemic relief funds shored up declines in state higher education finance in the short-term, long-term finance, tuition, and enrollment issues still require resolution. Meanwhile, the tides of economic and political development over the past 25 years have overthrown longstanding educational priorities, values, and practices.

Aside from the provision of essential medical and educational services, American systems foster an intolerable share of debt. Debt factors quite decisively in the equations of economic inequality, further widening the fissures of polarization.

Part XV
Finance Interludes

Chapter One:
Education, Deficits, Debts, GDP Interlude

The viability of higher education, among other markets, was particularly aggravated during and since the Great Recession. The 2008 "$700 billion bailout of the banking industry" under George Bush was seemingly financed out of thin air. It was exceeded by the 2009 "$813 billion American Recovery and Reinvestment Act" under Obama, meant to prop up healthcare and education systems and generally to re-stimulate the economy. (Wikipedia)

Both funding incidents continued the period of funny-money deficit spending without raising taxes, begun under Reagan, extended by the Clinton administration in the 1990s, and multiplied under the administrations of Bush, Obama, and Trump. And then came the Pandemic. As of May 1, 2023, "the national debt stood at $31.46 trillion." (USAFacts Team, *What Is the US National Debt and How Has It Grown Over Time?* usafacts.org, May 2, 2023) "The US has run a budget deficit over the last 20 years, substantially growing the national debt. The US government debt-to-GDP ratio in 2022 was 129%, an "all-time high" (ibid) The ratio was at a record-low of 31.8% of GDP in 1981. (Source: OMB, Bureau of Economic Analysis, the Census Bureau).

Critical economic analysis centers on the extent to which the US government finances its debt and interest owed on it by using/selling Treasury notes that guarantee investment returns. "However, since the interest on the debt must be paid back to creditors who buy government securities, the government must spend a growing amount of its budget to repay the national debt. Deficit finance not only creates a financial burden for the government, but also diverts federal funds from other important programs." (ibid, USAFacts Team) "As of February 2025," the U.S. Treasury reports, "it costs $478 billion to maintain the debt, which is 16%! of the total federal spending in fiscal year 2025. The national debt has increased every year over the past ten years" (Fiscal Data, *What Is the National Debt,* treasury.gov). This provides fodder for greater fiscal discipline and reorganization of federal budget management. You either have to spend less, or tax more. This economic benchmark is once again upended by Republican passage of 'Big, Beautiful Bill' legislation.

Education Finance Loses Out

The states of America are required to balance their budgets, except under conditions of duress. Their economies are tightly tied, however, to the roller-coaster of the broader national economy, controlled in large part by dominant corporate interests and their Republican Party cohorts, for whom raising taxes to bring down deficits and debt is like taking poison.

In such a high-debt/deficit, recession-prone environment controlled by private financial interests, the environment for social thinking, social policy, and social funding is thwarted. The enterprise of higher education, along with many others, is increasingly forced to somehow pay for itself. It has fallen victim to the mentality and reality of commodification, "that colleges and universities are, first and foremost, credential providers and commercial enterprises" (Inside Higher Ed, *Combating the*

Commodification of Higher Education, insidehighered.com, June 5, 2022).

Historically, American higher education was considered a public or social good, just as it continues to be in Europe. The wonderful liberal spirit of open inquiry and open interest that advances individual idealism and once guided undergraduate and graduate study now appears increasingly unaffordable.

Out of the Debt/Deficit Funding Impasse

The foregoing illustrates the depths of the current economic impasse, which affects the entire education finance system. To counteract these developments and find new budgetary accommodation for education, the Bipartisan Policy Center issued a reform proposal on "Higher Education Financing and Student Outcomes." (M. Aborn, N. Cahill, *Education Funding Takes a Hit During Recessions, But It Doesn't Have To*, Bipartisan Policy Center, Oct. 27, 2020)

The proposal envisions "implementing a federal-state partnership with a recessionary trigger to provide automatic additional support during recessions. States that increased higher education spending during good times would receive a generous match from the federal government, a portion of which would be set aside in a rainy-day fund. These resources would be used to mitigate the cycle of disinvestment and smooth over funding shortfalls, reducing the need for colleges to raise tuition and thereby lessening reliance on student debt to plug state funding gaps." (ibid)

Given the terms and conditions of the American marketplace behemoth at this point, advancing such a proposal would require great dexterity and public education. It would require great popular and political support; at the moment, this is more than a tall order, presupposing normal governmental function. May such function be restored.

The legislation, endorsed by prominent, progressive members of Congress, (Senator Bernie Sanders of Vermont and Representative Pramila Jayapal) "aims for free college tuition at all community colleges, public four-year colleges, and tribal colleges" and to "eliminate tuition fees for students from families making under $125,000 and to reduce the cost of attendance by doubling the maximum Pell Grant award." (Melanie Hanson, *How Much Would Free College Cost?* The Education Data Initiative, August 31, 2023)

This so-called "College for All Act" would be funded through separate legislation that taxes "Wall Street speculation on stock trades by 0.5%." It would raise an estimated "$2.4 trillion" over the long-term for tuition-free education" (ibid). The federal cost of the program is estimated at an annual "$48 billion," to be shared with state and tribal governments (ibid). It would also challenge the tuition structures and feasibility of 'private' college and university higher education. Perhaps, finally, the rising costs of private education become unaffordable and place it out of the market.

Other proposals, such as America's College Promise Act, promote tuition-subsidized plans to be funded through shared federal and state grants. At the moment, bets are off for all such plans, but may yet one day be revisited.

The Cost of Universal Tuition-Free Higher Education

The ongoing quest to make higher education in America more affordable and accessible draws on different schemes and different cost estimates. In a *New York Times* opinion piece, the author David Deming estimates that "at least some - and perhaps all - of the cost of universal tuition-free public higher education could be defrayed by redeploying money that the government is already spending." (David Deming, *Tuition-Free College Could Cost Less Than You Think*, NYT, July 19, 2019) His calculations are based on the 2016 expenditure analysis. It reveals that "the federal government spent $91 billion on policies that subsidized college attendance, more than the $79 billion for total tuition and fee revenue for public institutions." (ibid) The higher education landscape may be shifting.

Chapter Two:
Compare Higher Ed/Vo-Tech Education

The comparison of European and American higher education systems presents many "apple and orange" challenges. To name but a few, what can be called high school education in most of Europe is more selective, academically rigorous, and usually completed at the age of 19. There are few intramural activities. The panoply of sports pursued in American high schools is moved in Europe to entirely different and separate venues.

Once at the university, which is predominantly public in Europe, the normal duration of study for a bachelor's degree is three years. More often than not, students enter university with predetermined academic and/or degree interests and goals - such as, for example, completing a three-year, advanced environmental-engineering bachelor's degree, at the University of Vienna. University study is geared toward specific academic attainment and professional career development. Sports and other extracurriculars are pursued at non-league club levels.

European higher education is more Spartan compared to the cornucopia of academic, social, artistic, and athletic experiences cultivated at most American public and private colleges and universities - underwritten by comparatively lavish public and private investments. Room and board in Europe are provided by most universities on a limited first-come, first-served basis, with costs financed from home or through student loans. Campus life, such as it is, is more dispersed in Europe and left more to individual initiative than to college organization.

The chief difference between American and European higher education conditions is that most European universities are tuition-free, except for modest student-paid stipends or fees. It's a scramble in some countries to maintain budgetary education outlays, but a "typical European higher education institution still receives about two-thirds of its revenues as a basic state contribution." *(How are European Higher Education Institutions Funded? New Evidence from ETER Microdata,* European Tertiary Education Register, The ETER Project.com, 2019)

In Austria, to give but one example, "the total expenditure in the tertiary (undergraduate/graduate, sic) sector amounts to €6.75 billion. The share of public funding is 91.6%. (sic) 8.4% comes from private sources." (European Commission-Eurydice-Austria, *Funding in Education,* europe.eu/national education, Nov. 27, 2023)

A partial review of higher education funding in Europe reveals that Germany maintains virtually tuition-free university education for EU citizens, as does France. In Germany, the individual states or provinces assume most educational budgetary costs, over and against federal higher education outlays. In France, the ratio of federal -to-state funding is reversed.

In Italy, tuition is subsidized on a sliding scale depending on factors such as family income and size, providing access to all. Higher education tuition is highly subsidized for EU citizens in the Netherlands and all the Nordic countries, including Russia. (European Commission,

Eurydice, *Funding in Education, Higher Education Funding by Country*, 2023) The UK introduced means-based tuition fees with a cap under £10,000 beginning in 2012. Scotland, Wales, and Northern Ireland have each instituted their own university tuition fee systems. (Wikipedia, *Tuition Fees in the United Kingdom*, wikipedia.org, August 2023)

Room and board costs, as mentioned, are borne by student families and/or student loans. These arrangements vary from country to country. In Austria, so-called study grants to cover living costs are available for students whose families cannot afford such expenses. Eligible students can receive stipends of up to €8,580 per year. These are grants, not loans. At present, revealing the widespread income capacity of most Austrian households, only 16% of Austrian students qualify for and receive study grants to support their living expenses. (Austrian Federal Ministry of Education, Science, and Research, *University Report-Study Grant*, bmbwf.gv.at 2020)

High public funding for higher education is an outgrowth of the phenomenal development of Europe's post-war "welfare capitalist" states. After World Wars I and II, a general consensus pervaded the populations of most European states - people had had enough of aristocracies, nobilities, and elites, whether monarchical, or those in high finance and business, in the military, or within the church. This echoes the historical shift in consciousness that occurred in post-World War II Europe, cited earlier, as a token of historical progress. As previously cited author, Tony Judt observes, Europe underwent "an evolution in which it was the state that served its subjects, rather than the other way around." (Tony Judt, *Postwar: A History of*

Europe Since 1945, ibid, p. 360) In the 1960s and 1970s, before confidence in the state's ability flagged, it was widely perceived that the government could "do a better job than the unrestricted market" (ibid, p. 361). Laissez-faire capitalism was discredited. Now, the state was held better able to "dispense justice, provide security, distribute goods and services, and to design and apply strategies for social cohesion, moral sustenance, and cultural vitality." (ibid)

This was nowhere truer than in the realm of higher education. Where previously, higher education had been a domain of privilege for the well-to-do who could afford it, access to higher education in post-war European social democratic states was made "universal and equal." In 1965, "the Italian Ministry of Education abolished all university entrance examinations and fixed subject quotas. Higher education, once a privilege, would now be a right. The result was catastrophic." (ibid, p. 394) The expansion of university classrooms, halls, labs, and dormitories could not keep up with the enrollment boom, which at some sites, grew by 600% in just a few years. This has since settled down. (ibid) The grand commitments and expectations of the social state have been scaled back.

As noted, the EU follows the "subsidiarity principle," which holds that "higher education policies are decided at the level of the individual member states." (ibid) State policy, especially in Austria, continues to provide relatively generous support to higher education. Putting a finer point on it, cited Quora commentator, Per, son of Jürgen, notes the difference between European and American policies, is that in "European countries, the costs of educating the population are shared by everyone. Instead of you or your parents taking a massive hit all at once, the burden is spread out collectively (sic) via taxes…. In European countries, people tend to see higher education as a matter of national interest and an educated population as a necessity for continued technological, social, and cultural development as well as preservation of their history and values." (Per, son of Jürgen, B.Sc, journalism, U of Kansas, *Why is college free in a lot of European countries but so expensive in the U.S.?* Quora.com, 2020)

Such policies have individual and social benefits. As Per son continues, they "level the playing field, and thereby support (sic) social mobility, because they make higher education available to everyone regardless of their families' economic status. It means you are much freer to compete on an equal footing with people whose parents happen to have more money than yours." (ibid)

Vocational-Educational Training State governmental financial support for equal and universal higher education tuition, derived from relatively higher business and individual taxes, is widespread in Europe. It is supported logistically and administratively at the EU level. In conjunction with European states as well, the EU promotes work-based learning, "in particular apprenticeships. Involving the social partners in its governance, such dual VET (vocational-educational-training) is considered to have several positive societal and economic effects, most notably low youth unemployment." (P. Emmenegger & L. Seitzl, *Social Partner Involvement in Collective Skill Formation Governance: A Comparison of Austria, Denmark, Germany, Netherlands, and Switzerland,* Sage Journals-European Trade-Union Institute (ETUI), February 12, 2020)

In many European countries, apprenticeship and VE training begin at the ripe age of 15 years old, following a tiered design of educational organization. First, at the age of 10, and then again at the age of 15, a sort of culling takes place. Students with academic interests and aptitudes are tracked into schools that emphasize academic learning. This is true in Austria as well. At the second culling, when students are 14 or 15, some who have found an inclination and aptitude for academic learning in the intervening years will also enroll in the *Gymnasium*, or academic, pre-university high-schools. Since 2016, roughly "30%" of Austria's high school student population has attended such schools. (The Standard, OECD Report, *Austria: Breakdown of Students Attending Occupational Training Schools Rises*, September 16, 2016.)

Another one-third or so of Austrian high school students attend vo-tech occupational training schools that conclude with an academic degree, enabling graduates to enroll in universities. The occupational training involved covers a broad range of fields, from Teacher Training and Social Work to Agriculture and Forestry, Healthcare Assistants to Business/Accounting, and Chemical/Electrical and IT Computer Technology. (*Trans. Occupational High-Schools, oesterreich, gv.at*, March 20, 2023)

Finally, another one-third or so of Austrian high school students enroll in what are called *dual-apprenticeship* vo-tech programs, which offer *dual* educational and on-site training learning experiences. According to Statista, a firm that conducts statistical reviews for Austrian and German enterprises, the number of students in dual-apprenticeship programs rose to 40.7% in 2022 - some 108,000 students in all. Apparently, this number is insufficient to fill all available apprentice positions. (Trans. Statista, *Statistics for Training and Apprenticeship in Austria*, January 11, 2024)

Nonetheless, the VET programs recognize and respond to students for whom strict academic learning is just not their cup of tea. Such students are invited to develop more practical skills. At the moment, over 10,000 students are enrolled/employed in the *Construction, Architecture & Building Trades*, in the *Office & Commercial Finance* sector, in the *Machinery, Vehicles & Metal* trades, in *Tourism & Hospitality*, or in the field of *Electrical Engineering & Electronics*. (ibid) Lesser numbers are involved in a broad array of other trades.

Austria's apprentice program or system is similar to those in Germany, Denmark, the Netherlands, and Switzerland. They are described as *collective* in that they are "characterized by high public commitment (from the state, sic), high involvement of firms," and trade unions. (*Social Partner Involvement in Collective Skill Formation...*, ibid) In each of these countries, enrollment in such programs for secondary school-age students is above 33%, almost double the OECD average. (ibid)

Organization and implementation of VET systems in these countries involve broad and delicate institutional coordination, cooperation, and voluntary buy-in from each *neo-corporatist* (business-labor-government) interest. Crucially, programs depend on businesses and employers who are able and willing to take part in what is a collective, public-enterprise effort. They pay trade-union, collectively bargained apprentice wages and social benefits, and in return, they get a ready-trained stream of certified workers whose skills are *portable*. As is true for social partnership undertakings generally, the system is only viable to the extent that firms in the same sector are similarly involved. Trade unions, for their part, expand their ranks, contribute training guidelines at the training schools, and provide on-site instruction. The state funds the educational/training institutes involved. The state's interest is advanced through "improved social cohesion and boosted (sic) performance of the national economy." (ibid)

The Sage report cites the German apprenticeship system as the most successful of the modern era because of its strategic design, involving "employer associations, trade unions, educators and government representatives in a joint, multi-layered regulation along neo-corporatist or *social partnership* lines." (ibid) Everybody is pulling on the same set of oars. It is an organic operation. The "cooperation cannot be imposed by law, but happens on the ground." (ibid) This accounts for the variety of apprentice systems, even between countries that share the same *collective* design. Each state has its own governance arrangement, lines of authority, and decision-making processes shared between provincial and federal authorities.

In Austria, interestingly, and in contrast to German and Swiss VET systems, the social partners representing business and labor are excluded from federal ministry education and economic policy deliberations. Apparently, the political parties and their ministries take priority at this strategic policy level. Otherwise, at the technical-operational level, "the social partners are very involved in the definition of training content and firm-level training" (ibid) for the dual-apprenticeship programs. As is the case in other fields, as mentioned, social partnership involvement in vo-tech training is supported, but not stipulated by law. This allows the partners to maintain initiative and adaptation. Of course, in Austria, the partnership is reinforced by obligatory membership for both "employers in the Chamber of Commerce and for all employees in the Chamber of Labor." (ibid) This assures continuity and uniformity.

The case made for the *collective* implementation of such programs in Austria, and the other countries mentioned, demonstrates the advantages of streamlining educational, training, and employment systems. The advantage gained is not so much competitive as it is an equality of opportunity. State, business, and labor stakeholders find a utility that redounds not only to their own efficiency and productivity, but to the larger economy. Young people gain valuable training and extensive skills with which they can confidently enter the job market. There are certainly trade-offs in such a systemic organization, but the whole is designed and implemented to be responsive and adaptive. In all, these programs represent coordinated social adaptation and response to the standing and extensive social interest in education.

Equal opportunity pertains not only to partnership involvement in Vo-tech education, but also to the processes and services described above for collective bargaining and health care. All three fields stand in contrast to the more ad hoc systems characteristic of capitalist market economies, such as found particularly in the USA – where, educational, medical, and employment opportunities are more *competitive*, often matters of chance, good or bad fortune, and increasingly of financial privilege.

Such observations signify the profound social insight and commitment to social partnership that transcends political prejudice, or preference. As the cited historian Tony Judt appraises it, "the welfare state was avowedly social, but it was (and is, sic) far from socialist. In that sense, welfare capitalism, as it unfolded in Western Europe, was (and is, sic) truly post-ideological." (*Tony Judt, ibid*, p.362) This exemplifies the kind of pragmatic ideology referred to earlier and testifies to the great breadth of social thinking in Europe that augments dimensions of the private economy. It is possible and beneficial to harness the power of both public and private systems.

Chapter Three: Debt, Deficit & Taxation

This post-ideological consensus is revealed in taxation regimes across the European continent, which signal common commitment to public interest politics and policies. Though staunch conservative and liberal constituencies exist in all European states, upkeep of a broad social contract abides: the long-term welfare of society needs protection from the vicissitudes and depredations of unregulated markets, and also, presumably, from drastic shifts in political alignment

Percent of Government Spending to Gross Domestic Product (GDP) by Country 2021-2022 (International Monetary Fund, Government Expenditures, % of GDP, imf.org, 2022)

Country	Score (%)	Country	Score (%)
France	58.03	Japan	44.00
Italy	56.07	Poland	43.05
Austria	52.08	Canada	41.04
Germany	49.05	USA	36.02
Sweden	47.03	Russia	36.00
Spain	47.01	China	33.04
Brazil	46.04	Mexico	28.05
United Kingdom	44.00	Euro Zone	50.05

Commitment to the "social contract" finds many expressions, but perhaps none as transparent as in tables that indicate national taxation rates as a percentage of Gross Domestic Product (GDP). Higher levels of spending relative to GDP nominally reflect priorities of social unity and shared material well-being. You will notice the higher numbers associated with the EU.

While EU conditions are not panacean, they do indicate profound social and economic determination to resolve the historic and current inequities generated by liberal market capitalist economies. The numbers above offer only relative insight. So far, most European states maintain fiscal-monetary probity and balance, to stave off inflationary pressures and political conflict. However, EU budget and debt issues remain live-wire concerns.

Whether debt and taxation are managed appropriately depends on a country's economic and political situation. Many factors are involved -its GDP, its global trade balance, per capita income levels, currency strength, demographics, etc. Economics, at this level, resembles physics. By common consent, European countries are subject to EU disciplinary rules. It is the trade-off they make in order to maintain national taxation autonomy.

In contrast to the American taxation regime, individual European taxpayers are not subject to federal tax. Instead, a portion of their state taxes is filtered through the state to EU institutions in Brussels, Belgium. Legal and treaty mechanisms guide economic management both at the national and supranational EU level.

The EU Stability and Growth Pact, finalized by the Maastricht Treaty, mentioned above, stipulates that Eurozone members must adhere to certain rules. As noted earlier, "The treaty limits government deficits to 3% of GDP and public debt levels, as noted, to 60% of GDP, or sufficiently diminishing toward and approaching that level at a satisfactory pace, so as to enable countries to share a single currency." (European Commission-Economy and Finance, History of the Stability and Growth Pact, europa.eu, 2022)

Enforcement of the pact is somewhat contingent, but the EU does exert significant leverage. Nations, such as Austria at the current moment, are obliged to honor their agreements, or the collective union of European nations would simply fall apart. Enforcement procedures, known as EDPs (excessive deficit procedures), can be triggered when countries repeatedly and flagrantly exceed debt/deficit thresholds.

Offending countries can be required to "fix the problem through a program of fiscal adjustment." (Bruegel, To Unblock Fiscal Rule Reform, the EU Should Reinstate Its Excessive Deficit Procedure, bruegel.org, October 17, 2023) As the headline indicates, the rule was suspended on account of the pandemic. Its reinstatement requires rule adjustment and amendment.

In 2022, most of the 27 EU member states managed to stay below the deficit-to-GDP limit even after the pandemic crisis had thrown many budgetary plans and commitments up in the air. The current account deficit to GDP ratio "in Germany averaged 3.27 percent of GDP from 1980 until

2022." (EUROSTAT) "Government debt to GDP in Germany averaged 66.51 percent of GDP from 1995 until 2022, reaching an all-time high of 82.00% of GDP in 2010 and a record low of 54.90% of GDP in 1995." (Trading Economics, Germany Government *Debt to GDP*, tradingeconomics.com, 2022)

For its part, "Austria recorded a current account deficit of 0.30 percent of the country's Gross Domestic Product in 2022. Its government debt to GDP' ratio was 78.40% in 2022" (Trading Economics, *Austria's Current Account Deficit to GDP & Austria Government Debt to GDP*, tradingeconomics.com, 2022/2023). Austria's favorable deficit rating and lower interest rate payments are due to its high ranking as an arena for bond investment. At the moment, however, in 2025, as Statistics Austria reports "The ongoing economic crisis is having an impact on public finances and has caused the budget deficit to rise to 4.7% in 2024. This means that Austria has moved further away from the 3% Maastricht limit. In addition to the decline in economic output, the 8.8% increase in government expenditure particularly contributed to the deficit. This increase was driven primarily by the salary settlements for the public sector, pension adjustments and the valorization of social benefits. (*Government Deficit of 4.7% in 2024 above Maastricht Limit*, statistik.at, March 2025) Aside from the listed expenditures, un-budgeted governmental Covid pandemic outlays in 2020 and 2021 may be catching up as well. The current coalition government of 2025, as mentioned above, is itself now subject to EU-ordered EDP conditions. It is in for some fairly drastic budgetary belt-tightening.

As on other continents, taxation, debts, and deficits are quarterly and perennial issues of great concern. They pertain to the control of inflation - the great bugaboo for all countries, but, given European history, especially for the EU. The Maastricht agreements of 1992 are intended to guide and, to a certain extent, sequester economic management from political contest and contention.

Inflation control provides a litmus test by which political conflict can be contained. The Maastricht rules induce mutual, voluntary agreement and commitment to contain deficit spending, not only for economic reasons, but to protect the European social welfare, and social-partnership project. This project is endangered when excessive expenditures are required to service debt.

There will always be deficit fluctuations, reflecting discrepancies between government spending and the revenues of taxation, but Europeans are especially determined to keep deficits on a tight leash.

The American Contrast

As noted earlier, the USA's debt-to-GDP ratio of 129% would run afoul of European limits. The American economy is exceptional, if for no other reason than its size. But normal economic metrics still apply. In the USA, deficits-to-GDP ratios over the past 40 or so years have fluctuated between the high rate of 14.7% during the pandemic of 2020/2021 to the surplus rate of +2.3% in 2000. In 1982, under Reagan, the deficit stood at 3.8%. It increased and shrank until 2007, and then rose precipitously to 9.7% after the banking crisis of 2008/2009.

The deficit shrank to "2.4% in 2015" and then gradually increased before skyrocketing with the pandemic. (FRED Economic Data, *The Current Deficit as % of GDP*, fred.stlouisfed.org, October 24, 2023) In 2022, after Biden's pandemic relief and investment legislation, "the US deficit-to-GDP ratio was "3.7%, or 5.3%" depending on assessment methodologies. (Trading Economics) or (FRED Economic Data) As noted earlier in the Tax Accountant and Socail Worker chapter, (p. 213) America's deficit: GDP ratio over the past four years averages at 7.3%, including outlays to ameliorate the Pandemic.

Debts and deficits in the USA are quite the gnarled bone, or, as the case may be, political football. The so-called congressional balanced-budget provisos and debt-ceiling requirements don't seem to effectively resolve budgetary arguments or contain political contention and conflict. The political contest is ramped up by ideology. Stalemate prevails. The ball, so to speak, goes up one end of the field only to return the other way. In America, deficit hawks argue that high deficit spending is inflationary and raises interest rates on borrowing, imperiling investment that would have otherwise gone toward economic development. (Yet, many of their members refuse to increase taxes to pay down the debt.)

Deficit doves also believe that deficits pose a long-term economic burden, but can be useful in the short-term to manage economic downturns and invigorate the economy.

The US Congress has yet to invent a platform or restructure economic conditions so that debt/deficit/GDP issues can be efficiently resolved. This inability is at the crux of economic and political stalemate. It stokes dysfunction, reflecting brinkmanship, neglect, and incompetency but, more decisively, the retardation of American economic development.

The horrible polarization and stalemate in American affairs will only subside when American political, capital, and labor interests develop a new and different platform upon which conflicts over taxation, debt, and deficit spending issues find more reliable, viable, and sustainable resolutions. The EU provides an alternative model - not to be copied but to exemplify innovation.

Alternative Deficit Platforms

In America, Stefanie Kelton's work, among others, signifies an attempt to create a new and different platform, or framework to resolve the impasse of economic policy and debate. She describes herself as a "deficit owl", "one who proposes that deficits are justified to address urgent social deficits in employment, education, healthcare, and infrastructure - provided inflation is moderate and supply bottlenecks are absent" (Stephanie Kelton, *The Deficit Myth: Modern Monetary Theory and How to Build a Better Economy*, John Murray Publisher, p. 76, 2020).

In her book, Kelton contends that the debate between deficit hawks and doves, both of whom believe deficits need tight control, "is stuck in the faulty idea that deficits are sinful." She contends that modern economies demand wise deficit management to meet the requirements of a functional and productive society. Productivity is essential to hold down debt. High levels of productivity can be inspired and maintained by sagacious, deficit-supported finance.

She advocates the Modern Monetary Theory, which proposes that money should no longer be understood as a scarce resource, rooted in material value, but rather as a resource of relative social abundance. Rather than "crowding out" private business investment, as conventional deficit analysis holds, Kelton argues that "deficit spending, properly targeted, stimulates, or 'crowds in' private business growth" (*Ibid.*, p. 126). In this sense, fiscal management in the realm of politics and government budgets is more important than monetary policy determined by banks. As you might observe, this flies in the face of orthodox American finance, and the control banks exert over economic policy.

Kelton goes on to clarify economic function. The American economy is so large that bond investment is attractive and secure and provides the federal government with ongoing financial liquidity. The U.S. government "issues" currency. As long as inflation is held at bay, the government is not constrained by the same budgetary limits known to ordinary people who consume, or "use" currency. Kelton supports the notion that government budgets are relatively unlimited by pointing out recent incidents of government deficit finance.

Because of deficit spending anxiety, there never seems to be quite enough money at the national level to invest in public education and healthcare - except when it comes to "expanding the defense budget, bailing out banks, giving huge tax breaks to the wealthiest Americans," or injecting the economy with hundreds of billions of stimulus money in response to the Great Recession or the Pandemic" (*Ibid.*, p. 4).Such incidents appear *ipso facto* to support Kelton's case, remembering her *proviso* that there are conditions, especially inflationary ones, that impose budgetary limits.

Otherwise, as she has it, government deficit and debt finance won't cause bankruptcy. It is merely the government borrowing money from itself, through very attractive bond sales to entities such as China and Japan (which already hold considerable amounts of U.S) debt. In all, Kelton's theory supports building an economy that is geared "toward people over profits and people over balanced budgets" (ibid).

Social Market/ Partnership Platforms

It sounds like a very "European" theory. Except it is not. Europe is a long way from adopting Modern Monetary economic theories and the deficit spending free-for-all they at least partially imply.

Euro-currency solvency, as indicated, is still of bedrock value that keeps governmental and banking financial policies tethered to real economic conditions - notwithstanding disjointed European monetary and fiscal policy and the "mismatch" between banking and governmental institutions - as reviewed and alleged earlier, by Chartbook's Adam Tooze.

If you'll recall, Tooze's survey pointed to a European systemic shortfall when it came to managing the Great Recession (2007-2009), the "sovereign debt crisis" (2010-2015) and the Pandemic healthcare crisis of 2020-2021, not to mention challenges like the cutoff of Russian oil and the Ukraine war, which induced high levels of inflation.

Mismanagement and systemic barriers may be issues, but Tooze himself later admits that these are part of the

Eurozone design. Its constraints and rules are meant to rein in deficit spending, even at the expense of growth. (Adam Tooze, Chartbook 370, *America's Big Spending: Source, Centre for European Reform,* Aslak Berg, *Why Should Europe Not Worry about U.S. Out-Performance*, December 13, 2023). Growing pains, no pun intended, are involved, but the analysis also shows how European monetary and fiscal policy is juxtaposed to American policy - where fiscal and monetary measures combine to support growth even at the expense of higher deficit spending.

As also noted, the European economy, in its different parts, weathered the economic headwinds of the past 15 years through the resiliency and adjustments of its more decentralized, state-based national economies. Some states had to increase deficit spending to contain economic fallout. The financial tempests since 2007 are still not wholly vanquished. The resiliency of European society in its several states is also, if not more, attributable to the social partnership design or platform of their economic organization. Despite the systemic challenges of the past era, economic inequality and related social polarization have been contained.

The sociological term, "social capital" usually refers to the synergy produced by amicable and cooperative working relationships. It can also apply to the social synergy generated by the many manifestations of social partnership described above in healthcare, education, and with reference to employment conditions. Social partnership is so deeply embedded in the design of most European economies and the relationships it generates that it is almost taken for granted. It provides the binding, affirmative, and mutually exercised sinews of a social contract - the Social Market social contract. Certainly, such a contract comes with costs, but so far - its benefits have proven sustainable and beneficial to vast swaths of European populations.

To cite but one example, the case for German benefits was made recently in a thorough study by Jan Priewe, *Comparing Living and Working Conditions: Germany Outperforms the United States.* Utilizing the Purchasing Power Parity (PPP) metric referenced earlier, he first focuses on the issue of consumer consumption, so critical to GDP calculations. Higher mean-incomes allow for greater individual, private consumption of goods and services in America, but this, for Priewe, gets evened out in Germany by what he terms "collective consumption in-kind," or public financial support of common services. This refers to such things as "no tuition fees for university students, subsidization of public transport and culture, toll-free highways, healthcare, etc. Of course, this goes along with higher taxes and social security contributions. For instance, the European Commission's database AMECO shows Germany's public expenses for individual consumption in kind, valued here in PPP US$$, as $8,800 per person as compared to $2,876 in the U.S. (2021) (Jan Priewe, *Ibid.*, Nr. 91, Hans-Böckler-Stiftung, January 2024, p. 15).

These are so-called "shared benefits," the hallmark of social market economies, financed by individual and business taxes, redounding to the benefit of all. Similar scenarios can be found in most European countries. Priewe applies the Purchasing Power Parity (PPP) metric again to compare American and German wage structures. "Mean annual wages in the U.S. exceed the German ones, mainly because of higher annual working time. However, the German median wage exceeds the one in the U.S. despite much lower annual working time in Germany. Even median hourly wages are much higher in Germany (of course, all data in PPP US$)" (Jan Priewe, *Ibid,* p. 14).

Priewe accounts for such favorable comparisons by citing "stronger trade unions in Germany and the system of more centralized bargaining, despite its slowly fading impact." (*Ibid.*). Such things offer an additional glimpse of conditions in Europe that explain the social cohesion fostered by social partnership designs. Moreover, his assessment reinforces the central economic thrust of the social market capitalist system: when more people are paying into the system, (because of higher relative wages) business benefits, as do projects to extend higher education and healthcare for to the general benefit of society.

Part XVI
Contemporary American Realities

Chapter One:
The Social Contract

The old American social contract loses binding force because many segments of the population are not keeping up with the economic gains made by the upper two quintiles, or 40% of the population, -not to mention the so-called top 1%. Even as wages have gained on inflation since 2021 (Fortune Magazine, 12/12/2023) and cheerleaders for the economy broadcast hope, great segments of the population have been left behind since the Great Recession of 2007-2008.

A reminder of American disparity levels is worthwhile. In 2023, "the top three income quintiles, or 60% of American households, earned 87.4% of total income generated by the American economy. Rendered in different terms than those already given, **(See Appendix 4: World-Wide Income Shares)** the lower two income quintiles, or 40% of American households, earned just 12.6% of that income" (Statista Research Department, *Shares of household income of quintiles in the United States from 1973-2023*, statista.com, Sept. 17, 2024). The top 1% of households, extravagantly boosting top quintiles income levels, earned 14.6% of all wages in 2021, twice as high as their 7.3% share in 1979" (Julian Kagan, *Income and Wealth Disparities Between Top and Bottom Earners*, Investopedia.com, Sept. 2, 2024).

The ostensive, new financialized social contract leaves many vulnerable to the demagoguery of resentment and division, - even to the point of doubting the fundamental value of democratic self-government. A social contract has to be about more than income and wealth accumulation for the owning classes. To retain durable legitimacy, it has to be continuously reinforced in mutual benefit to the broadest spectrums of society.

In the recent era, social interest policies to bolster the old social contract were cruelly foreclosed when the American financial system nearly collapsed in 2008. Poor Barack Obama's administration was confronted with saving a sinking economic ship at the beginning of his presidency, radically limiting his policy options. He was in the midst of an emergency.

Contrast this with FDR's assumption of office in 1932, a full three years after the ship of the economy had run aground. He had more policy room and appetite, - if no less urgency, - to advance New Deal policies that reformed the economic system. In their article, *Why the Great Recession Made Inequality Worse*, Ken-Hou Lin and Megan Tobias argue that "whereas the New Deal took a bottom-up approach and brought governmental resources directly to unemployed workers, the recent recovery was largely top-down and finance-driven" (ibid, *Oxford University Press Blog*, February 10, 2020).

It was a cruel irony of Great Recession times and emblematic of systemic capture that the very culprits responsible for the crisis were the ones to get "bailed out" - in order to avert a total economic crash. The banks were not only bailed out; the system of which they are nominal proprietors was, in the main, perpetuated. As Lin and Tobias note, "The crisis was not only wasted. It made the United States even more unequal."

A lot of damage was done. The stock market might have recovered by 2013, but unemployment "was as high as 8%, and the single-family mortgage delinquency rate still hovered above 10%...In 2016, a typical American family owned 30% less wealth than it did in 2007" (ibid).

The social contract ink to secure and promote shared gain had long been evaporating, even as Obama administration programs attempted to broaden economic recovery. Considerable funds ($831 billion) were dedicated by the American Recovery and Reinvestment Act of 2009 to provide fiscal relief to state and municipal governments. These one-offs certainly helped, but reform and restructuring of the overall financial system languished, as did social contract reinvigoration. These things, as Lin and Tobias observe, were "deemed politically infeasible under the market-oriented governing model dominating in the late 2000s." (ibid).

This model continues to require unflinching support for the financial institutions of society as the ultimate custodians of economic welfare. Policies of "Quantitative Easing," among others adopted by the Federal Reserve, provided banks with a lot of cheap money and signified, according to Lin and Tobias, a "regressive shift in how American society organizes economic resources. Under such conditions, increase in productivity [must] first and foremost benefit the financial sector and investors." (ibid.) These developments reflect many things, but chiefly the capture of public policy by hyper-capitalist interests at the expense of American working-class populations, to the detriment of social unity and shared material prosperity. While people at the bottom 50% of income distribution scrape by, those at the top engage in speculative frenzies with all the left-over money that should have gone to support lower class wages. At their worst, these equity fund robber barons rival Marie Antoinette and her royal callousness to the fate of the people before the French revolution: "Let them eat cake."

Financialization and Private Equity Frenzy

Lin and Tobias point to three primary ways by which this "financialization" of the economy occurs: First, the financial sector creates extractive intermediaries that drain resources from other economic activities without providing commensurate benefit. Examples of this include mega-banks, shadow banks, and corporate financial arms" (ibid.) which exploit such things as financial student loan debt vulnerabilities (explaining, perhaps, why it's so difficult to reform student debt policies) and also take over public-sector pension funds, often leaving actual pensioners with their hats in hand.

"Second, the financial sector loosens the co-dependence between labor and capital, allowing investors to profit without production. Third, the proliferation of financial products among American households is invariably regressive: poor households pay the highest interests and fees, while rich households reap the largest investment gains." (ibid.)

It becomes increasingly hard to get a loan, or to refinance a mortgage for folks with less money to their name. The corporate financial arms cited above include the growing power of "private equity" firms. With names such as Apollo, Blackstone, the Carlyle Group, and Kohlberg Kravis Roberts.

According to Chris Hedges, writing -perhaps exaggeratedly - for *The Real News Network*, such firms "buy up and plunder businesses, piling on debt, refusing to reinvest, slashing staff, and often driving companies into bankruptcy." (ibid, *How Private Equity Conquered America*, realnewsnetwork.com, March 1, 2024). For equity firm owners, however, it's often quite a lucrative business. Hedges' interview with Gretchen Morgenson, who wrote the book, *These Are the Plunderers: How Private Equity Runs - and Wrecks - America*, reveals some of the scope and scurrilous practices overtaking all sorts of private and public business enterprises - from hospitals and nursing homes to educational institutions, public water utilities, mom-and-pop stores, and retail chains. As Hedges claims, "these private equity firms, like an invasive species, are ubiquitous." (Hedges, ibid.)

Morgenson explains the M.O. thus: "These firms, first of all, raise money for their buyouts. They don't use a lot of their own money for those buyouts. What they do is they go to public pensions, they go to endowments, they go to the big institutional investors and say, 'We're putting together a fund, we're going to buy-out companies, we're going to make them more efficient, and then we're going to sell them in five to seven years at a profit, and you will be able to reap those gains along with us.'

"But yes, the private equity titans do not put a lot of their own money at stake here. One to two percent of these funds are typically the private equity firm's money. So, after they have raised the money, they go out and look for companies to buy, and they home-in on companies that have assets they can strip." (ibid.) As Morgenson further notes, "It's an extraction business." (ibid.)

According to Hedges and Morgenson, shady business transactions of all sorts leave 'taken-over companies' little recourse. The private equity firms install their own representatives to govern company boards. "The deal is," as Hedges relates, "they get the pension funds to invest because supposedly the pension funds will make a profit. But then, as you write in the book, they force the pension funds to pay them management fees. You have cases in the book where they're not even doing anything, but if I remember, they're pulling like 10%, a lot of money. And these pension funds, in the end, don't make a profit." (ibid.)

"That's just one of the tricks of the trade," Morgenson rejoins, "that they do to generate billions of dollars for themselves while they're impoverishing so many other people." (ibid.) Remedy, it appears, is elusive. Morgenson continues, "One of the things that could improve our perception or educate people about how pervasive private equity has become is to force these firms to identify themselves as the owners. So, it should be the Carlyle nursing home or the Blackstone donut shop or whatever just so you are aware of who you are dealing with and whose pocket you're putting your money into." As the playwright wrote, 'something is rotten in the state of Denmark'. (William Shakespeare, *Hamlet*)

"Now, the secrecy is one thing. The political clout is immense. They have so much money. Their tax treatment is an outrage, and many presidents have tried to change it, but have not been able to do so." (ibid) In such and other profound ways, financialization represents a regressive shift in the American economy, one that has exacerbated income and wealth inequality. Wage growth in 2023, as noted, has only recently started to exceed inflation rates. However, it has a long way to go to regain lost ground and restore confidence in the economic system and the social contract it represents.

Perhaps massive governmental deficit spending - and even the massive corporate tax cut of 2017 - have both abetted the broad economic recovery touted by commentators, such as Adam Tooze. But this would overlook the behavior, also noted earlier, of corporations that "did not use the easy credit and tax cut to increase wages or create jobs. Rather, they took advantage of the low interest rate to finance stock buybacks, channeling other people's money to top executives and shareholders. "(ibid)

The financialization pattern appears again, in which economic growth is "wed to heightened inequality." (ibid) Maybe it will all work out, except for the ominous shadow of inequality, polarization, and stalemate that still hovers over the land, along with precarious amounts of deficit and debt.

Economic financialization is a real phenomenon perpetrated, as noted earlier, by doyens of the new executive class and corporate interests, certain elements of which are fomenting a class war from the top. It's no use vilifying an entire class of people, but stock trading firms, in particular, appear to be getting away with financial murder.

At a minimum, it's high time to support legislation introduced by Bernie Sanders in 2019. His bill "would tax trading of stocks bonds, and derivatives at rates ranging from 0.005% to 0.5%." (Irina Ivanova, *Bernie Sanders has a way to raise $2 Trillion - tax Wall Street trading*, CBS News, cbsnews.com, May 23, 2019). Economists estimate the "tax could raise between $776 billion and $2.4 trillion over 10 years." (ibid) It would raise money, but more importantly, constrain speculation. Such legislation must be accompanied by confrontive argument that advocates fundamental revision of American economic policy.

Such a tax, as the one Sanders proposes, is not uncommon in Europe. Austria doesn't have such a Financial Transaction Tax (FTT), but Switzerland does, along with others such as "Finland, Poland, Great Britain, France, Italy, and Turkey." (Elke Asen, *Financial Transaction Taxes in Europe*, taxfoundation.org, February 4, 2021). The EU Parliament and Germany are pushing for an EU-wide financial transaction tax, but have yet to achieve a unified response from all European countries.

Excessive financialization of the U.S. economy must find restraint. The phenomenon still contends with what remains strong - though tenuous - welfare state interests for the overall direction of American economic development. The Biden administration did its level best to uphold and extend the promise and potential of that state, but the case now appears to be threatened on multiple fronts.

Indeed, the phenomenon of financialization represents a breakdown of social welfare solidarity, and the hollowing out of effective labor interest leverage, both of which are necessary for the financialization takeover. The pluralist American social interest, once the preamble and substance of the American social contract, is left in shambles. Private economic interest overwhelms political and public interest. In the dialectical terms of physics, this must call forth an equal and opposite reaction.

However, the social/financial world does not always respond in physical-world terms -even though it will, eventually. The furor created by Trump's 2025 tariff policies should lead to countermanding policies. In the meantime, his decrees indicate to what extent the old social contract, guiding capital toward social ends, was weakened and rife for plunder. As noted earlier, a charitable reading of the Trump tariff agenda, is that he is somehow able to bend global trade to his will and policies and create a more balanced system – though exactly what that system is supposed to look like is impossible to say. Perhaps, he just wants to reverse China's global trade position. The time horizons in which manufacturing returns to America, or to all affected countries, is at the moment incalculable. Manufacturing without commitments to social security leads to unalloyed exploitation. In the meantime, even after Trump's tariff U-Turn, the unity, balance and predictability of the world order is upset. This opens the door to a world in rivalry and divided, contentious calculation; a world prone to conflict. The tragedy of the moment is that other, more beneficent and socially constructive and viable visions are within reach

A New Social Contract

Excessive financialization is only one aspect of the American economy that needs reversal. Beyond that, the need to reformulate and renew the American social contract becomes increasingly evident. As yet, Elizabeth Warren's proposals are among those that articulate the most concrete, yet groping vision of what that social contract might look like.

Her campaign for the Democratic Party presidential nomination in 2020 stoutly identified the growing financialization of the economy as a nemesis. "For decades," she wrote, "Washington has lived by a simple rule: If it's good for Wall Street, it's good for the economy. The financial sector has been sucking value out of the economy instead of benefiting it." (Deborah D'Souza, *Elizabeth Warren's Economic Plan: Break and Remake,* investopedia.com, August 15, 2023)

Warren's plans are still relevant a few years after she proposed them. She goes after all sorts of malignant, if not malfeasant, corporate and fund manager practices, - including *executive compensation;* the new, *sub-prime* loan maneuver in which *leveraged loans* are made to businesses with lower credit ratings and higher levels of debt; and the *carried interest loophole,* which provides a tax windfall to investment fund managers. (ibid)

The list goes on. She would advance laws to reverse *anti-competitive mergers* in the tech, banking, and agricultural sectors. She would also pass an updated version of the *Glass-Steagall Act* to prevent investment banks from accessing *taxpayer-subsidized insurance* plans. (ibid)

Ala Stephanie Kelton and *The Deficit Myth,* Warren advocates getting rid of *debt ceiling* requirements or adjusting them to governmental spending decisions. She supports Senator Bernie Sanders' single-payer, universal *Medicare for All* legislation. (ibid)

To pay for such proposals and plans, besides altering debt-ceiling requirements, Warren would overhaul the American tax system. Through her *Real Corporate Profits Tax* legislation, corporate abuse of tax loopholes would be closed. Further, she advocates a "7% tax on corporate profits over $100 million (domestic and foreign) in addition to regular tax liabilities." (ibid)

To pay for universal, single-payer Medicare, Warren advocates that *98% of the* monies businesses normally spend on employee health insurance be redirected to the federal government. She also advocates for a Wealth Tax of "2% to 6% on household net worth over $50 million." (ibid) This would raise $3 trillion over 10 years and affect 0.1% of the population, requiring an expansion of the Internal Revenue Service's ranks and authority — beyond such powers extended by President Biden's *Inflation Recovery Act* – and now withdrawn under Trump.

Such proposals go a long way toward addressing modern excesses of commodification, monopolization, and financialization, which distort economic balance and drive inequality in America. They make necessary inroads in redressing the great swindle — the notion that higher taxation rates (particularly for corporations and high earners) are socially and economically regressive.

Judging by the defeat of her 2020 candidacy for the Democratic presidential nomination, however, the people were not having it. This reflects, among other things, the capitalist capture of the American economic system and the deeply ingrained mindset against taxation. It also reflects the success by which the economic system's hyper-promotional, advertisement and public relations campaigns, as referenced earlier, *"manufacture consent."*

Ultimately, though, Warren's defeat and the defeat of many progressive campaigns in America occur due to a lack of:

1. Organized interest groups in the population: a receptive and galvanized trade-union movement, among other alignments, anchored in the population, would fit the bill
2. Progressive plans, despite being numerous, fail to clearly connect with targeted appraisals of the systemic failures they aim to address and remedy. The economic malfeasance of the system must be attacked.

As yet, progressive proposals appear too scattered and incoherent. They're somehow not reaching enough people *where they are*. Such proposals must serve not only to communicate but to galvanize, and reclaim ground lost over the past 40 years, and bring about social and political sea change. This especially pertains to income distribution and the deployment of higher taxes to serve all economic classes and interests, in the provision of healthcare and education, including those who drive business enterprise and economic development.

Welfare Revisited

Discussion of welfare, as earlier indicated, inevitably involves confronting issues of race and racism to re-adjust public perception. As argued, people of color, including especially those with black skin, are falsely associated with high levels of welfare need and support. In fact, the largest population of welfare recipients, if you recall, "are non-Hispanic white people who account for 44.6% of SNAP/food stamp benefits." (*What the Data Says About Food Stamps in the U.S* (ibid).

Such statistics provide a wedge to pry racial issues away from welfare provisions, depriving militant Republicans of their government spending, and welfare profligacy talking points. But the welfare system, as such, also needs to be revamped. This is central to re-purposing and envisioning a change in taxation regimes.

Despite President Bill Clinton's administration efforts in the 1990s to reform the system, and move people from welfare to work, welfare provision currently attains only mediocre results. According to a libertarian Cato Institute appraisal, "welfare reform may have reduced the growth in (food stamp) benefits, but that merely shifted spending to other programs, from Medicaid to housing and so on" (Michael Tanner, *How Did Bill Clinton's Welfare Reform Turn Out?*, Cato Institute/cato.org, August 22, 2016),

Welfare provision in America remains a "hot button" issue, but it needs to be reframed, even by erstwhile welfare advocates. A better system is both desirable and attainable. The Cato article concludes: "The federal government funds more than 100 separate anti-poverty programs, more than 70 of which provide benefits to individuals. Today, federal and state governments spend nearly $1.5 trillion (current rating) on anti-poverty programs. Yet, even if poverty rates haven't spiked as critics feared, neither have we lifted many people out of poverty. That's a great deal of money for pretty mediocre results." (ibid) Such observations impugn not only the efficacy of U.S. state and federal welfare systems, but also an economic system that produces so much poverty. Such assessments should train eyes especially on income distribution indices, and wage compensation, but also on the 'pre-distributive' systems in Europe and Austria that use higher taxes to give people a leg up before they fall behind – by extending universal healthcare, higher educational and collectively bargained fair wages. Wage level indices and poverty condition measurements are important to note. Even better, get over to the other part of town, on the other side of the economic tracks. Let yourself be convinced by the actual conditions of American economic welfare.

The American welfare system is stopgap and conceals the counter-productivity of the greater economic system. In her master's dissertation review of welfare systems across the globe, Margali Robbe identifies the American welfare system as a "liberal regime" alongside others such as Australia, the U.K., and Ireland. These liberal regimes are characterized by "low level(s) of decommodification and high level(s) of stratification." (Margali Robbe, Supervisor(s): Prof. Dr. Ronan Van Rossem, *Higher Education Policies from a Welfare State Perspective - The Role of Higher Education in the Provision of Welfare*, Sociology Dissertation, Ghent University, 2020-2021).

The system is commodified, for Robbe, in that most insurance is procured through private companies and financed through gainful employment. That leaves a large, but lesser part of the population dependent on state safety net coverage, driving and preserving class stratification and economic inequality.

Robbe's welfare system review goes on to consider more 'conservative' welfare regimes, including, "Austria, Belgium, France, Germany, Italy, Japan, the Netherlands, and Switzerland." These systems are more state-oriented and by Robbe's reckoning, achieve only "a medium degree of decommodification" because benefits are mostly tied to employment, privileging the employed and, therefore, fixing class-stratification.

True, but Europe in general, has far lower poverty rates, measured in 'relative' terms, between 3-16%, depending on the state and measure used. As noted earlier, Austria has an 'absolute poverty rate of 3.7 %., or some "300,000 people who say they cannot afford the expenses of daily life, which are considered the minimum standard of living according to the EU definition. (Statistic Austria, ibid) 'Conservative' welfare systems attempt to embed the insurance of social services (education, healthcare, and employment conditions) in the economic marketplace, while extricating them from strictly private marketplace control. Higher taxes and government-mediated services supplant insurance company control, manipulation, and profit-taking that comes at the expense of broad social security and social unity.

To complete the picture, Robbe reserves the highest praise for Nordic state - 'social-democratic' welfare models, including Norway, Denmark, Sweden, and Finland. These combine "a high degree of decommodification and a low degree of (class) stratification." (ibid). This indicates universal coverage, independent of employment status, funded through relatively high business and individual income taxes and heavier state involvement in insurance provision.

Social Contract Stakes

Alternatives exist not only in the provision of welfare, but also in re-structuring the economy in line with all social interests, revitalizing and rehabilitating the American social contract. Public support for a different, more socially constructive economic system is putatively high (which makes militant capitalists nervous), but it falters because of a lack of communication, awareness and organization, that viable alternatives exist.

Certainly, distrust of excessive state intervention in the economy is warranted. But what if state intervention can be diminished by integrating policies away from private insurance and more toward conditions of employment? This is the 'conservative' Austrian approach. Competitive economies can coexist with the upkeep of broad social interests.

But all this, the decommodification of social services and the conversion of America's welfare state into a social state, depends ultimately on systemic overhaul of the economy. In the first place, and essentially, this requires an adjustment of capital interests – business owners, investors, banks, stock brokers etc., and their valiant re-dedication to the upkeep of democratic processes and the American republic. In its turn, this requires an overhaul of industrial relations between employers and employees, who are likewise re-dedicated to the democratic reinvigoration of the American labor movement on a partnership basis.

Part XVII
The Old New Deal Social Contract

Chapter One:
American Labor History

So, when did the tide finally turn against the greater, old New Deal American social contract? It's a long, lamentable, and convoluted story that begins at the outset of FDR's New Deal policies between 1933 and 1939. The New Deal itself marked the end of an earlier laissez-faire economic social contract. These are the turnstiles of historical and dialectical processes, of which it is essential to be conscious; they make sense of what can appear as the randomness of social, economic and political life. The Hegelian lens that focuses on the role of the state and government is particularly applicable. First, the state held back from market intervention, then it attempted to guide market affairs.

Prior to the New Deal, there were several attempts by lawmakers, business associations, and commissions to reform American capitalism, so to speak, from within. In the name of national unity, World War I brokered a rapprochement between business and labor interests through the National War Labor Board. Trade-unions negotiated a cessation of labor strikes and unrest in exchange for contracts and negotiating concessions from businesses.

Some sought to continue this rapprochement after the war. As labor historian William Domhoff tells it: "Businessmen, through their trade associations over the next 12 years (from 1918 to 1930), encouraged industrial self-government as an alternative to government regulation." (G. William Domhoff, *The Rise and Fall of Labor Unions in the U.S., From the 1830s until 2012 (but mostly the 1930s-*

1980s), whorulesamerica.ucsc.edu/University of California, Santa Cruz, 2012). Such efforts didn't pan out, especially after the stock market crash of 1929 and the resultant economic depression.

The story of the New Deal has been told a hundred times, but new looks are still relevant and rewarding. It unfolds like a boxing match between labor and capital interests, mediated by popular opinion and federal executive, legislative, and judicial authority. The events of 1929-1932 pretty much overthrew the idea that American capitalism could be reformed from within through *industrial self-government*.

As much as business leaders groused about New Deal policies, and enactments, they were probably also relieved. Economic activity in production, trade, and commerce had ground to a halt for three long years. In his 1932 presidential nomination acceptance speech, FDR articulated: "A New Deal for the forgotten man." (Britannica Encyclopedia, *New Deal, U.S. history*, britannica.com, February 5, 2024). The New Deal would mandate federal regulation and investment into American "industry, agriculture, finance, waterpower, labor, and housing sectors", each of which had fallen apart, leaving millions of people without work. *(ibid.)*

The first steps were taken by the U.S. Congress in 1933, when it passed the National Industrial Recovery Act (NIRA) to resuscitate industrial production. Heralded by Roosevelt as a *partnership in planning* between business and government, the NIRA: "Authorized the promulgation of industrial codes of fair competition, guaranteed trade-union rights, and permitted the regulation of working standards."

(ibid,) To implement the law bolstering industrial recovery and public works projects, Congress established the National Recovery Administration (NRA) and the Public Works Administration (PWA). Roosevelt explained the NIRA's thrust in a fireside chat in the summer of 1933: "There is a clear way to reverse that process (the low wages — long hours) — *the economic hell of the past four years.* If all employers in each competitive group agree to pay their workers the same wages - reasonable wages - and require the same hours - reasonable hours - then higher wages and shorter hours will hurt no employer. Moreover, such action is better for the employer than unemployment and low wages because it makes more buyers for his product. That is the idea which is at the very heart of the NIRA" (Franklin D. Roosevelt, *The Fireside Chats*, Internet Archive, archive.org, July 24, 1933).

Though this particular program was errantly conceived, Roosevelt's statement remarkably articulates a principle, or rationale that guided and still guides European Social Partnership policy to this day - as long as all businesses share the same employment conditions, the competitive field is leveled for all. Equitable wages allow the 'social wage economy' and business alike to flourish.

Though Roosevelt's sentiments would carry over into subsequent federal legislation, the NIRA Act itself was too broad and too interventionist. It provides a telling illustration of ineffective governmental involvement in economic processes. By treating business as a unified entity, it inadvertently: "Promoted cartels and monopolies." (Wikipedia, *National Industrial Recovery Act of 1933*, wikipedia.org). The *promulgation of industrial codes* imposed ineffective and impractical governmental constraints on recovering free-market conditions. Congressional power to regulate interstate commerce overreached into areas of state commerce. Even NIRA advocates ended up: "Supporting free-market philosophies." *(ibid.)* It was a ham-handed governmental experiment.

Finally, the NIRA was ruled unconstitutional by the Supreme Court in 1935. Congress had authorized the executive branch to promulgate industrial codes. This offended the *doctrine of non-delegation*. The court held that: "The code-making authority thus conferred is an unconstitutional delegation of legislative power." *(ibid.)* Plus, the Court held that the NIRA was too vague about how code-making and code implementation was supposed to function.

By contrast, *code-making'* and *code implementation* were initiated and implemented in Austria and many European countries not through government mandate, but through the auspices of actual business and labor actors – through authentic social partnership. In this case, it can't go unsaid, such far-seeing industrial policy was brought on by the combined catastrophes of economic depression, two world wars, the decimation of national populations, and vast destruction of physical infrastructure

In America, in the 1930s, it was back to the drawing board. Other acts of this period in America were more successful. Federal intervention restored the capitalist system by mandating and securing the social interest in its operation, especially as to "wages, hours, child labor and collective bargaining." (ibid) The social interest mandated unemployment compensation and social security. It mandated reform of the financial system, providing FDIC federal insurance for bank deposits for all banks in the Federal Reserve System. The Securities and Exchange Commission (SEC) attempted to restore investor confidence in what had become the manipulated and misled U.S stock market. All these and other measures constituted a new American social contract, a new dialectic turn, or position. This new social contract is important to bear in mind as its social- interest tenets are increasingly tested by Trump's agenda in 2025.

Collective Bargaining in America

Back to 1935. The NIRA had misfired in finding the right balance between governmental, business, and labor interests, thus scuttling the emergence of durable partnership. The neo-corporatist model in America was unknown, or rejected out of hand. Nonetheless, one of the greatest New Deal initiatives was on behalf of working men and women. Roosevelt spoke to the rights of workers against those of: "A small group that had concentrated into their own hands almost complete control over other people's property, other people's money, other people's labor - other people's lives. For too many of us throughout the land, life was no longer free; liberty was no longer real. Men and women could no longer follow the pursuit of happiness" (Caleb Crain, *State of the Unions*, The New Yorker Magazine, August 26, 2019.

To a certain extent, The National Labor Relations Act (NLRA) of 1935, also known as the Wagner Act, repaired failed aspects of the NIRA. It provisionally settled years and decades of struggle between labor and capital interests, between the rights of workers to strike and the rights of owners to lock them out for striking. It carried forward elements of the Norris-LaGuardia Act, passed in the waning months of 1932, as the Herbert Hoover presidential administration finally expired. This Act: "Curbed the power of the courts to issue injunctions or restraining orders against strikes, absent violence or fraud" (*National Labor Relations Board, Pre-Wagner Act Labor Relations*, nlrb.com, 2024).

The Norris-LaGuardia Act further prohibited so-called *yellow-dog* contracts issued by businesses, which stipulated that employees who joined a union could and would be fired. It granted union workers: "Full freedom of association undisturbed by employers" and "barred federal courts from issuing injunctions to prevent strikes, picketing, or boycotts" (Encyclopedia Britannica Editors, *Norris-LaGuardia Act*, britannica.com, 2024). The act responded to popular demands for fair employment conditions. However, it didn't go far enough. Unchastised, business owners and employers continued to spy on, interrogate, and blacklist union organizers. In response: "A great wave of strikes occurred across the nation in the form of citywide general strikes and factory takeovers" (National Archives-Milestone Documents, *National Labor Relations Act, 1935*, archives.gov, 2024).

The Norris-LaGuardia Act, however, lacked oversight and enforcement provisions. The labor union strikes finally aided in the narrow passage of the NLRA Wagner Act in 1935. The Act sanctioned union rights to organize and go on strike. It made collective bargaining mandatory where and when unions were officially established. It also defined the governmental role in arbitrating industrial relations. New conditions were created for a partnership between government, labor, and business interests, forming the foundation of a viable social partnership.

The Wagner Act further created the National Labor Relations Board (NLRB) as a federal agency to mediate and adjudicate unresolved trade union and business disputes. The poignant and precise language of the Act warrants a longer quote: "Specifically, the National Labor Relations Board (NLRB) was empowered to decide, when petitioned by employees, if an appropriate bargaining unit of employees existed for collective bargaining; to conduct secret-ballot elections in which the employees in a business or industry could decide whether to be represented by labor unions; and to prevent or correct unfair labor practices by employers (later also by unions). The act prohibited employers from engaging in such unfair labor practices as setting up a company union and firing or otherwise discriminating against workers who organized or joined unions. The act also barred employers from refusing to bargain with any such union that had been certified by the NLRB as being the choice of a majority of employees" (Encyclopedia Britannica Editors, *Wagner Act, U.S. 1935*, britannica.com, 2024).

Institutions and a national framework to manage labor relations and encourage partnership were established, except for one major caveat. The labor-liberal-democratic coalition behind the NLRA/NLRB Wagner Act was brokered by excluding agricultural interests from its coverage. Southern state sharecropping and Jim Crow racial discrimination laws were thereby preserved.

As it stood, apparently, the Wagner Act was controversial enough. It was "fiercely opposed by Republicans and big business, and was challenged in the Supreme Court as a violation of the 'freedom of contract' of employers and employees and as an unconstitutional intrusion by the federal government in industries that were not directly engaged in interstate commerce, which Congress was empowered to regulate." *(ibid)*

Such disputes were provisionally settled by the U.S. Supreme Court in 1937, in favor of the Wagner Act, upholding union organizing rights and rights to collective bargaining. In a 5-4 case decision, *National Labor Relations Board v. Jones & Laughlin Steel Corp*, the Court upheld the Act's "constitutionality." *(ibid)* In so doing, it upheld the Wagner Act's most famous provision, Section 7a, which stated: "Employees shall have the right to organize and bargain collectively through representatives of their own choosing, and shall be free from the interference, restraint, or coercion of employers of labor, or their agents, in the designation of such representatives or in self-organization or in other concerted activities for the purpose of collective bargaining or other mutual aid or protection." *(ibid)*

Post-World War II Labor Conditions

This wonderfully clear statement would be challenged remorselessly in the following decades. In the meantime, World War II intervened. Following the war, wide-scale strike activity continued.

In 1947, the Republican-controlled Congress passed the Taft-Hartley Act over the veto of Democratic President

Harry S. Truman. Again, the precise language warrants a longer quotation:

"The Taft-Hartley Act prohibited the 'closed shop' (an arrangement that makes union membership a condition of employment), allowed states to prohibit the 'agency shop' (an arrangement that required employees who are not union members to pay fees to a union to cover the costs of its bargaining on their behalf), narrowed the definition of unfair labor practices, and specified unfair union practices, among other provisions. Following the adoption of the Taft-Hartley Act, a number of states enacted so-called 'right-to-work' laws, which banned both closed and agency shops." *(ibid)* Such prohibitions, not incidentally, are effectively offset in Austria. 'Closed shop' and 'agency shop' distortions are avoided by all-inclusive employee fee support of Chambers of Labor – that uphold the labor interests of all workers – private, public, industrial, retail and commercial, but without direct purview over employment conditions and negotiations. This resolution represents an oppositional dialectical position.

In America, as will be seen, right-to-work laws have made a modern comeback, inimical to maintaining and growing the interests of organized labor.

The Wagner and Taft-Hartley Acts were amended and extended by the Landrum-Griffin Act (1959), which further banned secondary boycotts and limited the right to picket." *(*Encyclopedia Britannica Editors, *Wagner Act, U.S. 1935, ibid)*

Many legal and structural curtailments contained and abridged the union movement, some of which were brought on by the unions themselves. The roots of the American labor movement were ultimately too shallow to sustain and extend the visionary language and acts of the New Deal. The movement was so hedged into adversarial status that it could not redeem the organizational potentials of partnership with business and industry. It had to box with one hand tied behind its back. It was stymied from without, but also from within, by lack of organizational cohesion and coordination. Likewise, business and governmental interests were dispersed for lack of organizational consolidation. 'Neo-corporate' alliances didn't develop, or were mutated.

These vexed conditions reflected the ambivalent legal and judicial environment created by congressional action, as the country moved into the period of post-war economic expansion. The social scientists Clawson and Clawson appraise labor relations as they evolved in the post-war era in more clinical terms: "Schizophrenia is the dominant characteristic of US labor law. For union recognition, American labor law grants/guarantees workers the right to 'self-organize' via the formation of unions, a right realized through the federally mandated and supervised representation election that establishes a particular union as the sole legally recognized bargaining agent for that workplace (or bargaining unit). At the same time, the law protects the right of employers to influence and intervene in this process: "Unique among industrial democracies, US labor law allows employers actively to oppose their employees' decision to unionize" (Dan and Mary Clawson, *What Has Happened to The US Labor Movement,* JSTOR, jstor.org, p. 100, 1999).

Golden Age Capitalism

Over time, the post-war legal and judicial environment successfully marginalized what was otherwise a fairly burgeoning labor movement. Despite barriers and challenges, "private sector union density (the % of the labor force in unions) rose to 39.2% in 1954." (William Dickens & Jonathan Leonard, *Accounting for the Decline in Union Membership, 1950-1980*, JSTOR, Industrial & Labor Relations Review, vol. 38, no. 3, p. 323, 1985) (There are an array of statistical measures, but they settle between 35 and 39 %)

Whatever the exact number, in the early decades of post-war economic expansion, union workers shared in the prosperity. The New Deal social contract proved beneficial to a growing majority of the American people. The position and status of working people reached a critical mass, enough so as to benefit non-union affiliated workers.

Social interest even percolated into the upper echelons of business management. An early gospel of this social interest, *The Modern Corporation and Private Property*, written in 1932 by Adolph Berle and Gardiner Means, argued that "companies were inextricably intertwined with their communities and ought to act with a sense of shared responsibility" (David Gelles, *The Man Who Broke Capitalism*, Simon & Schuster Paperbacks, p. 24, 2022).

Such an attitude was carried forward in practice during the post-war "golden age of capitalism." This period, as described by Gelles, lasted from the "post-war boom to the stagflation of the 1970s - a stretch when many of the great American employers were at their best." (ibid, p. 25)

Companies like GE, GM, and Johnson & Johnson upheld the earlier ideas of "industrial self-government." Such businesses were particularly paternalistic. "In the postwar years, companies poured profits back into their workforces, ensuring a stable, skilled employee base. Labor unions offered employees a measure of job security and the assurance of steadily increasing wages. The gap in pay between a machinist and a manager was meaningful but not too extreme" (ibid, p. 25).

In what sounds like holy writ, circa 1943, the chairman of Johnson & Johnson, Robert Johnson, engraved a credo of corporate commitments to the social interest. The company's "first responsibility is to our customers, doctors, and nurses, to mothers and fathers" … and second to its employees, to provide a "sense of security in their jobs, and wages fair and adequate, management just, hours short." Third, to management, executives would be "persons of talent, education, experience, and ability." Fourth, "to our owners and stockholders, business must make a sound profit, high taxes paid, new factories built and new products launched. When these things have been done, the owners and stockholders should receive a fair return" (ibid, p. 25). This signifies, to a tentative extent, dialectic resolution between governmental, business and labor interests involved.

Such ideas now appear quaint, or even naïve, as if they belonged on another planet. However, as Gelles is quick to note, this was an American reality. Companies were "actually sharing their profits with their employees. From 1948 to 1979, worker pay grew in tandem with worker productivity" (ibid). So, that was when America was great, except for the part where it unjustifiably, murderously and tragically prosecuted the war in Vietnam.

Otherwise, the American social contract was further extended and renewed by the great Civil Rights movement of the 1960s. This era, combined with high trade-union membership, which stood at "26.3% of the private sector" in 1975, represents a high-water mark, or dialectical resolution of American material and ideal interests. (Leo Troy, Neil Sheflin, *Labor Market Reporter: U.S. Trade-Union Membership*, U.S. Dept. of Labor - Bureau of Labor Statistics, publicpurpose.com, 2015). America was living up to its ideals, for broad stretches of the populace, of being a land of fair opportunity. What there was of material plenty was more broadly shared. A glance back in time, as noted, reveals that the American middle class has shrunk in the last 50 years. "In 1971, 61% of Americans lived in middle-class households. By 2023, the share had fallen to 51%, according to a new Pew Research Center analysis of government data" (Rakesh Kochhar, *The State of the American Middle Class,* Pew Research Center, pewresearch.org, May 31, 2024).

The Hegelian resolution, or fusion of material, productive conditions, however, and their counterparts in the realm of democratic ideology was fairly fleeting.

Chapter Two:
Labor Movement Plight

Throughout this post-war time period until 1979, the trade-union labor movement and collective bargaining gradually lost footing: the 'hollowing out', referred to earlier. By 1984, trade-union membership had plummeted by almost 11 points to 15.5%. Thus, began the long slide of growing U.S. economic inequality.

As Wikipedia notes: "There is a substantial wage gap between union and nonunion workers in the U.S.; unionized workers average higher pay than comparable nonunion workers (when controlling for individual, job, and labor market characteristics. Research shows that the union wage gaps are higher in the private sector than in the public sector, and higher for men than for women. Private-sector union strength positively affects the wages of nonunion private-sector workers (when controlling for background conditions, such as industry, the automation risk, offshoring, public-sector union strength, overall employment levels, and other factors); this is called the union "spillover effect" (Wikipedia, Labor Unions in the United States, wikipedia.org, March 17, 2024). **(See Appendix 2)**

As noted earlier, this spillover effect sustains collective bargaining and social partnership conditions in Austria and other European countries.

But back in America - private-sector union density was between 35% and 39% in 1954 (depending on the reporting source). That number crumbled to *15.7%* in 1992 and today stands at about *6%*. Public-sector workforce union density is much higher, at *32%*, but it involves fewer overall workers. In 2022, *10.1%* of the total U.S. workforce was unionized. (Bureau of Labor Statistics, *Union Member Survey*, bls.gov, January 23, 2024)

There are multiple explanations for the breakdown of the U.S. labor movement. These bear scrutiny, as cautionary tales, and in relation to parallel social partnership developments in Europe and Austria.

Racketeering

Union racketeering was one reason the movement faltered. In a kind of knockout round of the great U.S. labor vs. capital boxing match, the bipartisan Landrum-Griffin Act of 1959, referenced earlier, further curtailed trade-union secondary boycotts and picketing. This law prohibited labor unions from picketing businesses associated with those resisting and blocking union representation. While restrictive, the Act also aimed to protect unions from organized crime. It:

- Outlawed union loan activity,
  - Strengthened rank-and-file democratic secret election procedure
- Provided recourse to federal courts to enforce union member rights, and
- Declared a union member Bill of Rights (James Jacobs, Ellen Peters, *Labor Racketeering: The Mafia and the Unions*, jstor.org, University of Chicago, 2005, p. 235)

Such matters are vital. The collective protections afforded Austrian workers were dismantled in America and so left their interests vulnerable to retrenchment, revision and marginalization in ensuing decades. This failure represents a missed opportunity of pragmatic accommodation between all interests in society. America's 'Business First' and individualist mentality superseded the formation of a collective, social consciousness, at the foundation of a social state. The prior dialectic resolution of prevailing social interests was outmoded.

It transpired that unions were subject to abuse and intimidation from mafia infiltration and control. This corruption was exposed in several famous congressional hearings. The *Kefauver Hearings* of 1950-1951 provide one example, as do the *McClellan Senate Select Committee* hearings (1957-1960) on *Improper Activities in the Labor Management Field*, which ultimately led to the 1964 conviction of Jimmy Hoffa, the Teamsters Union president.

Certain unions, both large and small, allowed illicit and illegal mafia involvement in their operations. The hearings revealed organized crime infiltration into The International Brotherhood of Teamsters

- The International Longshoremen
- The Hotel and Restaurant Employees International
- Several smaller unions

There was a general pattern of extortion in which non-compliant employers were threatened with unlawful strikes, work stoppages, picketing, and workplace sabotage. (ibid) Evidence of theft and embezzlement of union pension and welfare funds was conclusive, as was intimidation and violence against rank-and-file union member dissidents.

(ibid, p. 230) Mafia interests came to control union executive committees and meddle with union purse strings. There were shakedowns and felonious malfeasances at many levels and in many industries. One union leader, David Dubinsky, called labor racketeering *"A cancer that almost destroyed the American labor movement."* (ibid, p. 229)

Racketeering tendencies were only stemmed beginning in the 1980s, with the introduction and enforcement of the 1970 *Racketeer Influenced and Corrupt Organizations Act (RICO)* statutes. As a result, among other things, a series of *consent decrees* - agreements in court between litigant parties - allowed for administrative oversight and takeover of corrupt union operations until they could demonstrate consistent remedy and reform.

But a lot of damage had already been done.

Racketeering undermined the union movement's public standing and credibility, as well as efforts to recruit new members. Unions became insular. But racketeering and insularity were merely symptoms of deeper, broader internal and external trade-union miscarriages. All these developments reveal the malign shortcomings of adversarial relations between business and labor.

In their 1999 analysis, *'What Has Happened to the U.S. Labor Movement?'* sociologists Clawson and Clawson identified five proximate causes for decline:

1. Demographics
2. The union's role
3. The state and legal system
4. Globalization and neoliberalism
5. The employer offensive (ibid, p. 97)

The State and Legal System

In its executive, legislative, and judicial capacities, the state adopted inconsistent, if not *schizophrenic* - policies toward organized labor and its right to organize for collective bargaining.

In theory, unions can be organized, but in practice, it is much more difficult. This constrained trade-union initiative and shoved the movement into isolated corners. Such truncation and enforced weakness may itself explain the turn toward racketeering that developed.

Legal support for unions was abridged, but trade unions still represented large constituencies and controlled large budgets supported by union membership fees. Their powers, apparently, needed to be augmented by whatever means necessary — legal, corrupt, or otherwise.

Schizophrenic policy compelled schizophrenic behavior.

Trade-union collective bargaining conditions remain similar to those described in 1999. Trade-union organization and representation are both allowed and restricted. The fortunes of the labor union movement often depend on which party controls the Senate, the White House, and the corresponding makeup of the National Labor Relations Board (NLRB).

"The NLRB is governed by a five-person board and a general counsel, all of whom are appointed by the President with the consent of the Senate." (Wikipedia, *National Labor Relations Board*) The NLRB was established under the original *1935 Wagner Act* provisions. It is supposed to be an independent federal agency that: "Enforces U.S. labor law in relation to collective bargaining and unfair labor practices." (ibid)

But again, that independence is relative. NLRB function was curtailed in the first month of Trump's second presidential term. He had fired an NLRB member, preventing the Board's quorum. On March 6, 2025, however "a federal judge ruled that President Donald Trump illegally fired former National Labor Relations Board (NLRB) chair Gwynne Wilcox. The judge ordered that she be restored and allowed to fulfill her duties as a duly-appointed member of the NLRB" (Alejandro Agustin Ortiz, *Trump's Attempt to Deride NLRB Won't Stop Power of Collective Actions,* ACLU, aclu.org, March 21, 2025). The NLRB survives to fight another day, but its status and standing remains precarious.

Card-Checks

The NLRB is putatively independent, but its enforcement powers depend on political winds and the corresponding favor of business or labor interests. Up until recently, for example, NLRB rules favored employer efforts to impede union representation, by requiring formal union elections.

In 1969, in a case decided by the U.S. Supreme Court - *NLRB v. Gissel Packing Company* - the court reversed a long-standing policy - the so-called *Joy Silk doctrine*, "that allowed workers to form a union by collecting signed authorization cards from a majority of their bargaining unit, rather than participating in a formal NLRB-supervised election" (Ian Ward, *The Lie That Helped Kill the Labor Movement*, Politico Magazine, politico.com, June 2022).

The *card-check* reversal of the *Joy Silk* doctrine exposed union formation efforts to litigation and employer-sponsored anti-union campaigns in the run-up to union authorization elections. Now, 50 years later, (and perhaps at risk) signed authorization card procedures to form a union have been reinstated. In fact, the NLRB recently created two new mechanisms "for unions to represent workers via 'card-check and without conducting a secret-ballot election" (Grant T. Collins, *NLRB Creates Two New Pathways to Card-Check Unionization*, NLRB, felhaber.com, September 13, 2023).

The first mechanism basically reinstates the above-mentioned *Joy Silk* doctrine. When sufficient signatures are gathered and presented, the NLRB ruling states further conditions:

"If the employer fails to act within 14 days of the union's demand, then the NLRB will consider the employer to have waived its right to a secret-ballot election and, if the union truly represents a majority, then the employer will have violated the NLRA by failing to bargain with the union" (ibid).

The second mechanism for obtaining union representation is triggered "if the employer commits 'any' unfair labor practice ('ULP') that "requires setting aside the election" (ibid). Such practices, in the intervening years, are fairly common. In the case at hand, "after reviewing the evidence, the NLRB concluded that the employer "engaged in a large number of severe unfair labor practices and otherwise coercive conduct throughout the critical period" (ibid).

Despite such encouraging instances, the governmental sphere has not done much to bolster the cause of organized labor. It has been an uphill battle, even when Democratic administrations are in power. The Economic Policy Institute notes that: "During the Great Society era, when Democrats were at their peak congressional power (in the 1960s and 70s), and under each successive Democratic president - Carter in 1978, Clinton in 1993, and Obama in 2009 - efforts to strengthen the NLRA's protections of workers' rights to collective bargaining were all defeated, despite majority support in both the House and Senate and by the president. The tool employed in each defeat was the filibuster, spearheaded by a minority of senators representing an even smaller share of the population. The result has been policy drift in labor law, allowing outcomes to shift in favor of corporate employers and their allies" (H. Shierholz, M. Poydock, C. McNichols, *Unionization Increased by 200,000 in 2022*, epi.org, January 19, 2023).

Such developments reflect the gradual devolution of effective governmental action on behalf of America's working-class citizenry, comprising at least 50% of the population. They mirror the corresponding ascendency and overthrow of the American economy by the interests of capital. Ultimately, in conjunction with movements of popular, social, and labor advocacy, the reconstitution of the American economy depends on the voting public and its representatives determined to revamp economic conditions - through greater partnership reconfiguration of industrial relations. By such means can the dialectic between democracy and capitalism be resolved, along with the accomplishment of an American social democracy. It has been and will be an uphill battle.

Chapter Three:
Employer Offensives I

As noted earlier, employer resistance has been ongoing since "freedom of contract" issues were first raised at the dawn of the New Deal. The "card-check" reversal was only one skirmish in a long battle. Sociologists Clawson and Clawson recount systemic attempts to "maintain union-free workplaces, through delays, intimidation, and election prevention without NLRB involvement" (ibid, p. 102).

In earlier times, "employers agreed to hold the union representation election without contesting the process through the National Labor Relations Board. In 1962, 46.1 percent of all NLRB elections were conducted as consent elections," contrasted with only 8.6% in 1977 (Prosten 1979) (ibid).

The employer offensive continues today, in earnest, utilizing time-proven tactics in use since at least 1986. In Hegelian terms, this is an outgrowth of neo-liberal, capitalist ideology.

Clawson and Clawson report studies from that earlier time which found that "87% of employers used outside consultants while 64% held five or more captive audience meetings, in which the company requires all employees to listen to anti-union presentations during work hours - a level of access, within a coercive atmosphere, that cannot be equaled by union organizers, who are barred from company property and can talk to workers only away from the job" (ibid, p. 102). Employer determination to maintain an orderly workplace would be better served by promoting worker councils, as generally in Europe, and Austria, and even co-determination to improve relations in the workplace. In the meantime, however, more radical business measures are pursued to abrogate the enforcement of union rights altogether

Business titans Jeff Bezos, Amazon's CEO, Tesla's Elon Musk, and Trader Joe's Albrecht family are in the midst of legal suits that challenge the very standing of the National Labor Relations Board. Each ask "federal courts to declare the core functions of the NLRA," of 1935 New Deal vintage, "unconstitutional on the grounds that the NLRB administrative courts, like those of other regulatory agencies, mix judicial functions with executive branch functions" (Harold Myerson, *America's Richest Men Ask the Courts to Make Unions Illegal*, The American Prospect, prospect.org, 2/22/2024).

A ruling in their favor would effectively reverse the *NLRB v. Jones & Laughlin Steel* case of 1937, which declared the NLRA/NLRB constitutional. That decision affirmed the legality of trade-unions and collective bargaining, as well as the special function of the NLRB to adjudicate and resolve disputes between organized labor and business employers.

To disband the NLRB would remand all such disputes to federal courts at-large and consign issues requiring explicit and timely resolution to judicial limbo, if not oblivion. Which dialectic tide of interest — the oligarchic material, or the ideal of democratic representation — will prevail? In Myerson's words, union approval ratings are at their "highest levels in 60 years, with young workers particularly bent on winning a say in their work lives. Joe Biden's NLRB appointments would have augmented that approval, "working to restore some teeth to the NLRA, which had been largely defanged by decades of decisions from pro-corporate courts" (ibid)

As stated at the outset of this essay, all historic times and many matters are inundated with dialectical processes, perhaps none more so than the conflict between capital and labor interests. At such a moment, it is useful to recall Abraham Lincoln's remarks at the 1859 Wisconsin State Agricultural Fair.

He affirmed the reasoning then and there that: "Labor is prior to, and independent of, capital; that, in fact, capital is the fruit of labor and could never have existed if labor had not *first* existed - that labor can exist without capital, but that capital could never have existed without labor. Hence labor is the superior - greatly the superior - of capital." (Abraham Lincoln, *Address before the Wisconsin State Agricultural Society/Fair,* abrahamlincolnonline.org, Milwaukee, Wisc., September 30, 1859) It goes without saying, without subtracting from Lincoln's conclusive conviction, that capital interests are co-equal with those of labor, in that capital brings labor into employment. This is the foundation of social partnership between capital and labor interests.

Today's (PRO) Act: Protecting the Right to Organize

Lincoln's conclusion, as the last Myerson quote attests, is under duress today, but the attitude is still alive and well, or at least it was until the second Trump administration. It may be that Bezos, Musk, the Albrecht family, and their ilk get their way, and force the dialectic pendulum to swing conclusively, and permanently in favor of corporate interests. Legislative attempts in 2019 at the federal level, however, sought to bring the NLRA up to date and at long last bolster trade-union and labor interests.

The *Protecting the Right to Organize Act*, or *PRO Act* proposed to "amend previous labor laws, such as the National Labor Relations Act, for the purpose of expanding various labor protections, related to employees' rights to organize and collectively bargain in the workplace" *(*Wikipedia*, Protecting the Right to Organize Act*, wikipedia.org).

This would have pushed the dialectic pendulum in the other direction. Such declarations recall the language of the original Wagner Act. The PRO Act would have addressed and reversed the cavalcade of pro-business rulings over at least the past 60 years.

It would "prevent employers from holding mandatory meetings for the purpose of counteracting labor organization, and strengthen the legal right of employees to join a labor union. The bill would also permit labor unions to encourage secondary strikes (reversing *Taft-Hartley* and *Landrum-Griffin* edicts)" It would allow the National Labor Relations Board to fine employers for violations of labor law, and provide compensation to employees involved in such cases" (ibid).

The PRO Act offers renewed protections for employees who seek to join a labor union "from being fired. It would allow unions to override "right-to-work" laws, and also enable labor unions to collect dues from all employees in a workplace, regardless of whether they are union members. It prevents an employer from using citizenship status against an employee" (ibid). It would also empower the National Labor Relations Board0, as noted, to levy hefty fines on employers who violate the law, particularly repeat offenders. Employees whose rights are violated in such cases would receive "monetary compensation" (ibid).

Furthermore, the PRO Act would re-designate "independent contractors" whose status is often used by employers to evade fair employment conditions, as "employees." (ibid)

Such amendments to NLRB/government policy may well have contributed to growing union enrollment. The *Economic Policy Institute* reports that in 2022 "more than 16 million workers in the United States were represented by a union - an increase of 200,000 from 2021." At the same time, however, non-union jobs were added at a faster rate, which accounts for a decline from "11.6% to 11.3%" of workers represented overall (in public and private sectors) by a union.

As noted, the legislation was introduced in 2019. Its House sponsor was Representative Robert C. Scott (D-Va). Patty Murray, Democrat of Washington, is the Senate sponsor. The bill passed in the Democratic-controlled House and was referred to a committee in the Senate, despite having "41 co-sponsors" (ibid).

Such legislation would surely have turned the tables on neo-liberal and corporate interests, then and now reigning in Congress and over the economy, at-large. The thrust of such legislation, however, remains critically adversarial. The aim should not be to overthrow capital interests, owners, managers, and investors, but to create a system in which labor and capital can maintain relations of mutual accommodation.

Adversarial wrangling between American labor and capital interests is hugely inefficient and costly. It is juvenile. It stems from a premise that one side must subdue the other. It is high time to grow up and recognize that economic progress for all interests -not to mention social harmony, - that can be achieved by social partnership. In Austria, for instance, business account ledgers are shared with Works Council representatives to establish worker-management trust and open channels for collaboration. Collectively bargained contracts provide financial bottom lines.

In America, the litany of transgressions against the labor interest must still be recounted. Contemporary right-to-work laws militate against social partnership, not to mention the PRO Act legislation that gropes in the direction of greater accommodation. In America, despite pockets of robust union representation, the contemporary labor movement is hobbled by adversarial and counterproductive relations with commerce - and vice versa. It has gone so far that so-called "Right to Work" laws are now upheld in 27 American states.

Right-to-Work Laws

As noted, 'right-to-work' legislation emerged after passage of the Taft-Hartley Act of 1947, which marked off boundaries in which organized labor could operate. Subsequently, many states outright banned both closed and agency union shops, effectively preventing unions from funding themselves.

In certain sections of the country, hostility to trade unions was high. As also noted, the reach of the Wagner Act trade union organizing rights excluded agricultural interests in the South from its coverage.

The story of Right-to-Work laws actually antedates the Taft-Hartley Act. It goes way back to 1941, when William Ruggles, publisher of the *Dallas Morning News*, and Vance Muse, director of the Christian American Association, teamed up to vilify and thwart the trade-union movement as a front for "Jewish Marxism" (Michael Pierce, *Vance Muse and the Racist Origins of Right-to-Work*, Expert Forum-Law and Policy Analysis, February 22, 2018).

At first, these anti-union voices advocated for a national ban on closed union shops, - an arrangement where all workers in the employ of a business were required to be union members. Fair enough. Such compulsion clearly restricts rights to association and free speech and, as noted, was banned outright by the Taft-Hartley Act, which mandated employee protections from unfair union practices.

The original thrust of 'right-to-work' legislation was to enforce guardrails on union-organizing activities. The Soviet Union's command economy, and universal union measures were rightfully targeted bugaboos. Under the blanket condemnation of Soviet-style communism, Muse, Ruggles, and others, also attacked the labor union organizing activities of the Congress of Industrial Organizations (CIO) in southern industries and among Black sharecroppers - "challenging the legal underpinnings of white supremacy." (ibid)

Himself an avowed white supremacist, and anti-union crusader, Muse complained that the CIO was "sending organizers to the rural South to inflame the contented but gullible African-American population." The point was to maintain the South's "Jim Crow" color line. (ibid) To achieve this, he and his ilk supported draconian anti-union strikebreaking laws. This crippled union ability to challenge company segregation policies. Combined with the 'divide and conquer' tactics cited in the chapter on Racism, such maneuvers irrevocably set back the union movement in the South and, by extension, the entire country.

Alternating gains and setbacks characterize American labor movement history, but ultimately leave its role in the economy and the status of industrial relations at a decided disadvantage. In dialectical terms, this gives corporate and financial interests every incentive to pursue their advantage. There must be a counter-vailing challenge.

The prospects of broad-based trade-union organization were delivered a further blow when the U.S. Supreme Court recently struck down the ability of public sector unions to assess a "fair share fee" to finance their services. (Michael Artz, *The Impact of Janus on the Labor Movement, Five Years Later*, American Bar Association - Human Rights, October 31, 2023).

This marks the latest incarnation of anti-union, so-called 'right-to-work' law gaining a hold on the country from Alabama to Wisconsin and almost every 'red state' in between. "First," as Arty notes, it was that nobody should be forced, as a condition of employment, to join a union. Now, it's that — and that unions can't finance themselves for services they provide to all workers, union member or not. A fair share fee is a percentage of total union dues paid by an employee covered by a collective bargaining agreement but who chooses not to join the union as a member. In the 2018 *Janus v. AFSCME* case, conservative judges, led by Samuel Alito, made the case that such fees "are an affront to the free speech clause (sic) of the First Amendment." (ibid)

By so doing, conservative judges overturned 40 years of case law that sprang from a 1977 U.S. Supreme Court ruling that 'fair share fees' violated neither the First Amendment nor the 14th Amendment on interstate commerce. This ruling established that public and private unions must be held to the same standards, "while insisting that objectors to union membership or policy may not have their dues used for other ideological or political purposes." (*Wikipedia, Abood v. Detroit Bd of Education*). First Amendment protections were duly recognized.

Whether the *Abood* case "had failed to properly assess the First Amendment principles in its decision," as the Alito opinion argued, it is obvious that a union can't pay for the legitimate services it renders to all covered by collectively bargained contracts without some kind of fee. (*Wikipedia, ibid*) In Austria, as will be seen, such fees are assessed for all workers. They do not, however, flow into union coffers, but to the Chamber of Labor, which provides research on economic and employment conditions, and advocacy and representation for all workers, union or not.

In America, the fallout from the Abood case on public sector unions was calculated to be enormous, further debilitating the status and unity of trade-union negotiated agreements, - both public and private. The Alito/corporate strategy appears to abolish the collective power of worker contracts, leaving individual workers to fend for themselves at the whim of cost-cutting employers. This clearly demonstrates the need for 'Austrian-style' Chambers of Labor.

Up until recently, fortunately, the projected reversal of public-union strength has not come to pass. Public sector trade unions have been able to conduct counter-campaigns. "By convincing existing members of the value of their union, persuading some non-members to join, and recruiting new hires into the union, these unions softened the blow" perpetrated by the Supreme Court decision. (*Janus v. AFSCME, ibid*) But now, it more than appears, the second Trump administration is determined to curtail and dismantle the mandated union rights of federal agency employees. Thousands of federal workers have been laid off. The legal standing of their release is up in the air.

American labor relations are still too dominated by and dependent on governmental intercession. Authentic and enduring social partnership must have its origins at the grass roots – in industrial and business interests coinciding to a certain, negotiated extent, with the interests of organized labor - in the name of greater overall economic productivity, efficiency and social fairness. At the same time, organized labor in America must outgrow legacies of collusion, malfeasance and isolation in favor of coordination and consolidation.

Part XVIII
Austrian and European Parallels

Chapter One:
Social Partnership Institutions and Agencies

Over time, haltingly and sometimes torturously, Austrians and other Europeans confronted and solved many of the same trade-union issues that are currently so at stake in America - especially union formation and representation issues. The fundamental difference between America and Europe on this score is that worker and trade union rights have been fully integrated into economic and industrial relations.

At the close of World War, I, in 1918, the Austrian Social Democratic and Christian Social parties overthrew the Habsburg monarchy to establish a parliamentary government. Owing to food shortages and other privations caused by the war and its internationally destabilizing effects, strike activity grew massively in Austria.

"Unlike the strikes of 1914-16, which were almost exclusively 'economic' in their aims - demanding better wages and shorter hours, for instance - the strikes of 1917-18 often featured 'political' demands such as immediate peace, amnesty for political prisoners, or national independence." (Jako Benes, *Labor, Labor Movements, Trade-Unions and Strikes in Austria-Hungary,* International Encyclopedia of the First World War, April, 2016)

Influenced by Marxist proponents and precepts, these strikes reflected a growing awareness among Austro-Hungarian rank-and-file workers of the revolutionary capacities developing throughout Europe, particularly in Russia. It was all their putative Social-Democratic party leaders could do to maintain discipline and prevent protesting masses from running amok. Politics and principles played a definite role, but they weren't nearly as urgent as the food shortages that engulfed the Austrian-Hungarian population in 1918.

"These hunger protests were mostly held by women, who thus won influence over 'high politics.' When the flour allocations were restricted yet again in January 1918, strikes broke out in almost every region of the monarchy. Social democracy positioned itself at the head of the strikes and articulated both economic and political demands. The strikes continued throughout 1918, with protests against price increases, poor working conditions, and the miserable food supply situation." (Judith Fritz, *"Hunger and Protest - Social Tensions Escalate,* The First World War, The World of the Habsburgs, 2014)

Amidst the revolutionary commotion and party rivalry, the conservative Christian Socials ultimately took office and signed the constitution of Austria's First Republic. One of the new government's first initiatives, due to revolutionary conditions and pressure from the Social Democratic Party, was passage of the original Works Council Act in 1919.

Today, after many amendments and in conformity with European law, the Labor Constitution Act, "stipulates the rights of 'works council' bodies regarding consultation and co-determination in social, staff, and economic matters. The works council is the main employee representative body within the work establishment." (Franz Marhold, *2003/EC, Supplementing the Statute for a European Cooperative*

Society with Regard to the Involvement of Employees, National Implementation Report – Austria, 2003)

The Works Council Act specifies and authorizes the ways and means of employee representation in firms with five or more workers. It stipulates quarterly or even monthly employer consultations on matters of workforce interest, including personnel data, monitoring obligations, and 'intervention rights if employment infractions occur'.

Hiring plans must be disclosed, as must information regarding the firm's economic and financial situation. Works Council representatives have the right to inspect the firm's ledger sheets and accounting books. In corporations, any controlling company's reorganization or restructuring plans must be shared. Additionally, in firms with more than 40 employees, one-third of the supervisory board, or Board of Directors, must be comprised of worker-elected representatives. *(ibid.)*

These measures protect the status, standing, and interests of virtually all Austrian employees. As observed earlier, you will note the Works Council representatives' right to assess company accounting books as a measure of enforceable partnership - not only for monitoring internal business affairs, but also to ensure that management complies with collectively bargained wage and benefit conditions. Especially in light of the review of workplace and labor union conditions in the U.S., the greatest service of such Works Councils may be that they keep both union and management activities and practices honest.

Many firms and employees in Austria, however, do not entertain or inaugurate Works Councils. Many firms remain family-run and owned, and are often managed along traditional, paternalistic lines. Yet, they comply, as noted, with larger collectively negotiated labor settlements. Worker rights are respected, - efficiency, productivity, and control are maintained, but company hierarchies largely go unchallenged.

Most small firms with fewer than 10 employees and even some with up to 40 workers don't have Works Councils. Collegiality and cooperation are presumably upheld by smaller workforce numbers. As the number of employees grows, so does the likelihood of Works Council representation.

"A separate study based on the 2013 European Company Survey, which only looks at workplaces with 10 or more employees, found that 47% had a Works Council, or a public sector equivalent, with the percentage increasing in larger workplaces." *(Service of the ETU -European Trade Union, Worker-participation.eu, Austria, 2016)*

In all, these Social Partnership innovations and others address and to a certain extent resolve the Hegelian master-slave perspective on social development. While questions of domination and subservience invariably accompany human relationships, social partnership accomplishes a framework for formal parity in which productive interests are respected.as co-equal. Cooperation supersedes adversarial competition.

Chapter Two:
Social Partnership on the Ground in Austria

The Social Partnership system works not only for employees, but in the main, also for managers. In Austria's province of Vorarlberg, small and medium enterprise CEO and General Manager, Felix Rippe, has directed and revived several different business operations over the years - including firms producing coffee machine technology, small machine manufacturing, and the packaging industry. He sums up his experience working with Works Councils in somewhat ambivalent, but generally positive terms.

As he says, "Relations and outcomes depend on management. Works Councils can be very powerful when both parties (management and WC) work hand in hand for the success of the company. Some managers lack confidence and trust in the process and don't want to be seen as pushovers in granting additional worker rights and benefits. But the system also depends on Works Council cooperation and their ability to see beyond immediate interests to the welfare of the company. This was my (Felix's) position. Works Council representatives and management were not always of the same opinion, but we could respect each other in discussion and seek the best outcome for all concerned. So, it depends." (Felix Rippe, CEO Perspective on Works Council Interview, 2024)

There are, of course, countless issues involved in Management - Works Council affairs. Works Council representatives ensure that employees enjoy further on-the-job training and educational opportunities. At larger companies, as noted, they contribute to a constructive work climate and can be helpful to businesses in the implementation of necessary, but perhaps unpopular management policies.

Works Councils occupy a delicate position mediating between employee and employer interests. Works Council representatives are legally protected from being fired for openly, and honestly advocating in the interests of their fellow employees, but management brings pressures to bear.

At first glance, giving workers such status in the USA appears unthinkable and foreign. The PRO Act encompasses a vision by which worker participation in actual production planning in the workplace can be realized, outlining and defining the necessary employment protections for this to happen. Again, when such practices are generalized, no business would be at a competitive disadvantage, but could instead reap the benefits of a 'co-determination' culture.

A Works Council Graphic Design Editor

The Austrian province of Vorarlberg's provincial newspaper, *Die VN*, engages a Works Council, on which its Graphic Design editor, Christian Stuppner, served for 12 years. Along with five others, he eventually represented the interests of 360 fellow employees. His participation stemmed initially from a challenge that he and other associates mounted to the then current Works Council configuration - whose representation was found to yield too much ground to management priorities. Such Councils are termed 'yellow.'

Again, it is a delicate balancing act. Management has various ways and means to influence Works Council representative behavior, including providing paycheck premiums. Stuppner himself conveys a deferential, rather than confrontational attitude toward management. He had to respect the capital holders' self-evident prior stake in the enterprise. But still, he expected mutual recognition and respect for his role as Works Council representative and for the workers he represented. This is the hallmark of partnership.

In any case, Stuppner's work colleagues proposed a new list of representatives who at first won two seats in an initial election, breaking the hold of the old Works Council guard. In the next scheduled Works Council election, five years later, the group's list of representatives won over half the votes and inaugurated a new era of Works Council-Management relations.

In the end, membership in the Works Council appreciably increased. For Stuppner himself, the whole experience illustrates an exemplary case of democratic procedure and process creating better workplace conditions, and conditions for productivity.

Works Council conditions are ever-evolving. They have rightfully earned a permanent status and position in Austrian industrial relations. They are established with different names in various forms in several European countries, including Germany, France, Great Britain, Italy, Spain, the Netherlands, and Belgium, but all share the 'co-determination' moniker.

Works Councils serve worker interests on the ground and in real-time and are nominally and functionally independent from larger trade-union regional and national institutions. This is essential. It provides companies and their workforces with autonomy and adaptive flexibility.

By the same token, Works Councils are informed of and contribute to larger trade union negotiations and settlements, but their members do not have to be union members, nor do they have to implement union dictates. As noted, they hold the larger trade-union representative bodies accountable and honest.

European Works Councils

At the federal European level, Works Councils are mandated not only on a national basis, but also through European Union Directives. (Wikipedia, Works Council). In 1994, the Council of the European Union mandated the establishment of the European Works Council "or similar bodies (sic) for the purposes of informing and consulting employees in companies that operate at the European Union level. The directive applies to companies with at least 1,000 employees within the EU and at least 150 employees in each of at least two European Economic Area (EEA) countries. (ibid)

The European Works Council came into being through the passage of the Single European Act, described earlier, creating Europe's unified market. The European Works Council gives representation to workers in big, multinational companies and provides a "direct line of communication to top management. It also ensures that workers in different countries are all told the same thing at the same time ... lastly, they give workers' representatives in unions and national works councils the opportunity to consult with each other and to develop a common European response to employers' transnational plans, which management must then consider before those plans are implemented." (ibid)

In an era of mergers and acquisitions, as will be seen, such awareness and leverage are of paramount importance in restraining corporate control over national markets and worker interests.

Works Councils protect employee interests at the local level. In Austria, and elsewhere in Europe, other bodies represent labor interests at regional and national levels. Austria is somewhat singular in that worker interests are represented not only at the industrial, sectoral, and national levels through their respective unions, but also by Chambers of Labor.

"The existence of these separate structures has implemented a dual-channel system of representation." These 'supplement' the Statute for a European Cooperative Society with regard to the involvement of employees, ibid)

In short, Works Councils, Union representation and Chambers of Labor provide the channels through which social market capitalism upholds a collective commitment to worker inclusion and prosperity.

The likelihood of any of this happening in America may appear far-fetched at the moment, but a movement for employee rights on the shop floor could emerge at any time. Such a movement would be predicated on union membership growth and increased networking and solidarity between already existing American trade unions. In this internet day and age, such organization and coordination are entirely conceivable.

Chambers of Labor

The 'dual-channel system of company level and regional labor representation is further extended through regional and federal Chambers of Labor. Besides and in coordination with Works Councils, these Chambers of Labor enact worker stake-holdership in the economic system. They balance the aforementioned dominance exercised by employers/owners in industrial relations, providing an explicit social dimension to employment, augmenting that of the private contract.

Chambers of Labor serve to inform and uphold worker rights. They help workers identify their interests as a class not only in itself, but for itself. In their research capacities, moreover, they provide economic information that is vital to both business and labor enterprise.

Chambers of Labor, as noted above, are funded by compulsory membership fees. These amount to 0.5% of gross (before tax) wages. So, if you make 2,500 euros a month, 12.50 euros is forwarded to the Chamber of Labor in your province with every monthly paycheck.

Compulsory membership is a contested political issue. Employees generally support it, however, because the efficacy of their collective interest depends on uniformity and unity - and because workers get a lot back in return for their dues. Chambers of Labor provide free information to all workers on issues "related to labor law, social insurance, tax law, women's and family policy, worker protection, the protection of apprentices and young workers, unemployment insurance, and consumer protection. In labor-law disputes between employees and employers, the Labor Chamber provides legal assistance ranging from oral or written interventions with employers to free representation of employees before the Labor and Social Tribunals." (European Trade Union Institute (ETUI), Austria, *The Chamber of Labor - Role and Functioning,* etui.org, May 2, 2017)

"Of Austrian citizens surveyed, 75% stated that the Chamber of Labor is a reliable organization." (ibid)

"Further of note is that employment issues in Austria are represented and resolved through these independent Chamber agencies. They operate (sic) outside the formal purview of the Austrian court litigation system. This produces efficiency and efficacy. The Chamber of Labor is unique in Europe. No other country has such a formalized, legalized, institutionalized interest group representing employees. The unique thing in Austria is this legally established, self-administering, complete infrastructure of professionals." (Joan Traub, Co-determination... ibid, p. 619)

Public votes for provincial Chamber of Labor General Assemblies (employee parliaments) are held every five years in direct, secret ballot elections. All Chamber of Labor members (all employees, in effect) are entitled to vote.

These elections are non-partisan, but candidate lists are proposed and reflect the interests, nonetheless, of the biggest established Social Democratic, Conservative, Freedom, Green, and Neo-Liberal political parties.

General Assembly representatives are elected and serve on a proportional basis. *'Proporz,'* as it is known, serves to share and balance political party participation at all governmental and, in the case of the Chambers, all non-governmental organizational and administrative levels. In this manner, all political interests are proportionally represented.

At this point, it makes sense to survey the political landscape and learn how political parties are involved in social partnership procedures and activities.

Social Partnership Parliamentary Involvement

Bernie Weber, erstwhile Green Party parliamentarian and spokesman, describes these Social Partnership affairs as contested and fractious, but also "effective and essential." (Bernie Weber Interview, Vorarlberg Green Party representative, April 9, 2024)

Such a perspective reveals the difference and rub between theory and practice.

Weber took up his seat after the Green Party won 18.9% of the vote in Vorarlberg's 2019 state election, second to the Conservative Party, which won 43.5%. The two parties then served in a majority coalition government until 2024.

Weber served as the Green Party spokesman on economic issues, land development and zoning, municipality affairs, citizens' initiatives for democracy, and art and culture. By European and worldwide standards, Weber considers the institutions of Austria's Social Partnership "unique" in their standing and influence.

"They provide an institutional setting, a green table, as it were, for the conflict and resolution of class interests." (ibid)

The heyday of Social Partnership may be associated with past achievements of Austria's Grand Coalition between the Socialist and Conservative parties through the 1990s, but its utility still comes to the fore, especially in times of national stress.

The period after the Great Recession, (2008-2011) and, more recently, during and after the COVID-19 public health crisis (2020-2022,) called for greater governmental intervention and reliance on the Social Partnership to arrive at and execute policies.

Even as union power wanes in an economy more geared toward international trade and more regulated by the EU, the Social Partnership still exerts influence to integrate labor and capital interests in the social market capitalist economy; both at the national and provincial level. Its role might be more crucial than ever in restraining the disintegrating effects of global hyper-capitalism.

Along with other political party groups, groups aligned with Green Party interests play an instrumental role in the councils of Social Partnership institutions, whether at the national and/or regional trade- union level, or in the councils of the Chamber of Labor and Chamber of Commerce.

At times in 2003 and 2017, when the governing Conservative and Freedom Party coalitions aimed to reduce the scope and power of the Social Partnership, the Green Party stood in "critical solidarity." As Weber says: "The Green Party has always defended the institutions of the Social Partnership, especially the Chamber of Labor and National Trade-Union, against Freedom Party attacks." (ibid)

Though opposed and resisted at times, Green Party-affiliated representatives continue expressing their views in Social Partnership councils and affairs to this day. It is not always easy. Green Party environmental positions and social inclusion initiatives often meet resistance from Chamber of Commerce representatives, who tend to support their Conservative Party counterparts when such issues come to the parliamentary floor. The Green Party Economy faction has seats within the Chamber of Commerce and, according to Weber, it "is far more oppositional than its Green counterparts in the Chamber of Labor." (ibid)

Green Party-affiliated lists in National Trade-Union councils also express "critical solidarity," but they often differ from or oppose some union positions and policies. In the past, these have included union support for industrial development over environmental protection.

In the 1970s and 1980s, for example, nascent Green Party environmental groups and vociferous public sentiment successfully blocked the construction and development of nuclear and hydroelectric power plants at "Zwentendorf" and "Hainburg on the river Au," respectively. (ibid)

Further, the current Green Party opposes large highway projects supported by the National Trade Union. They argue, instead, that different, non-car modes of transportation should be encouraged.

The Greens also advocate for more open and democratic processes at the Trade Union level. There may be employee Works Council co-determination at the company or industrial level, but not enough within Trade Union councils themselves. Hence, Green Party - affiliated list representatives "call for more representation of under-represented part-time, gig, and women workers and for more participation in Trade-Union primary elections and strike ballot" decision processes." (ibid)

These disagreements receive substantial airing, if not always satisfactory resolution. Still, as Weber notes: "The Green Party will always support the Trade Unions and the vital role they play in a social democracy. There are numerous overlaps and areas of agreement "in the social and labor market policy demands of both the Green Party and the unions." (ibid)

Austria has a spectrum of political parties and interests. The Socialist Party, as would be expected, is closely aligned in policy matters with the National Trade Union. For Weber, however, "This is not always constructive for either organization." He would prefer both to exercise more independence.

Weber further cites the Austrian Conservative Party as excessively "critical of the Chamber of Labor and the National Trade-Union. It targets each, as would be expected, as 'socialist organizations.'" This, for Weber, is unwarranted because Conservative Party members, affiliated with business and agricultural interests, are fully represented in Labor Chamber and Trade-Union councils. (ibid) In this respect, political party interests fully inter-penetrate and are represented in social partnership institutions and councils.

For the past 75 years, representing broad but differentiated public support, Austria's Socialist Party and Conservative Party have sustained the Social Partnership, through both high and low times.

The so-called Freedom Party, representing fairly extreme nationalist positions, is "antagonistic toward the Social Partnership because "it privileges economic class interest, or social interest, over nationalist ethnic/racist aspiration." At least, this is the position of the Freedom Party when it shares governmental power. When out of power, however, it recognizes the utility of forging "alliances within the Chamber of Labor and National Trade-Union."

The Neos are a go-go capitalist, neo-liberal economic party. They are also "antagonistic toward the Social Partnership and would abolish Chamber of Commerce and Chamber of Labor mandatory memberships." (ibid) Like their rivals in the Freedom Party, they would presumably alter, if not unravel Austria's social state.

A picture emerges here of political party affiliates engaged in Social Partnership processes, each pressing their claims in non-governmental agencies that nonetheless influence parliamentary parties and lawmakers. Furthermore, a picture of united plurality emerges, wherein political, governmental, and economic interests are expressed and addressed in tandem.

The influence between these governmental and non-governmental entities is reflexive. However, the economic and social expertise produced in partnership, through deliberative processes, provides legitimacy and removes some of the politics from policymaking. Though the standing of the Social Partnership is continually contested, its relevance remains, as does its broad support among the Austrian citizenry.

Among Social Partnership institutions, the Green Party most favors the Chamber of Labor, according to Weber, because of its "advocacy for employees and their participation in the productive economy." (ibid)

In addition, the Chamber of Labor provides research expertise to all parties, which "improves the legislative negotiating process and creates better legislative outcomes."

The Greens strenuously support mandatory membership fees because they provide financial wherewithal, both for the Chamber of Commerce among businesses and the Chamber of Labor among employees.

Chambers of Labor & Chambers of Commerce As noted earlier, elected provincial "Chamber of Labor assemblies vote in turn to designate National Chamber of Labor representatives. At both provincial and national levels, with combined staffs of 2,600, Chambers of Labor conduct extensive research and advocacy on a range of labor, consumer legislation and policy issues, providing a scientific basis for debate and decision-making." (Austria, *The Chamber of Labor Role and Functioning*, ibid)

The Labor Chambers serve as a bridge between Works Councils, the Employer Chamber of Commerce, and the National Trade-Unions. "They act jointly with other social partners in conducting and publishing studies on social and economic issues. Besides this, they provide financial support for education, vocational/technical training, and cultural productions – including theater troupes and monthly newspapers that reach every household, maintaining and advancing issues and topics relevant and vital to the interests of all working people.

Parallel to the Chambers of Labor, the Austrian Chambers of Commerce are similarly elected, but serve different functions. Here, as with the Chambers of Labor, membership is mandatory for all business owners and employers. Every five years, Chamber of Commerce members elect representatives to provincial chambers, who then vote to constitute the Austrian Federal Chamber of Commerce, "the parent organization for the nine provincial chambers and 110 trade associations for different Austrian industrial and business concerns." (Wikipedia, Austrian Economic Chamber, wikipedia.org, November 2023)

Both Chamber of Commerce and Chamber of Labor elections, as noted, are officially non-partisan, but candidate lists are proposed nonetheless in conjunction with the major political parties.

In the 2015 Chamber of Commerce federal elections, for example, the Economic League list, supported by the conservative party, won 66.6% of the vote. The Socialist-supported Business Association and the Freedom Party's Economic Initiative list each won 10.8%, the Green Economy Group secured 9.1%, and the neo-liberal party Neos received just over 2%.

The committees and the federal chamber contribute to and represent the interests of commerce in the yearly collective contract negotiations conducted with the national trade union organization, the Austrian Trade-Union Federation (ÖGB). (Eurofund, Austria: Elections Take Place in the Austrian Economic Chambers, Eurofund, europa.eu, May 2015)

Austrian National Trade-Union

The Austrian Trade Union Federation (ÖGB) augments Works Council and Chamber of Labor representation at the national level. It represents some 4.3 million employees in industrial sector wage and benefit negotiations with their counter-parts from the Chamber of Commerce. Twenty-eight percent of the workforce, or 1.4 million workers, are trade-union members. This means, the national trade union must continually maintain and grow its standing among the Austrian workforce. ÖGB-negotiated, collectively bargained contracts cover 96% of the Austrian workforce, whether for unionized members or not. (Wikipedia, Austrian Trade-Union Federation) Negotiation involve:

- Labor compensation and benefits negotiations are, of course, conducted on the basis of numerous complex but stable factors. The "Benya rule," for instance, is one influential measure that calculates inflation and sectoral productivity-profit rates to determine the extent of wage growth. Besides Benya, other factors are considered, such as:
- Economic cycle factors and specific labor market shocks, such as changes in labor market participation rates and/or migration.
- Structural factors, including how other Social Partnership institutions weigh in.
- European Union and European Monetary Union factors.
- Growing internationalization and the rise of both non-standard and part-time contracts in the labor market."

(Gerhard Fenz, Christian Ragacs, Alfred Stiglbauer, *Aggregate Wage Developments in Austria Since the Introduction of the Euro*, Austrian National Bank, *Monetary Policy and the Economy*, Q1-Q2, 2019)

These factors are numerous and complex, but their studied, continuous inclusion provides shared reference, reliability, and stability to partner negotiations. The Benya Rule, as mentioned, provides a measure by which rising productivity creates efficiencies that support wage increases to keep pace with inflation, without, presumably, exacerbating it. As you can imagine, there is quite a bit of give and take involved.

The Austrian National Trade Union (ÖGB) is the umbrella organization for seven consolidated, smaller trade-union sectors, including those for:

1. Production workers in manufacturing (including the metal industry), agriculture, and mining.
2. Construction workers.
3. Postal and telecommunications workers.
4. The largest union, representing private sector employees and employees in the printing, journalism, and paper industries, as well as apprentices, students, and part-time employees.
5. Public service workers (including teachers and university professors.
6. Transport and service industry workers.
7. Municipal workers and workers in the media and the arts.
8. (ibid)

Provincial Representation

Reinhard Stemmer represents the national trade-union (ÖGB) in Austria's Vorarlberg province. Herr Stemmer exercises provincial oversight and is a member himself of the transport and service industry union (VIDA), which represents 136,000 employees nationwide. (vida.at, August, 19, 2024) This includes airplane, railroad, and bus system workers, workers in the caregiving professions, barber salon workers, and restaurant and hotel industry workers.

He is also the Works Council representative in the union division for train engineers in Vorarlberg, numbering some 240 members. (Stemmer Interview I - 2023), (Austrian Federal Railways (ÖBB), *About the Group*, konzern.oebb.at, 2024) Stemmer has his hands full, but he notes that several of his functions "overlap" because negotiation conditions follow well-laid tracks. (Stemmer Interview I, 2023)

At the moment, (2024) however, Stemmer has misgivings about the status of labor conditions, relations and interests. Despite the well-laid tracks of negotiation, recent success in rounds of collective bargaining, and Austria's impressive labor representation and organizational frameworks, he notes that across the union front - whether for Austrian Airline workers, metal industry workers, teachers, or restaurant workers - Chamber of Commerce and Conservative Party pushback threatens the foundation of Austrian industrial relations and Social Partnership compatibility, like seldom before. (Stemmer Interview II, 2024)

Political Influence

Conservative Party and Chamber of Commerce agitation, now abetted by a resurgent authoritarian, so-called Freedom Party, predates the 2020 pandemic, the Ukrainian War oil price shock, and the inflation upsurge. Business and industry economic interests, along with their representatives in the Conservative Folk (sic) Party in parliament, started efforts in 2018 to repeal Social Partnership provisions that mandate obligatory employee membership in Chambers of Labor and business membership in the Chamber of Commerce. Without these clauses, many believe the unity of the Social Partnership would slowly, but surely unravel.

For some, including businessman Felix Rippe, cited earlier, mandatory membership in a partnership is a misnomer.

"Partnerships" Rippe believes, "should be of such mutual benefit as to be substantially voluntary. That's how the Social Partnership works and flourishes" in his native Netherlands.

Others, perhaps more closely attuned to the intricacies of Austrian Social Partnership arrangements and the fragility of market conditions, believe mandatory membership promotes the stability, continuity, and security upon which Austrian Social Partnership and its many benefits depend.

In 2019, efforts to reverse obligatory Partnership conditions were set back only by a fluke of history. The ruling Conservative Party and its Freedom Party coalition partners were caught in a surreptitiously filmed scandal. The film featured Austria's Freedom Party Vice Chancellor, Christian Strache in a potentially illicit, if not illegal transaction. He's caught offering interest in lucrative Austrian public contracts and/or interest in a major Austrian newspaper publication, the *Krone* (or *Crown*) to the supposed niece of a Russian oligarch. In return, she was to facilitate contributions to the Freedom Party.

The 2017 tape, recorded on the Spanish island of Ibiza, was released two years later. It reveals Strache saying he wanted to "build a media landscape like (sic) autocratic Hungarian President Viktor Orban." (Wikipedia, Ibiza Affair, April 28, 2024)

Strache's almost instant mea culpa confession before a national TV audience and the ensuing public outcry, resulted in the ultimate and almost immediate downfall of the Conservative Party and Freedom Party coalition, testimony to Austria's self-correcting and functional political culture. Social Partnership conditions survived.

In the intervening years, however, and separate from the repudiation and scandalous downfall of the Freedom Party-Volks/Folk Party coalition, trade-union representative Stemmer points out that business and "management tactics have grown more provocative." (Stemmer Interview II, ibid) Continued economic inflationary pressures apparently goad business interests to resist sustained union demands that wages and benefits for Austrian workers keep pace. Businesses want more elbow room.

The consumer 'purchasing power' argument still sustains the union's negotiation position, but pressure mounts. Austrian pro-business advertisements on YouTube and other social media outlets increasingly appear to at least indirectly flaunt, if not undermine the Partnership. Union coffers themselves are not plentiful enough to finance sustained public relations campaigns of their own. Moreover, Social Partnership conditions, until now, restrain public airing of labor interest grievances, let alone censure of business behavior. Curiously, the social partnership foundations of Austrian governance are not broadly taught in the upper grades of Austrian schools. You would think such instrumental structures would be a mainstay of the high school civics curriculum.

A Social Partnership Business Owner

Individual business owner support for the Social Partnership, though, is still widespread, if in some precincts grown thin. Vorarlberg business owner, Christian Bickel esteems the Social Partnership for its social and economic benefits. He owns and manages an 'office management' software company, *Consolidate*, which serves around 400 customers in German-speaking Austria, Switzerland, and Germany. In business since 1996, the company employs 22 people.

Bickel regards the 'social market' economy and Social Partnership as instrumental not only in forging the prosperous economy that is a priority for everybody, as he says, but one "which impedes exploitation." (Bickel Interview, trans. May 18, 2022) The Partnership prevents the bottom from falling out of the economy. It ensures collectively bargained basic wages and prevents downward wage competition, which is especially important during economic downturns when job opportunities become scarce.

"The social market economy itself, not the government," Bickel notes, provides a social safety net.

"People are incentivized to work. Basic living conditions of food, clothing, and shelter should be assured," he adds, "but people should not be overindulged. As he says, "there should be a safety net, but not a hammock."

At the same time, Bickel notes that businesses need to operate in competitive market conditions. In general, most employees are compensated at "higher market rates" than the collectively bargained minimum rate. (Bickel Interview, ibid) Hence, there is a combination of social and market values integrated into the employment system.

He especially values the system because of the uniform benefits it provides, including legally mandated "maximal and minimal vacation periods, sick leave and socially insured healthcare." Because the financial obligations to support these conditions are equally shared, "damage to the economic system as a whole is prevented." (sic) (ibid)

Otherwise, if only some employers and/or employees paid into the system, others would seek competitive advantage, leading to a "downward spiral" in economic relations and economic security. (ibid)

The Partnership keeps party politics and governmental intervention in the economy to a minimum. The government delegates "important economic decisions" to business and labor bodies, which render their own seal of approval and legitimacy.

Bickel himself can testify to the non-partisan nature of the Commerce Chamber and Trade-Union negotiation processes. For 12 years, he was the head of a provincial Chamber of Commerce Information Technology (IT) sub-group that evolved into his participation on a 13-member negotiating committee, along with other Commerce Chamber and Trade-Union representatives.

"In the years that he served," he says, "he never knew the political orientation of fellow committee members and would have stood up and left the minute political partisanship became an issue." (ibid)

When he first joined the IT sub-group, Bickel doubted the utility of mandatory membership in the Chamber of Commerce for businesses and employees in the Chamber of Labor. Over the years, however, the experience changed his opinion.

"Mandatory membership, whether in the Commerce or Labor Chambers, saves managers the hassle and time expended to recruit members," Bickel says. "It saves energy. And cross-the-board contributions certainly reduces membership fees - making participation "easier, cheaper, and more productive." (ibid) Most tellingly, Bickel continues, "Chamber activity in the areas of labor and commerce regulation, limits governmental involvement and protects such matters from "becoming over-politicized." (sic) (ibid)

Austrian Works Councils, Chambers of Labor and Commerce, and the Trade Union Federation provide the institutional sinews by which the social interest in a market economy is upheld. They make it a 'social market', over and against, but still in synch with the capitalist market. Each institution, in its own way, contributes to greater economic equality and mitigates the causes of polarization endemic to modern society.

They provide bridges and avenues by which Austrian citizens are included in the larger social, economic, and political structures of society. These structures support civic identity and freedom and provide essential definition, expression, and connection to the larger society. They stave off the social effects of alienation which can otherwise tempt people, as Erich Fromm pointed out, to surrender their freedom and escape from individual responsibility.

Furthermore, the Austrian social partnership continues to renew itself, as it did at the beginning of the century, during and after the Great Recession years, and now in 2025 the partners are called upon again to forge compromises and concessions to reduce the country's high deficits and budgetary overdrafts.

Part XIX
More American Labor History

Chapter One:
Right-to-Work Revisited

The portrait of the many economic structures and agencies in Austria provides a distinct picture. It demonstrates a viable and compelling model for the maintenance and representation of labor and capital interests. It is unique in some ways, but nonetheless provides beacons to guide the way forward.

It is precisely because of inefficient and costly strike actions, not to mention their social fallout, that Austria creates uniform conditions of collective bargaining strength and peaceful industrial relations at all levels of the economy. This has not yet come to pass in the USA, which remains entangled in historic economic and legal traditions. Untangling these snarls should prompt new industrial policy initiatives from government, business and labor entities to recalibrate economic policy and development. Such initiatives, however, inevitably clash with existing systemic realities and, at best, achieve only piecemeal progress. A crisis of Democracy is at hand. More thoroughgoing reform, leadership and advocacy must find forward thrust.

Certainly, on the face of it, the Austrian system of Social Partnership, - and, for that matter, the social markets of Europe, - are not easily replicable on the American continent. The Austrian example, minuscule in comparison with the American economy, appears too rare, or special to be of any practical guidance. However, the social solidarity principles that sustain European social markets possess basic viability. They have world-wide applicability.

Elements of the Austrian Social Partnership may have more than merely local viability. It is not entirely far-fetched, for example, to envision the emergence of a new Labor Party in the USA, or more robust support from the Democratic Party, proposing the establishment of Chambers of Labor in each state. Beyond the protections rendered by the U.S. Department of Labor, these offices, - modeled after Austria's case, - would be more deeply integrated into the working economy, giving workers a more effective voice and status. Business owners and managers already have their Chambers of Commerce. Given the right circumstances and pressures, Commerce Chambers too could undergo greater amalgamation and coordination. Chambers of Labor, of course, would be further strengthened by shop-floor works councils and stronger unions. But first, labor interests themselves must attain greater amalgamation and coordination.

Alternatively, speculation may be warranted that all these industrial relations matters are being outmoded by the intercession of AI and other IT innovations, such as quantum computation. These could conceivably provide post-modern resolution to the perennial and inadequately settled disputes between labor and capital. It is conceivable, at least on the surface, (and beyond the formal purview of this essay), that parameters for an 'equitable, parity' economy, could be programmed, and maintained in real-time. 'Benya rule' calculations, related to rates of inflation and productivity/profit, among a host of others, could be supplied by duly constituted and delegated labor and capital interests - to better regulate and reduce the mayhem, untoward inequality, and at times venal and vapid tendencies of market capitalist economic enterprise. Newly constituted 'coordinated market economies' could be achieved. The interests of commerce and labor would find new, non-adversarial, or belligerent modes of organization and representation. It is not unimaginable. Of course, such prospects are fraught with challenges and perhaps threats to individual and social autonomy, and to the very economic interests they are meant to serve. Conversely, constructive, and accountable application of advanced IT and quantum capacities may contribute to greater and more broadly distributed economic empowerment. In the meantime, the hard, economic realities of history and of the current moment must still be confronted.

Chapter Two:
Trade-Union Role Retrospective

Protecting the Right to Organize (PRO) campaigns and contemporary strike initiatives notwithstanding, the American labor movement must tap new wells and networks to forge a renaissance of labor interests in America. To rejoin the analysis of sociologists Clawson and Clawson, they also cite the role of trade-unions themselves as a cause for labor's historic decline.

Despite its militant history of active strike confrontation and disputes over wage and employment conditions, the trade-union movement grew *accommodationist* after World War II. The Taft-Hartley Act of 1947 and the subsequent Landrum-Griffin Act of 1959 limited public space for trade-union advocacy, protest, and organization, but they also recognized trade-union status as a legitimate partner in the development of American industrial relations. Clawson and Clawson observe that industrial relations "assumed the existence of a postwar 'accord' between management and labor, an arrangement whereby business accepted unions and unions became the de facto allies of management, helping to regulate and co-opt worker discontent." *(ibid, p. 96)* This was a far cry from mutual partnership.

Such *accommodation* is evident even today. Michael Kuitu, a retired unionist, was a heavy equipment operator and an erstwhile member of the International Union of Operating Engineers. He was an elected delegate to the Duluth (MN) Central Labor Body, the Duluth Building Trades and the Carlton County Central Labor Body. In 1997, he was elected as one of two rank-and-file members to the 12 - member Executive Board of Local 49, which held oversight jurisdiction for Minnesota and North and South Dakota. While serving on that board, it often occurred to him that "the other board members believed the main function of the board was to manage the membership for the contractors." *(Mike Kuitu Interview, August 2024)*

To alter these circumstances, he and other rank-and-file members sought elected union officer positions, but were unsuccessful. As an example of union inefficacy, he maintains that "union failure to organize broadly, deeply, and in opposition prevented a national single-payer health care system." "Instead," he noted, "individual unions negotiated only in their own limited interests."

"The current 2024 leadership of Local 49," he continued, "endorsed Trump supporter, Pete Stauber to represent us in Congress. So, unions like that have only themselves to blame for having to deal with the Guardians of Privilege that are the bane of existence for 98% of Americans." *(Mike* Kuitu *Interview, ibid)*

Accommodationist tendencies continue. The Kuitu interview reveals a few things: union leaders in Kuitu's time perceived their interests in isolation, disassociated from broad public understanding and broader support of a larger union movement. Their interest was to maintain their 'locals' status and standing, not in the risks associated with confrontation, nor in holding out for 'national health insurance' when their own insurance coverage was on the line. There is a labor interest 'for itself', but the labor interest 'in itself' lacks organizational cohesion and articulation.

Parochial, over-accommodation is not social partnership. Hence, a candidate and a party are supported that kowtow to industry, without upholding the interests of labor.

Anti-communism

The constriction of the trade-union movement and working-class consciousness has many roots, but perhaps none so tangled as the anti-communist hysteria that gripped American society in the early post-war period. It took real hold in the land of opportunity, not only via propaganda and Joe McCarthy's blacklisting witch hunt, - terrible as these were, - but because wider society itself was predisposed to endorse the prospects of individual opportunity and capacities of self-determination. Collectivism, associated with communist and socialist states, didn't take hold in the land of wide-open prairies and opportunity.

Even after the worst of his machinations brought McCarthy down in 1954, social sentiment still supported the Landrum-Griffin Act of 1959. Besides curtailing union organizational room to maneuver, it further stipulated that suspected communist sympathizers were to be rooted out and disqualified from union membership. *(Wikipedia – Landrum-Griffin Act)* Anti-communism sowed suspicion and distrust and demonized the utterly justifiable cause of organized labor to advocate on behalf of a fair wage for a fair day's work. Workers' rights to these market-based claims have been normalized in Europe, over and against any communist affiliation. They are the basis of *good faith* not only in the labor movement, but in the whole phenomenon of social partnership.

As it was (and still is) in America, trade-unions were compelled to throttle their wide-ranging demands and recede into the narrow confines of individual union halls. Many union members and leaders," Kuitu observes, "seldom will engage in helping other unions and focus only on their own issues." Expressions of political solidarity and the formation of union alliances were stymied by the legacy and perceived consensus of anti-communism, but also by market conditions.

Kuitu laments the long-standing decline of labor movement prospects. "I believe and will carry to my last breath that the struggles of the generations that created the labor movement got lost in translation to the generations that followed. When northern unionized industries were sent down to the former slave states, unions were defeated. There was little outcry and too few boycotts. The same happened when union jobs went overseas. The labor movement died one job at a time." *(Kuitu Interview, ibid)*

Trade-Union Historical Hang-Ups/Divisions

The labor movement became self-inhibited, lending credence to anti-communist innuendo. Widespread racketeering practices, noted above, didn't help.

The trade union movement was also limited by its own historical, institutional hang-ups and prejudices. The first national and more inclusive labor confederation, the Knights of Labor, (KOL), suffered setbacks after the violent and terrible Chicago Haymarket Massacre of 1886. The KOL sought to involve member craft-unions in "social and political disputes that did not represent the unions' own direct interest." (Editors of Encyclopedia Britannica, *Labor*

Organization, britannica.com, March 13, 2024) That direct interest focused narrowly on immediate gains, such as the "right to collective bargaining for wages, benefits, hours, and working conditions." *(ibid)*

Such interests were taken up by the more conservative American Federation of Labor (AFL) under the leadership of Samuel Gompers. The AFL would come to represent "approximately a hundred" *(ibid)* skilled craft-union trades, including carpenters, typographers, cigar makers, and iron and steel workers. (G. William Dornhoff, *The Rise and Fall of Labor Unions in the U.S.*, University of California Santa Cruz, whorulesamerica.ucsc.edu, 2012)

The AFL didn't dictate national standards but respected regional and local craft-union autonomy. This led to *"jurisdictional disputes between unions affiliated with the Federation,"* but membership still grew in pre-Depression years. *(Encyclopedia Britannica, ibid)* Craft unions held special leverage over businesses because their members' skill levels were hard to replace.

The influx of European immigrants in the late 19th and early 20th centuries, along with increasing industrialization, provided businesses with a workforce by which they could hire cheap labor to bypass and undercut trade-union worker employment conditions. AFL craft unions, in particular, "opposed the continuing influx of non-skilled industrial workers into the country because they saw the introduction of more workers and mass-production technologies as detrimental for their wages and social status." *(The Rise and Fall of the American Labor Movement, ibid)*

American '*white-male nativism,* as Dornhoff describes it, was at play against immigrants, many of whom were from Eastern Europe. The economic incentive to preserve high wages by limiting employee numbers outweighed solidarity and the prospects of increased union membership and organizational strength.

The ideological fervor and commitment to socialist principles that raised prospects for all workers in Europe didn't catch on as much in the United States. By the same token, Americans were swept up by more practical concerns and the social, economic, and political realities of a relatively young society, still settling a vast continent.

AFL-CIO

The AFL's defensive, if not parochial, insularity - favoring craft-unions over industrial worker unionization - was at least temporarily overcome in 1934 on the issue of majority vs. proportional union rule and representation. Industrial workers involved in the United Mine Workers, under the leadership of John Lewis, and the Union for Garment Workers rejected the conciliation of proportional representation, favored by business.

The issue was fraught. "Majority-rule" meant that once a majority of employees voted for union representation "at a plant, factory, or office," the union would be the sole negotiator for employee interests. (G. William Dornhoff, *Who Rules America*, Chapter - *The Rockefeller Network Creates a Labor Disputes Board*, ibid)

"Proportional rule," on the other hand, favored by business interests on the National Labor Board, meant the company could organize and represent those employees in the minority who voted not to have union representation. Though argued ostensibly in the name of minority interests, it was seen at the time as a fairly naked "divide-and-conquer" strategy that would allow companies to avoid serious negotiations with unions." (ibid)

This issue, among others, mobilized industrial strikes that precipitated the passage of the National Industrial Relations Act (NIRA) and the National Recovery Act. However, the industry-wide wage and price code-setting and the transfer of legislative powers these Acts authorized, were ruled unconstitutional in 1935.

Subsequent strikes in 1935, among other developments, led to the passage of the NLRA-Wagner Act and the establishment of the NLRB. Both faced Supreme Court legal challenges but were ruled constitutional in 1937, becoming the law of the land. According to Dornhoff, the "AFL was slow to pursue" the momentum prompted by the NLRA and related industrial strikes in 1936. (ibid) The AFL'S 1935 convention had rejected a resolution, stating that "in the great mass production industries…industrial organization is the only solution." (Editors of Encyclopedia Britannica, *AFL-CIO Labor Organization*, britannica.com, March 13, 2024)

Such resistance triggered defections from AFL ranks and the creation of the Congress of Industrial Organizations (CIO), which eventually put the representation of industrial mining, steel, rubber, and auto workers under one umbrella. It was John Lewis who spurred the 1936 "sit-down-strike" against GM with the motto "one shop, one union." (Editors of Encyclopedia Britannica, *John L. Lewis*, britannica.com, February 8, 2024)

The post-World War II congressional ascendancy of conservative political and business interests led to the promulgation of the 1947 Taft-Hartley Act. As noted above, this act restricted spheres for union organizing, protest, and advocacy. Such developments, along with shifting labor demographics from the industrial North to the South – where there was strong opposition to union inclusion of Black workers - as noted above, created environments inimical to the union movement.

These political and demographic developments galvanized the AFL and CIO toward greater political alliance but "only gradually translated into union solidarity." (*AFL-CIO Labor Organization*, ibid) Under the leadership of the CIO's United Auto Worker (UAW) president, Walter Reuther, and former AFL president George Meany, the two unions eventually merged in 1955. Combined, the AFL-CIO represented "about 1/3 of all nonagricultural workers" in America. However, membership declined steadily thereafter." (ibid)

The largest trade-union, the Teamsters, was expelled in 1957 from the Meany-led AFL-CIO, due to suspected racketeering practices. Ultimately, to the lasting detriment of the union movement and union solidarity, the merger of the AFL-CIO never quite mended strategic organizational differences and visions. "The conservative Meany and the liberal Reuther never achieved more than an icy cordiality." (ibid)

As leader of the numerically stronger AFL, Meany took over the merged unions. His early craft-union bias later extended to protecting the interests of existing union members at the expense of new and/or unintegrated labor groups, such as women and black-skinned workers. He was anti-communist and tended to be accommodationist. "He transformed the nature of the U.S. labor movement from radical to conservative, preferring to achieve goals through lobbying and dispute arbitration rather than through strikes and marches." *(*Britannica Encyclopedia Editors, Amy Tikkanen, *George Meany*, March 13, 2024) Under Meany's tenure, *Britannica* reports, "union membership as a percentage of the non-agricultural U.S. workforce declined from 33 percent in 1955 to 23 percent in 1979." (ibid) There were splits, divisions, and departures.

Meany comes in for a lot of criticism from different quarters, including from what was then the New Left. His predecessor, Samuel Gompers, and successor, Wayne Kirkland, are also assailed "for having undermined true social democracy in favor of personal gain and corporate accommodation with employers and the state." (*JSTOR Review*, Edmund Wehrle, *Taking Care of Business - Samuel Gompers, George Meany, Lane Kirkland and the Tragedy of American Labor* by Paul Buhle, *International Labor & Working Class*, #61, Spring, 2002, pp. 216-218)

Walter Reuther & the Alliance for Labor Action

Meany saw to it that UAW president Reuther, and CIO allies were expelled from the AFL-CIO's Executive Board in 1968. The rift was deep. Under Reuther's leadership, in the run-up to that year's presidential election, the UAW withheld its per capita federation membership dues to force a debate at the AFL-CIO national convention.

At issue was "whether the federation met its responsibilities to the changing needs of the labor movement and the nation." (Emily Straus, *Alliance for Labor Action*, encyclopedia.com, March 22, 2024) Reuther's challenge was an unsuccessful attempt at reform. After prospects were dashed by the Democratic party's defeat in the 1968 presidential election, "the UAW disaffiliated with the federation." "(ibid) Philosophical differences were at the crux of the matter. "Meany backed away from broaching political class struggle, and Reuther believed in activist unions." (ibid) Reuther sought systemic change, while Meany sought accommodation with larger political powers and interests. The differences between Meany and Reuther went way back.

On behalf of the UAW. - of which he was president, but still part of the CIO, Reuther joined an alliance in 1964 with "Martin Luther King, Jr. and the Farmer's Union, among others, to form the Citizen's Crusade Against Poverty." (ibid) This and other motions were a bid to extend the reach of President Lyndon Johnson's "inadequate" War on Poverty. To extend collective bargaining, reminiscent of similar developments in Austria, Reuther advocated for a "Price-Wage Public Review Board and a progressive spending tax." (ibid)

The AFL-CIO Executive Council censored such actions, which launched Reuther and his allies on a campaign to challenge the "stodgy bureaucratic leadership of the AFL-CIO for being inactive politically and socially." (ibid)

Fundamental trade-union differences were cited, such as "the need to increase unionization among the unorganized industrial, construction, office, technical, and professional workers." (ibid) All combined, leading up to the 1968 convention challenge, such statements and events provide just a flavor of an alternative social, and strategic vision represented by Reuther, his UAW, and erstwhile CIO allies. They held that the "progressive, modern labor movement" should be characterized by "dynamic thrust and crusading spirit." (ibid)

After disaffiliation, Reuther and the UAW departed from the AFL-CIO to form the Alliance for Labor Action (ALA). They were joined in this enterprise by the other largest American labor union, the now nominally rehabilitated Teamsters under Frank Fitzsimmons. The Alliance advocated a "far-reaching program, committed to working with any group willing to help organize the nonunionized workers and to strengthening collective bargaining by embracing the concept of coordinated bargaining." (ibid) In other words, they advocated for an over-arching national trade-union organization.

The ALA represented "four million workers" and their families. Though large, the ALA couldn't gain traction with many smaller unions after Meany "identified it as a dual union and threatened to expel AFL-CIO affiliates that joined it." (ibid) Then, in 1970, Walter Reuther himself was killed in an airplane-crash in Michigan. Internecine division ensued, and the ALA disbanded in 1972.

The 'union role' in the breakup of the labor union movement was hence significant. Each setback and course-setting can be attributed to circumstances specific, though not exceptional to America and the country's relative youth. Part of Meany's shortcomings can be traced to America's post-war 'new frontier' mentality. America was triumphant after World War II and possessed apparently unlimited horizons for free enterprise, and capitalist development. Many labor leaders got on board.

Despite the capitalist calamity of the 1930s, suffered in the then more recent and memorable economic Depression, unlimited economic expansion appeared plausible against all ideological concerns and protests. Still, Meany regrettably lacked a confident, practical vision for the entire class of working employees in America.

As the section on Walter Reuther and the UAW demonstrates, however, it was, for a moment, a close-run thing. What if the Democrats under Humphrey had won that year's presidential election? What if, on another front, Martin Luther King and his 1968 Poor People's Campaign in support of Memphis sanitation workers' fight to unionize, hadn't been terminated by his assassination?

King was ready to bring the Civil Rights movement into a new stage, proclaiming, "Now our struggle is for genuine equality, which means economic equality." (Martin Bennett, *1968, King, Memphis and the Poor People's Campaign,* California Labor Federation, colaborfed.org, June 1, 2018) What if there had been a merger between the Civil Rights and labor movements? Outlooks and positions taken up by Reuther, the UAW, and the ALA were similar to the practical social partnership platforms constructed by labor interests in Europe and Austria a little ahead of, but also in, the same period. The union movement in Europe was galvanized by the historical calamity of World War II and more ideological clarity. Such clarity, outlined in this essay's chapter on Marxism, along with conditions on the ground, allowed labor leaders to perceive the shortcomings and dangers posed by unchecked capital interests.

Empirical conditions have changed, warranting the critical analysis featured here, among other places, of labor and capital's respective positions. Retrospective protest is warranted. The largest trade-unions failed at partnership. Parochial tactics and accommodation prevented broad alliance formations with which the working class could be organized at sectoral industrial levels.

This leaves the labor movement to fight for concessions without broad solidarity to advance labor interests on the national level. Wide swaths of working people in America are hence left with inadequate income, and prone to alienation, powerlessness, and demagoguery - not to mention getting laid off due to rampant merger and acquisition conditions.

Trade-union alliances at the industrial sector level can compel national agreements and, hence, leverage government and business cooperation. All this requires a labor movement that equates its claims with civil rights, broadcasting them with the help of the internet and social media, through a new understanding and articulation of collective identity.

It also requires a revamped governmental industrial policy, chastened by the realities of the moment and inspired by visions of a future in which practical social partnership is attainable.

As it happened, after decades of relative union strength and after the brief ALA interlude, failed vision and further membership declines and divisions thwarted the AFL-CIO and the greater trade-union movement. It became easy pickings for the doyens of hyper-capitalism who came to power in the Reagan era.

Chapter Three:
Employer Offensive II

The section here on American labor history began with the question of when the tide irrevocably turned against the old New Deal social contract. That tide continues to churn. It brings in the already noted wash of financialization, private equity machinations, and merger and acquisition frenzy that drive increased economic inequality. It brings in the wave of anti-union, 'right-to-work' laws in several states, which make union dues optional and reduce union leverage. But first, a requiem needs to be sung for the old New Deal social contract.

The hallmarks of that contract, you will recall, were articulated even at the corporate level after World War II to include all American social interests. Recall that Johnson & Johnson corporation CEO Robert Johnson proclaimed a range of ordered corporate commitments: first to 'mother, father, and medical business customers,' then to 'employees,' then to managers,' and finally to 'owners and stockholders,' who could claim a reasonable profit after the other commitments had been fulfilled.

This view represented a revival of the pre-war "industrial self-government" belief system, noted previously, which supposed capitalism could be reformed from within. It found wide subscription and implementation across the American corporate spectrum by such companies as "GE, Exxon, General Motors, Ford, Westinghouse, US Steel, IBM, and Xerox" (Gelles, *The Man Who Broke Capitalism*, ibid, p.18, 2022). The record shows, again, that "from 1948 to 1979, worker pay grew in tandem with worker productivity" (ibid, p. 25).

As surveyed earlier, the misbegotten 1970s inflationary surges intervened to convulse the American economic system and crack broad support for welfare capitalism. Then came the formation of 'the new executive class' and class war designs to wrest economic direction and control away from government entrusted with upholding public interests. Then came Ronald Reagan.

The protracted and lamentable downfall of the American labor movement was decades in the making. One of the quintessential chapters unfolded, as noted, during the Reagan years. A strike for higher wages conducted by 11,000 unionized air traffic controllers was broken. Prior to that event, as Caleb Crain of *The New Yorker* reports," there were 289 large strikes a year, on average, during the 1970s but only 83 a year in the 1980s" (*State of the Unions*, ibid, p. 80). In the current decade, the yearly rate is 14.

After the defeat of the air controllers' strike, the ground began to shift. As a copper mine owner summed it up at the time, "Suddenly people realized, hell, you can beat a union" (ibid). This state of affairs, as indicated, had many untoward causes and even more untoward consequences. "Real hourly pay," Crain further elaborates, is lower today than it was in 1973" (ibid).

During the economic seizures of the 1970s the economic philosophies of Friedrich Hayek and Milton Friedman gained prominence. By then, the depredations of state socialism in Eastern Europe's communist bloc countries had become quite evident. In his seminal work,

The Road to Serfdom, Hayek lumped these developments in with the social economies being innovated and constructed in Western European countries. Hayek championed all-out free-market competition, "unencumbered by regulations," as the only reliable mechanism "to address society's needs" (*The Man Who Broke Capitalism*, ibid, p. 35).

Friedman, who won the 1976 Economics Nobel Prize for his efforts, held up the same banner. "The social responsibility of business is to increase profits" (ibid). He completely rejected the idea that businesses have social responsibility other than to make money. In Gelles' words, this sanctioned a "wholesale rewriting of the American social contract" (ibid, p. 36). It also stands in fundamental contradiction to the social contract being forged at the time in Western Europe. There, as noted, businesses are not only private institutions but, in equal measures, social enterprises. As businesses take and gain from the public hand, so they must contribute to its broader social upkeep. But more than this, as noted, it's all in the actuarial calculations: efficient provision of high-quality social insurance (and 'pre-distributed' services) can be sustained when all employed and productive sectors of the economy are able to contribute to its upkeep. When all contribute, premiums are reduced.

This was the road not taken in America.

GE & Jack Welch

As faith in governmental institutions and policies wavered in 1970s America, - as Watergate unfolded, as gas prices and inflation rates increased economic insecurity, - diatribes against federal regulation and taxation took hold. The neo-laissez-faire shift advocated by the likes of Hayek and Friedman found receptive audiences. The dormant, if not failing, American economy was taken hostage by a phalanx of capital interests. This takeover, however, was first predicated, as mentioned, on the overthrow of the trade-union movement and the position of labor in American society.

It was the renowned and, for some, notorious president of General Electric (GE), Jack Welch, who perhaps most took advantage of the scrambled moment and breakdown of the old economic paradigm. As Gelles observes, "No one (until Welch, sic) had yet dared to explicitly, relentlessly put shareholders ahead of employees, communities, and the environment" (ibid, p. 39).

The New Deal social contract, which extended a stake to broad social constituencies, was now replaced by a contract that favored corporate shareholders. Thus, was inaugurated "a new cutthroat era of American capitalism" (ibid). "Before Welch came along," Gelles continues, "employees were regarded as a company's greatest asset" (ibid, p.43).

During Welch's reign, a counter-mentality made its imprint across American corporate culture: "Labor was a cost, not an asset" (ibid, p. 44). The strategy was to cut costs, increase profits, and boost Wall Street stock valuations. 'Downsizing,' 'outsourcing,' 'offshoring jobs were the hallmark tactics to accomplish this strategy. Such methods are now so commonplace that they barely merit mentioning. But then, "hundreds of thousands of people lost their jobs at GE while Welch was CEO" (ibid, p.45).

Communities were blighted. Trade-unions were unable to counter these business maneuvers. Their power and leverage were dispersed and in decline. "Welch managed to wage his sustained and sweeping campaign against loyalty (to employees, sic) without going to war with the unions, avoiding a major strike during his time as CEO" (ibid, p. 46).

Trade-union interests were bypassed. They were no longer recognized as essential partners, but as an unnecessary burden. "Welch simply moved jobs away from pro-labor areas whenever he could, thereby drastically reducing the proportion of the GE workforce that was unionized" (ibid). Even worse, when cost-cutting and downsizing reached a limit, work was shifted from unionized factories in America to foreign countries, wherever labor was cheap

The human fallout of such tactics is self-evident. As Gelles observes, "Gone was Generous Electric (of the bygone golden age era, sic), replaced by an enterprise that seemed to lack institutional memory and was consumed with reducing costs and boosting revenues, no matter the fallout." As one manager told Welch in 1988:" If this is the best business in the world, why do I go home feeling so miserable?" (ibid p. 48).

This is the world now familiar to our own times, where management loyalty to employees is tenuous at best. This is a result of a shareholder mentality that gradually, but steadily overtook business practices. Gelles concludes: "Thanks in part to the example set by GE, shedding employees became an acceptable - even routine - way for companies to improve their profitability." (ibid, p. 49)

As labor unions declined, "everyday Americans got an even smaller slice of the economic pie. After growing between 5 and 9% annually from the late 1960s until 1981, blue-collar workers saw those (income, sic) gains erased." (ibid, p. 50)

Now, trade-union interests are largely supine. Welch's success, however, was apparently indisputable. GE stock prices continued to rise. The 'stock-value' bandwagon rolled across the economy, from one industry to another. Jack Welch became an economic guru. "Everywhere he went, he continued to preach the gospel of shareholder primacy, suggesting that companies put investors first and remain unsentimental in the face of layoffs." (Gelles, ibid, p. 132)

Seen in dialectical terms, the hollowing out of the organized labor movement in America set the stage for the ongoing overthrow of the American capitalist system by global, hyper-capitalist interests. For democratic capitalism to succeed, however, as the cited economic commentator Martin Wolf argues, a benign fusion between business and government interests is essential for the maintenance of a democratic society. The groundwork for the ongoing disintegration of business and government interests, - ushered in by Jack Welch, among others, - was advanced by the substantive removal of working people and their organized labor interests from the industrial policy equation.

Welch's methods didn't stop with 'downsizing,' 'outsourcing,' and 'offshoring, even though such practices would continue and grow in the next 'buyout' phase. The object wasn't production anymore, but to make money at all costs. Welch perceived early on in his 20-year GE tenure from 1980 to 2000, as Gelles notes, that "real money was going to be made not in the factories of the American heartland, but from buying (sic), rather than building." (ibid, p. 56)

Manufacturing and maintaining GE power plants, jet engines, and appliances would only generate so much earnings, and this was always dependent on economic conditions. Consistent earnings growth, at the heart of shareholder capitalism, could only be sustained by buying other companies. One GE commentator noted: "The model Welch (sic) had was really the Pac-Man model - just eat up companies. Acquire growth, acquire growth, acquire growth." (ibid, p. 50)

Hence was born GE Capital, financial engineering, and the era of business acquisitions and mergers. Gelles explains, "The deal making boom Welch unleashed re-ordered the economy well beyond GE." (ibid, p. 57) Prior to his time, annual business merger transactions numbered a couple thousand. "With Welch setting the pace at GE, those numbers exploded. By the end of his tenure, the number of deals soared to upward of 14,000 a year.... Of the companies that were in the Fortune 500 in 1980, a full 143 of them – 28% - had been acquired by the end of the decade." (ibid)

Along the way, a number of New Deal laws that restrained breakaway capitalism had to be rewritten or replaced altogether. In 1985, Welch became enamored of NBC, one of several holdings in the RCA conglomerate, which included a "large consumer electronics business, a satellite operation, semiconductor manufacturing, and much more." (ibid, p. 51)

Old Social Contract Torn

As Gelles recounts, the Reagan administration was instrumental in paving the way for GE's acquisition of RCA. Formerly, by New Deal edict, "GE had been expressly prohibited from owning RCA," as a matter of obvious anti-trust enforcement. Two companies in the same industry (which GE and RCA definitively were) should be prevented from colluding with each other to augment or monopolize market control. In the New Deal era, both companies signed off on the ruling with a 'consent decree'. The Reagan administration "conveniently threw out the 'consent decree' that had kept the two companies apart" (ibid, p.51). Welch and GE acquired "RCA for $6.3 billion, making it, at the time, the largest non-oil deal in history" (ibid).

The old Securities Act of 1933 expressly barred companies from "intentionally meddling with their own share price" (ibid, p.659). This included the practice of stock buy-backs, which set the stage for manipulating share value. In another 'gift' from the Reagan administration, the Securities Exchange Commission changed the law so that companies could indeed start buying back their own stock.

The current essay recounts Robert Reich's appraisal of contemporary corporate behavior, in which the greedy, if not usurious effects of these 'buyback' maneuvers were examined. In theory, buy-back revenues were supposed to be re-invested in the economy - in 'R&D', in worker wages, in capital (equipment) improvement. They were supposed to 'trickle down' to support things like worker 401(k) "retirement accounts." They were not supposed to vastly increase managerial portfolio wealth. But this is what happened. In practice, as Gelles asserts, "research has shown that buybacks exacerbate inequality" (ibid). It was morning in America. GE set records in the buy-back field, even as it was considered unorthodox, if not unethical, by other American industrialists. The CEO of US Steel "likened the practice of buybacks" to "eating your own mother" (ibid).

By 1997, the earnings contagion had seized the economy. GE led the way. The strategy was to reach quarterly earnings projections to maintain and raise stock prices. GE Capital expanded its acquisition appetite by going after overseas companies. Employing the old 'buyout', 'downsize' tactics to generate bottom-line value, GE started a craze. But taxes on overseas operations were an intolerable cost. They had to be expunged. "GE and other companies won a change to American law that allowed them to avoid paying billions of dollars to the IRS. Known as the 'active financing' exception, the new twist in the law let GE (and other US companies) claim that money the company made from its international financing activity was actually being generated abroad. So long as it kept the profits offshore, GE could essentially avoid paying taxes on its ever-expanding lending operations across the globe, all the while amassing additional tax credits, depreciation, and write-offs that it used to offset profits it made elsewhere in the company" (ibid, p. 62).

So, began the search for tax havens and offshoring profits. Altogether, the old New Deal social contract was rewritten or replaced in many of its essentials. The law now privileges the finance and investment capital class. Between 2003 and 2012, S&P 500 companies "deployed a full 54% of their earnings - some $2.4 trillion - to buy back their own stock" (ibid, p. 66). Stock-based monetary instruments, buybacks, and dividends don't benefit workers, who, anyway, don't own much stock. The wages and wealth of company executives, on the other hand, depend on stock prices. As one expert on the buyback phenomenon notes, "the very people we rely on to make investments in the productive capabilities that will increase our shared prosperity are instead devoting most of their companies' profits to uses that will increase their own prosperity" (ibid, p.66).

As Gelles points out, "financial services" involved in private equity, real estate, consumer finance, banking, insurance, and investment comprised "under 5%" of GDP in 1980" (ibid, p. 67). Today, according to Statista, financial services comprise the biggest part of the American GDP, standing at 20.2% (Statista Research Dept, *Share of value added to the GDP of the U.S. in 2022, by industry,* statista.com, November 3, 2023). This would all be well and good, except for the 'reverse distribution' going on those benefits only a small and privileged sector of the American population. All well and good except it becomes ever clearer that these interests will fight to maintain their ill-got, account-ledger cooking, illicit gains no matter the cost; so illicit that the plutocratic end-game heaves evermore into view. The aim is to sever society from its democratic heritage and the rule of law, the few remaining means left by which their gains can be restrained and directed toward the public good and democratic hope for the future.

Part XX
The Modern World in America and Europe

Chapter One:
Comparisons

The picture in Europe on these issues is not as bleak, but it appears that European corporate titans came rather late to the stock buyback party. The French newspaper Les *Echos* (*The Echo*) wrote in 2022, that "Large European companies have massively turned to share buybacks since the pandemic. They have tripled in the space of a year, reaching 70 billion euros in the first half of the year in Europe, including 15 billion in France." (Elisabeth Wallins, *Share Buybacks, Regulations Still Too Timid in the Face of Market Excesses,* University of Montpellier Science-Society, 2022)

This is practically nothing compared to the American market, where, by the end of 2021, "Share buybacks had even exceeded $1 trillion in annual flows for the S&P 500 alone." (ibid)

Whether in America or Europe, the story remains the same: „The main purpose of the share buyback announcements is to please shareholders in the short term by bolstering the share prices of the companies concerned. The executives who propose such maneuvers also benefit from them, as good stock prices have become a major expression of their ability to 'create value." (ibid)

This, of course, raises the value of *stock options* by which corporate executives are remunerated. The overall effect of these operations is the creation of a share buyback quasi-derivative market, divorced from other market and social values. As the *Les Echos* article points out, reminiscent of Daniel Bensaid's Marxist appraisal given earlier, "In some years, the total flow of dividends and share buybacks even exceeded the flow of new share issues, thus reversing the financing function of the financial markets." (ibid)

Hyper indeed. To what extent European regulators will catch up to these *stock price manipulation* trends remains an open question. On the face of it, social partnership restraints should kick in during the next round of negotiations.

Unchecked capitalist designs, as noted earlier in this treatise, are par for the course. Free markets, as you may recall, operate through the „law of motion," which holds that, in a capitalist system, those in private business – capitalists - must constantly step up the rate of *capital* accumulation. *(Marx's Theory of Surplus Value*, International Viewpoint, ibid)

American, European, and Austrian regulatory agencies are charged with reining in controversial, if not illicit, share buybacks along with profligate merger and acquisition practices. These damage market and social values, which demand at least a basic amount of honesty and accountability. It is a game of catch-up.

In America, in the immediate aftermath of the 2021 COVID epidemic, "Ballooning stock prices have driven up company valuations, resulting in more companies willing to sell at today's high prices. Corporate buyers, armed with their own high valuations, are on the hunt. Incentivized by cheap capital and huge cash reserves, dealmakers have created an unprecedented merger wave, pushing already-overtaxed antitrust enforcement capacity to its limit." (Sarah Miller and Krista Brown, *To Save Jobs and Slow Inequality,*

Stop the Merger Frenzy, American Economic Liberties Project – Anti-Monopoly Policies & Enforcement, January 11, 2022)

Despite the troubling history of massive merger and acquisition effects, bipartisan consensus holds that business and industrial consolidation serves consumer welfare. The efficiency achieved, the argument goes, contributes to lower consumer prices, despite evidence to the contrary. Recalling Robert Reich's admonitions, cited earlier, "recent research suggests: "Mergers in industries that result in six or fewer significant competitors see price hikes in 95 percent of cases." (ibid)

According to the article, the effects of rampant, contemporary merger activity "have compounding effects on workers' earning ability and job security. Mergers eviscerate competition, increasing dominant firms' market power and leading to depressed worker wages - even as consumer costs and shareholder profits rise, further increasing income inequality." *(ibid,* Gauti B. Eggertsson et al., *"Kaldor and Piketty's Facts: The Rise of Monopoly Power in the United States*, National Bureau of Economic Research, Working Paper No. 24, 2018)

One perhaps unintended consequence of the first Trump administration's CARES Act, - legislated to capitalize the American economy during the pandemic, - was its bolstering of Wall Street and corporate ledger sheets. The business downturn was buoyed and an economic spiral was prevented, but the CARES Act "helped unleash today's unprecedented merger wave." (ibid)

While one might argue that mergers and acquisitions spur economic dynamism, - components of the *creative destruction* apparently necessary for an economy continually producing new technologies or products, - the contemporary mergers and acquisitions phase is more about capital finance and greed.

"When it comes to mergers, this much is clear: workers, even those that keep their jobs, are worse off - but executives, their bankers, and shareholders certainly aren't. CEOs are awarded eye-popping payments for selling their firms. In 2018, AT&T's $85 billion takeover of Time Warner netted the latter's CEO, Jeff Bewkes, a $97.7 million payday - and even massive Trump-era tax cuts didn't prevent the company from firing 45,000 workers in the years since." (ibid)

All the protections in the world, including the Worker Adjustment and Retraining Notification Act (WARN) of 2008, don't seem to slow the mergers and acquisitions juggernaut. With all the business consolidation and labor fallout, the Biden administration acted to bolster anti-trust enforcement at both the Federal Trade Commission (FTC) and the Department of Justice (DOJ). Biden appointed FTC Chairwoman, Lina Khan stated, "The current merger boom will further exacerbate deep asymmetries of power across our economy, further enabling abuses." (ibid)

Since what seems like time eternal, the then new Assistant Attorney General and head of the DOJ's Antitrust Division, Jonathan Kanter reiterated the government's commitment to reigning in the monopolization of the American economy. In his testimony before the Senate

Judiciary Committee, he stated: "The critical mission of the antitrust laws is to protect competition for people in the workplace to ensure that thriving competitive markets lead to adequate compensation." (ibid) Kastner's and Khan's sentiments are a bygone balm to what is now under way in the new Trump administration.

But even then, before Trump II, you might have said that the economic lifeboat had already left the harbor.

In 2022, in response to President Biden's call for greater merger and acquisition control, the FTC and DOJ issued new guidelines to "reverse corporate consolidation and protect American workers from its destructive effects." (ibid) And indeed, antitrust cases did see a marked increase, but the guidelines introduced are not laws. In the then meantime, merger and acquisition activity also appeared to be taking full advantage of funds released to support infrastructure projects. (Dolly Mirchandani, *Infrastructure M&A Forges ahead Even before Government Boost*, White & Case Law, July, 2021)

Chapter Two:
M&A in Europe

The merger and acquisition scene in Europe has a different regulatory backstory, but is in its own throes. From the beginning of the EU monetary union in 2001, the European Parliament called for a strengthening of the rights of workers and their representatives in corporate restructuring.

In general, where an M&A involves a transfer of undertakings, under the terms of the EU Directive:

"The rights and obligations of the transfer organization arising from a contract of employment or employment relationship are transferred to the transferee. Furthermore, following the transfer, the transferee must observe the terms and conditions in any applicable collective agreement until the agreement expires or is replaced. All the countries considered here have implemented these provisions in their national regulation." *(Industrial* Relations Aspects *of* Mergers *and Takeovers,* European Public Service Union - epsu.org, 2001)

The EU Parliament issued a further series of directives (not binding laws) that member states were to fulfill on their own terms, and they did so to varying extents. These directives included worker "rights to information and consultation" and the "right to expert assistance" in identifying the precise terms of mergers or acquisitions and their related impact on given workforces. These rights are upheld in most core European Union member states.

Another directive specified the worker's "right of opposition," which, of all the countries surveyed, only the Netherlands upheld. There: "The managements of companies involved in an M&A have to ask their respective works councils for their opinion. When the opinion of the works council is negative, management has to postpone the implementation of its decision for a period of one month. During that period, the works council can go to court to fight the merger decision." *(ibid)*

In Austria:

"In the event of major company changes, including mergers, takeovers, and changes of ownership, the Works Constitution Act provides that management should inform works councils as early as possible, preferably in the planning phase, and at the latest at a time which makes consultation possible. The information must cover the reasons for the restructuring, and the numbers, qualifications, and employment duration of the employees affected. In companies with over 20 employees, compulsory social plans must be established in the event of a basic deterioration of labor standards. The works council may present proposals to prevent or mitigate negative consequences for employees." *(ibid)*

Notice here the prerogative given to company Works Councils. As noted earlier, social partnership institutions do indeed exert restraint, if not control.

In political terms, however, these directives were issued a long time ago. In 2004, a Takeover Bids Directive was issued to bring more clarity and unified implementation across the EU. It was then periodically amended. In 2016, market evolution and globalization increased pressure on EU worker protection regulatory frameworks. "At the start, there was at least lip service to a corporate governance model with a well-balanced division of power between the different stakeholders. Capital owners, management, and labor cooperated in a productive environment and kept the real economy going. But this engagement and involvement of the different stakeholders within the company has been eroded in the past three decades." (Jan Cremers, Sigurt Vitols, *Takeovers with or without Workers' Voice: Workers' Rights Under the EU Takeover Bids Directive*, European Trade-Union Institute, worker-participation.eu, 2016, p. 16)

This, at least, was the view circa 2016 of the *European Worker Participation Competence Center (EWPCC)*. The EWPCC is built on the conviction that workers' participation is a key vehicle for trade-union presence and activism at the company level; this arguably holds even more truth at the cross-border level, since it is here that involvement rights can be strategically combined." *(ibid, p. 10)*

The 'stakeholder view' stated here challenges the mainstream 'shareholder view'. In 2016, it still held valence. The 'stakeholder' view, as described earlier in this text, upends traditional 'shareholder customs and rules', especially the private right to business privacy invoked in all such merger and acquisition transactions.

The *Takeover Bids Directive* also addresses this:

"Member States shall provide that, within the conditions and limits laid down by national legislation, the employees' representatives and any experts who assist them are not authorized to reveal to employees or to third parties any information that, in the legitimate interest of the undertaking or establishment, has expressly been provided to them in confidence.

This obligation shall continue to apply, wherever they said representatives or experts are, even after the expiry of their terms of office. However, a Member State may authorize the employees' representatives and anyone assisting them to pass on confidential information to employees and to third parties bound by an obligation of confidentiality." (ibid, p.20)

It appears that the Directive is comprehensive in defining and protecting worker rights in the event of M&A proceedings. Shareholder rights are, to a degree, abridged.

Critics argue, however, that the Directive on Takeover Bids does not go far enough: "From the stakeholder perspective, the passage of the Directive represents a clear victory for the shareholder paradigm in European company and securities law." *(Horn 2012; Johnston 2009; Sjåffell 2009)* In particular, the decision on whether or not a bid gets accepted is clearly placed in the hands of the shareholders of the target company, to the exclusion of workers or the management of the target company." (ibid, p. 21) The stakeholder position, as quoted above, is in the throes of erosion. The world seems to change at an ever more hyper pace. The way in which labor and capital interests are established and integrated lies at the crux of this ultramodern moment.

The contemporary international industrial relations situation warrants extensive analysis and citation. First, it is essential to note that, in important respects, "Labor is not a commodity. There are substantial limits to the ways in which labor (power) can be bought and sold, often imposed through elaborate employment protection legislation, while 'decommodification' *(*Esping-Andersen, *1990)* is reinforced by extensive welfare systems." *(ibid)* This is a forthright statement of labor rights holding social and ethical value, extending beyond those values bestowed by the markets.

"Second, partly as a corollary, collective agreements usually have priority over individual employment contracts, further limiting the freedom of individual labor market actors. Moreover, centralized bargaining – and, in some countries, legal extension mechanisms - result in high levels of coverage (even when union density is low). Collectively bargained labor agreements are adopted and ratified in synchronization with market conditions. They provide a bulwark against current and future exploitation." (ibid)

"Third, there is broad social and political acceptance that labor possesses distinctive collective interests which (whether or not defined as antagonistic to those of the employer) need independent representation. From this follows the idea of labor as a 'social partner,' often with a key role in shaping social policy and administering public welfare." (ibid) This expresses *Social Partnership* foundational principles.

"Fourth, almost universally, there is a standardized system of workplace representation at least partially independent of management (underwritten by law or peak-level agreement, or both). The autonomy of employers is thus constrained to a degree unknown elsewhere in the world." (Richard Hyman, *Trade-Unions and the Politics of the European Social Model, Sage Publications, London School of Economics, 2005)*

In the great struggle between labor and capital interests, the *American (Anglo-Saxon) model* is differentiated from the *continental* model of European social market capitalism. America still has a long way to go in catching up to the labor prognosis quoted above. Europe is in the midst of sorting it out.

Chapter Three:
Competition Law Revisited

The precise meaning and reach of contemporary EU Competition Law come under contested scrutiny. The Danish Executive Vice-President of the European Commission, Margrethe Vestager, heads the EU's competition authority and is also its 'digital czar.' In the latter capacity, her agency "fined some of the world's biggest tech giants over violations of antitrust rules" and is spearheading the creation of the EU Artificial Intelligence Act, which, if adopted, stands to become the world's first comprehensive AI law." (Yasmeen Serhan, *Time 100AI*, time.com, September 7, 2023)

However, it is in her capacity as a free-market champion and in the name of the EU's competition authority that she recently "hit back at calls for a wholesale overhaul of the EU's merger regulations, amid rising pressure from France and Germany to help spur the emergence of "European champions." (Javier Espinoza & Henry Foy, *Competition Chief Warns against Weakening Rules to Create Champions*, Financial Times, ft.com, September 17, 2024) The French-German idea here supports the vested consolidation of large European, supranational champion corporations to protect Europe's global market position.

In her capacity as head of the EU's Competition Authority, Vestager was instrumental in ruling against the merger of large German and French railway companies on the grounds that "neither party was prepared to make sufficient remedies to stamp out industry and consumer concerns over unfair competition." (Neil Hodge, *Intercontinental Champions and the Case for Reform*, International Bar Association, iba.org, February 2019) Germany and France were unhappy about the ruling. They pointed out that a positive ruling "was necessary to preserve the EU market for EU companies and to stave off competition from American, Chinese (sic), and other competitors." (ibid)

So, the wheels of commerce turn. Global market competition is fierce. Such discontent as expressed by Germany and France led to the "EU Commission President Ursula von der Leyen's nomination of (sic) the Spanish Socialist, Teresa Ribera, as Vestager's successor, tasking her with developing a "new approach to competition policy, one that is more supportive of companies scaling up in global markets." (*Competition chief warns*...ibid)

As a liberal free-market politician, Vestager insists that any changes "should be 'surgical', noting that merger rules, which allow Brussels to block deals when there is a risk of market domination, have rarely changed since their adoption in 1989. The problem with a more radical overhaul was not that it would allow big businesses to merge" (sic), she says - "The problem is whether or not you want that big business to be challenged." (ibid)[2]

---

[2] Please use the sharing tools found via the share button at the top or side of articles. Copying articles to share with others is a breach of FT.com T&Cs and Copyright Policy. Email licensing@ft.com to buy additional rights.

Subscribers may share up to 10 or 20 articles per month using the gift article service. More information can be found here: https://www.ft.com/content/e89ddf05-d311-4291-acbe-e4fa915995bd

Conclusion

The whole discussion leads back to several issues previously raised in this essay. Adam Tooze's observations on 'state capitalism' come to mind, as does the portrait of the Eurozone and the European Union's Court of Justice (CJEU) adjudication of Competition Law. Also relevant is the intricate tango between Europe's member states and federal authority and the principle of 'subsidiarity' - so central to the whole social market and social partnership enterprise.

As Reinhard Stemmer of the Austrian National Trade-Union (ÖGB) somewhat nervously noted, business support for the Social Partnership appears to be shifting. Will the tide turn on this historically significant enterprise, or are these more momentary rip-tides? This question and the issues it involves are very alive. Resolution will require business, labor, and governmental social partners at national levels, as well as their representatives in the European Parliament and EU federal bureaucracy to come to terms with and set the future course of Europe's Social Market economy.

That economy, and the Social Partnerships it embodies across Europe, are vulnerable to the tides of contemporary political and economic development. Its institutions and commitments are deeply rooted, but competitive global market forces necessitate new institutional alignment and recalibration of commitments.

Recall the materialist 'mode of production' - ideological spectrum raised earlier. The ever-growing, consolidated market materialist forces appear to overthrow the historical experience that fostered the ideals, insights and adaptations of social capitalist market economies - and their promise to take history in a different direction.

Dialectical analysis, reinvigorated but un-dictated by Friedrich Hegel and Karl Marx, on ideal and materialist planes, prognosticate that these systemic tensions will be resolved over time at different levels. Historical progress, however halting and vexed, is possible. In its economic class analysis, the dialectic provides ballast and bulwark by which, in the name of democratic interests, the ideals of greater shared social and economic equality can be revived, protected and extended.

The last word has not been written on the innovations and impressive contributions of Europe's Social Partnerships to durable political economy. It'll be a close-run thing within the European sphere. Will Europe become yet another mere *free trade* zone, or will it preserve social partnership templates of solidarity and shared prosperity? Will it reinvigorate itself to tame gargantuan and impersonal global market interests?

Perhaps, the EU is still too young to more forcefully advocate for itself as the outstanding developmental model it represents. As this essay adamantly argues, the adaptations of the European and Austrian social market capitalist economies exert their own dialectical force that should tilt and propel future global economic and political developments. But, of course, other forces exert their own dialectic pressures. American, Chinese, and Russian interests brood on the horizon with all their weight and unresolved historic baggage. Reactionary and oligarchic interests come to the fore in America. But it is far from a foregone conclusion that they will gain their goals. The dialectic is not predictive, but it does seem to indicate that the pendulum has swung in one direction just about as far as it can go, (especially with regard to market financialization, as well as to merger & acquisition patterns) enough to be called back and recalibrated by the broader social and economic interests of the American, not to mention European, working public.

In America, the reinvigoration of those interests and their long-overdue legitimate claims can be awakened by a new labor movement. But it is far from certain. History is ever contingent and malleable. Instead of democratic empowerment, that pendulum and all the history it embodies can indeed fly right off its hinges, where inhuman autocracy looms.

Part XXI

Chapter One:
The Tragedy of Russian Autocracy

Sheer autocratic examples are current, even if rather far afield, aside from what is going on in the U.S.A. It is not a digression to draw Russia into the picture. Indeed, to differing degrees, current and historical American, European, and Russian affairs are intertwined. Plutocratic (rule by the wealthy) and oligarchic (rule by the few) interests are alive and well in Russia, both as underwriters and beneficiaries of what has become an autocratic Russian state. This follows a litany of misfortunes and ruptures in Russian affairs, which extend back beyond the last century, but redound to this day.

The United States played an unintended and unfortunate role in Russia's more recent sordid, autocratic transformation. The breakup of the Soviet Union was catastrophic and revolutionary. Russia's reconstruction under Boris Yeltsin after 1991 required hasty adaptation to forestall a counter-coup from old communist parties and interests. Though reluctant to do so, Yeltsin persuaded leading Russian economists to adopt policies of "shock privatization", long advocated by American economists (such as Milton Friedman) for foreign economic systems in crisis.

The task in Russia was to turn what had been the 'command and control' economy of Soviet times into a functioning market economy -and fast! Esteemed American economists, such as Larry Summers and Jeffrey Sachs, came onto the scene and counseled broad privatization and other provisions, such as Russian debt forgiveness and financial aid. The aid and the forgiveness were not supported by the American government, but privatization was nonetheless introduced.

In 1991, "Yeltsin delivered the first big privatization shock to the Russian economy when he lifted price controls," which by 1994 caused prices to rise by "almost 2000%" (Greg Rosalsky, *How Shock Therapy Created Russian Oligarchs and Paved the Path for Putin*, NPR, npr.com, March 22, 2022). Then came the hard part. Russian ministers of economics were ordered to transfer state-controlled industries - from manufacturing and oil refineries to mines, media outlets, and biscuit factories - into private enterprises. "It was, to date, surely the biggest transfer of state assets to private owners in world history" (*ibid*).

After many convolutions and convulsions, the transfers resulted in the huge concentration of businesses and properties into the hands of a few - the oligarchy.

The scenario displays elements of tragedy. After the recent fall of the Berlin Wall in November of 1989, capitalism appeared to be triumphant - not only in the Cold War struggle against communism, but as the ultimate and inevitably best way to organize an economic system. When American economists and businesspeople came to assist and aid fallen Russia, it is not hard to imagine their confidence, if not a certain hubris. Assurances might have been given that privatization would attract huge foreign and American investment.

Apparent vindication of free-market values created a blind spot. As Tim Snyder, Yale historian, and expert on

Eastern European affairs, puts it: "American conventional wisdom contributed to the disaster (of Russian autocracy) by suggesting that markets would create institutions, rather than stressing that institutions were needed for markets." (Tim Snyder, *The Road to Unfreedom*, Penguin Random House UK, 2018, p. 34) Institutions such as independent courts, functioning capital markets, and strong regulatory bodies take time to develop. (NPR, ibid) Russia didn't have time for such things.

Remember, this was a hyper-capitalist moment. Instead of institutions, Russia got an oligarchy and no dependable rule of law. Investment conditions were dicey, at best. On this account, among others, the big promises that might have been made about foreign investment as an inducement to privatize evaporated like water in the desert. Snyder spells out how the turn to outright autocracy in Russia occurred, as Vladimir Putin started his illicit, if not illegal, third term of office in 2012.

Putin's Reign

A third presidential term for Putin had been proscribed by the Russian Constitution. He was term-limited in 2008, but this was canceled by his appointed successor, Dmitry Medvedev, who served an interim term and managed to alter the constitution. Now Putin could run again for president without term limits.

At the end of his current term in 2030, Putin will have controlled the Russian government for almost 30 years. As Snyder describes: "Democracy never took hold in Russia, in the sense that power never changed hands after freely contested elections … the end of Soviet economic planning created a violent rush for profitable industries and resources and inspired arbitrage schemes, quickly creating a new class of wealthy men." (*ibid*, p.43)

These groups made out like literal bandits in the 1990s and during Putin's first two presidential terms in the early 2000s. Even as Putin made diplomatic overtures to normalize relations with European countries and NATO, the Russian oligarchs exerted ever more power and control.

At the same time, the EU admitted the former Soviet states of Lithuania, Latvia, and Estonia into its fold between 2004 and 2007, "along with several other European states that had been Soviet satellites" (*ibid*, p. 46). The thing was, each of these states "had to demonstrate their sovereignty in specific ways that Russia had not: by creating a market that could bear competition, a governmental administration that could implement EU law, and a democracy that held free and fair elections" (*ibid*).

And so, Russia came to a fork in the road. One route involved rule-of-law reform, accountability, and an open market economy. The other route led to rogue-state status and oligarchic market control. In 2012, against the "largest protests in the history of the Russian Federation" and aided by electronic-digital manipulation of the vote, Putin and his party - *United Russia*, were installed to take open-ended control of the Russian government. (*ibid*, p. 49). The oligarchs who controlled the economy were so powerful that they could disdain the democratic reforms required by the EU for cooperation and membership.

They followed the road to autocratic unfreedom instead.

Russian Nationalist Fabrications

To pull this stunt off, both before and after, horrendous ideological invention and state - managed propaganda were and are required. Conjectures of the old, Russian fascist philosopher - a contradiction in terms - Ivan Ilyin (1883-1954) were exhumed, broadcast, and hoisted on official levels for all to hear and see. His crypto-religious outlook was that the "world of empirical existence cannot be theologically justified" (ibid, p.21). For Ilyin, "passions are evil. God erred in his creation by releasing 'the evil nature of the sensual'" (ibid). Well, this stands both Hegel and Marx on their heads and kicks them in the ass, asserting instead arbitrary and enforced state autocratic dictate, power and control.

That's not all.

Removing God as a reliable actor allowed Ilyin to glorify the state on high at an abstract, invisible level. As Snyder observes, "he saw his own nation as righteous, and the purity of that vision was more important than anything Russians actually did" (ibid, p.23). Ilyin saw Russia as a pristine, ahistorical state that endures over and beyond historic cycles of foreign conflict, attack, and injury. To hell with the dialectic. Everybody in Russia partakes in this martyrdom and thereby finds collective salvation. Such fictions are supposed to imbue Putin with demi-god status. His claims to total authority enable national redemption. "The nation is not God," wrote Ilyin, "but the strength of its soul is from God" (ibid).

This rhetoric all gets retrofitted to lend legitimacy to a Russian regime that has absconded with any earthly claim to legitimacy, especially the legitimacy of political succession. The ideology removes the state from temporal responsibility as it foists a 'politics of eternity' on the population. It allows more current fascist philosophers – again, a contradiction in terms - like Alexander Dugin (1962) to claim that there is a 'Russian truth,' apart from the truth that involves seeing, hearing, and touching. His "life's work" is, as Snyder says, "to bring fascism to Russia" (ibid, p. 88).

What the 'politics of eternity' does, according to Snyder, is place "one nation (Russia, sic) at the center of a cyclical story of victimhood. Time is no longer a line into the future, but a circle that endlessly returns the same threats from the past" (ibid, p. 8). To maintain such nonsense, all organs of state media are mobilized to create a fictional reality. "To end factuality is to begin eternity. If citizens are led to doubt everything, they cannot carry out sensible discussion about reform, and cannot trust one another enough to organize for political change. A plausible future requires a factual present" (ibid, p. 160).

The main message of Russian news programs was/is the "denial of factuality" (ibid, p. 161). This induces popular surrender and diminishes meaningful social and political agency. Agency, apparently, is solely a possession of the state, whose function now is to incite "crisis and spectacle. Law ceases to signify neutral norms that allow social advance, and comes to mean subordination to the status quo: the right to watch, the duty to be entertained" (ibid, p. 28).

Special doubt is propagated about the world beyond Russian borders, whose alternative models are always portrayed as alien, corrupt, and threatening. Hence the foundation and rationale for cyber and media warfare against America was laid, the underwritten manipulation of parties in Europe opposed to the EU, and the eventual military invasion of Ukraine. Europe is and was perceived as a hostile rival, for it, unlike Russia, has been integrated in a way that maintains national sovereignty. Snyder observes key subtleties: "The EU was like an empire in that it was a large economic space. It was unlike an empire in that its organizing principle was equality rather than inequality" (ibid, p.73).

By 2013, this European identity was manifest. "With its democratic procedures, welfare states, and environmental protections, the EU offered an alternative model to American, Russian, and Chinese inequality" (ibid, p. 75). Instead of level-headed reception and recognition, the EU model represented a threat to un-reconstructed states like Russia. "Russia was the first European post-imperial power not to see the EU as a safe landing for itself, as well as the first to attack integration in order to deny the possibility of sovereignty, prosperity, and democracy to others" (ibid, p. 78).

For Russia, by the early 2010s, such benefits were intolerable. The overtures Putin had made to align Russia with the EU were now reversed. On the basis of Russia's hyper-nationalistic 'philosophies', the Europe of legal, economic, and political legitimacy and integration should be subdued and made to be more like Russia. Since the downfall of the Soviet Union in 1991, Russia was unable to achieve reliable economic and political transformation. As Snyder explains it, "Russia managed no democratic changes of executive power. What had been an oligarchy of contending clans in the 1990s, was transformed into a kleptocracy, in which the state itself became the single oligarchical clan" (ibid, p. 79),

The Russian wars in Georgia (1991- 1993/2008), Chechnya (1994-1996/1999-2009), and Dagestan (1999) were aimed at holding together the old Soviet Union confederation. They were just warm-ups to the war of conquest Russia launched on Ukraine in 2014 and 2022. These wars were now justified by fascist ideologies to protect the pristine innocence of Russia's national identity, ever-threatened by foreign, Western influences and designs. The new Russian ultra-nationalist identity warranted imperial expansion, which should overthrow Europe itself and extend to Asia. Russia, as Snyder notes would be the center of the "empire of Eurasia." (ibid)

Though such realities, scenarios, and fictive narratives result from Russia's particular history, autocratic echoes and designs are also present in the West. When Trump spokeswoman Kellyanne Conway invoked 'alternative facts' into the American political lexicon in 2017 to explain U.S. governmental perspective and policy, an autocratic-like assault on 'facticity' was launched. The MAGA shift of the erstwhile Republican Party embraces multiple autocratic tendencies, especially the Big Lie it propagates about the outcome of the 2020 presidential election. More saliently, as mentioned earlier in this treatise, the program detailed in the '2025 Project' by the treasonous, once conservative Heritage Foundation broadcasts volumes of hateful perfidy that would undo America's constitutional heritage.

Insinuations of autocracy are evident in Europe as well. The Western world appears poised at a crossroads between the false road of autocratic unfreedom and a way forward where the ambiguities, uncertainties, and challenges of freedom and self-government can still be navigated – transporting the human spirit and destiny with dignity, and integrity, to the benefit of all.

In Conclusion The foregoing essay and analysis surveyed conditions that indicate a course to follow at the crossroads. It outlined the Hegelian and Marxist perspectives, not to be taken whole cloth, but as providing essential templates for critical evaluation of political regimes, the ideologies to which they subscribe, and the industrial relations by which they are constituted. These provide essential gauges to measure conditions of social unity and material prosperity; so essential in determining social viability. They present applicable frameworks for gauging parameters and horizons of human progress at individual and collective levels.

The essay employed such lenses in survey of the roots and realities of American political, economic and socio-economic polarization, particularly as it results from income and wealth inequality, and its capitalist market system of wage distribution. The diagnosis was further grounded by Heather McGhee's analysis of American racism and how it has crippled the achievement of a more united and equitable society. Combined, such pressures, as delineated by Martin Wolf, undermine the contemporary ideological-materialist fusion of American democratic capitalism.

The different way forward represented generally by the social democratic market economies of Europe, and by Austria, in particular, was described in detail. It encompasses the essential features of a social economy in which equitable wage compensation structures, mediated and negotiated by ongoing social partnership institutions, maintain broad material prosperity and competitive economic enterprise. European progressive tax systems underpin 'pre-distribution economic policies, which support the social provision of near universal, healthcare and higher and vo-tech tuition-free education. These constitute vital elements of the social market economy and offer models for alternative economic organization and development. They show a way forward out of the impasse and peril of current American political and economic circumstances.

At stake in this analysis are the conditions in which individual and collective consciousness can develop in socially beneficial terms, on into the future. These depend on social and economic institutions that support the incentive, orientation, and inclusion of all economic classes. The essay demonstrates the indispensable need for adaptable fusion of ideological and materialist metrics to ensure the further evolution of economic prosperity, social unity, human ingenuity, and socio-ethical, creative capacities. Such a fusion is being approached by the social democracies of Europe.

By maintaining this fusion, the false roads conjectured by both the politics of eternity, of inevitability and autocracy, as Snyder defines them, can be evaded. These represent a tragic attenuation of individual and social capacities that are so critical to the human spirit and horizons of future, historical progress.

Appendices

Appendix 1:
Environmental Consciousness p. XVII

Indeed, the 'materialist paradigm', whose main cornerstone is the scientific method, promotes comprehension, manipulation, and exploitation of the natural environment, not to mention an economy premised on over-consumption. As much as humanity appears to hold mastery over the environment and its vast and manifold resources, depletion and pollution of these stores undermine that quest, and threaten unsustainable ecological and climatological degradation. The materialist economy must incorporate greater ecological efficiency, conservation and preservation into its operations. Doing so, certainly depends on ascertainable knowledge, education and policy, but perhaps even more so on an ethical/spiritual-environmental conversion. This has thus far fundamentally eluded the nominal and substantial grasp of 'materialist' proceedings.

The current essay addresses the shortcomings (and blessings) of the 'materialist paradigm' in more conventional terms, as it applies to political, economic and social usage. Resolving the contradictions involved on these levels may allow humanity greater mental and spiritual space to focus and grasp a more fulsome environmental consciousness. This essay leaves the issues, questions and challenges of such a conversion in abeyance, as it is and will be taken up more profoundly by other, current and future voices and treatises.

Appendix 2:
Collective Bargaining and Wage Inequality pp. 55, 112, 251, 286, 487

"A major factor depressing wage growth for middle earners and driving the growth of wage inequality over the last four decades has been the erosion of collective bargaining" (Mishel, Lawrence, *The Enormous Impact of Eroded Collective Bargaining on Wages*, Economic Policy Institute, April 8, 2021). This factor should be appraised as an instrumental, if not a near-final cause of polarization in America.

"For the "typical" or median worker, declining unionization translates to a loss of $1.56 per hour worked, the equivalent of $3,250 for a full-time, full-year worker. The erosion of collective bargaining lowered the median hourly wage by $1.56, a 7.9% decline (0.2% annually), from 1979 to 2017. De-unionization lowered the male median hourly wage by $2.49, an 11.6% (0.29% annual) decline, over the 1979–2017 period. These losses from de-unionization are the equivalent of annual losses for a full-time, full-year median worker and median male worker, respectively, of $3,250 and $5,171. This impact is due to both the direct effect on wages of union workers and the spillover effect on wages of nonunion workers." (ibid)

"Declining unionization widened inequality between high-wage earners and middle-wage earners. De-unionization widened the 90/50 wage gap (the gap between earners at the 90th percentile of the wage distribution and the 50th percentile, measured in logs) by 7.7 points and therefore explains 33.1% of the 23.2-point growth of the wage gap between high- and middle-wage earners over the 1979–2017 period (ibid)

"**Unions disproportionately benefit those with low and moderate wages, those with lower levels of education, and nonwhites**, and this has been the case since the birth of the modern labor movement in the New Deal. The erosion of collective bargaining, correspondingly, has therefore increased wage inequality." (ibid)

In all, these numbers may not appear to add up to much, but could very well be the difference between staying economically-socially afloat, or sinking, between falling behind, or just being able to keep up; to say nothing of other benefits, like health insurance, that are collectively bargained.

Appendix 3: Net National Wealth Chart p. 66

Net National Income Ratio (selected) (in %) 2023

China	877	USA	577.7
Australia	875.9	Austria	570.3
Switzerland	844.8	India	479.4
Germany	692.4	U. Kingdom	441
France	621	Russia	431
Scandinavia Av	619.6	Brazil	390.5

(World Inequality Database, Worldview, wid.world, 2023)

Appendix 4:
World-Wide Income Shares pp, 211, 457

Selected Top 1% of Population National Income Shares in 2023

Country	%	Country	%
Russia	23.8	Germany	12.7
India	22.6	France	12.6
Brazil	21	Spain	11.9
USA	20.7	Canada	11.6
S. Africa	19.2	Austria	11.3
China	15.7	Scandinavia	10.3
U. Kingdom	13.1	Australia	9.9

(World Inequality Database, Worldview, wid.world, 2023

Top 10% of Population National Income Share (selected) (in %) 2023

Country	%	Country	%
S. Africa	65.1	Canada	36.3
Brazil	59.2	U. Kingdom	36.2
India	57.7	Austria	34.4
USA	46.8	Spain	33.6
China	43.3	Australia	32.9
Germany	36.7	Scandinavia Av	31.5

(World Inequality Database, Worldview, wid.world, 2023

Bottom 50% of Population National Income Share (selected) (in %) 2023

Country	%	Country	%
S. Africa	6.4	Australia	17.2
Brazil	*9.1*	Germany	19.9
USA	13.4	U. Kingdom	20.1
China	13.7	France	20.5
India	15	Spain	22.5
Russia	15.7	Austria	23.7
Canada	17.3	Scandinavia Av	23.9

(World Inequality Database, Worldview, wid.world, 2023)

Bibliography

A Different Way Forward: Social Market Capitalism & Social-Partnership in Europe, Austria and the USA

Adorno, T.W. and Horkheimer, M. (1944). *Dialectic of Enlightenment*. London: Verso.

Bensaïd, D. and Elliott, G. (2009). *Marx for our times: adventures and misadventures of a critique*. London; New York: Verso.

Brunner, U. (2020). *Lernen S' Geschichte, Herr Reporter!* ecoWing.

Desmond, M. (2023). *Poverty, by America*. Crown Publishing Group

Ferri, D. and Cortese, F. (2019). *The EU social market economy and the law: theoretical perspectives and practical challenges for the EU*. London: Routledge.

Fromm, E. (1941). *Escape from Freedom*. Henry Holt.

Gelles, D. (2022). *The man who broke capitalism: how Jack Welch gutted the heartland and crushed the soul of corporate America--and how to undo his legacy*. New York: Simon & Schuster.

Hudelson, R. and Ross, C. (2006). *By the Ore Docks*. U of Minnesota Press

Judt, T. (2005). *Postwar: A History of Europe Since 1945*. New York: Penguin Books.

Kelly, K. (2022). *Fight Like Hell*. Simon and Schuster

Kelton, S. (2020). *The Deficit Myth*. John Murray Publishers Ltd.

McAlevey, J. 2020. *A Collective Bargain, Unions, Organizing, and the Fight for Democracy,* New York: Harper Collins

McGhee, H.C. (2021). *The Sum of Us: What Racism Costs Everyone and How We Can Prosper Together.* New York: One World.

Piketty, T. (2020). *Capital and ideology.* Cambridge, Massachusetts: Harvard University Press.

Piketty, T. (2014). *Capital in the Twenty-First Century.* London: Harvard University Press.

Snyder, T. (2018). *The road to unfreedom: Russia, Europe, America.* London: Bodley Head, An Imprint Of Vintage.

Thomas, A. (2017). *Republic of equals: predistribution and property-owning democracy.* New York, Ny: Oxford University Press.

Wilkinson, R. (2009). *The Impact of Inequality.* The New Press

Wolf, M. (2023). *The Crisis of Democratic Capitalism.* Penguin.

Wolin, Sheldon, *Politics and Vision, Continuity and Innovation in Western Political Thought,* Princeton University Press, 1960, 2004

Citations

Scott Green, Michelle Falkenbach, Social Partnership, Civil Society and healthcare, National Library of Medicine, 2016

Index

A

Adorno, Theodor, 366, 369

Age of Enlightenment, 85-6

AI, 80, 84-5

Alliance for Labor Action (ALA), 545-48

AFL-CIO, 543-547, 550

Alternative Deficit Platforms, 450

American Collective Bargaining, 284-87, 478-81

American Economic History, 190-94

American Labor History, 474-80

American Slavery, 233-35

American Social Contract, 457-59

Anti-Communism, 339, 539

American Survey, I-V, 40-8, 187-90, 228-32, 320-22, 361-64

Anti-Trust Enforcement/Austria, 314-18

Atwood, Margaret, 136

Auschwitz-Birkenau, 80

Austrian, Authoritarian Parallels, 374-77

Austrian Chamber of Commerce, 174, 213, 522-23, 527

Austrian Chamber of Labor, 174-76, 213

Austrian Collective Bargaining, 213-17, 202

Austrian Income Tax, 208-213

Austrian National Trade Union (ÖGB), 174-76, 524-26

Austrian Neo-Corporatism, 173-80

Austrian Partnership Institutions, 173-80, 506-09

Austrian School of Economics, 295-96

Austrian Social Partnership, 189, 292, 527, 532, 535

Austrian Works Council, 507-09, 510-13

Austro-fascism, 168-71, 178

Austro-Hungarian Empire, 162-64, 166

Austro-Marxism, 166-68

Authoritarianism, 265, 269, 273

Autocracy, 127, 164, 263, 577, 579, 581, 587-588

B

Bensaid, Daniel, *Marx for Our Times,* 101, 104, 109, 111, 113-14

Benya Negotiating Rule, 524-25, 535

Bickel Christian, Vorarlberg Business Owner, Chamber of Commerce, 529-31

Bicycle Reaction, 333-37

Biden, Joseph, U. S. President, 52-3, 280, 566

C

Capitalism, xvii, 36-7, 41, 43, 45, 51-2, 130, 196, 340

Card Checks, 492-3, 495

Carter, James, U.S, President, 191, 193

CEO Wages, 68, 152, 193, 292

Citizens United, 275

Civil & Class War – Austria, America, 166-68, 279-80

Cohen, Leonard, musician, 390, 392

College for All Act, 432

Competition in the E.U. 314-18

Corporate Income Taxes, U.S. 200, 46-8

Cortez, Alexandria, U.S Rep, 336

Critical Race Theory (CRT), 231, 240-45,

D

Deficits, Debts, GDP, 429-30

Deficit Management-Europe, USA, 445-48, 453-54

Democratic Capitalism, 119-23, 131, 158, 556

Democratic Party, 41, 58-9, 136, 189-90, 196-98 268, 273, 336 380-82, 386-87, 389, 548

Desmond, Matthew, 50-1, 326

Dialectics Defined, 78-9, 93-5, 133-34, 281

Dialectic Issues Today, 134-139

Dialectic Zombie, 132-34

Dictatorship of the Proletariat, 115

Dollfuss, Engelbart, 168

Dugin, Alexander, Fascist Philosopher, 584

Dystopia, 136, 388

E

Edsall, Thomas, political analyst, 263-64, 266

Employer Offensive vs. Org. Labor I-III, 495-97, 551-53

European Central Bank (ECB), 31-3

European Competition Law, 573-74, 309-12

European Post- World War II Treaties, 394-406

European Social Dialogue, 345-48

European Social Mkt. Capitalism, 131, 271

European Social Partnership, 338, 409-10, 570-71, 575-76

European Soc. Part. Appraisal, 339-42

European/American Market Conditions, 385-388, 389-391

European Union (EU), 28, 30-9, 165, 220, 307-12

F

FDR's New Deal, 458, 474-76, 478

Federalist Society, 264, 275

Financialization and Private Equity Frenzy, 460-65

Financial Services, 353, 560, 563

Floyd, George, 239

French Revolution, 86, 89, 120

Friedman, Milton, 553-54, 579,

Fromm, Erich, *Escape from Freedom,* 68, 72, 367-68

Fukuyama, Francis, *End of History,* xiv-xvii

G

GE & Jack Welch, 553-57

GINI Index Graph, 56

Golden Age Capitalism, 484-86

Gov't Spending: GDP graph, 444-46

Great Recession, 70, 157, 303, 351, 424, 429, 457-59

H

Hammond, Samuel, philosopher, 86-7

Hayek, Friedrich, *Road to Serfdom,* 552-53

Health Insurance Comparisons, 418-23

Hegel, Friedrich, xvi, 81-94, 95, 98-100, 139, 576

Historical Materialism, xxi, xxiv 77-9,

Historical Progress/ Consciousness, xiii-xviii, 79-83, 86, 88-94, 96-100, 179-180, 438, 588

Hitler, Adolph, 170-72

Humanist View, 126-27

I

Ideology & Marx, 100, 128-30

Ideology, 81, 94, 102, 154, 587

Illiberalism, 182

Ilyin, Ivan, fascist philosopher, 583

Inequality- Income & Wealth, 55-60, 62-8, 69-72, 203-04, 271, 285-86, 321-22, 324-29; and Status, 372-74

Intergenerational Income Elasticity, 331-32

Iron Law of Wages, 111-12

J

Johnson, Lyndon, U.S. Pres. Great Society, 130, 191, 546

K

Kelton Stefanie, Alternative Deficit Platform, 450-52

Keynes, John Maynard, Economist, 35, 192, 302

Kreisky, Bruno, Austrian Chancellor, 341

Kuito, Michael, American Labor Union rep., 537-540

Kuznets, Simon, 63

L

Law of Motion, 116, 147, 563

Liberalism, xvii, 31, 43, 98, 159, 177, 182, 187-88, 229,

Lincoln, Abraham, 74, 189, 237, 497

M

MAGA Constituencies, 57, 336, 378, 381-383

Malthus, Thomas, 61

Manufactured Consent, Chomsky, Noam, 57-8

Marshall Plan, 289-90, 292-93

Marx, Karl/Class Analysis, 62, 77-9, 81-3, 100-05, 109-18, 119-20, 124-26

Material Incentives, 106-07

McGhee, Heather, 231-32, 236, 238, 245-53, 581

Mergers & Acquisitions, 567-70, 564-66

Minimum Wage, 54, 215, 245, 328-29

Modern Monetary Theory, Kelton, Stefanie, 54, 451-52

Moscow Declaration, 172

N

Napoleon II, Dictatorship, 114

National Industrial Recovery Act, (NIRA) 475-78,

Nat'l Labor Relations Act, NLRA, Wagner Act, 478-82, 498, 501

National Labor Relations Board (NLRB) 480-82, 492-94, 495-96, 498-99

Neo-liberal Capitalism, 303

New Deal Social Contract, 474-76

New Executive Class, 378-83

New Social Contract, 465-68

Ng, Karen, Philosopher, 81-2, 93-4

Nosko, Ulrich, Vorarlberg Tax Acct/Advisor, 223-26, 318

Nutrition Assistance Program (SNAP) 232

O

Obama, Barack, U.S. President, 254-56

P

Personality Cult, 365-74

Philanthropy-NFL, 148-49

Piketty, Tom, French Economist, 61-8, 108, 139, 190, 204, 323

Pillar of Social Rights, EU, 359

Polarization, 41, 236, 336, 412,

Post-Marxism, 125-26

Post-WW II Treaties, Europe, 394-98, 399-404

Poverty, 50-1, 238, 323-26, 326-29

Poverty Measures, 323-25

Pre-Distribution, 217-22

Private & Public Goods, 48-55

Project 2025, 136, 277-78, 586

Protecting the Right to Organize Act (PRO), 497-500

Purchasing Power Parity (PPP) 30, 454

Putin, Vladimir, Russian President, 581-83, 585

R

Racism, 236-240

Racketeering, 488-90

Reagan, Ronald, U.S. Pres. 45, 192, 203, 231, 281-83

Reich, Robert, U.S. Labor Sec., 199, 274, 282, 304-05, 564

Republican Party, 193-94, 204, 235, 265-67, 283

Reuther, Walter, Alliance for Labor Action, 547-48

Ricardo, David, 61-2

Right-to-Work Laws, 500-04

Rippe, Felix, European business manager, 510, 527

Roster Depreciation Allowance (RDA), 144-48

Russian Autocracy, 579-81

S

Sanders, Bernie, U.S. Senate, 118, 336, 432, 463-64, 467

Santayana, George, philosopher, 95

Schedule F, 276-78

Schuschnigg, Kurt, Austrian Chancellor, 169-70

Schüssel, Wolfgang, Austrian Chancellor, 378-79

Self-consciousness, 81-3

Smith, Adam, 63

Social Democracies, xii, xviii, 37, 97, 110, 116-17, 156

Social Mkt.Capitalism. xiii, 117, 131, 182, 216, 301, 303,344, 572

Socio-psychological, 72, 279, 321, 330, 333, 344, 372

Social Values, 195-96

Stability & Growth Pact, EU, 446-47

Stakeholder Capitalism, 331-32

State Capitalism, 34-7

Status Anxiety, 364-74

Status & Inequality, 372-74

Stemmer, Reinhard, Austrian Trade Union Rep., 526, 575

Student Debt, Debt Relief, 424-26, 426-7

Stuppner, Christian, Works Council Rep. 511-12

Sum of Us, 231, 236, 245-253

Surplus Value, 102-106

T

Taft-Hartley Act, 482, 500-01, 537, 544

Taxation Doesn't Pay, 196-99, 251

Taxation Income -Graphs, American/Austrian, 205, 208

Teamsters Trade Union, 251-52, 489, 544,

Tooze, Adam, Historian, 31-39, 452

Trade Unions, 112-13, 174-76, 345, 416-17

Transcendentalists (Footnote), 87

Trump, Donald, U.S. President, 50, 54, 198, 263, 328

Trump Personality Cult, 367-69

Trump Administration II, 43, 188, 198, 465

Trump Tax Cuts, 46-8, 199

U

United Auto Workers (UAW) 137, 252, 416, 545-48

V

von Mises, Ludwig, Austrian Economist, 295, 302-03

Vo-Tech/Ed Comparison, 434-37, 438-43

Vranitzky, Franz, Austrian Chancellor, 173

W

Wage & Price Parity Commission, 180-81

Wage Earners, 57

Warren, Elizabeth, U.S. Senator, 465-68

Weber, Bernie, Vorarlberg Parliamentarian, 517-22

Welfare State, xxii, 42-3, 49, 198-199, 228-232

Wolf, Martin, Economic Journalist, 42-3, 130-31, 156-58

Works Council Act, 507-09

World Economic Forum, 329-31

Y

Yeltzin Boris, Russian President, 580-81

Z

Zero-Sum Attitude, 247-49, 251

www.ingramcontent.com/pod-product-compliance
Lightning Source LLC
LaVergne TN
LVHW011029111125
825482LV00007B/50